DIABETIC COOKBOOK

FOR THE NEWLY DIAGNOSED

500 Simple and Easy Recipes for Balanced Meals and Healthy Living (21 Day Meal Plan Included)

JAMIE PRESS

Table of Content

Introduction...1

Chapter 1
All You Need to Know about Diabetes.............................2

How Insulin Works.. 2
Treating Type 2 Diabetes 2
Healthy Eating 3
Exercise and Diabetes 3
Make Time to Meditate 3
When You Need Insulin Therapy 3

Chapter 2
A Healthy Plate 5

Why We Need Carbs 5
Good Carbs vs. Bad Carbs 6
4 Tips for Counting Carbs 6
A Healthy Plate 6

Chapter 3
Essential Things You Need to Know About Sugar 7

Do I need to eliminate sugar entirely from my diet?... 7
Which Foods Are High in Sugar? 8
What Ingredients Should I Avoid? 9
How Much Sugar Can I Eat in a Day? 9
What are the Best Substitutes for Sugar?.. 10
How to Use this Book 10

Chapter 4
21 Day Meal Plan 12

Chapter 5 - Breakfast Recipe...15

Apple Cheddar Muffins 15
Blueberry Cinnamon Muffins 15
Cafe Mocha Smoothies 15
Apple Cinnamon Muffins 15
Apple Cinnamon Scones 16
Apple Filled Swedish Pancake 16
Berry Breakfast Bark.............................. 16
Apple Topped French Toast..................... 17
Coconut Breakfast Porridge.................... 17
Apple Walnut Pancakes.......................... 17
Ham & Cheese Breakfast Biscuits............ 17
Cauliflower Breakfast Hash 18
Blueberry English Muffin Loaf 18
Blueberry Stuffed French Toast............... 18
Mocha Java Smoothies 18
Breakfast Pizza...................................... 19
Cheese Spinach Waffles.......................... 19
Cranberry Coffeecake............................. 19
Cinnamon Apple Granola 20
Holiday Strata 20
Cottage Cheese Pancakes 20
Crab & Spinach Frittata 21

Cinnamon Rolls 21
Pumpkin Muffins.................................... 21
Italian Breakfast Bake 22
Eggnog Breakfast Pudding 22
Strawberry Coconut Scones 22
Ham & Broccoli Breakfast Bake............... 23
Ham & Jicama Hash 23
Hawaiian Breakfast Bake 23
Peanut Butter Waffles............................. 23
Hot Maple Porridge 24
Strawberry & Ricotta Crepes 24
Spinach Cheddar Squares....................... 24
Mango Strawberry Smoothies.................. 24
Olive & Mushroom Frittata 25
Mini Mushroom Egg Stacks 25
Spinach & Tomato Egg Muffins................ 25
Pumpkin Pancakes 26
Poached Eggs & Grits 26
"Bacon" & Egg Muffins............................ 26
Summer Breakfast Parfait....................... 26
Waffle or Pancake Mix 27
Sunrise Smoothies................................. 27

Jicama Hash Browns 27
Pumpkin Spice French Toast 27
Vanilla Mango Smoothies 28
Pumpkin Pie Smoothie 28

Strawberry Kiwi Smoothies 28
Yogurt & Granola Breakfast Popsicles 28
Lemon Glazed Blueberry Bread 29
Tex Mex Breakfast Bake 29

Chapter 6 - Snacks Recipe 30

Almond Cheesecake Bites 30
Almond Flour Crackers 30
Asian Chicken Wings 30
Banana Nut Cookies 30
BLT Stuffed Cucumbers 31
Buffalo Bites 31
Candied Pecans 31
Cheese Crisp Crackers 31
Cheesy Pita Crisps 32
Mozzarella Sticks 32
Cheesy Taco Chips 32
Honeydew & Ginger Smoothies 32
Chewy Granola Bars 33
Italian Eggplant Rollups 33
Chili Lime Tortilla Chips 33
Cauliflower Hummus 34
Popcorn Style Cauliflower 34
Chocolate Chip Blondies 34
Cinnamon Apple Chips 34
Raspberry Walnut Parfaits 35
Cinnamon Apple Popcorn 35
Crab & Spinach Dip 35
Crispy Baked Cheese Puffs 35
Hot & Spicy Mixed Nuts 36
Crunchy Apple Fries 36
Cranberry & Almond Granola Bars 36
Tex Mex Popcorn 36
Watermelon & Shrimp Ceviche 37

Fig Cookie Bars 37
Fluffy Lemon Bars 37
Pesto Stuffed Mushrooms 38
Gingerbread Cookies 38
Tortilla Chips 38
Orange Oatmeal Cookies 39
Almond Coconut Biscotti 39
Freezer Fudge 39
Pickled Cucumbers 40
Fried Zucchini 40
Oatmeal Peanut Butter Bars 40
Cheesy Onion Dip 40
Zucchini Chips 41
Rum Spiced Nuts 41
Double Chocolate Biscotti 41
Homemade Cheetos 42
Soft Pretzel Bites 42
Peanut Butter Oatmeal Cookies 42
Honey & Cinnamon Shortbread 43
Mini Eggplant Pizzas 43
Honey Roasted Pumpkin Seeds 43
Margarita Chicken Dip 44
Onion Rings 44
Parmesan Truffle Chips 44
Pistachio Cookies 45
Rosemary Potato Chips 45
Tangy Almond Shortbread Cookies 45

Chapter 7 - Salads Recipe 46

Asian Style Slaw 46
Asparagus & Bacon Salad 46
Autumn Slaw 46
Cantaloupe & Prosciutto Salad 46
Avocado & Citrus Shrimp Salad 47
Southwest Chicken Salad 47
Baked "Potato" Salad 47
Chopped Veggie Salad 47
Broccoli & Bacon Salad 48
Festive Holiday Salad 48
Broccoli & Mushroom Salad 48
Creamy Crab Slaw 48
Caprese Salad 49
Shrimp & Avocado Salad 49
Celery Apple Salad 49

Chicken Guacamole Salad 49
Grilled Vegetable & Noodle Salad 50
Layered Salad 50
Pomegranate & Brussels Sprouts Salad 50
Healthy Taco Salad 50
Strawberry & Avocado Salad 51
Lobster Roll Salad with Bacon Vinaigrette . 51
Mustard "Potato" Salad 51
Harvest Salad 52
Watermelon & Arugula Salad 52
Pickled Cucumber & Onion Salad 52
Pecan Pear Salad 52
Warm Portobello Salad 53
Asian Noodle Salad 53
Zucchini "Pasta" Salad 53

Chapter 8 - Desserts Recipe....................................54

Summer Corn Salad................................ 54
Holiday Apple & Cranberry Salad 54
Strawberry Cheesecake.......................... 54
Cappuccino Mousse................................ 55
Apple Pear & Pecan Dessert Squares 55
Cream Cheese Pound Cake 55
Broiled Stone Fruit................................. 56
Blueberry Lemon "Cup" Cakes 56
Peach Custard Tart................................. 56
Blueberry No Bake Cheesecake 57
Apricot Soufflé 57
Autumn Skillet Cake 57
Peanut Butter Pie.................................. 58
Chocolate Cherry Cake Roll 58
Strawberry Sorbet 58
Baked Maple Custard 59
Tiramisu.. 59
Cheesecake 59
Dark Chocolate Coffee Cupcakes............. 60
Blackberry Crostata 60
German Chocolate Cake Bars 60
Coconut Milk Shakes 61
Blackberry Soufflés 61
Caramel Pecan Pie 61
Chocolate Orange Bread Pudding 62
Chocolate Torte 62
Sticky Ginger Cake 62

Lemon Meringue Ice Cream 63
Cinnamon Bread Pudding........................ 63
Apple Crisp.. 63
Coconut Cream Pie 64
No-Bake Chocolate Swirl 64
No Bake Lemon Tart.............................. 64
Coconutty Pudding Clouds 64
Gingerbread Soufflés 65
Mini Key Lime Tarts 65
Sangria Jello Cups 65
Moist Butter Cake................................. 66
Peach Ice Cream 66
Watermelon Ice.................................... 66
Pineapple Frozen Yogurt 67
Pumpkin Ice Cream with Candied Pecans .. 67
Raspberry & Dark Chocolate Mini Soufflés . 67
Raspberry Lemon Cheesecake Squares 68
Pomegranate Panna Cotta....................... 68
Toffee Apple Mini Pies........................... 68
Mini Bread Puddings.............................. 69
Raspberry Peach Cobbler 69
Raspberry Almond Clafoutis 69
Carrot Cupcakes................................... 70
Café Mocha Torte................................. 70
Sweet Potato Crème Brule 71
Tropical Fruit Tart 71

Chapter 9 - Soups and Stews Recipe 72

Guinness Beef Stew with Cauliflower Mash 72
Chicken Pappardelle............................... 72
African Christmas Stew 73
Asian Meatball Soup.............................. 73
Bacon & Cabbage Soup 73
Beef & Lentil Soup 74
Beef Burgundy & Mushroom Stew 74
Cioppino.. 74
Beef Vegetable Soup 75
Beef Zoodle Stew 75
Chipotle Chicken & Corn Soup 75
Beer Cheese & Chicken Soup.................. 76
Clam & Bacon Soup 76
Crab & Cauliflower Bisque...................... 76
Salmon Dill Soup.................................. 77
Cajun Seafood Stew.............................. 77
Chipotle Bacon & Chicken Chowder 77
Chicken & Pepper Stew 78
Chorizo & Corn Chowder........................ 78
Creamy Sweet Potato & Cauliflower Bisque 78
Tuscan Sausage Soup 79
Cheesy Ham & Broccoli Soup.................. 79

Beef & Sweet Potato Stew 79
Chunky Chicken Noodle Soup 80
Creamy Chicken & Cauliflower Rice Soup .. 80
Southwest Chicken Soup 80
Curried Chicken Soup............................. 81
Easy Seafood Chowder........................... 81
Mexican Beef Stew 81
French Onion Soup 82
Hearty Bell Pepper Stew 82
Irish Stew 82
Italian Sausage Soup 83
Italian Veggie Soup............................... 83
Roasted Mushroom & Cauliflower Soup 83
Harvest Vegetable Soup 84
Korean Beef Soup 84
Pork Posole 84
Sausage & Pepper Soup 85
Spicy Shrimp Soup 85
Tomato Soup with Seafood 85
Smoky Lentil & Leek Soup 86
Steak & Broccoli Soup........................... 86
Turkey & Bacon Chowder....................... 86

Tangy Asparagus Bisque 86
Vegetable Noodle Soup........................ 87
White Bean & Chicken Soup 87

Smoky Pumpkin Soup 88
South American Fish Stew 88
Spicy Tomato Chicken Soup 88

Chapter 10 - Poultry Recipe...89

Slow Cooker Poblano Soup..................... 89
Creamy Italian Chicken & Pasta 89
Honey Garlic Chicken 90
Hot Chicken Salad Casserole 90
Cajun Chicken & Pasta 90
Arroz Con Pollo 91
Balsamic Chicken & Vegetable Skillet........ 91
Middle East Chicken Skewers 91
Asian Roasted Duck Legs 92
BBQ Chicken & Noodles 92
Cheesy Chicken & Spinach 92
Cheesy Chicken & "Potato" Casserole 93
Cheesy Stuffed Chicken 93
Jalapeno Turkey Burgers....................... 93
Chicken Stuffed with Mushrooms 94
Roasted Duck Legs with Balsamic
Mushrooms...................................... 94
Chicken & Shrimp Satay 95
Turkey Stuffed Poblano Peppers.............. 95
Chicken Marsala 96
Chicken Tuscany................................. 96
Hawaiian Chicken 96
Chicken Zucchini Patties with Salsa 97
Turkey Meatballs with Spaghetti Squash ... 97
Ranch Chicken Casserole 97
Roast Turkey & Rosemary Gravy 98
Chutney Turkey Burgers 98
Chicken & Spinach Pasta Skillet 98
Creamy Chicken Tenders 99
Creamy Turkey & Peas with Noodles........ 99
Spicy Lettuce Wraps 99

Crunchy Grilled Chicken.........................100
Orange Chicken...................................100
Curried Chicken & Apples.......................100
Korean Chicken 101
Turkey & Mushroom Casserole.................101
Chicken Cordon Bleu 101
Mediterranean Grilled Chicken 102
Lemon Chicken 102
Creole Chicken 102
Crispy Italian Chicken with Zucchini 103
French Onion Chicken & Vegetables 103
Healthy Turkey Chili 103
Mediterranean Stuffed Chicken 104
Pecan Chicken Enchiladas 104
Sweet & Sour Chicken 105
Turkey Sloppy Joes 105
Spiced Chicken Breasts with Peach Pepper
Relish 105
Slow Cooker Lemon Chicken with Gravy ..105
South of the Border Chicken Casserole 106
Seared Duck Breast with Red Wine & Figs 106
Southwest Turkey Lasagna......................107
Turkey Stuffed Peppers.........................107
Teriyaki Turkey Bowls...........................108
Thai Turkey Stir Fry 108
Peppered Duck Breasts with Grilled Plums 109
Spicy Grilled Turkey Breast 109
Turkey Noodle Casserole.......................110
Turkey & Pepper Skillet 110
Turkey Roulade 111
Zesty Chicken & Asparagus Pasta............111

Chapter 11 - Fish and Seafood Recipe 112

Turkey Enchiladas................................112
Cajun Catfish 112
Cajun Flounder & Tomatoes 112
Baked Salmon with Garlic Parmesan
Topping..113
Pan Seared Trout & Salsa......................113
Jambalaya 113
Baked Seafood Casserole......................114
Monterey Crab Quiche..........................114
Spanish Halibut...................................115
Seafood Enchiladas..............................115
BBQ Oysters with Bacon 116
Fisherman's Pie 116
Cajun Shrimp & Roasted Vegetables........116
Cilantro Lime Grilled Shrimp 117

Blackened Shrimp.................................117
Coconut Shrimp 117
Grilled Tuna Steaks..............................117
Crab Cakes...118
Crab Frittata 118
Shrimp in Coconut Curry 118
Crock Pot Fish & Tomatoes....................119
Crunchy Lemon Shrimp 119
Dill Smoked Salmon over Noodles..........119
Shrimp & Artichoke Skillet 119
Paella 120
Seafood Gumbo 120
Crispy Baked Flounder with Green Beans .121
Garlic Shrimp with Sun Dried Tomatoes ...121
Sweet & Spicy Seafood Pasta 121

Maple Glazed Salmon 122
Seafood Medley over Pasta 122
Shrimp Pasta in Red Pepper Sauce 122
Lobster Chowder 123
Maple Orange Salmon 123
Tangy Orange Roughy 123
Shrimp with Pumpkin Risotto 123

Red Clam Sauce & Pasta 124
Mediterranean Shrimp Pasta 124
Seafood & Broccoli Pasta 124
Italian Steamed Mussels.....................125
Salmon Milano 125
Margarita Grilled Salmon 125

Chapter 12 - Vegetable Mains Recipe 126

Tuna Carbonara.............................126
Cauliflower Mushroom Risotto 126
Asian Fried Eggplant 127
Garden Vegetable Pasta.....................127
Tex Mex Veggie Bake 127
Butternut Fritters 128
Roasted Cauliflower with Tomatoes 128
Crust Less Broccoli Quiche 128
Chili Relleno Casserole 129

Eggplant-Zucchini Parmesan 129
Creamy Pasta with Peas 129
Grilled Portobello & Zucchini Burger 129
Faux Chow Mein 130
Florentine Pizza 130
Pizza Stuffed Portobello's...................130
Fiesta Casserole 131
Zucchini Fritters 131

Chapter 13 - Pork Lamb and Beef Recipe 132

Chestnut Stuffed Pork Roast..................132
Beef Tenderloin Steaks with Brandied
Mushrooms.................................132
Hearty Beef Chili 133
Herb Crusted Baked Ham 133
Pork Chops with Creamy Marsala Sauce ..133
Alfredo Sausage & Vegetables 134
Beef & Veggie Quesadillas...................134
Bacon & Cauliflower Casserole..............134
Asian Beef Bowls 135
BBQ Pork Tacos 135
Kielbasa & Lamb Cassoulet 135
Beef & Broccoli Skillet 136
Beef Picadillo 136
Honey Bourbon Pork Chops.................136
Beef Goulash 136
Horseradish Meatloaf 137
Beef Tenderloin with Roasted Vegetables .137
Mississippi Style Pot Roast 137
Beer Braised Brisket 138
Grilled Lamb & Apricot Kebabs.............138
Zucchini Lasagna...........................138
Blue Cheese Crusted Beef Tenderloin.......139
French Onion Casserole.....................139
Creamy Braised Oxtails 139
Cajun Beef & Rice Skillet 140
Cajun Smothered Pork Chops...............140
Garlic Honey Pork Chops 140
Cheesesteak Stuffed Peppers 141
Cheesy Beef & Noodles......................141
Deconstructed Philly Cheesesteaks..........141

Crock Pot Beef Roast with Gravy.............142
Crock Pot Carnitas 142
Italian Sausage & Zucchini Warm Salad ...142
Crust Less Pizza 143
Easy Carbonara.............................143
Ham & Brie Turnovers 143
Garlic Butter Steak 144
Grilled Cajun Beef Tenderloin 144
Grilled Pork Tenderloin Sandwiches 144
Herb Crusted Pork Tenderloin 145
Lamb Ragu 145
Italian Pork Medallions 145
Tangy Balsamic Beef 145
Maple Bourbon Glazed Ham 146
Pasta Bolognese............................146
Sirloin Strips & "Rice"........................146
Spicy BBQ Beef Brisket.....................147
Pork Paprika 147
One Pot Beef & Veggies 147
Poblano & Cheese Burgers 148
Shepherd's Pie 148
Southwest Braised Beef.....................148
Moroccan Beef Skewers.....................149
Stuffed Flank Steak 149
Stuffed Grilled Pork Tenderloin 149
Sausage & Spinach Frittata 150
Tandoori Lamb 150
Swedish Meatballs 150
Spicy Grilled Flank Steak....................151
Pork Loin with Onion Beer Sauce 151
Swedish Beef Noodles 151

Chapter 14 - Meatless Main Dishes Recipe.................152

Taco Casserole 152
Crispy Tofu with Chili Garlic Noodles........152
Black Pepper & Garlic Tofu 153
Tempeh Lettuce Wraps 153
Teriyaki Tofu Burger..............................153
Crock Pot Stroganoff..............................154
Cauliflower "Mac" and Cheese 154
Mexican Scrambled Eggs & Greens...........154

Orange Tofu 155
Grilled Tofu & Veggie Skewers 155
Tofu in Peanut Sauce............................155
Tofu Salad Sandwiches 155
Tofu Curry 156
Pad Thai..156
Tofu Bento...156

Chapter 15 - Grains, Legumes & Pasta Recipe..........157

"Flour" Tortillas 157
Fried Rice...157
Flourless "Burger Buns".........................157
Cheesy Cauliflower Puree 157
Cauliflower Puree 158
Mexican "Rice" 158
Cauliflower "Rice" 158
No Corn "Cornbread" 158
Chickpea Tortillas 159

Cheese Biscuits 159
Light Beer Bread 159
Quick Coconut Flour Buns 159
Cauliflower Pizza Crust 160
"Cornbread" Stuffing............................160
Garlic Basil Breadsticks 160
Healthy Loaf of Bread............................161
Homemade Pasta 161
Homemade Noodles..............................161

Chapter 16 - Sauces, Dips & Dressings Recipe.........162

Pizza Crust 162
Alfredo Sauce 162
Creamy Poppy Seed Dressing.................162
Almond Vanilla Fruit Dip 163
Garlic Dipping Sauce 163
Orange Marmalade 163
Basic Salsa 163
Herb Vinaigrette...................................164
Blueberry Orange Dessert Sauce 164
Spaghetti Sauce 164
All Purpose Beef Marinade 164
All Purpose Chicken Marinade.................165
Apple Cider Vinaigrette..........................165
BBQ Sauce 165
Pear & Poppy Jam.................................165
Bacon Cheeseburger Dip 166
Caramel Sauce.....................................166
Berry Dessert Sauce 166
Blackberry Spread.................................166
Cheesy Jalapeno Dip.............................167
Chinese Hot Mustard.............................167
Cinnamon Blueberry Sauce 167
Citrus Vinaigrette 167
Cranberry Orange Compote 168

Marinara Sauce 168
Dry Rub for Pork...................................168
Easy Cheesy Dipping Sauce 168
Horseradish Mustard Sauce.....................169
Italian Salad Dressing 169
Italian Salsa 169
Maple Mustard Salad Dressing.................169
Walnut Vinaigrette................................169
Maple Shallot Vinaigrette 170
Pizza Sauce 170
Pineapple Mango Hot Sauce 170
Peach Pepper Relish 170
Queso Verde 171
Raspberry & Basil Jam...........................171
Roasted Tomato Salsa 171
Spicy Asian Vinaigrette..........................171
Spicy Peanut Sauce 172
Spicy Sweet Dipping Sauce 172
Sriracha Dipping Sauce 172
Strawberry Rhubarb Jelly.......................172
Sugar Free Ketchup 173
Teriyaki Sauce.....................................173
Tangy Mexican salad dressing.................173
Warm Bacon Vinaigrette Dressing 173

Appendix 1 Measurement Conversion Chart 174

Appendix 2 Recipe Index.. 175

Introduction

If you are reading this, then like me, you or someone you love is struggling with Type 2 Diabetes. For me, it is a loved one, my son. He was diagnosed with diabetes when he was 12. He was already an extremely picky eater, so having to completely change his diet in order to control his blood sugar was hard on both of us.

It took me many trials, and errors, to learn how to understand the effects that different food had on his overall health. I decided that I wanted to help other people in this same situation, so they did not have to struggle as I did.

Most people do not understand what diabetes is or have even a basic idea on how to manage it. Before my son was diagnosed, I thought diabetes was all about watching your sugar intake. Oh, how wrong I was. After a two-week training course, while my son was in the hospital, I was completely overwhelmed by information overload.

The first time I went grocery shopping after we left the hospital, I ended up spending eight hours just reading and comparing nutrition labels on products. This was an eye-opening experience, as I realized just how unhealthy most of the processed food in the store is. I made a decision then to only cook meals made from "real food".

My goal with this book is that you will have an easier time shopping and preparing healthy meals for your family. I have included the vital information you need to understand and control your Type 2 diabetes, along with strategies for meal planning, choosing good carbs, and carb counting tips.

So, let's begin!

Chapter 1 - All You Need to Know about Diabetes

According to the Diabetes Research Institute, over 422 million people suffer from diabetes worldwide. In the US, the number of people diagnosed with Type 2 Diabetes has increased dramatically over the last few years. Just what is diabetes?

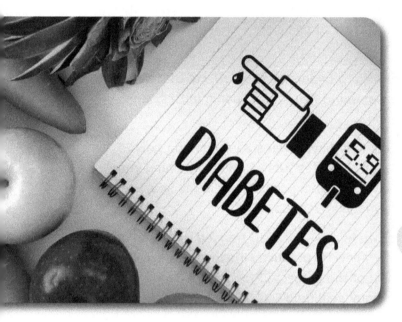

How Insulin Works

Your body processes the food that you eat and turns some of into glucose, or blood sugar. Glucose is what our bodies use for fuel to keep us moving. When the body creates glucose, the pancreas is supposed to release insulin which helps the body move glucose from the blood to the cells. When this system breaks down, diabetes occurs.

Traditionally, two types of diabetes were all that medical professionals focused on. Today, there are more types, like gestational diabetes that occurs when a woman is pregnant. For this book, we are going to just focus on Type 2 Diabetes.

Type 2 Diabetes is more commonly known as "adult onset diabetes". It tends to be diagnosed after the age of 35 and is most often found in people who are overweight and not leading an active lifestyle. While the body is producing some insulin, in many cases, it is not enough to move the glucose from the blood into the cells. Or, some type 2 diabetics are insulin resistant.

Treating Type 2 Diabetes

Managing your diabetes can often feel like walking a tight rope without a net. For some, it becomes a daily struggle to maintain a healthy glucose level, no matter how hard they try. Your blood sugar can drop, or spike, depending on several different factors.

Since the body is still producing some insulin, conventional treatments for type 2 diabetes focus on diet and exercise. Most people don't understand the effects that stress has on the body, and it can even cause your blood sugar to increase or decrease. The most common treatment for diabetes is insulin therapy. So let's look at each of these elements and see how they can benefit you.

Healthy Eating

Many people assume that overeating sugar is the reason their glucose levels are too high. But they are wrong. While paying attention to how much sugar you eat is essential, it is more important to keep track of the carbohydrates you consume.

Our bodies turn all carbohydrates into sugar for fuel. So while you may think a particular food is okay, since it doesn't have a lot of sugar, it may be high in carbs and cause your blood sugar to soar. We will discuss carbs in more detail in the next chapter. But for now, just know that a healthy diet which pays attention to carbohydrate levels is one of the best ways to manage Type 2 Diabetes.

Exercise and Diabetes

Exercise, along with a healthy diet, can help you to keep your blood sugar in a healthy range. You don't need to run out and buy an expensive gym membership or any fancy equipment. You need to follow a simple, easy exercise routine. Most importantly, you need to be consistent, whatever exercise you choose, make sure you do it every day.

Since Type 2 diabetes is most often found in adults who are overweight and tend to be sedimentary, simply walking every day can be beneficial. When your blood sugar is too high, a casual stroll around the neighborhood can help bring it down to a reasonable level again. Start small if you must, get up and move more throughout your day.

Make Time to Meditate

Stress has a horrible effect on our bodies. And for diabetics, stress can cause a rise in your blood sugar. Some studies have shown that meditating regularly can help to lower these levels. Meditation helps to reduce stress by slowing the heart rate, lowering blood pressure, reducing oxygen intake, and naturally, lowering stress levels. This relaxed state helps the body function as it is intended and helps to maintain blood sugar levels.

When You Need Insulin Therapy

Most type 2 diabetics do not require daily injections of insulin, thankfully. Insulin therapy is not a perfect science since how much insulin you need varies according to your health, weight, blood sugar levels, and other factors. Type 2 diabetics may need insulin therapy, especially if you are insulin resistant, but you can usually take medication for this rather than having to inject it. In many cases, just eating right and exercising can reduce the need for medications. The number one goal of this book is to prevent insulin therapy if we can.

Chapter 2 – A Healthy Plate

Eating a healthy, balanced diet is the best way to control your Type 2 diabetes. While this is not a new idea, diabetics need to pay attention to key elements in the foods they eat. **Let's take a look at some of those:**

Portion size is everything. Maintaining a normal glucose level needs to be the first goal, but losing, or maintaining your weight should be a close second. Reading nutrition labels on food will quickly become your newest hobby, and understanding them is based on portion size. If you double the portion listed, you must double the carb, fat, calories, and other items listed on the label.

The most important thing to look for is the number of carbs in your food. The total carbs in a food item include dietary fiber and sugar. You also need to look for fat content, cholesterol, and sodium. All of these can affect the health of your heart. To keep your heart healthy, you should limit cholesterol intake to less than 300mg, saturated fats to 20g or less, and keep your sodium intake under 2300mg per day.

Fiber is something else you should be paying attention to. Eating the recommended amount of fiber will keep you feeling full between meals so that you won't be easily tempted by an afternoon snack. A good range is 20-30 grams of fiber every day.

Why We Need Carbs

As mentioned earlier, carbs are what our bodies use for fuel. When they are broken down and turned into glucose, the body either uses the energy right away or stores it in our cells for later. A diet without carbs causes the body to break down protein and fat for energy. Most carbohydrates come from dairy, pasta, bread, fruits, and vegetables.

Diabetics also need to understand the difference between "fast" and "slow" carbs. When carbs are paired with food high in protein, they are absorbed by the body more slowly. Fast carbs do not have protein, so the body processes them quicker. This is important to understand because fast and slow carbs can create a rapid change in your glucose levels.

For example, when trying to raise a dangerously low glucose level, you would need a fast carb. Orange juice is an excellent example of a fast carb. But once the glucose level starts to come up, a slow-carb might be needed to maintain it, something like a granola bar with protein would work.

Good Carbs vs. Bad Carbs

Now that we understand why we need carbs, we need to realize that not all carbs are good. The Dietary Guidelines for Americans by the USDA states that good carbs also have a lot of fiber. Your body processes them slower, so no quick rise in glucose and they have the most vitamins and nutrients. Source of good carbs would be fruit, vegetables, and whole grains.

Bad carbs come from refined and processed foods. These foods have some of the grains removed from them during the baking or cooking process. They will also have sugar added to make them taste better. Bad carbs come from white bread, cookies, and cake. As soon as I typed that, I could hear you all sob. Don't worry; I will show you how to have your cake and eat it too.

4 Tips for Counting Carbs

①.**Look at the label.** Most foods today, except for fresh foods like meat and produce, have a nutrition label. Reading this label is the best way to know what you are putting in your body. And you will see that the recipes in this book have nutrition facts to guide you.

a. **Know proper portion sizes.** When reading the label, the information on it is based on the portion size. If it says ¼ cup, then eat just ¼ cup.

b. **Look at the total carbohydrates;** this will include all of the carbs plus the dietary fiber and the sugars.

②.**Use your kitchen tools to keep your portion sizes on track.** These tools include measuring cups, spoons, and a kitchen scale will be an excellent investment.

③.**Dining out can get tricky.** Most restaurants now feature nutrition information on their website. If you know ahead of time where you are going, check the website first. This makes ordering so much easier.

④.**Also,** when dining out, it is not possible to measure portion sizes as you do at home. To give you a better picture, keep in mind that 2 cups would fit in both of your hands, 1 cup would be the size of your fist, and ½ cup would fit in your palm.

A Healthy Plate

To keep your body functioning at its best, and your blood sugar levels in a healthy range, you need to balance your meals. A good rule to follow is to make one-quarter of your plate protein, one-quarter whole grains, and half your plate vegetables or fruit. Following this guideline for lunch and dinner will provide you with the necessary fuel your body needs to keep you going throughout the day.

Another tip is to eat smaller meals for breakfast, lunch, and dinner, and add a mid-morning and mid-afternoon snack. This is helpful if you find yourself getting hungry between mealtimes. Doing this will also help to keep your blood sugar at a "normal" level, without any drops between meals. Try to avoid snacks full of refined sugars, and go for those with good carbs with fiber.

Chapter 3 - Essential Things You Need to Know About Sugar

Developing diabetes later in life can be caused by a variety of things. One of these is being overweight. Eating a lot of sugary foods and sweets does not cause diabetes, but it does lead to obesity and other health problems.

Having type 2 diabetes means that you have to monitor the food that you eat and balance out your intake of carbohydrates and sugars throughout the day. To help you do that, let's look at some of the most frequently asked questions for other diabetics about sugar.

Do I need to eliminate sugar entirely from my diet?

It is impossible to eliminate all sugar from any diet. Many foods contain sugar naturally, like fruit. Plus, our bodies turn all carbohydrates into glucose for energy, which is a fancy word for blood sugar.

What you can do is watch the amount of sugar you eat and make sure to avoid eating foods that have added sugar in them. In the last chapter, we went over nutrition labels and how to understand them. When you look at the "total carbohydrates" on a label, know this number includes complex carbohydrates, sugar, and fiber. Monitoring your carbohydrate intake is the best way for a diabetic to keep glucose levels within a normal range.

Which Foods Are High in Sugar?

You will be surprised to learn that many food items labeled "healthy" are actually quite high in sugar. Here are 15 of the worst culprits that you should try to avoid, **or eat only occasionally:**

1. **Barbecue Sauce,** a single serving, about two tablespoons may have as many as three teaspoons of sugar.

2. **Ketchup,** like its cousin, BBQ sauce, it is full of sugar.

3. **Fruit juice,** you get more health benefits, and less sugar, by eating the actual fruit than drinking the juice.

4. **Spaghetti Sauce,** tomatoes naturally have some sugar in them, but many companies add sugar to their pasta sauces.

5. **Sports Drinks,** these are high in added sugars since they were designed for athletes, who burn sugar quicker than the average human.

6. **Chocolate Milk,** while it delivers all the healthy nutrients of plain milk, it also contains added sugar.

7. **Granola,** the oats used to make granola are full of fiber, carbs, and nutrients, but most granola contains over six teaspoons of sugar per 100 grams.

8. **Flavored coffee,** those tasty, trendy drinks can have up to 25 added teaspoons of sugar in every cup.

9. **Iced Tea,** if you buy yours premade, it may have as much sugar as a can of soda.

10. **Protein Bars,** while eating protein can help you feel fuller longer and help with weight loss, most commercial protein bars are high in added sugar.

11. **Vitamin water,** just like other "healthy" drinks, these have added sugars, some may have as many as 32 grams per bottle.

12. **Canned Soup,** this one may surprise you, the vegetables used in the soup have natural sugars, but many companies add sugar to the soup.

13. **Cereal Bars,** just like sweetened breakfast cereals, they have more sugar than you should eat in a day.

14. **Canned or Processed Fruit,** most canned fruit is packed in syrup which adds more sugar, also canned fruit loses most of its healthy fiber and nutrients during the processing.

15. **Bottled Smoothies,** mixing fruit and milk can provide many health benefits, but commercially made smoothies can have as many as 24 teaspoons of sugar in just one serving.

What Ingredients Should I Avoid?

Most processed food in the US is full of artificial chemicals, preservatives, and sugar. The easiest way to avoid them is to cook at home, this way you know what is in the food you eat. But when you have to buy something processed, read the label and avoid the following ingredients

- High fructose corn syrup
- Dextrose
- Lactose
- Fructose
- Sucrose
- Malt syrup
- White granulated sugar
- Honey
- Agave nectar
- Maltodextrin
- Glucose

How Much Sugar Can I Eat in a Day?

As you can see, avoiding sugar completely is just not possible. According to the American Heart Association, your sugar intake should be 10%, or less, of your daily calorie intake. For a diet of 1,200 calories per day, you should shoot for 120 – 100 grams of sugar or less.

You can increase your energy by eating foods high in fiber, lean proteins, and healthy fats. Also, eat smaller meals throughout the day, which will prevent the urge to snack on sugary foods and keep your blood sugar from spiking.

What are the Best Substitutes for Sugar?

Luckily, you will find plenty of sugar substitutes in the grocery store today. **Sugar substitutes come in three primary varieties:**

1. **Artificial sweeteners,** these synthetic substitutes will not affect glucose levels, but they do tend to have an unpleasant aftertaste. Artificial sweeteners include saccharin, aspartame, sucralose, and neotame.

2. **Sugar Alcohols,** these occur naturally in some foods and are created to be added to others. Unlike artificial and natural sweeteners, these do have calories and can affect your glucose levels. Sugar alcohols include; sorbitol, lactitol, glycerol, and xylitol.

3. **Natural sweeteners include honey,** molasses, maple syrup, fruit juices, and nectars. You need to monitor the amount you use because they act just like sugar.

However, there is a natural sweetener that has no calories and will not cause a spike in glucose. Stevia is a sweetener extracted from the Stevia rebaudiana. Substitutes made from the stevia plant include Splenda, Truvia, and Pur Via.

I like Splenda the best, it tastes a little sweeter than sugar and has some great alternatives for baking, like brown sugar and powdered sugar versions. When the recipe says 1 cup sugar substitute, be sure to check the label on the product you choose and use the equivalent it states for 1 cup of sugar.

How to Use this Book

You will find that all of the recipes in this book include information for calories, total carbs, net carbs, and protein. Net carbs are what you get when you subtract the fiber content from the total carbs if you don't see a net carb count listed, that recipe is not high in fiber.

None of the recipes use refined sugars or processed foods. Chapter 14 is full of recipes to make your own healthy condiments, dips, sauces, and salad dressings. Also, since carbs are such a vital part of controlling diabetes, I didn't label the recipes as "low carb" but trust me, they are.

Now, let's get cooking!

Chapter 4 – 21 Day Meal Plan

I f all of this information seems overwhelming, don't stress about it. With a little preparation, strategy, and this book, you can sail through the week without the hassle of wondering what you are going to cook today. Spend less time grocery shopping by preparing a meal plan for the week ahead.

The optimum meal plan will keep your blood sugar regulated while allowing you to drop some weight too. Pick your recipes so that you end up with no more than 1,200 calories a day. Balance your carbs, so you are getting the right amount to fuel your body throughout the day. Breakfast, lunch, and dinner should total no more than 30-45 grams of carbs. Eat two snacks a day that total around 15 grams, and you will be on track.

	Breakfast	Lunch	Dinner	Snacks	Daily Total
Day-1	Apple Cinnamon Muffins + 8 oz. skim milk	Smoky Lentil & Leek Soup	Chicken Stuffed with Mushrooms + ½ cup green beans + Broiled Stone Fruit	¼ cup Cauliflower Hummus + ½ cup each broccoli & turnip	1028 Calories, 102 Carbs, 52 Sugar
Day-2	Spinach Cheddar Squares + 8 oz. skim milk	Butternut Fritters	Asian Beef Bowl + Fluffy Lemon Bar	Tortilla Chips & Salsa	1043 Calories, 83g Carbs, 43g Sugar
Day-3	Poached Eggs & Grits + 8 oz. skim milk	Celery Apple Salad	Beef & Sweet Potato Stew + Cornbread+ Mini Key Lime Tart	½ cup green grapes	1171 Calories, 83 Carbs, 61g Sugar
Day-4	Bacon & Egg Muffins + 8 oz. unsweetened orange juice	Lobster Roll Salad	BBQ Chicken & Noodles + Chopped Veggie Salad + Pistachio Cookies	½ banana	1076 Calories, 89 Carbs, 51 Sugar

Day-5	Breakfast Pizza + 8 oz. unsweetened orange juice	Beef & Veggie Quesadilla	Cajun Flounder & Tomatoes + ½ cup steamed asparagus + Chocolate Cherry Cake Roll	Buffalo Bites	1136 Calories, 100g Carbs, 48g Sugar
Day-6	Apple Walnut Pancakes + 8 oz. glass skim milk	Chicken & Pepper Stew	Asian Roasted Duck Legs + Cauliflower Puree + Steamed Spinach + Sangria Jello Cup	Almond Coconut Biscotti + cup of coffee	1094 Calories, 79g Carbs, 57g Sugar
Day-7	Blueberry Stuffed French Toast + 8 oz. skim milk	Beef Picadillo + Cauliflower Rice	French Onion Casserole + ½ cup green beans	Honey Cinnamon Shortbread	1022 Calories, 72g Carbs, 44g Sugar
Day-8	Café Mocha Smoothie + ½ cup strawberries + 2 slices toast	Spicy Lettuce Wraps	BBQ Pork Tacos + Layered Salad + Cinnamon Apple Chips	Tex Mex Popcorn	851 Calories, 70g Carbs, 39g Sugar
Day-9	Cauliflower Breakfast Hash + 8 oz. skim milk	Cheesy Ham & Broccoli Soup	Cashew Chicken + Fried Rice	Rosemary Potato Chips	1127 Calories, 76g Carbs, 28g Sugar
Day-10	Apple Cinnamon Scones + ½ cup green grapes + 4 oz. skim milk	Crab Cakes + Celery Apple Salad	Healthy Taco Salad + Peanut Butter Pie	1 cup plain popcorn	1188 Calories, 79g Carbs, 45g Sugar
Day-11	Crab & Spinach Frittata + 8 oz. skim milk	Beef Vegetable Soup	Warm Portobello Salad with Bacon Vinaigrette + Dark Chocolate Coffee Cupcake	½ cup strawberries	995 Calories, 76g Carbs, 44g Sugar
Day-12	Ham & Broccoli Breakfast Bake + 8 oz. skim milk	Easy Carbonara	Teriyaki Turkey Bowls + Peach Custard Tart	Chili Lime Tortilla Chips + Salsa	1059 Calories, 81g Carbs, 40g Sugar
Day-13	Cheese Spinach Waffles + 8 oz. orange juice	Chutney Turkey Burgers + Onion Rings	Cajun Beef & Rice Skillet + Raspberry Peach Cobbler	Tex Mex Popcorn	1020 Calories, 62g Carbs, 48g Sugar

Day-14	Cinnamon Roll + 8 oz. skim milk	Monterey Crab Quiche + Orange Oatmeal Cookies	Blue Cheese Crusted Beef Tenderloin + Broccoli & Mushroom Salad + Orange Oatmeal Cookies	Popcorn Cauliflower	1082 Calories, 85g Carbs, 53g Sugar
Day-15	Ham & Jicama Hash + 8 oz. skim milk	Crustless Pizza + Summer Corn Salad	Crunchy Lemon Shrimp + Rosemary Potato Chips	Cinnamon Apple Popcorn	1111 Calories, 64g Carbs, 21g Sugar
Day-16	Hot Maple Porridge + 8 oz. skim milk	Shrimp & Avocado Salad	Creamy Turkey, Peas & Noodles + Lemon Meringue Ice Cream	Cheesy Pita Crisp	1171 Calories, 60g Carbs, 18g Sugar
Day-17	Italian Breakfast Bake + 4 oz. orange juice	Watermelon & Arugula Salad	Cheesy Stuffed Chicken + Cauliflower Puree + ½ cup asparagus	Mini Bread Pudding	1012 Calories, 46 Carbs, 36g Sugar
Day-18	Mango Strawberry Smoothie	Tangy Asparagus Bisque	Grilled Lamb & Apricot Kebabs + Cauliflower Rice + Chocolate Orange Bread Pudding	Honey Cinnamon Shortbread	971 Calories, 77g Carbs, 51g Sugar
Day-19	Peanut Butter Waffles + 8 oz. skim milk	Fiesta Casserole + Cheese Biscuit	Cajun Seafood Stew + Peach Ice Cream	Honeydew & Ginger Smoothie	1095 Calories, 77g Carbs, 45g Sugar
Day-20	Spinach & Tomato Egg Muffins + Jicama Hash Browns	Chipotle Chicken & Corn Soup + Cornbread	Cajun Smothered Pork Chops + Cauliflower Puree + ½ cup asparagus	Cinnamon Apple Chips	1095 Calories, 67g Carbs, 37g Sugar
Day-21	Tex Mex Breakfast Bake + 8 oz. skim milk	Grilled Pork Tenderloin Sandwich + Mustard Potato Salad	Cheesesteak Stuffed Peppers + Banana Nut Cookies	Fried Zucchini + Garlic Dipping Sauce	1049 Calories, 71g Carbs, 44g Sugar

Chapter 5 - Breakfast Recipe

Apple Cheddar Muffins

Prep time: 10 minutes, Cook time: 20 minutes, Serves: 12

Ingredients:

1 egg	fat cheddar cheese,
¾ cup tart apple,	grated
peel & chop	2/3 cup skim milk
2/3 cup reduced	

What you'll need from store cupboard:

2 cup low carb baking	2 tbsp. vegetable oil
mix	1 tsp cinnamon.

Instructions:

1. Heat oven to 400 degrees F. Line a 12 cup muffin pan with paper liners.
2. In a medium bowl, lightly beat the egg. Stir in remaining Ingredients just until moistened. Divide evenly between prepared muffin cups.
3. Bake 17-20 minutes or until golden brown. Serve warm.

Nutrition Facts Per Serving
Calories 162 Total Carbs 17g Net Carbs 13g Protein 10g Fat 5g Sugar 8g Fiber 4g

Blueberry Cinnamon Muffins

Prep time: 10 minutes, Cook time: 30 minutes, Serves: 10

Ingredients:

3 eggs	¼ cup margarine,
1 cup blueberries	melted
1/3 cup half-n-half	

What you'll need from store cupboard:

1½ cup almond flour	1 tsp baking powder
⅓ cup Splenda	1 tsp cinnamon

Instructions:

1. Heat oven to 350 degrees. Line 10 muffin cups with paper liners.
2. In a large mixing bowl, combine dry Ingredients.
3. Stir in wet Ingredients and mix well.
4. Fold in the blueberries and spoon evenly into lined muffin pan.
5. Bake 25-30 minutes or they pass the toothpick test.

Nutrition Facts Per Serving
Calories 194 Total Carbs 12g Net Carbs 10g Protein 5g Fat 14g Sugar 9g Fiber 2g

Cafe Mocha Smoothies

Total time: 5 minutes, Serves: 3

Ingredients:

1 avocado, remove	unsweetened
pit and cut in half	½ cup canned
1 ½ cup almond milk,	coconut milk

What you'll need from store cupboard:

3 tbsp. Splenda	2 tsp instant coffee
3 tbsp. unsweetened	1 tsp vanilla
cocoa powder	

Instructions:

1. Place everything but the avocado in the blender. Process until smooth.
2. Add the avocado and blend until smooth and no chunks remain.
3. Pour into glasses and serve.

Nutrition Facts Per Serving
Calories 109 Total Carbs 15g Protein 6g Fat 1g Sugar 13g Fiber 0g

Apple Cinnamon Muffins

Prep time: 15 minutes, Cook time: 25 minutes, Serves: 12

Ingredients:

1 cup apple, diced	calorie margarine,
fine	melted
2/3 cup skim milk	1 egg, lightly beaten
¼ cup reduced-	

What you'll need from store cupboard:

1 2/3 cups flour	½ tsp sea salt
1 tbsp. Stevia	¼ tsp nutmeg
2 ½ tsp baking	Nonstick cooking
powder	spray
1 tsp cinnamon	

Instructions:

1. Heat oven to 400 degrees F. Spray a 12-cup muffin pan with cooking spray.
2. In a large bowl, combine dry Ingredients and stir to mix.
3. In another bowl, beat milk, margarine, and egg to combine.
4. Pour wet Ingredients into dry Ingredients and stir just until moistened. Gently fold in apples.
5. Spoon into prepared muffin pan. Bake 25 minutes, or until tops are lightly browned.

Nutrition Facts Per Serving
Calories 119 Total Carbs 17g Net Carbs 16g Protein 3g Fat 4g Sugar 3g Fiber 1g

Apple Cinnamon Scones

Prep time: 5 minutes, Cook time: 25 minutes, Serves: 16

Ingredients:

2 large eggs	margarine, melted
1 apple, diced	and divided
¼ cup + ½ tbsp.	1 tbsp. half-n-half

What you'll need from store cupboard:

3 cups almond flour	2 tsp cinnamon
1/3 cup + 2 tsp	1 tsp vanilla
Splenda	¼ tsp salt
2 tsp baking powder	

Instructions:

1. Heat oven to 325 degrees. Line a large baking sheet with parchment paper.
2. In a large bowl, whisk flour, 1/3 cup Splenda, baking powder, 1 ½ teaspoons cinnamon, and salt together. Stir in apple.
3. Add the eggs, ¼ cup melted margarine, cream, and vanilla. Stir until the mixture forms a soft dough.
4. Divide the dough in half and pat into 2 circles, about 1-inch thick, and 7-8 inches around.
5. In a small bowl, stir together remaining 2 teaspoons Splenda, and ½ teaspoon cinnamon.
6. Brush the ½ tablespoon melted margarine over dough and sprinkle with cinnamon mixture. Cut each into 8 equal pieces and place on prepared baking sheet.
7. Bake 20-25 minutes, or until golden brown and firm to the touch.

Nutrition Facts Per Serving

Calories 176 Total Carbs 12g Net Carbs 9g Protein 5g Fat 12g Sugar 8g Fiber 3g

Apple Filled Swedish Pancake

Prep time: 25 minutes, Cook time: 20 minutes, Serves: 6

Ingredients:

2 apples, cored and	½ cup sugar-free
sliced thin	caramel sauce
¾ cup egg substitute	1 tbsp. reduced
½ cup fat-free milk	calorie margarine

What you'll need from store cupboard:

½ cup flour	1/8 tsp cloves
1`1/2 tbsp. brown	1/8 tsp salt
sugar substitute	Nonstick cooking
2 tsp water	spray
¼ tsp cinnamon	

Instructions:

1. Heat oven to 400 degrees. Place margarine in cast iron, or ovenproof, skillet and place in oven until margarine is melted.
2. In a medium bowl, whisk together flour, milk, egg substitute, cinnamon, cloves and salt until smooth.
3. Pour batter in hot skillet and bake 20 – 25 minutes until puffed and golden brown.
4. Spray a medium saucepan with cooking spray. Heat over medium heat.
5. Add apples, brown sugar and water. Cook, stirring occasionally, until apples are tender and golden brown, about 4 – 6 minutes.
6. Pour the caramel sauce into a microwave-proof measuring glass and heat 30 – 45 seconds, or until warmed through.
7. To serve, spoon apples into pancake and drizzle with caramel. Cut into wedges.

Nutrition Facts Per Serving

Calories 193 Total Carbs 25g Net Carbs 23g Protein 6g Fat 2g Sugar 12g Fiber 2g

Berry Breakfast Bark

Prep time: 10 minutes, freeze time:2 hours, Serves: 6

Ingredients:

3-4 strawberries,	yogurt
sliced	½ cup blueberries
1 ½ cup plain Greek	

What you'll need from store cupboard:

½ cup low fat granola	maple syrup
3 tbsp. sugar free	

Instructions:

1. Line a baking sheet with parchment paper.
2. In a medium bowl, mix yogurt and syrup until combined. Pour into prepared pan and spread in a thin even layer.
3. Top with remaining Ingredients. Cover with foil and freeze two hours or overnight.
4. To serve: slice into squares and serve immediately. If bark thaws too much it will lose its shape. Store any remaining bark in an airtight container in the freezer.

Nutrition Facts Per Serving

Calories 69 Total Carbs 18g Net Carbs 16g Protein 7g Fat 6g Sugar 7g Fiber 2g

Apple Topped French Toast

Prep time: 10 minutes, Cook time: 10 minutes, Serves: 2

Ingredients:

1 apple, peel and slice thin	¼ cup skim milk
1 egg	2 tbsp. margarine, divided

What you'll need from store cupboard:

4 slices Healthy Loaf Bread, (chapter 14)	brown sugar
1 tbsp. Splenda	1 tsp vanilla
	¼ tsp cinnamon

Instructions:

1. Melt 1 tablespoon margarine in a large skillet over med-high heat. Add apples, Splenda, and cinnamon and cook, stirring frequently, until apples are tender.
2. In a shallow dish, whisk together egg, milk, and vanilla.
3. Melt the remaining margarine in a separate skillet over med-high heat. Dip each slice of bread in the egg mixture and cook until golden brown on both sides.
4. Place two slices of French toast on plates, and top with apples. Serve immediately.

Nutrition Facts Per Serving

Calories 394 Total Carbs 27g Net Carbs 22g Protein 10g Fat 23g Sugar 19g Fiber 5g

Apple Walnut Pancakes

Prep time: 15 minutes, Cook time: 30 minutes, Serves: 18

Ingredients:

1 apple, peeled and diced	2 egg whites
2 cup skim milk	1 egg, beaten

What you'll need from store cupboard:

1 cup flour	1 tbsp. Splenda brown sugar
1 cup whole wheat flour	2 tsp baking powder
½ cup walnuts, chopped	1 tsp salt
2 tbsp. sunflower oil	Nonstick cooking spray

Instructions:

1. In a large bowl, combine dry Ingredients.
2. In a separate bowl, combine egg whites, egg, milk, and oil and add to dry Ingredients. Stir just until moistened. Fold in apple and walnuts.
3. Spray a large griddle with cooking spray and heat. Pour batter, ¼ cup on to hot griddle. Flip when bubbles form on top. Cook until second side is golden brown. Serve with sugar free syrup.

Nutrition Facts Per Serving

Calories 120 Total Carbs 15g Net Carbs 13g Protein 4g Fat 5g Sugar 3g Fiber 2g

Coconut Breakfast Porridge

Prep time: 2 minutes, Cook time: 10 minutes, Serves: 4

Ingredients:

4 cup vanilla almond milk, unsweetened

What you'll need from store cupboard:

1 cup unsweetened coconut, grated	8 tsp coconut flour

Instructions:

1. Add coconut to a saucepan and cook over med-high heat until it is lightly toasted. Be careful not to let it burn.
2. Add milk and bring to a boil. While stirring, slowly add flour, cook and stir until mixture starts to thicken, about 5 minutes.
3. Remove from heat, mixture will thicken more as it cools. Ladle into bowls, add blueberries, or drizzle with a little honey if desired.

Nutrition Facts Per Serving

Calories 231 Total Carbs 21g Net Carbs 8g Protein 6g Fat 14g Sugar 4g Fiber 13g

Ham & Cheese Breakfast Biscuits

Prep time: 5 minutes, Cook time: 15 minutes, Serves: 4

Ingredients:

1 cup ham, diced	½ cup low fat cheddar cheese, grated
2 eggs	
¾ cup mozzarella cheese, grated	

What you'll need from store cupboard:

½ cup reduced fat grated parmesan, grated

Instructions:

1. Heat oven to 375 degrees. Line a baking sheet with parchment paper.
2. In a large bowl, combine the cheeses and eggs until fully combined. Stir in the ham.
3. Divide the mixture evenly into 8 parts and form into round tolls. Bake 15-20 minutes or until cheese is completely melted and the rolls are nicely browned.

Nutrition Facts Per Serving

Calories 192 Total Carbs 2g Protein 16g Fat 13g Sugar 0g Fiber 0g

Cauliflower Breakfast Hash

Prep time: 10 minutes, Cook time: 20 minutes, Serves: 2

Ingredients:

4 cups cauliflower, grated	¾ cup onion, diced
1 cup mushrooms, diced	3 slices bacon
	¼ cup sharp cheddar cheese, grated

Instructions:

1. In a medium skillet, over med-high heat, fry bacon, set aside.
2. Add vegetables to the skillet and cook, stirring occasionally, until golden brown.
3. Cut bacon into pieces and return to skillet.
4. Top with cheese and allow it to melt. Serve immediately.

Nutrition Facts Per Serving

Calories 155 Total Carbs 16g Net Carbs 10g Protein 10g Fat 7g Sugar 7g Fiber 6g

Blueberry English Muffin Loaf

Prep time: 15 minutes, Cook time: 1 hour, Serves: 12

Ingredients:

6 eggs beaten	unsweetened
½ cup almond milk,	½ cup blueberries

What you'll need from store cupboard:

½ cup cashew butter	½ tsp salt
½ cup almond flour	Nonstick cooking spray
¼ cup coconut oil	
2 tsp baking powder	

Instructions:

1. Heat oven to 350 degrees. Line a loaf pan with parchment paper and spray lightly with cooking spray.
2. In a small glass bowl, melt cashew butter and oil together in the microwave for 30 seconds. Stir until well combined.
3. In a large bowl, stir together the dry Ingredients. Add cashew butter mixture and stir well.
4. In a separate bowl, whisk the milk and eggs together. Add to flour mixture and stir well. Fold in blueberries.
5. Pour into the prepared pan and bake 45 minutes, or until it passes the toothpick test.
6. Cook 30 minutes, remove from pan and slice.

Nutrition Facts Per Serving

Calories 162 Total Carbs 5g Net Carbs 4g Protein 6g Fat 14g Sugar 1g Fiber 1g

Blueberry Stuffed French Toast

Prep time: 15 minutes, Cook time: 20 minutes, Serves: 8

Ingredients:

4 eggs	½ cup orange juice
1 ½ cup blueberries	1 tsp orange zest

What you'll need from store cupboard:

16 slices bread, (chapter 14)	Blueberry Orange Dessert Sauce, (chapter 16)
3 tbsp. Splenda, divided	Nonstick cooking spray
1/8 tsp salt	

Instructions:

1. Heat oven to 400 degrees. Spray a large baking sheet with cooking spray.
2. In a small bowl, combine berries with 2 tablespoons of Splenda.
3. Lay 8 slices of bread on work surface. Top with about 3 tablespoons of berries and place second slice of bread on top. Flatten slightly.
4. In a shallow dish, whisk remaining Ingredients together. Carefully dip both sides of bread in egg mixture and place on prepared pan.
5. Bake 7-12 minutes per side, or until lightly browned.
6. Heat up dessert sauce until warm. Plate the French toast and top with 1-2 tablespoons of the sauce. Serve.

Nutrition Facts Per Serving

Calories 208 Total Carbs 20g Net Carbs 18g Protein 7g Fat 10g Sugar 14g Fiber 2g

Mocha Java Smoothies

Prep time: 5 minutes, blend time: 3 minutes, Serves: 4

Ingredients:

3 cup skim milk	cholesterol free
¼ cup egg substitute,	

What you'll need from store cupboard:

3 tbsp. Splenda	2 tsp instant coffee granules
3 tbsp. unsweetened cocoa	1 ½ tsp vanilla

Instructions:

1. Place all Ingredients in a blender and process until smooth. Pour into glasses and serve immediately.

Nutrition Facts Per Serving

Calories 151 Total Carbs 21g Net Carbs 20g Protein 12g Fat 1g Sugar 19g Fiber 1g

Breakfast Pizza

**Prep time: 10 minutes, Cook time: 30 minutes,
Serves: 8**

Ingredients:

12 eggs
½ lb. breakfast sausage
1 cup bell pepper, sliced
1 cup red pepper, sliced
1 cup cheddar cheese, grated
½ cup half-n-half

What you'll need from store cupboard:

½ tsp salt
¼ tsp pepper

Instructions:

1. Heat oven to 350 degrees.
2. In a large cast iron skillet, brown sausage. Transfer to bowl.
3. Add peppers and cook 3-5 minutes or until they begin to soften. Transfer to a bowl.
4. In a small bowl, whisk together the eggs, cream, salt and pepper. Pour into skillet. Cook 5 minutes or until the sides start to set.
5. Bake 15 minutes.
6. Remove from oven and set it to broil. Top "crust" with sausage, peppers, and cheese. Broil 3 minutes, or until cheese is melted and starts to brown.
7. Let rest 5 minutes before slicing and serving.

Nutrition Facts Per Serving

Calories 230 Total Carbs 4g Protein 16g Fat 17g Sugar 2g Fiber 0g

Cheese Spinach Waffles

**Prep time: 10 minutes, Cook time: 20 minutes,
Serves: 4**

Ingredients:

2 strips of bacon, cooked and crumbled
2 eggs, lightly beaten
½ cup cauliflower, grated
½ cup frozen spinach, chopped (squeeze water out first)
½ cup low fat mozzarella cheese, grated
½ cup low fat cheddar cheese, grated
1 tbsp. margarine, melted

What you'll need from store cupboard:

¼ cup reduced fat Parmesan cheese, grated
1 tsp onion powder
1 tsp garlic powder
Nonstick cooking spray

Instructions:

1. Thaw spinach and squeeze out as much of the water as you, place in a large bowl.
2. Heat your waffle iron and spray with cooking spray.
3. Add remaining Ingredients to the spinach and mix well.
4. Pour small amounts on the waffle iron and cook like you would for regular waffles. Serve warm.

Nutrition Facts Per Serving

Calories 186 Total Carbs 2g Protein 14g Fat 14g Sugar 1g Fiber 0g

Cranberry Coffeecake

**Prep time: 10minutes,Cook time: 20-25 minutes,
Serves: 12**

Ingredients:

1 cup whole fresh cranberries
4 large eggs

What you'll need from store cupboard:

1 ¼ cup flax seed meal
½ cup Splenda
½ cup sugar free vanilla syrup
¼ cup olive oil
3 tbsp. cinnamon
1 tbsp. vanilla
1 tsp baking powder
1 tsp nutmeg
½ tsp salt
Nonstick cooking spray

Instructions:

1. Heat oven to 350 degrees. Coat a Bundt cake pan with cooking spray.
2. Put cranberries in a microwave safe bowl and cover with plastic wrap. Cook on high 1-2 minutes or the berries are tender.
3. In a medium mixing bowl combine all the wet Ingredients. Mix until thoroughly combined.
4. Add the dry Ingredients and mix well. Let sit for 10 minutes so the mixture thickens.
5. Fold in the cranberries and pour into prepared pan.
6. Bake 20-25 minutes or until the coffeecake passes the toothpick test. Let cook 5 minutes in pan then invert onto serving plate.

Nutrition Facts Per Serving

Calories 122 Total Carbs 11g Net Carbs 9g Protein 2g Fat 6g Sugar 9g Fiber 2g

Cinnamon Apple Granola

Prep time: 5 minutes, Cook time: 35 minutes, Serves: 4

Ingredients:

1 apple, peel and dice fine	¼ cup margarine, melted

What you'll need from store cupboard:

1 cup walnuts or pecans	½ cup hemp seeds
1 cup almond flour	1/3 cup Splenda
¾ cup flaked coconut	2 tsp cinnamon
½ cup sunflower seeds	2 tsp vanilla
	½ tsp salt

Instructions:

1. Heat oven to 300 degrees. Line a large baking sheet with parchment paper.
2. Place the nuts, flour, coconut, seeds, Splenda, and salt in a food processor. Pulse until mixture resembles coarse crumbs but leave some chunks.
3. Transfer to a bowl and add apple and cinnamon. Stir in margarine and vanilla until well coated and mixture starts to clump together.
4. Pour onto prepared pan and spread out evenly. Bake 25 minutes, stirring a couple of times, until it starts to brown.
5. Turn the oven off and let granola sit inside 5-10 minutes. Remove from oven and cool completely, it will crisp up more as it cools. Store in airtight container.

Nutrition Facts Per Serving
Calories 360 Total Carbs 19g Net Carbs 14g Protein 10g Fat 28g Sugar 12g Fiber 5g

Holiday Strata

Prep time: 25 minutes, Cook time: 1 hour, Serves: 8

Ingredients:

8 eggs	tomatoes
6 slices bacon, diced	4 cup spinach
4 breakfast sausages, casings removed and meat crumbled	3 cup skim milk
	1 cup reduced fat cheddar cheese, grated
1 onion, diced fine	
1 pint cherry	

What you'll need from store cupboard:

½ loaf Italian bread, cut in 2-inch cubes	¼ tsp pepper
2 tsp Dijon mustard	Butter flavored cooking spray
1 tsp salt	

Instructions:

1. Spray a 13x9-inch baking dish with cooking spray.
2. Heat a large non-stick skillet over medium heat. Add bacon and sausage and cook until bacon is crisp, and sausage is cooked through, about 5-7 minutes. Transfer to paper towel lined plate. Drain all but 1 tablespoon of fat from the pan.
3. Add onion and cook until soft and golden brown, about 6 minutes.
4. Add tomatoes and spinach and cook until tomatoes start to soften and spinach wilts, about 2 minutes. Remove from heat and set aside to cool.
5. In a large bowl, beat eggs with milk, Dijon, salt and pepper. Mix in cheese, bread, bacon, sausage, and spinach mixture. Pour into prepared pan and cover with plastic wrap.
6. Refrigerate for two hours or overnight.
7. Heat oven to 359 degrees. Uncover and bake 1 hour, or until set in the center. Cool slightly before serving.

Nutrition Facts Per Serving
Calories 343 Total Carbs 24g Net Carbs 22g Protein 25g Fat 16g Sugar 7g Fiber 2g

Cottage Cheese Pancakes

Prep time: 5 minutes, Cook time: 5 minutes, Serves: 2

Ingredients:

1 cup low-fat cottage cheese	4 egg whites

What you'll need from store cupboard:

½ cup oats	1 tsp vanilla
1 tbsp. Stevia, raw, optional	Nonstick cooking spray

Instructions:

1. Place all Ingredients into a blender and process until smooth.
2. Spray a medium skillet with cooking spray and heat over medium heat.
3. Pour about ¼ cup batter into hot pan and cook until golden brown on both sides.
4. Serve with sugar-free syrup, fresh berries, or topping of your choice.

Nutrition Facts Per Serving
Calories 250 Total carbs 25g Net Carbs 23g Protein 25g Fat 4g Sugar 7g Fiber 2g

Crab & Spinach Frittata

Prep time: 10 minutes, Cook time: 30 minutes, Serves: 10

Ingredients:

¾ lb. crabmeat	1 cup Swiss cheese
8 eggs	½ cup onion, diced
10 oz. spinach, frozen and thawed, squeeze dry	½ cup red pepper, diced
2 stalks celery, diced	¼ cup mushrooms, diced
2 cup half-n-half	2 tbsp. margarine

What you'll need from store cupboard:

1 cup bread crumbs	¼ tsp nutmeg
½ tsp salt	Nonstick cooking spray
¼ tsp pepper	

Instructions:

1. Heat oven to 375 degrees. Spray a large casserole, or baking dish with cooking spray.
2. In a large bowl, beat eggs and half-n-half. Stir in crab, spinach, bread crumbs, cheese, and seasonings.
3. Melt butter in a large skillet over medium heat. Add celery, onion, rep pepper, and mushrooms. Cook, stirring occasionally, until vegetables are tender, about 5 minutes. Add to egg mixture.
4. Pour mixture into prepared baking dish and bake 30-35 minutes, or until eggs are set and top is light brown. Cool 10 minutes before serving.

Nutrition Facts Per Serving

Calories 261 Total Carbs 18g Net Carbs 16g Protein 14g Fat 15g Sugar 4g Fiber 2g

Cinnamon Rolls

Prep time: 15 minutes, Cook time: 20 minutes, Serves: 6

Ingredients:

4 eggs	1 ripe banana

What you'll need from store cupboard:

2/3 cup coconut flour	1 tsp vanilla
6 tbsp. honey, divided	1 tsp baking soda
	½ tsp salt
6 tbsp. coconut oil, soft, divided	1 tbsp. + ½ tsp cinnamon

Instructions:

1. Heat oven to 350 degrees. Line a cookie sheet with parchment paper.
2. In a medium bowl, lightly beat eggs. Beat in the banana. Add 2 tablespoons honey, 2 tablespoons melted coconut oil, and vanilla and mix to combine.
3. Mix in flour, salt, baking soda, and ½ teaspoon cinnamon until thoroughly combined. If dough is too sticky add more flour, a little at a time.
4. Line a work surface with parchment paper and place dough on top. Place another sheet of parchment paper on top and roll out into a large rectangle.
5. In a small bowl, combine 2 tablespoons honey, 2 tablespoons coconut oil, and 1 tablespoons of cinnamon and spread on dough.
6. Roll up and cut into 6 equal pieces. Place on prepared pan and bake 15-30 minutes, or until golden brown.
7. Let cool 10 minutes. Stir together the remaining 2 tablespoons of honey and coconut oil and spread over warm rolls. Serve.

Nutrition Facts Per Serving

Calories 247 Total Carbs 23g Protein 4g Fat 17g Sugar 20g Fiber 1g

Pumpkin Muffins

Prep time: 5 minutes, Cook time: 20 minutes, Serves: 10

Ingredients:

2 eggs	¼ cup butter, melted

What you'll need from store cupboard:

2 cup almond flour	2 tsp baking powder
¾ cup pumpkin	1 tsp cinnamon
⅓ cup Splenda	1 tsp vanilla
2 tbsp. pumpkin seeds	½ tsp salt

Instructions:

1. Heat oven to 400 degrees. Line a muffin pan with paper liners.
2. In a large bowl, combine butter, pumpkin, eggs and vanilla. Whisk until smooth.
3. In another bowl, combine flour, Splenda, baking powder, cinnamon and salt. Add to pumpkin mixture and stir to combine. Divide evenly between muffin cups.
4. Sprinkle the pumpkin seeds on the top and bake 20 minutes, or they pass the toothpick test.
5. Let cool 10 minutes before serving.

Nutrition Facts Per Serving

Calories 212 Total Carbs 13g Net Carbs 10g Protein 6g Fat 16g Sugar 8g Fiber 3g

Italian Breakfast Bake

Prep time: 10 minutes, Cook time: 1 hour, Serves: 8

Ingredients:

19 oz. pkg. mild Italian sausages, remove casings
1 yellow onion, diced
8 eggs
2 cup half-and-half

2 cup reduced fat cheddar cheese, grated
¼ cup fresh parsley, diced
2 tbsp. butter, divided

What you'll need from store cupboard:

1/2 loaf bread, (chapter 14), cut in cubes
1 tsp salt
¼ tsp pepper

¼ tsp red pepper flakes
Nonstick cooking spray

Instructions:

1. Spray a 9x13-inch baking dish with cooking spray.
2. Melt 1 tablespoon butter in a skillet over medium heat. Add sausage and cook, breaking up with a spatula, until no longer pink. Transfer to a large bowl.
3. Add remaining tablespoon butter to the skillet with the onion and cook until soft, 3-5 minutes. Add to sausage with the cheese and bread cubes.
4. In a separate bowl, whisk together eggs, half-n-half, and seasonings. Pour over sausage mixture, tossing to mix all Ingredients. Pour into prepared baking dish, cover and chill 2 hours, or overnight.
5. Heat oven to 350 degrees. Remove cover and bake 50-60 minutes, or a knife inserted in center comes out clean. Serve immediately garnished with parsley.

Nutrition Facts Per Serving
Calories 300 Total Carbs 6g Net Carbs 5g Protein 22g Fat 20g Sugar 4g Fiber 1g

Eggnog Breakfast Pudding

Prep time: 15 minutes, Cook time: 1 hour, Serves: 10

Ingredients:

6 eggs
3 cup eggnog
1 cup skim milk

4 tbsp. butter, soft, divided

What you'll need from store cupboard:

1 loaf bread (chapter 14), cut in 1-inch-thick slices
1/2 cup Splenda

2 tbsp. bourbon
1/8 tsp salt
Powdered sugar substitute for dusting

Instructions:

1. Heat oven to 350 degrees.
2. Lay bread, in a single layer, on a baking sheet. Bake 8-10 minutes until dry and lightly toasted. Let cool slightly.
3. Grease 9x13-inch baking dish with ½ tablespoon of butter.
4. Spread one side of bread with remaining butter. Cut, or tear, bread into 1-inch cubes and place them in prepared dish.
5. In a large bowl, whisk together remaining Ingredients and pour over bread. Cover with foil and chill 1 hour.
6. Remove the foil and bake 45-50 minutes, or a knife inserted in center comes out clean. Remove from oven and let cool 10 minutes before serving. Dust lightly with powdered sugar substitute and serve.

Nutrition Facts Per Serving
Calories 326 Total Carbs 23g Net Carbs 22g Protein 10g Fat 20g Sugar 17g Fiber 1g

Strawberry Coconut Scones

Prep time: 5 minutes, Cook time: 40 minutes, Serves: 8

Ingredients:

1 ½ cup strawberries, chopped
1 large egg

What you'll need from store cupboard:

1 ½ cups almond flour
¼ cup coconut oil, melted
¼ cup Splenda

¼ cup unsweetened coconut, grated
2 tbsp. cornstarch
1 tsp vanilla
1 tsp baking powder

Instructions:

1. Heat oven to 350 degrees. Line a 9-inch round baking dish with parchment paper.
2. In a large bowl, beat egg, oil, Splenda, and vanilla until smooth. Scrape sides as needed.
3. Turn mixer to low, and add flour, cornstarch, coconut, and baking powder until incorporated.
4. Fold in strawberries. Spread batter evenly in prepared pan. Bake 35-40 minutes.
5. Let cool 15 minutes before removing from pan. Slice into 8 pieces.

Nutrition Facts Per Serving
Calories 225 Total Carbs 14g Net Carbs 11g Protein 5g Fat 17g Sugar 8g Fiber 3g

Ham & Broccoli Breakfast Bake

**Prep time: 10 minutes, Cook time: 35 minutes,
Serves: 8**
Ingredients:

8-10 eggs, beaten
4-6 cup small broccoli
florets, blanch for 2
minutes, then drain
well

1-2 cup ham, diced
1 cup mozzarella
cheese, grated
1/3 cup green onion,
sliced thin

What you'll need from store cupboard:

1 tsp all-purpose
seasoning
Fresh-ground black

pepper, to taste
Nonstick cooking
spray

Instructions:

1. Heat oven to 375. Spray a 9x12-inch
   baking dish with cooking spray.
2. Layer broccoli, ham, cheese and onions
   in the dish. Sprinkle with seasoning and
   pepper. Pour eggs over everything.
3. Using a fork, stir the mixture to make
   sure everything is coated with the egg.
4. Bake 35-40 minutes, or until eggs are
   set and top is starting to brown. Serve
   immediately.

Nutrition Facts Per Serving
Calories 159 Total Carbs 7g Net Carbs 5g
Protein 15g Fat 9g Sugar 2g Fiber 2g

Ham & Jicama Hash

**Prep time: 10 minutes, Cook time: 15 minutes,
Serves: 4**
Ingredients:

6 eggs, beaten
2 cups jicama, grated
1 cup low fat cheddar

cheese, grated
1 cup ham, diced

What you'll need from store cupboard:

Salt and pepper, to
taste

Nonstick cooking
spray

Instructions:

1. Spray a large nonstick skillet with
   cooking spray and place over medium-
   high heat. Add jicama and cook, stirring
   occasionally, until it starts to brown,
   about 5 minutes.
2. Add remaining Ingredients and reduce
   heat to medium. Cook about 3 minutes,
   then flip over and cook until eggs are
   set, about 3-5 minutes more. Season
   with salt and pepper and serve.

Nutrition Facts Per Serving
Calories 221 Total Carbs 8g Net Carbs 5g
Protein 21g Fat 11g Sugar 2g Fiber 3g

Hawaiian Breakfast Bake

**Prep time: 10 minutes, Cook time: 20 minutes,
Serves: 6**
Ingredients:

6 slice ham, sliced
thin
6 eggs

¼ cup reduced fat
cheddar cheese,
grated

What you'll need from store cupboard:

6 pineapple slices
2 tbsp. salsa

½ tsp seasoning
blend, salt-free

Instructions:

1. Heat oven to 350 degrees.
2. Line 6 muffin cups, or ramekins with
   sliced ham. Layer with cheese, salsa, and
   pineapple.
3. Crack one egg into each cup, sprinkle
   with seasoning blend.
4. If using ramekins place them on a baking
   sheet, bake 20-25 minutes or until egg
   whites are completely set but yolks are
   still soft. Serve immediately.

Nutrition Facts Per Serving
Calories 135 Total Carbs 5g Net Carbs 4g
Protein 12g Fat 8g Sugar 3g Fiber 1g

Peanut Butter Waffles

**Prep time: 5 minutes, Cook time: 10 minutes,
Serves: 4**
Ingredients:

4 eggs
½ cup low fat cream
cheese

½ cup half-n-half
2 tbsp. margarine

What you'll need from store cupboard:

2/3 cup low fat
peanut butter
2 tsp Splenda

1 tsp baking powder
Nonstick cooking
spray

Instructions:

1. Lightly spray waffle iron with cooking
   spray and preheat.
2. In a medium glass bowl, place peanut
   butter, margarine, and cream cheese.
   Microwave 30 seconds and stir to
   combine.
3. Stir in the cream, baking powder, and
   Splenda and mix until all the Ingredients
   are combined. Stir in eggs and mix well.
4. Ladle into waffle iron and cook until
   golden brown and crisp on the outside.
   Serve.

Nutrition Facts Per Serving
Calories 214 Total Carbs 9g Net Carbs 8g
Protein 9g Fat 15g Sugar 2g Fiber 1g

Hot Maple Porridge

Prep time: 2 minutes, Cook time: 1 minute, serves 1

Ingredients:

1 tsp margarine

What you'll need from store cupboard:

1/2 cup water	1 tsp Splenda
2 tbsp. flax meal	¼ tsp maple extract
1 tbsp. almond flour	Pinch salt
1 tbsp. coconut flour	

Instructions:

1. In a microwave safe bowl, combine all Ingredients, except margarine, and mix thoroughly.
2. Microwave on high for one minute.
3. Stir in margarine and serve.

Nutrition Facts Per Serving

Calories 143 Total Carbs 9g Net Carbs 2g Protein 5g Fat 1g Sugar 0g Fiber 7g

Strawberry & Ricotta Crepes

Prep time: 5 minutes, Cook time: 15 minutes, Serves: 4

Ingredients:

8 eggs	1 cup low-fat ricotta cheese
1 cup strawberries, sliced	

What you'll need from store cupboard:

2 tsp Splenda	Nonstick cooking spray
2 tsp vanilla	

Instructions:

1. In a small bowl, place strawberries and sprinkle with 1 teaspoon Splenda, set aside.
2. In a large mixing bowl, whisk ½ cup ricotta cheese with remaining Ingredients.
3. Spray a small nonstick skillet with cooking spray and heat over medium heat.
4. Pour ¼ cup batter at a time into hot pan, swirling the pan to cover the bottom. Cook until bottom is brown, about 1-2 minutes. Flip over and cook 1 minute more.
5. To serve, spread each crepe with 2 tablespoons ricotta cheese and fold over. Top with strawberries.

Nutrition Facts Per Serving

Calories 230 Total Carbs 10g Net Carbs 8g Protein 17g Fat 14g Sugar 9g Fiber 2g

Spinach Cheddar Squares

Prep time: 15 minutes, Cook time: 40 minutes, Serves: 4

Ingredients:

10 oz. spinach, frozen, thaw and squeeze dry	¾ cup reduced fat cheddar cheese, grated
1 ½ cup egg substitute	¼ cup red pepper, diced
¾ cup skim milk	

What you'll need from store cupboard:

2 tbsp. reduced fat parmesan cheese	½ tsp salt
1 tbsp. bread crumbs	¼ tsp garlic powder
½ tsp minced onion, dried	¼ tsp pepper
	Nonstick cooking spray

Instructions:

1. Heat oven to 350 degrees. Spray an 8-inch square baking dish with cooking spray.
2. Sprinkle bread crumbs over the bottom of prepared dish. Top with ½ cup cheese, spinach, and red pepper.
3. In a small bowl, whisk together remaining Ingredients. Pour over vegetables.
4. Bake 35 minutes. Sprinkle with remaining cheese and bake 2-3 minutes more, or until cheese is melted and a knife inserted in the center comes out clean.
5. Let cool 15 minutes before cutting and serving.

Nutrition Facts Per Serving

Calories 159 Total Carbs 7g Net Carbs 5g Protein 22g Fat 5g Sugar 4g Fiber 2g

Mango Strawberry Smoothies

Prep time: 5 minutes, Total time: 10 minutes, Serves: 2

Ingredients:

½ mango, peeled and diced	halved
¾ cup strawberries,	½ cup skim milk
	¼ cup vanilla yogurt

What you'll need from store cupboard:

3 ice cubes	2 tsp Splenda

Instructions:

1. Combine all Ingredients in a blender. Process until smooth. Pour into chilled glasses and serve immediately.

Nutrition Facts Per Serving

Calories 132 Total Carbs 26g Net Carbs 24g Protein 5g Fat 1g Sugar 23g Fiber 2g

Olive & Mushroom Frittata

Prep time: 10 minutes, Cook time: 20 minutes, Serves: 4

Ingredients:

2 cups fresh spinach, chopped	Parmesan cheese, grated
1 cup cremini mushrooms, sliced	¼ cup Kalamata olives, pitted and sliced thin
4 eggs	
2 egg whites	1 large shallot, sliced thin
1/3 cup reduced-fat	

What you'll need from store cupboard:

1 tbsp. olive oil	¼ tsp black pepper
½ tsp rosemary	1/8 tsp salt

Instructions:

1. Preheat broiler.
2. In a nonstick, broiler proof skillet, heat oil over medium heat. Add mushrooms and cook 3 minutes, stirring occasionally. Add spinach and shallot and cook until mushrooms and spinach are tender, about 5 minutes.
3. In a medium bowl, whisk together eggs and seasonings. Pour egg mixture into skillet. Cook, as it cooks, use a spatula around the edge of skillet, lifting the frittata so uncooked eggs flow underneath. Cook until eggs are almost set.
4. Sprinkle the olives and cheese over the top. Broil 4-inches from heat until top is lightly browned, about 2 minutes. Let stand 5 minutes before cutting into 4 wedges to serve.

Nutrition Facts Per Serving

Calories 146 Total Carbs 3g Protein 10g Fat 11g Sugar 0g Fiber 0g

Mini Mushroom Egg Stacks

Prep time: 10 minutes, Cook time: 25 minutes, Serves: 3

Ingredients:

6 mini Portobello mushrooms, rinse and remove stems	3 slices bacon, cooked crisp and crumbled
4 cup of mixed baby kale	½ red pepper, diced
4 eggs, beaten	6 tbsp. low fat cheddar cheese, grated
3 green onions, diced	

What you'll need from store cupboard:

3 tbsp. olive oil, divided	Salt and pepper

Instructions:

1. Heat oven to 350 degrees.
2. Lay mushrooms on baking sheet and brush with 1 tablespoon oil. Sprinkle with salt and pepper and bake 10-15 minutes, or until tender but firm enough to hold their shape.
3. Heat 1 tablespoon oil in a large skillet over med-high heat. Add vegetables and salt and pepper to taste. Cook, stirring frequently until kale has wilted and peppers are tender. Transfer to a bowl.
4. Wipe skillet clean and heat remaining tablespoon oil. Add eggs and scramble to desired doneness.
5. To assemble, top each mushroom with the kale mixture, then eggs. Sprinkle one tablespoon cheese on top then the bacon. One serving is 2 mushroom stacks.

Nutrition Facts Per Serving

Calories 256 Total Carbs 10g Net Carbs 8g Protein 21g Fat 15g Sugar 2g Fiber 2g

Spinach & Tomato Egg Muffins

Prep time: 5 minutes, Cook time: 25 minutes, Serves: 6

Ingredients:

6 eggs	diced
2 green onions, sliced	1/3 cup reduced-fat cheddar cheese, grated
1 avocado, sliced	
½ cup fresh spinach, diced	¼ cup almond milk, unsweetened
1/3 cup tomatoes,	

What you'll need from store cupboard:

Salt and pepper	spray
Nonstick cooking	

Instructions:

1. Heat oven to 350 degrees. Spray a muffin pan with cooking spray.
2. In a large bowl, beat together eggs, milk, and salt and pepper to taste.
3. Add remaining Ingredients and mix well.
4. Divide evenly between 6 muffin cups. Bake 20-25 minutes or until egg is set in the middle.
5. Remove from oven let cool 5 minutes. Serve topped with sliced avocado.

Nutrition Facts Per Serving

Calories 176 Total Carbs 5g Net Carbs 2g Protein 8g Fat 15g Sugar 1g Fiber 3g

Pumpkin Pancakes

Prep time: 10 minutes, Cook time: 10 minutes, Serves: 2

Ingredients:

4 eggs

What you'll need from store cupboard:

1 cup fine ground almond flour	1 teaspoon baking powder
½ cup pumpkin puree	½ tsp cinnamon
2 teaspoon liquid stevia	Nonstick cooking spray

Instructions:

1. Mix all Ingredients in a medium bowl and whisk until thoroughly combined.
2. Spray a small nonstick skillet with cooking spray and place over med-high heat.
3. Pour about ¼-1/3 cup batter into skillet, spreading out evenly. Cook until brown on the bottom. Flip and repeat with the other side.
4. Serve with a pat of margarine and sugar-free syrup if desired.

Nutrition Facts Per Serving

Calories 444 Total Carbs 22g Net Carbs 14g Protein 22g Fat 16g Sugar 8g Fiber 8g

Poached Eggs & Grits

Prep time: 1 minute, Cook time: 10 minutes, Serves: 4

Ingredients:

4 eggs, poached	¼ cup Colby cheese, grated
3 cups skim milk	

What you'll need from store cupboard:

1 cup grits	parmesan cheese, grated
2 tsp reduced fat	

Instructions:

1. In a large microwavable bowl, stir together the grits and most of the milk, save a little to stir in later. Cook 8-10 minutes, stirring every couple of minutes.
2. Meanwhile, poach the eggs in a large pot of boiling water.
3. When grits are done, stir in the cheese until melted and smooth. If they seem too stiff, add the remaining milk.
4. Ladle into 4 bowls and top each with a poached egg, serve.

Nutrition Facts Per Serving

Calories 180 Total Carbs 15g Net Carbs 14g Protein 13g Fat 6g Sugar 10g Fiber 1g

"Bacon" & Egg Muffins

Prep time: 10 minutes, Cook time: 15 minutes, Serves: 6

Ingredients:

1 ¼ cups frozen hash browns, thawed	2 tbsp. turkey bacon, cooked and chopped
1 cup egg substitute	2 tbsp. Monterey Jack cheese, grated
2 turkey sausage patties, diced	1 tbsp. fat-free sour cream
2 tbsp. onion, diced fine	

What you'll need from store cupboard:

1 clove garlic, diced fine	¼ tsp salt
1 tsp vegetable oil	1/8 tsp black pepper

Instructions:

1. Heat oven to 400 degrees. Spray a 6-cup muffin pan with cooking spray.
2. Divide the hash browns evenly among the muffin cups, pressing firmly on the bottoms and up the sides.
3. In a large skillet, over medium heat, heat oil until hot. Add onion, and cook stirring frequently until tender.
4. Add garlic and sausage and cook for one minute.
5. Remove the skillet from heat and stir in sour cream.
6. In a medium bowl, beat egg substitute with salt and pepper. Pour egg mixture evenly over the potatoes.
7. Top with sausage mixture, bacon and cheese. Bake 15 – 18 minutes, or until eggs are set. Serve immediately.

Nutrition Facts Per Serving

Calories 165 Total Carbs 13g Net Carbs 12g Protein 11g Fat 7g Sugar 1g Fiber 1g

Summer Breakfast Parfait

Prep time: 5 minutes, Total time: 10 minutes, Serves: 1

Ingredients:

1 5-oz. container vanilla Greek yogurt	1 peach, sliced thin
	¼ cup blueberries

What you'll need from store cupboard:

1/3 cup granola

Instructions:

1. Layer half the yogurt on the bottom of a glass or Mason jar. Top with half the granola, half the peaches and half the berries. Repeat. Eat immediately.

Nutrition Facts Per Serving

Calories 78 Total Carbs 20g Net Carbs 17g Protein 6g Fat 6g Sugar 12g Fiber 3g

Waffle or Pancake Mix

Prep time: 2 minutes, Cook time: 5 minutes, Serves: 4
Ingredients:
2 eggs
What you'll need from store cupboard:

1 cup almond flour	1 tsp nutmeg
¼ cup sparkling water	¼ tsp salt
2 tbsp. vegetable oil	Nonstick cooking spray
1 tbsp. Stevia	Sugar-free syrup
1 tsp cinnamon	

Optional: dark chocolate chips, carob chips, pecans, or blueberries
Instructions:
1. Lightly spray waffle iron with cooking spray and preheat.
2. In a medium bowl, stir together all Ingredients until smooth.
3. Pour ¼ cup batter into waffle iron and cook according to manufactures directions, about 3-4 minutes.
4. Serve with sugar-free syrup or your favorite toppings.

Nutrition Facts Per Serving
Calories 248 Total Carbs 9g Net Carbs 6g
Protein 8g Fat 21g Sugar 4g Fiber 3g

Sunrise Smoothies

Prep time: 5 minutes, Total time: 10 minutes, serves; 3
Ingredients:

1 banana, frozen and sliced	½ cup fresh pineapple, cubed
¾ cup ruby red grapefruit juice	½ cup peach slices, unsweetened

What you'll need from store cupboard:

4 ice cubes	1 tbsp. Splenda

Instructions:
1. Combine all Ingredients in a blender. Process until smooth. Pour into chilled glasses and serve.

Nutrition Facts Per Serving
Calories 97 Total Carbs 24g Net Carbs 22g
Protein 1g Fat 0g Sugar 18g Fiber 2g

Jicama Hash Browns

Prep time: 10 minutes, Cook time: 20 minutes, Serves: 2
Ingredients:

2 cups jicama, peeled	½ small onion, diced and grated

What you'll need from store cupboard:

1 tbsp. vegetable oil	A pinch of pepper to taste
A pinch of salt to taste	

Instructions:
1. Add the oil to a large skillet and heat over med-high heat.
2. Add the onion and cook until translucent.
3. Add the jicama and salt and pepper to taste. Cook until nicely browned on both sides. Serve immediately.

Nutrition Facts Per Serving
Calories 113 Total Carbs 12g Net Carbs 6g
Protein 1g Fat 7g Sugar 3g Fiber 6g

Pumpkin Spice French Toast

Prep time: 5 minutes, Cook time: 20 minutes, Serves: 4
Ingredients:

6 eggs	1 ½ cup skim milk

What you'll need from store cupboard:

8 slices Healthy Loaf Bread, (chapter 15)	spice
¼ cup pumpkin	1 tsp vanilla
1 tsp salt	Butter flavored cooking spray
1 tsp pumpkin pie	

Instructions:
1. In a large bowl, whisk together all Ingredients, except bread, until combined. Add the bread slices and toss to coat.
2. Spray a large, nonstick skillet with cooking spray and place over medium heat. Add bread, two slices, or what fits in the pan, at a time and cook 2-3 minutes per side. Serve as is, or with sugar-free maple syrup.

Nutrition Facts Per Serving
Calories 295 Total Carbs 10g net Carbs 8g
Protein 17g Fat 20g Sugar 5g Fiber 2g

Vanilla Mango Smoothies

Prep time: 5 minutes, Total time: 5 minutes, Serves: 3

Ingredients:

1 cup mango, frozen chunks

½ cup orange juice, unsweetened

6 oz. vanilla yogurt

What you'll need from store cupboard:

1 tbsp. honey

Instructions:

1. Place all Ingredients in a blender. Process until smooth. Pour into chilled glasses and serve.

Nutrition Facts Per Serving

Calories 112 Total Carbs 22g Net Carbs 21g Protein 4g Fat 1g Sugar 21g Fiber 1g

Strawberry Kiwi Smoothies

Prep time: 5 minutes, blend time: 3 minutes, Serves: 4

Ingredients:

2 kiwi, peel & quarter

6 oz. strawberry yogurt

1 cup strawberries, frozen

½ cup skim milk

What you'll need from store cupboard:

2 tbsp. honey

Instructions:

1. Place all Ingredients in a blender and process until smooth.
2. Pour into glasses and serve immediately.

Nutrition Facts Per Serving

Calories 120 Total Carbs 26g Net Carbs 24g Protein 3g Fat 1g Sugar 23g Fiber 2g

Pumpkin Pie Smoothie

Total time: 5 minutes, serves 2

Ingredients:

1 ½ cup almond milk, unsweetened

4 oz. reduced fat

cream cheese, soft

½ cup Greek yogurt

What you'll need from store cupboard:

¼ cup pumpkin puree

2 tbsp. Splenda

1/8 tsp cinnamon

Pinch ginger

Instructions:

1. Place all Ingredients in a blender. Process until smooth and everything is combined.
2. Pour into two glasses and garnish with the pinch of ginger on top.

Nutrition Facts Per Serving

Calories 220 Total Carbs 27g Net Carbs 25g Protein 13g Fat 5g Sugar 15g Fiber 2g

Yogurt & Granola Breakfast Popsicles

Prep time: 20 minutes, Cook time: 8 hours, Serves: 6

Ingredients:

1 ½ cups fresh berries, chopped

1 ¼ cups plain low-fat yogurt

What you'll need from store cupboard:

6 tbsp. granola, crumbled

4 tsp sugar free

maple syrup, divided

1 tsp vanilla

6 3-oz Popsicle molds

Instructions:

1. In a medium bowl, stir together yogurt, berries, 2 teaspoons maple syrup, and vanilla together.
2. Pour evenly into Popsicle molds.
3. In a small bowl, stir together remaining syrup and granola together. Top each Popsicle with 1 tablespoon of the granola mixture. Insert sticks and freeze 8 hours, or overnight. Popsicles can be stored in the freezer up to 1 week.

Nutrition Facts Per Serving

Calories 73 Total Carbs 20g Net Carbs 18g Protein 5g Fat 4g Sugar 7g Fiber 2g

Lemon Glazed Blueberry Bread

Prep time: 10 minutes, Cook time: 50 minutes, Serves: 12

Ingredients:

5 eggs	divided
½ cup blueberries	3 tbsp. butter, soft
5 tbsp. half-n-half,	

What you'll need from store cupboard:

2 cup almond flour, sifted	1 ½ tsp baking powder
½ cup Splenda	1 tsp vanilla
2 tbsp. coconut flour	Butter flavored cooking spray
2 tbsp. Swerve confectioners	

Instructions:

1. Heat oven to 350 degrees. Spray an 8.5-inch loaf pan with cooking spray.
2. In a large bowl, beat the eggs, ½ cup Splenda, and vanilla 2-3 minutes or until the eggs look frothy. Add 3 tablespoons half-n-half and mix again.
3. In a separate bowl, combine flours and baking powder. Add to egg mixture and beat to combine. Beat in the butter then fold in berries.
4. Transfer to prepared pan and bake 45-50 minutes or it passes the toothpick test.
5. Let cool 10 minutes in the pan, then invert onto serving plate.
6. In a small bowl, whisk together remaining 2 tablespoons half-n-half, powdered Splenda and lemon juice. When bread has cooled drizzle glaze over top, letting it drip down the sides. Slice and serve.

Nutrition Facts Per Serving

Calories 185 Total Carbs 14g Net Carbs 11g Protein 5g Fat 12g Sugar 10g Fiber 3g

Tex Mex Breakfast Bake

Prep time: 15 minutes, Cook time: 40 minutes, Serves: 9

Ingredients:

2 cups egg substitute	¾ cup bell pepper, diced
4 scallions, sliced	½ cup fat-free milk
1 cup reduced-fat Monterey Jack cheese, grated and divided	½ cup Italian salsa, (chapter 16)

What you'll need from store cupboard:

10 slices light whole-grain bread, cut into 1-inch pieces	½ tsp chili powder
	½ tsp garlic powder
1 (4-ounce) can green chilies, diced and drained	¼ tsp black pepper
	Nonstick cooking spray

Instructions:

1. Spray a 9x13-inch baking dish with cooking spray. Place bread evenly on the bottom.
2. Spray a small skillet with cooking spray and place over medium heat. Add bell pepper and cook until tender, about 5 minutes.
3. In a medium bowl, whisk together remaining Ingredients, reserving ½ cup cheese.
4. Place the cooked peppers over the bread, then pour in the egg mixture. Cover and chill at least 2 hours or overnight.
5. Heat oven to 350 degrees. Sprinkle the reserved ½ cheese over the top of casserole and bake, covered, 20 minutes. Remove the cover and bake 15 – 20 minutes more, or until the eggs are firm in the center.
6. Serve immediately topped salsa.

Nutrition Facts Per Serving

Calories 197 Total Carbs 25g Net Carbs 19g Protein 16g Fat 4g Sugar 9g Fiber 6g

Chapter 6 - Snacks Recipe

Almond Cheesecake Bites

Prep time: 5 minutes, chill time: 30 minutes, Serves: 6
Ingredients:
½ cup reduced-fat cream cheese, soft
What you'll need from store cupboard:
½ cup almonds, ground fine   ¼ cup almond butter
2 drops liquid stevia
Instructions:
1. In a large bowl, beat cream cheese, almond butter and stevia on high speed until mixture is smooth and creamy. Cover and chill 30 minutes.
2. Use your hands to shape the mixture into 12 balls.
3. Place the ground almonds in a shallow plate. Roll the balls in the nuts completely covering all sides. Store in an airtight container in the refrigerator.
Nutrition Facts Per Serving
Calories 68 Total Carbs 3g Net Carbs 2 Protein 5g Fat 5g Sugar 0g Fiber 1g

Almond Flour Crackers

Prep time: 5 minutes, Cook time: 15 minutes, Serves: 8
Ingredients:
½ cup coconut oil, melted
What you'll need from store cupboard:
1 ½ cups almond flour   ¼ cup Stevia
Instructions:
1. Heat oven to 350 degrees. Line a cookie sheet with parchment paper.
2. In a mixing bowl, combine all Ingredients and mix well.
3. Spread dough onto prepared cookie sheet, ¼-inch thick. Use a paring knife to score into 24 crackers.
4. Bake 10 – 15 minutes or until golden brown.
5. Separate and store in air-tight container.
Nutrition Facts Per Serving
Calories 281 Total Carbs 16g Net Carbs 14g Protein 4g Fat 23g Sugar 13g Fiber 2g

Asian Chicken Wings

Prep time: 5 minutes, Cook time: 30 minutes, Serves: 3
Ingredients:
24 chicken wings
What you'll need from store cupboard:
6 tbsp. soy sauce   Salt & pepper
6 tbsp. Chinese 5 spice   Nonstick cooking spray
Instructions:
1. Heat oven to 350 degrees. Spray a baking sheet with cooking spray.
2. Combine the soy sauce, 5 spice, salt, and pepper in a large bowl. Add the wings and toss to coat.
3. Pour the wings onto the prepared pan. Bake 15 minutes. Turn chicken over and cook another 15 minutes until chicken is cooked through.
4. Serve with your favorite low carb dipping sauce (see chapter 16).
Nutrition Facts Per Serving
Calories 178 Total Carbs 8g Protein 12g Fat 11g Sugar 1g Fiber 0g

Banana Nut Cookies

Prep time: 10 minutes, Cook time: 15 minutes, Serves: 18
Ingredients:
1 ½ cup banana, mashed
What you'll need from store cupboard:
2 cup oats   1/3 cup sunflower oil
1 cup raisins   1 tsp vanilla
1 cup walnuts   ½ tsp salt
Instructions:
1. Heat oven to 350 degrees.
2. In a large bowl, combine oats, raisins, walnuts, and salt.
3. In a medium bowl, mix banana, oil, and vanilla. Stir into oat mixture until combined. Let rest 15 minutes.
4. Drop by rounded tablespoonful onto 2 ungreased cookie sheets. Bake 15 minutes, or until a light golden brown. Cool and store in an airtight container. Serving size is 2 cookies.
Nutrition Facts Per Serving
Calories 148 Total Carbs 16g Net Carbs 14g Protein 3g Fat 9g Sugar 6g Fiber 2g

BLT Stuffed Cucumbers

Prep time: 15 minutes, Serves: 4
Ingredients:

3 slices bacon, cooked crisp and crumbled
1 large cucumber
½ cup lettuce, diced fine
½ cup baby spinach, diced fine
¼ cup tomato, diced fine

What you'll need from store cupboard:

1 tbsp. + ½ tsp fat-free mayonnaise
¼ tsp black pepper
1/8 tsp salt

Instructions:

1. Peel the cucumber and slice in half lengthwise. Use a spoon to remove the seeds.
2. In a medium bowl, combine remaining Ingredients and stir well.
3. Spoon the bacon mixture into the cucumber halves. Cut into 2-inch pieces and serve.

Nutrition Facts Per Serving
Calories 95 Total Carbs 4g Net Carbs 3g Protein 6g Fat 6g Sugar 2g Fiber 1g

Buffalo Bites

Prep time: 5 minutes, Cook time: 10 minutes, Serves: 4
Ingredients:

1 egg
½ head of cauliflower, separated into florets

What you'll need from store cupboard:

1 cup panko bread crumbs
1 cup low-fat ranch dressing
½ cup hot sauce
½ tsp salt
½ tsp garlic powder
Black pepper
Nonstick cooking spray

Instructions:

1. Heat oven to 400 degrees. Spray a baking sheet with cooking spray.
2. Place the egg in a medium bowl and mix in the salt, pepper and garlic. Place the panko crumbs into a small bowl.
3. Dip the florets first in the egg then into the panko crumbs. Place in a single layer on prepared pan.
4. Bake 8-10 minutes, stirring halfway through, until cauliflower is golden brown and crisp on the outside.
5. In a small bowl stir the dressing and hot sauce together. Use for dipping.

Nutrition Facts Per Serving
Calories 132 Total Carbs 15g Net Carbs 14g Protein 6g Fat 5g Sugar 4g Fiber 1g

Candied Pecans

Prep time: 5 minutes, Cook time: 10 minutes, Serves: 6
Ingredients:

1 ½ tsp butter

What you'll need from store cupboard:

1 ½ cup pecan halves
2 ½ tbsp. Splenda, divided
1 tsp cinnamon
¼ tsp ginger
1/8 tsp cardamom
1/8 tsp salt

Instructions:

1. In a small bowl, stir together 1 1/2 teaspoons Splenda, cinnamon, ginger, cardamom and salt. Set aside.
2. Melt butter in a medium skillet over med-low heat. Add pecans, and two tablespoons Splenda. Reduce heat to low and cook, stirring occasionally, until sweetener melts, about 5 to 8 minutes.
3. Add spice mixture to the skillet and stir to coat pecans. Spread mixture to parchment paper and let cool for 10-15 minutes. Store in an airtight container. Serving size is ¼ cup.

Nutrition Facts Per Serving
Calories 173 Total Carbs 8g Net Carbs 6g Protein 2g Fat 16g Sugar 6g Fiber 2g

Cheese Crisp Crackers

Prep time: 5 minutes, Cook time: 10 minutes, Serves: 4
Ingredients:

4 slices pepper Jack cheese, quartered
4 slices Colby Jack
cheese, quartered
4 slices cheddar cheese, quartered

Instructions:

1. Heat oven to 400 degrees. Line a cooking sheet with parchment paper.
2. Place cheese in a single layer on prepared pan and bake 10 minutes, or until cheese gets firm.
3. Transfer to paper towel line surface to absorb excess oil. Let cool, cheese will crisp up more as it cools.
4. Store in airtight container, or Ziploc bag. Serve with your favorite dip or salsa.

Nutrition Facts Per Serving
Calories 253 Total Carbs 1g Protein 15g Fat 20g Sugar 0g Fiber 0g

Cheesy Pita Crisps

Prep time: 5 minutes, Cook time: 15 minutes, Serves: 8
Ingredients:

½ cup mozzarella cheese ¼ cup margarine, melted

What you'll need from store cupboard:

4 whole-wheat pita pocket halves
3 tbsp. reduced fat parmesan
½ tsp garlic powder
½ tsp onion powder
¼ tsp salt
¼ tsp pepper
Nonstick cooking spray

Instructions:

1. Heat oven to 400 degrees. Spray a baking sheet with cooking spray.
2. Cut each pita pocket in half. Cut each half into 2 triangles. Place, rough side up, on prepared pan.
3. In a small bowl, whisk together margarine, parmesan and seasonings. Spread each triangle with margarine mixture. Sprinkle mozzarella over top.
4. Bake 12-15 minutes or until golden brown.

Nutrition Facts Per Serving

Calories 131 Total Carbs 14g Net Carbs 12g Protein 4g Fat 7g Sugar 1g Fiber 2g

Mozzarella Sticks

Prep time: 1 hour 10 minutes, Cook time: 30 minutes, Serves: 4
Ingredients:

8 string cheese sticks, halved
2 eggs, beaten

What you'll need from store cupboard:

1 cup reduced fat parmesan cheese
½ cup sunflower oil
1 tbsp. Italian
seasoning
1 clove garlic, diced fine

Instructions:

1. Heat oil in a pot over med-high heat.
2. In a medium bowl, combine parmesan cheese, Italian seasoning and garlic.
3. In a small bowl, beat the eggs.
4. Dip string cheese in eggs then in parmesan mixture to coat, pressing coating into cheese.
5. Place in hot oil and cook until golden brown. Transfer to paper towel lined plate. Serve warm with marinara sauce, (chapter 16).

Nutrition Facts Per Serving

Calories 290 Total Carbs 3g Protein 24g Fat 20g Sugar 0g Fiber 0g

Cheesy Taco Chips

Prep time: 15 minutes, Cook time: 40 minutes, Serves: 6
Ingredients:

1 cup Mexican blend cheese, grated
2 large egg whites

What you'll need from store cupboard:

1 1/2 cup crushed pork rinds
1 tbsp. taco
seasoning
¼ tsp salt

Instructions:

1. Heat oven to 300 degrees. Line a large baking sheet with parchment paper.
2. In a large bowl, whisk egg whites and salt until frothy. Stir in pork rinds, cheese, and seasoning and stir until thoroughly combined.
3. Turn out onto prepared pan. Place another sheet of parchment paper on top and roll out very thin, about 12x12-inches. Remove top sheet of parchment paper, and using a pizza cutter, score dough in 2-inch squares, then score each square in half diagonally.
4. Bake 20 minutes until they start to brown. Turn off oven and let them sit inside the oven until they are firm to the touch, about 10-20 minutes.
5. Remove from oven and cool completely before breaking apart. Eat them as is or with your favorite dip.

Nutrition Facts Per Serving

Calories 260 Total Carbs 1g Protein 25g Fat 17g Sugar 0g Fiber 0g

Honeydew & Ginger Smoothies

Prep time: 5 minutes, blend time: 3 minutes, Serves: 3
Ingredients:

1 ½ cup honeydew melon, cubed
½ cup banana
½ cup nonfat vanilla
yogurt
¼ tsp fresh ginger, grated

What you'll need from store cupboard:

½ cup ice cubes

Instructions:

1. Place all Ingredients in a blender and pulse until smooth. Pour into glasses and serve immediately.

Nutrition Facts Per Serving

Calories 68 Total Carbs 16g Net Carbs 15g Protein 2g Fat 0g Sugar 12g Fiber 1g

Chewy Granola Bars

Prep time: 10 minutes, Cook time: 35 minutes, Serves: 36

Ingredients:

1 egg, beaten
2/3 cup margarine, melted

What you'll need from store cupboard:

3 ½ cup quick oats	½ cup dried
1 cup almonds, chopped	cranberries
½ cup honey	½ cup Splenda brown sugar
½ cup sunflower kernels	1 tsp vanilla
½ cup coconut, unsweetened	½ tsp cinnamon
½ cup dried apples	Nonstick cooking spray

Instructions:

1. Heat oven to 350 degrees. Spray a large baking sheet with cooking spray.
2. Spread oats and almonds on prepared pan. Bake 12-15 minutes until toasted, stirring every few minutes.
3. In a large bowl, combine egg, margarine, honey, and vanilla. Stir in remaining Ingredients.
4. Stir in oat mixture. Press into baking sheet and bake 13-18 minutes, or until edges are light brown.
5. Cool on a wire rack. Cut into bars and store in an airtight container.

Nutrition Facts Per Serving
Calories 119 Total Carbs 13g Net Carbs 12g Protein 2g Fat 6g Sugar 7g Fiber 1g

Italian Eggplant Rollups

Prep time: 10 minutes, Cook time: 25 minutes, Serves: 8

Ingredients:

16 fresh spinach leaves	1 green onion, diced fine
4 sun-dried tomatoes, rinsed, drained and diced fine	4 tbsp. fat-free cream cheese, soft
2 medium eggplants	2 tbsp. fat-free sour cream

What you'll need from store cupboard:

1 cup spaghetti sauce (chapter 16)	fine
2 tbsp. lemon juice	¼ tsp oregano
1 tsp olive oil	1/8 tsp black pepper
1 clove garlic, diced	Nonstick cooking spray

Instructions:

1. Heat oven to 450 degrees. Spray 2 large cookie sheets with cooking spray.
2. Trim the ends of the eggplant. Slice them lengthwise in ¼-inch slices. Discard the ones that are mostly skin, there should be about 16 slices. Arrange them in a single layer on prepared pans.
3. In a small bowl, whisk together the lemon juice and oil and brush over both sides of the eggplant. Bake 20-25 minutes or until the eggplant starts to turn a golden brown color. Transfer to a plate to cool.
4. In a mixing bowl, combine remaining Ingredients, except spinach, until thoroughly combined.
5. To assemble, spread 1 teaspoon cream cheese mixture evenly over sliced eggplant, leaving ½-inch border around the edges .Top with a spinach leaf and roll up, starting at small end. Lay rolls, seam side down, on serving plate. Serve with warm spaghetti sauce (chapter 16).

Nutrition Facts Per Serving
Calories 78 Total Carbs 12g Net Carbs 6g Protein 3g Fat 3g Sugar 6g Fiber 6g

Chili Lime Tortilla Chips

Prep time: 5 minutes, Cook time: 15 minutes, Serves: 10

Ingredients:

12 6-inch corn tortillas, cut into 8 triangles
3 tbsp. lime juice

What you'll need from store cupboard:

1 tsp cumin
1 tsp chili powder

Instructions:

1. Heat oven to 350 degrees.
2. Place tortilla triangles in a single layer on a large baking sheet.
3. In a small bowl stir together spices.
4. Sprinkle half the lime juice over tortillas, followed by ½ the spice mixture. Bake 7 minutes.
5. Remove from oven and turn tortillas over. Sprinkle with remaining lime juice and spices. Bake another 8 minutes or until crisp, but not brown. Serve with your favorite salsa, serving size is 10 chips.

Nutrition Facts Per Serving
Calories 65 Total Carbs 14g Net Carbs 12g Protein 2g Fat 1g Sugar 0g Fiber 2g

Cauliflower Hummus

Prep time: 5 minutes, Cook time: 15 minutes, serves 6

Ingredients:

3 cup cauliflower florets

3 tbsp. fresh lemon juice

What you'll need from store cupboard:

5 cloves garlic, divided

5 tbsp. olive oil, divided

2 tbsp. water

1 ½ tbsp. Tahini

paste

1 ¼ tsp salt, divided

Smoked paprika and extra olive oil for serving

Instructions:

1. In a microwave safe bowl, combine cauliflower, water, 2 tablespoons oil, ½ teaspoon salt, and 3 whole cloves garlic. Microwave on high 15 minutes, or until cauliflower is soft and darkened.
2. Transfer mixture to a food processor or blender and process until almost smooth. Add tahini paste, lemon juice, remaining garlic cloves, remaining oil, and salt. Blend until almost smooth.
3. Place the hummus in a bowl and drizzle lightly with olive oil and a sprinkle or two of paprika. Serve with your favorite raw vegetables.

Nutrition Facts Per Serving

Calories 107 Total Carbs 5g Net Carbs 3g Protein 2g Fat 10g Sugar 1g Fiber 2g

Popcorn Style Cauliflower

Prep time: 5 minutes, Cook time: 20 minutes, Serves: 4

Ingredients:

1 head cauliflower, separated into bite-sized florets

What you'll need from the store cupboard

¼ tsp garlic powder

¼ tsp salt

1/8 tsp black pepper

Butter-flavored cooking spray

Instructions:

1. Heat oven to 400 degrees.
2. Place cauliflower in a large bowl and spray with cooking spray, making sure to coat all sides. Sprinkle with seasonings and toss to coat.
3. Place in a single layer on a cookie sheet. Bake 20 – 25 minutes or until cauliflower starts to brown. Serve warm.

Nutrition Facts Per Serving

Calories 53 Total Carbs 11g Net Carbs 6g Protein 4g Fat 0g Sugar 5g Fiber 5g

Chocolate Chip Blondies

Prep time: 5 minutes, Cook time: 20 minutes, Serves: 12

Ingredients:

1 egg

What you'll need from store cupboard:

½ cup semi-sweet chocolate chips

1/3 cup flour

1/3 cup whole wheat flour

¼ cup Splenda brown sugar

¼ cup sunflower oil

2 tbsp. honey

1 tsp vanilla

½ tsp baking powder

¼ tsp salt

Nonstick cooking spray

Instructions:

1. Heat oven to 350 degrees. Spray an 8-inch square baking dish with cooking spray.
2. In a small bowl, combine dry Ingredients.
3. In a large bowl, whisk together egg, oil, honey, and vanilla. Stir in dry Ingredients just until combined. Stir in chocolate chips.
4. Spread batter in prepared dish. Bake 20-22 minutes or until they pass the toothpick test. Cool on a wire rack then cut into bars.

Nutrition Facts Per Serving

Calories 136 Total Carbs 18g Net Carbs 16g Protein 2g Fat 6g Sugar 9g Fiber 2g

Cinnamon Apple Chips

Prep time: 5 minutes, Cook time: 10 minutes, Serves: 2

Ingredients:

1 medium apple, sliced thin

What you'll need from store cupboard:

¼ tsp cinnamon

¼ tsp nutmeg

Nonstick cooking spray

Instructions:

1. Heat oven to 375. Spray a baking sheet with cooking spray.
2. Place apples in a mixing bowl and add spices. Toss to coat.
3. Arrange apples, in a single layer, on prepared pan. Bake 4 minutes, turn apples over and bake 4 minutes more.
4. Serve immediately or store in airtight container.

Nutrition Facts Per Serving

Calories 58 Total Carbs 15g Protein 0g Fat 0g Sugar 11g Fiber 3g

Raspberry Walnut Parfaits

Prep time: 10 minutes, chill time: 1 hour, Serves: 4

Ingredients:

1 can coconut milk, chilled (not low fat)
½ cup fresh raspberries, rinsed and dried

What you'll need from store cupboard:

¼ cup walnuts, coarsely chopped
1 tbsp. Splenda
1 tsp vanilla

Instructions:

1. In a medium bowl, combine the berries and walnuts.
2. In a large bowl, beat coconut milk, Splenda and vanilla until combined. Let rest 5 minutes.
3. In 4 small mason jars, spoon half the vanilla cream evenly. Top with berries. Repeat. Screw on the lids and chill at least one hour.

Nutrition Facts Per Serving

Calories 213 Total Carbs 8g Net Carbs 6g Protein 4g Fat 20g Sugar 4g Fiber 2g

Cinnamon Apple Popcorn

Prep time: 30 minutes, Cook time: 50 minutes, Serves: 11

Ingredients:

4 tbsp. margarine, melted
What you'll need from store cupboard
10 cup plain popcorn
2 cup dried apple rings, unsweetened
and chopped
½ cup walnuts, chopped
2 tbsp. Splenda brown sugar
1 tsp cinnamon
½ tsp vanilla

Instructions:

1. Heat oven to 250 degrees.
2. Place chopped apples in a 9x13-inch baking dish and bake 20 minutes. Remove from oven and stir in popcorn and nuts.
3. In a small bowl, whisk together margarine, vanilla, Splenda, and cinnamon. Drizzle evenly over popcorn and toss to coat.
4. Bake 30 minutes, stirring quickly every 10 minutes. If apples start to turn a dark brown, remove immediately.
5. Pout onto waxed paper to cool at least 30 minutes. Store in an airtight container. Serving size is 1 cup.

Nutrition Facts Per Serving

Calories 133 Total Carbs 14g Net Carbs 11g Protein 3g Fat 8g Sugar 7g Fiber 3g

Crab & Spinach Dip

Prep time: 10 minutes, Cook time: 2 hours, Serves: 10

Ingredients:

1 pkg. frozen chopped spinach, thawed and squeezed
nearly dry
8 oz. reduced-fat cream cheese

What you'll need from store cupboard:

6 ½ oz. can crabmeat, drained and shredded
6 oz. jar marinated artichoke hearts, drained and diced
fine
¼ tsp hot pepper sauce
Melba toast or whole grain crackers (optional)

Instructions:

1. Remove any shells or cartilage from crab.
2. Place all Ingredients in a small crock pot. Cover and cook on high 1 ½ - 2 hours, or until heated through and cream cheese is melted. Stir after 1 hour.
3. Serve with Melba toast or whole grain crackers. Serving size is ¼ cup.

Nutrition Facts Per Serving

Calories 106 Total Carbs 7g Net Carbs 6g Protein 5g Fat 8g Sugar 3g Fiber 1g

Crispy Baked Cheese Puffs

Prep time: 5 minutes, Cook time: 10 minutes, Serves: 4

Ingredients:

2 eggs
½ cup cheddar cheese, grated
¼ cup mozzarella, grated

What you'll need from store cupboard:

½ cup almond flour
¼ cup reduced fat Parmesan
½ tsp baking powder
Black pepper

Instructions:

1. Heat oven to 400 degrees. Line a baking sheet with parchment paper.
2. In a large bowl, whisk eggs until lightly beaten. Add remaining Ingredients and mix well.
3. Divide into 8 pieces and roll into balls. Place on prepared baking sheet. Bake 10-12 minutes or until golden brown. Serve as is or with your favorite dipping sauce.

Nutrition Facts Per Serving

Calories 129 Total Carbs 2g Net Carbs 1g Protein 8g Fat 10g Sugar 0g Fiber 1g

Hot & Spicy Mixed Nuts

Prep time: 5 minutes, Cook time: 10 minutes, Serves: 6

What you'll need from store cupboard:

½ cup whole almonds
½ cup pecan halves
½ cup walnut halves
1 tsp sunflower oil
½ tsp cumin
½ tsp curry powder
1/8 tsp cayenne pepper
Dash of white pepper

Instructions:

1. Heat oven to 350 degrees.
2. Place the nuts in a large bowl. Add the oil and toss to coat.
3. Stir the spices together in a small bowl. Add to nuts and toss to coat.
4. Spread nuts on a large baking sheet in a single layer. Bake 10 minutes.
5. Remove from oven and let cool. Store in airtight container. Serving size is ¼ cup.

Nutrition Facts Per Serving

Calories 257 Total Carbs 5g Net Carbs 1g Protein 6g Fat 25g Sugar 1g Fiber 4g

Crunchy Apple Fries

Prep time: 15 minutes, Cook time: 10 minutes, Serves: 8

Ingredients:

3 apples, peeled, cored, and sliced into ½-inch pieces
¼ cup reduced fat margarine, melted
2 tbsp. walnuts, chopped
What you'll need from the store cupboard
¼ cup quick oats
3 tbsp. light brown sugar
2 tbsp. whole wheat flour
1 tsp cinnamon
1/8 tsp salt

Instructions:

1. Heat oven to 425 degrees. Put a wire rack on a large cookie sheet.
2. Add oats and walnuts to a food processor or blender and process until the mixture resembles flour.
3. Place the oat mixture in a shallow pan and add brown sugar, flour, cinnamon, and salt, mix well. Pour melted butter in a separate shallow pan.
4. Dip apple slices in margarine, then roll in oat mixture to coat completely. Place on wire rack.
5. Bake 10 – 12 minutes or until golden brown. Let cool before serving.

Nutrition Facts Per Serving

Calories 146 Total Carbs 20g Net Carbs 17g Protein 1g Fat 7g Sugar 13g Fiber 3g

Cranberry & Almond Granola Bars

Prep time: 15 minutes, Cook time: 20 minutes, Serves: 12

Ingredients:

1 egg
1 egg white

What you'll need from store cupboard:

2 cup low-fat granola
¼ cup dried cranberries, sweetened
¼ cup almonds, chopped
2 tbsp. Splenda
1 teaspoon almond extract
½ tsp cinnamon

Instructions:

1. Heat oven to 350 degrees. Line the bottom and sides of an 8-inch baking dish with parchment paper.
2. In a large bowl, combine dry Ingredients including the cranberries.
3. In a small bowl, whisk together egg, egg white and extract. Pour over dry Ingredients and mix until combined.
4. Press mixture into the prepared pan. Bake 20 minutes or until light brown.
5. Cool in the pan for 5 minutes. Then carefully lift the bars from the pan onto a cutting board. Use a sharp knife to cut into 12 bars. Cool completely and store in an airtight container.

Nutrition Facts Per Serving

Calories 85 Total Carbs 14g Net Carbs 13g Protein 3g Fat 3g Sugar 5g Fiber 1g

Tex Mex Popcorn

Prep time: 5 minutes, Cook time: 5 minutes, Serves: 4

Ingredients:

¼ cup cilantro, diced
Refrigerated butter-flavor spray

What you'll need from store cupboard:

4 cup popcorn
1 tsp chili powder
½ tsp salt
½ tsp cumin seeds
½ tsp garlic powder
1/8 tsp smoked paprika

Instructions:

1. Place popcorn in a large bowl and spritz with butter spray. Add remaining Ingredients and toss to coat. Continue spritzing and tossing until popcorn is well coated.
2. Store in an airtight container. Serving size is 1 cup.

Nutrition Facts Per Serving

Calories 32 Total Carbs 6g Net Carbs 5g Protein 1g Fat 0g Sugar 0g Fiber 1g

Watermelon & Shrimp Ceviche

Prep time: 20 minutes, chill time: 1hour 30 minutes, Serves: 14

Ingredients:

1 lb. medium shrimp, peeled, deveined and tails removed	½ cup + 2 tbsp. lime juice, divided
1 jalapeño pepper, diced fine	½ cup jicama, diced fine
1 cup seedless watermelon, diced fine	½ cup red onion, diced fine
	½ cup fresh cilantro, chopped

What you'll need from store cupboard:

Salt and pepper, to taste

Instructions:

1. Chop shrimp into small pieces.
2. In a medium bowl, combine shrimp and ½ cup lime juice. Cover and chill 1 hour or until shrimp turn pink. Drain and discard juice.
3. In a large mixing bowl, combine all Ingredients. Salt and pepper to taste. Cover and chill at least 30 minutes.
4. Serve with, or on, your favorite crackers. Serving size is ¼ cup.

Nutrition Facts Per Serving

Calories 47 Total Carbs 3g Protein 8g Fat 1g Sugar 1g Fiber 0g

Fig Cookie Bars

Prep time: 5 minutes, Cook time: 20 minutes, Serves: 12

Ingredients:

½ cup dried figs	cream cheese
1/8 cup reduced-fat	3 tbsp. skim milk

What you'll need from store cupboard:

2/3 cup flour	1 tbsp. Splenda
½ cup quick oats	¾ tsp baking powder
1/3 cup powdered sugar substitute	½ tsp vanilla
6 tbsp. hot water	¼ tsp salt
2 tbsp. sunflower oil	Nonstick cooking spray

Instructions:

1. Heat oven to 400 degrees. Spray a cookie sheet with cooking spray.
2. Add the figs, water and Splenda to a blender and process until figs are finely chopped.
3. In a large bowl, stir together flour, oats, baking powder, and salt. Add oil, and milk 1 tablespoon at a time, until mixture forms a ball.
4. Roll dough out on a lightly floured surface to a 12x9-inch rectangle. Place on prepared pan. Spread fig mixture in a 2 ½-inch wide strip down the middle. At ½ inch intervals, use a sharp knife to cut the dough almost to the figs on both long sides. Fold strips over filling, overlapping and crossing in the middle.
5. Bake 15-20 minutes or until light brown. Remove from oven and let cool.
6. In a small bowl, beat cream cheese, powdered sugar substitute, and vanilla until smooth. Drizzle over bars and cut into 12 pieces.

Nutrition Facts Per Serving

Calories 105 Total Carbs 17g Net Carbs 16g Protein 2g Fat 3g Sugar 9g Fiber 1g

Fluffy Lemon Bars

Prep time: 15 minutes, chill time: 2 hours, Serves: 20

Ingredients:

8 oz. low fat cream cheese, soft	melted
1/3 cup butter,	3 tbsp. fresh lemon juice

What you'll need from store cupboard:

12 oz. evaporated milk	cracker crumbs
1 pkg. lemon gelatin, sugar free	1 cup boiling water
	¾ cup Splenda
1 ½ cup graham	1 tsp vanilla

Instructions:

1. Pour milk into a large, metal bowl, place beaters in the bowl, cover and chill 2 hours.
2. In a small bowl, combine cracker crumbs and butter, reserve 1 tablespoon. Press the remaining mixture on the bottom of a 13x9-inch baking dish. Cover and chill until set.
3. In a small bowl, dissolve gelatin in boiling water. Stir in lemon juice and let cool.
4. In a large bowl, beat cream cheese, Splenda and vanilla until smooth. Add gelatin and mix well.
5. Beat the chilled milk until soft peaks form. Fold into cream cheese mixture. Pour over chilled crust and sprinkle with reserved crumbs. Cover and chill 2 hours before serving.

Nutrition Facts Per Serving

Calories 126 Total Carbs 15g Protein 3g Fat 5g Sugar 10g Fiber 0g

Pesto Stuffed Mushrooms

Prep time: 5 minutes, Cook time: 20 minutes, Serves: 4

Ingredients:
12 cremini mushrooms, stems removed
4 oz. low fat cream cheese, soft
½ cup mozzarella cheese, grated

What you'll need from store cupboard:
1/3 cup reduced fat Parmesan cheese
6 tbsp. basil pesto
Nonstick cooking spray

Instructions:
1. Heat oven to 375 degrees. Line a square baking dish with foil and spray with cooking spray. Arrange the mushrooms in the baking pan. Set aside.
2. In a medium bowl, beat cream cheese, pesto and parmesan until smooth and creamy. Spoon mixture into mushroom caps. Top with a heaping teaspoon of mozzarella.
3. Bake 20-23 minutes or until cheese is melted and golden brown. Let cook 5-10 minutes before serving.

Nutrition Facts Per Serving
Calories 76 Total Carbs 4g Protein 8g Fat 3g Sugar 1g Fiber 0g

Gingerbread Cookies

Prep time: 15 minutes, Cook time: 10 minutes, Serves: 10

Ingredients:
1 egg   ¼ cup butter, soft

What you'll need from store cupboard:
2 cup almond flour,   1 tsp vanilla
sifted   ½ tsp baking powder
¼ cup Splenda   ¼ tsp cloves
1 tbsp. cinnamon   ¼ tsp nutmeg
1 ½ tsp ginger

Instructions:
1. In a medium bowl, stir together the almond flour, cinnamon, ginger, cloves, nutmeg, and baking powder.
2. In a large bowl, beat the butter and Splenda for 1-2 minutes, until fluffy. Beat in the egg and vanilla. Beat in the almond flour mixture until a dough forms.
3. Form the dough into a ball, wrap with plastic wrap and refrigerate for at least 30 minutes.
4. Heat the oven to 350 degrees. Line a cookie sheet with parchment paper.

5. Roll the dough out between two sheets of parchment paper to ¼-inch thick. Cut out desired shapes with cookie cutter and place on prepared pan. Or you can drop dough by teaspoonful onto pan.
6. Bake 10-15 minutes or until edges are golden brown. Remove to wire rack and cool. Store in airtight container. Serving size is 1 large, or 2 small cookies.

Nutrition Facts Per Serving
Calories 181 Total Carbs 9g Net Carbs 7g Protein 5g Fat 15g Sugar 6g Fiber 2g

Tortilla Chips

Prep time: 10 minutes, Cook time: 10 minutes, Serves: 4

Ingredients:
2 cup part-skim grated mozzarella cheese, grated

What you'll need from store cupboard:
¾ cup super fine   ½ tsp salt
almond flour   ½ tsp chili powder

Instructions:
1. Heat oven to 375 degrees.
2. Prepare a double boiler. Over high heat, bring the water in the pot to a simmer, then turn heat to low. Add all the Ingredients to the top of the double boiler and stir constantly until cheese melts and mixture holds together in a ball. Turn out onto a large piece of parchment paper and let cool 5 minutes.
3. Knead the dough to thoroughly combine all the Ingredients. Separate into 2 equal portions. Working with one portion at a time, roll dough out between two pieces of parchment paper into 9x15-inch rectangle.
4. Remove top piece of parchment and with a pizza cutter, or sharp knife, cut rectangle into squares or triangles. Slide the parchment paper onto a cookie sheet and arrange dough shapes so they have ½-inch space between them. Repeat with second dough portion.
5. Bake 5-8 minutes, or until centers are golden brown. Remove from oven and transfer to wire rack to cool. Chips will crisp up as they cool. Store in an airtight container.

Nutrition Facts Per Serving
Calories 95 Total Carbs 3g Net Carbs 2g Protein 5g Fat 8g Sugar 0g Fiber 1g

Orange Oatmeal Cookies

Prep time: 10 minutes, Cook time: 10 minutes,

Serves: 18 (2 cookies per serving)

Ingredients:

1 orange, zested and juiced
½ cup margarine

1 egg white
1 tbsp. orange juice

What you'll need from store cupboard:

1 cup whole wheat pastry flour
1 cup oats
¼ cup stevia
¼ cup dark brown sugar substitute

¼ cup applesauce, unsweetened
1/3 cup wheat bran
½ tsp baking soda
½ tsp cream of tartar
¼ tsp cinnamon

Instructions:

1. Heat oven to 350 degrees. Line two cookie sheets with parchment paper.
2. In a medium mixing bowl, cream butter. Gradually add the sugars and beat 2 -3 minutes.
3. Add egg white and applesauce and beat just to combine.
4. Sift the dry Ingredients together in a large mixing bowl. Add the wet Ingredients, the orange juice, and the zest.
5. Drop the dough by tablespoons onto the prepared cookie sheets. Bake 10 minutes, or until the bottoms are brown. Cool on wire rack. Store in an airtight container.

Nutrition Facts Per Serving

Calories 129 Total Carbs 17g Net Carbs 16g Protein 2g Fat 6g Sugar 8g Fiber 1g

Almond Coconut Biscotti

Prep time: 5 minutes, Cook time: 50 minutes,

Serves: 16

Ingredients:

1 egg, room temperature
1 egg white, room

temperature
½ cup margarine, melted

What you'll need from store cupboard:

2 ½ cup flour
1 1/3 cup unsweetened coconut, grated
¾ cup almonds,

sliced
2/3 cup Splenda
2 tsp baking powder
1 tsp vanilla
½ tsp salt

Instructions:

1. Heat oven to 350 degrees. Line a baking sheet with parchment paper.

2. In a large bowl, combine dry Ingredients.
3. In a separate mixing bowl, beat other Ingredients together. Add to dry Ingredients and mix until thoroughly combined.
4. Divide dough in half. Shape each half into a loaf measuring 8x2 ¾-inches. Place loaves on pan 3 inches apart.
5. Bake 25-30 minutes or until set and golden brown. Cool on wire rack 10 minutes.
6. With a serrated knife, cut loaf diagonally into ½-inch slices. Place the cookies, cut side down, back on the pan and bake another 20 minutes, or until firm and nicely browned. Store in airtight container. Serving size is 2 cookies.

Nutrition Facts Per Serving

Calories 234 Total Carbs 13g Net Carbs 10g Protein 5g Fat 18g Sugar 9g Fiber 3g

Freezer Fudge

Prep time: 15 minutes, chill time: 2 hours,

Serves: 16

Ingredients:

¼ cup margarine
¼ cup creamed

coconut

What you'll need from store cupboard:

1 ¼ cup coconut oil
1 cup pecans, ground fine
6 tbsp. cocoa powder,

unsweetened
2 tbsp. honey
1 tbsp. vanilla
¼ tsp sea salt

Instructions:

1. Line an 8x8 inch glass baking dish with wax paper.
2. Add the oil and margarine to a glass measuring cup. Fill a medium saucepan about half full of water and bring to a boil.
3. Place the measuring cup in the pan and stir until they are melted and combined.
4. Pour into a blender or food processor and add everything but the nuts. Process until smooth. And the nuts and pulse just to combine.
5. Pour into the prepared pan and freeze until the fudge is set.
6. Remove from the pan and cut into 32 pieces. Store in a plastic container in the freezer. Serving size is 2 pieces.

Nutrition Facts Per Serving

Calories 254 Total Carbs 7g Net Carbs 6g Protein 1g Fat 26g Sugar 5g Fiber 1g

Pickled Cucumbers

Prep time: 15 minutes, Cook time: 5 minutes, Serves: 10
Ingredients:
2 cucumbers, cut into 1/4-inch slices
½ onion, sliced thin
What you'll need from store cupboard:

1 ½ cups vinegar	1 tsp peppercorns
2 tbsp. stevia	1 tsp coriander seeds
1 tbsp. dill	½ tsp salt
2 cloves garlic, sliced thin	¼ tsp red pepper flakes

Instructions:
1. In a medium saucepan, combine vinegar and spices. Bring to a boil over high heat. Set aside.
2. Place the cucumbers, onions, and garlic into a quart-sized jar, or plastic container, with an air tight lid. Pour hot liquid over the vegetables, making sure they are completely covered.
3. Add the lid and chill at least a day before serving.

Nutrition Facts Per Serving
Calories 33 Total Carbs 6g Net Carbs 0g Protein 0g Fat 0g Sugar 4g Fiber 0g

Fried Zucchini

Prep time: 10 minutes, Cook time: 10 minutes, Serves: 4
Ingredients:
3 zucchini, slice ¼ - 1/8-inch thick
2 eggs
What you'll need from store cupboard:

½ cup sunflower oil	Parmesan cheese
1/3 cup coconut flour	1 tbsp. water
¼ cup reduced fat	

Instructions:
1. Heat oil in a large skillet over medium heat.
2. In a shallow bowl whisk the egg and water together.
3. In another shallow bowl, stir flour and parmesan together.
4. Coat zucchini in the egg then flour mixture. Add, in a single layer, to the skillet. Cook 2 minutes per side until golden brown. Transfer to paper towel lined plate. Repeat.
5. Serve immediately with your favorite dipping sauce.

Nutrition Facts Per Serving
Calories 138 Total Carbs 6g Net Carbs 4g Protein 6g Fat 11g Sugar 3g Fiber 2g

Oatmeal Peanut Butter Bars

Prep time: 5 minutes, Cook time: 10 minutes, Serves: 10
Ingredients:
½ cup almond milk, unsweetened
What you'll need from store cupboard:

1 cup oats	2 tbsp. peanuts, chopped
¼ cup agave syrup	
6tbsp. raw peanut butter	1 tsp pure vanilla

Instructions:
1. Heat oven to 325 degrees. Line a cookie sheet with parchment paper.
2. Place all Ingredients, except the peanuts, into a food processor. Process until you have a sticky dough. Use your hands to mix in the peanuts.
3. Separate the dough into 10 equal balls on the prepared cookie sheet. Shape into squares or bars. Press the bars flat to ¼-inch thickness.
4. Bake 8-12 minutes, or until the tops are nicely browned. Remove from oven and cool completely. The bars will be soft at first but will stiffen as they cool.

Nutrition Facts Per Serving
Calories 125 Total Carbs 14g Net Carbs 12g Protein 4g Fat 6g Sugar 1g Fiber 2g

Cheesy Onion Dip

Prep time: 5 minutes, Cook time: 5 minutes, Serves: 8
Ingredients:

8 oz. low fat cream cheese, soft	1 cup low fat Swiss cheese, grated
1 cup onions, grated	

What you'll need from store cupboard:
1 cup lite mayonnaise
Instructions:
1. Heat oven to broil.
2. Combine all Ingredients in a small casserole dish. Microwave on high, stirring every 30 seconds, until cheese is melted and Ingredients are combined.
3. Place under the broiler for 1-2 minutes until the top is nicely browned. Serve warm with vegetables for dipping.

Nutrition Facts Per Serving
Calories 158 Total Carbs 5g Protein 9g Fat 11g Sugar 1g Fiber 0g

Zucchini Chips

Prep time: 5 minutes, Cook time: 10 minutes, Serves: 6

Ingredients:

1 large zucchini, sliced into ¼-inch circle

1/4 cup reduced fat, Parmesan cheese, grated fine

3 tbsp. low-fat milk

What you'll need from the store cupboard

1/3 cup whole wheat breadcrumbs

½ tsp garlic powder

1/8 tsp cayenne pepper

Nonstick cooking spray

Instructions:

1. After slicing zucchini pat dry with paper towels. Let sit for 60 minutes before using. Then pat dry again.
2. Heat oven to 425 degrees. Spray a wire rack with cooking spray and place on cookie sheet.
3. In a medium bowl combine all Ingredients except milk and zucchini. Pour milk into a shallow bowl.
4. Dip zucchini into milk the coat with bread crumb mixture. Place on wire rack and bake 10 -15 minutes or until browned and crisp. Serve immediately.

Nutrition Facts Per Serving

Calories 25 Total Carbs 3g Protein 2g Fat 1g Sugar 1g Fiber 0g

Rum Spiced Nuts

Prep time: 5 minutes, Cook time: 10 minutes, Serves: 12

Ingredients:

2 tbsp. Margarine

What you'll need from store cupboard:

3 cups mixed nuts, unsalted

2 tbsp. dark rum

2 tbsp. Splenda

2 tsp curry powder

1 tsp salt

1 tsp ancho chili powder

1 tsp cinnamon

1 tsp cumin

Instructions:

1. Place a medium, nonstick, skillet over medium heat. Add nuts and cook, stirring frequently, about 3-5 minutes, to lightly toast them.
2. Add the margarine and rum and cook until most of the liquid evaporates.
3. Combine the remaining Ingredients in a large bowl. Add the nuts and toss to coat.
4. Dump out onto a large baking sheet to cool. Store in an airtight container. Serving size is ¼ cup.

Nutrition Facts Per Serving

Calories 254 Total Carbs 10g Net Carbs 8g Protein 6g Fat 22g Sugar 4g Fiber 2g

Double Chocolate Biscotti

Prep time: 15 minutes, Cook time: 30 minutes, Serves: 27

Ingredients:

3 egg whites, divided

2 eggs

1 tbsp. orange zest

What you'll need from store cupboard:

2 cup flour

½ cup Splenda

½ cup almonds, toasted and chopped

1/3 cup cocoa, unsweetened

¼ cup mini chocolate chips

1 tsp vanilla

1 tsp instant coffee granules

1 tsp water

½ tsp salt

½ tsp baking soda

Nonstick cooking spray

Instructions:

1. Heat oven to 350 degrees. Spray a large baking sheet with cooking spray.
2. In a large bowl, combine flour, Splenda, cocoa, salt, and baking soda.
3. In a small bowl, whisk the eggs, 2 egg whites, vanilla, and coffee. Let rest 3-4 minutes to dissolve the coffee.
4. Stir in the orange zest and add to dry Ingredients, stir to thoroughly combine. Fold in the nuts and chocolate chips.
5. Divide dough in half and place on prepared pan. Shape each half into 14x1 ¾-inch rectangle.
6. Stir water and remaining egg white together. Brush over the top of the dough. Bake 20-25 minutes, or until firm to the touch. Cool on wire racks 5 minutes.
7. Transfer biscotti to a cutting board. Use a serrated knife to cut diagonally into ½-inch slice. Place cut side down on baking sheet and bake 5-7 minutes per side. Store in airtight container. Serving size is 2 pieces.

Nutrition Facts Per Serving

Calories 86 Total Carbs 13g Net Carbs 12g Protein 3g Fat 3g Sugar 5g Fiber 1g

Homemade Cheetos

Prep time: 10 minutes, Cook time: 30 minutes, Serves: 6

Ingredients:
3 egg whites
½ cup cheddar cheese, grated and frozen

What you'll need from store cupboard:
¼ cup reduced fat parmesan cheese
1/8 tsp cream of tartar

Instructions:
1. Heat oven to 300 degrees. Line a baking sheet with parchment paper.
2. Put the frozen cheese in a food processor/blender and pulse, until it's in tiny little pieces.
3. In a large mixing bowl, beat egg whites and cream of tartar until very stiff peaks from. Gently fold in chopped cheese. Spoon mixture into a piping bag with ½-inch hole. Gently pipe "cheeto" shapes onto prepared pan. Sprinkle with parmesan cheese.
4. Bake 20-30 minutes. Turn off oven and leave the puffs inside another 30 minutes. Let cool completely and store in an airtight container.

Nutrition Facts Per Serving
Calories 102 Total Carbs 1g Protein 9g Fat 7g Sugar 0g Fiber 0g

Soft Pretzel Bites

Prep time: 15 minutes, Cook time: 15 minutes, Serves: 8

Ingredients:
3 cups mozzarella cheese, grated
3 large eggs
½ cup cream cheese

What you'll need from store cupboard:
2 cups almond flour, super fine
powder
1 tbsp. coarse salt
1 tbsp. baking

Instructions:
1. Heat oven to 400 degrees. Line a large cookie sheet with parchment paper.
2. Stir almond flour and baking powder together in a small bowl.
3. Place the mozzarella and cream cheese in a large glass bowl. Be sure to surround the cream cheese with the mozzarella. Melt the cheese in 30 second intervals on high, stirring after each interval. Continue this step until they are completely melted, about 2 – 2 ½ minutes.

4. Place the cheese, 2 eggs, and flour mixture into a food processor with a dough blade. Pulse on high until the mixture forms a uniform dough.
5. Wrap a pastry board with plastic wrap making sure it is taut. Lightly coat your hands with vegetable oil and separate dough into 8 equal parts. Roll each into 1-inch thick ropes.
6. With a sharp knife, cut dough into ¾-inch pieces. Place on prepared cookie sheet.
7. In a small bowl, whisk the remaining egg. Brush the dough pieces with egg then sprinkle with salt.
8. Bake 12 minutes, or until lightly browned. Set oven to broil and cook another 2 minutes to crisp up the outside of the pretzels. Serve warm by themselves or dip them in cheese sauce (chapter 16).

Nutrition Facts Per Serving
Calories 242 Total Carbs 6g Net Carbs 3g Protein 11g Fat 20g Sugar 1g Fiber 3g

Peanut Butter Oatmeal Cookies

Prep time: 5 minutes, Cook time: 30 minutes, Serves: 20

Ingredients:
2 egg whites
½ cup margarine, soft

What you'll need from store cupboard:
1 cup flour
1 cup quick oats
½ cup reduced-fat peanut butter
1/3 cup Splenda
1/3 Splenda brown sugar
½ tsp baking soda
½ tsp vanilla

Instructions:
1. Heat oven to 350 degrees.
2. In a large mixing bowl, combine dry Ingredients and stir to combine.
3. In a separate bowl, beat together the egg whites and margarine. Add to dry Ingredients and mix well.
4. Drop by teaspoonful onto nonstick cookie sheets. Bake 8-10 minutes or until edges start to brown.
5. Remove to wire rack and cool completely. Store in an airtight container. Serving size is 2 cookies.

Nutrition Facts Per Serving
Calories 151 Total Carbs 17g Net Carbs 16g Protein 3g Fat 7g Sugar 7g Fiber 1g

Honey & Cinnamon Shortbread

Prep time: 15 minutes, Cook time: 20 minutes, Serves: 22

Ingredients:

½ cup margarine, soft

What you'll need from store cupboard:

1 2/3 cup flour

3 ½ tbsp. honey

1 tsp cinnamon

1/8 tsp baking powder

Instructions:

1. Heat oven to 350 degrees. Line a baking sheet with parchment paper.
2. In a large bowl, beat margarine and honey until smooth and creamy.
3. Mix in the flour and baking powder to create a smooth dough. Shape dough into a rectangle, wrap with plastic wrap and chill 15 minutes.
4. Roll dough out on a lightly floured surface to ¼-inch thick. Cut into rectangles and place on prepared baking sheet. If you like use a fork to make patterns on the dough. Chill 20 minutes.
5. Bake 15-20 minutes, or until they start to turn golden brown. Transfer to wire rack to cool completely. Store in an airtight container.

Nutrition Facts Per Serving

Calories 82 Total Carbs 10g Protein 1g Fat 4g Sugar 3g Fiber 0g

Mini Eggplant Pizzas

Prep time: 10 minutes, Cook time: 35 minutes, Serves: 4

Ingredients:

1 large eggplant, peeled and sliced into ¼ - inch circles

2 cup spaghetti sauce, (chapter 16)

½ cup reduced-fat mozzarella cheese, grated

2 eggs

What you'll need from store cupboard:

1 ¼ cups Italian bread crumbs

1 tbsp. water

¼ tsp black pepper

Nonstick cooking spray

Instructions:

1. Heat oven to 350 degrees. Line 2 large cookie sheets with foil and spray well with cooking spray.
2. In a shallow dish, beat eggs, water and pepper. Place the bread crumbs in a separate shallow dish.
3. Dip eggplant pieces in egg mixture, then coat completely with bread crumbs. Place on prepared cookie sheets. Spray the tops with cooking spray and bake 15 minutes.
4. Turn the eggplant over and spray with cooking spray again. Bake another 15 minutes.
5. Remove from oven and top each piece with 1 tablespoon spaghetti sauce. Sprinkle cheese over sauce and bake another 4 – 5 minutes, or until sauce is bubbly and cheese is melted.

Nutrition Facts Per Serving

Calories 171 Total Carbs 24g Net Carbs 20g Protein 9g Fat 5g Sugar 6g Fiber 4g

Honey Roasted Pumpkin Seeds

Prep time: 10 minutes, Cook time: 30 minutes, Serves: 8

Ingredients:

2 cup raw fresh pumpkin seeds, wash and pat dry

1 tbsp. butter

What you'll need from store cupboard:

3 tbsp. honey

1 tbsp. coconut oil

1 tsp cinnamon

Instructions:

1. Heat oven to 275 degrees. Line a baking sheet with parchment paper, making sure it hangs over both ends.
2. Place the pumpkin seeds in a medium bowl.
3. In a small microwave safe bowl, add butter, coconut oil, and honey. Microwave until the butter melts and the honey is runny. Pour the honey mixture over the pumpkin seeds and stir. Add the cinnamon and stir again.
4. Dump the pumpkin seeds into the middle of the paper and place it in the oven. Bake for 30-40 minutes until the seeds and honey are a deep golden brown, stirring every 10 minutes.
5. When the seeds are roasted, remove from the oven and stir again. Stir a few times as they cool to keep them from sticking in one big lump. Enjoy the seeds once they are cool enough to eat. Store uncovered for up to one week. Serving size is ¼ cup.

Nutrition Facts Per Serving

Calories 267 Total Carbs 13g Net Carbs 12g Protein 8g Fat 22g Sugar 7g Fiber 1g

Margarita Chicken Dip

Prep time: 10 minutes, Cook time: 1 hour, Serves: 12
Ingredients:

2 ½ cup Monterrey jack cheese, grated
1 ½ cup chicken, cooked and shredded
1 ½ blocks cream cheese, soft, cut into cubes
¼ cup fresh lime juice
2 tbsp. fresh orange juice
2 tbsp. Pico de Gallo
1 tbsp. lime zest

What you'll need from store cupboard:

¼ cup tequila
2 cloves garlic, diced fine
1 tsp cumin
1 tsp salt

Instructions:

1. Place the cream cheese on bottom of crock pot. Top with chicken, then grated cheese. Add remaining Ingredients, except the Pico de Gallo.
2. Cover and cook on low 60 minutes. Stir the dip occasionally to combine Ingredients.
3. When dip is done transfer to serving bowl. Top with Pico de Gallo and serve with tortilla chips.

Nutrition Facts Per Serving
Calories 169 Total Carbs 5g Protein 14g Fat 8g Sugar 1g Fiber 0g

Onion Rings

Prep time: 5 minutes, Cook time: 15 minutes, Serves: 4
Ingredients:

1 large onion, slice ½-inch thick
1 egg

What you'll need from store cupboard:

¼ cup sunflower oil
2 tbsp. coconut flour
2 tbsp. reduced fat parmesan cheese
¼ tsp parsley flakes
1/8 tsp garlic powder
1/8 tsp cayenne pepper
Salt to taste

Instructions:

1. Heat oil in a large skillet over med-high heat.
2. In a shallow bowl, combine flour, parmesan, and seasonings.
3. Beat the egg.
4. Separate onion slices into individual rings and place in large bowl, add beaten egg and toss to coat well. Let rest 1-2 minutes.
5. In small batches, coat onion in flour mixture and add to skillet. Cook 1-2 minutes per side, or until golden brown. Transfer to paper towel lined cookie sheet.
6. Serve with sugar free ketchup, (chapter 16), or your favorite dipping sauce.

Nutrition Facts Per Serving
Calories 184 Total Carbs 8g Net Carbs 5g Protein 3g Fat 16g Sugar 2g Fiber 3g

Parmesan Truffle Chips

Prep time: 10 minutes, Cook time: 20 minutes, Serves: 4
Ingredients:

4 egg whites
½ tsp fresh parsley, diced fine

What you'll need from store cupboard:

3 tbsp. reduced fat parmesan cheese, divided
2 tsp water
½ tsp salt
Truffle oil to taste
Nonstick cooking spray

Instructions:

1. Heat oven to 400 degrees. Spray two muffin pans with cooking spray.
2. In a small bowl, whisk together egg whites, water, and salt until combined.
3. Spoon just enough egg white mixture into each muffin cup to barely cover the bottom. Sprinkle a small pinch of parmesan on each egg white.
4. Bake 10-15 minutes or until the edges are dark brown, be careful not to burn them.
5. Let cool in the pans 3-4 minutes then transfer to a small bowl and drizzle lightly with truffle oil. Add parsley and ½ tablespoon parmesan and toss to coat. Serve.

Nutrition Facts Per Serving
Calories 47 Total Carbs 0g Protein 4g Fat 3g Sugar 0g Fiber 0g

Pistachio Cookies

Prep time: 5 minutes, Cook time: 15 minutes, Serves: 13-14

Ingredients:

2 eggs, beaten

What you'll need from store cupboard:

1 2/3 cup almond flour	3/4 cup + 50 pistachio nuts, shelled
1 cup + 2 tbsp. Splenda	

Instructions:

1. Add the ¾ cup nuts and 2 tablespoons Splenda to a food processor. Process until nuts are ground fine.
2. Pour the ground nuts into a large bowl, and stir in flour and remaining Splenda until combined.
3. Add eggs and mix Ingredients thoroughly. Wrap dough with plastic wrap and chill at least 8 hours or overnight.
4. Heat oven 325 degrees. Line a cookie sheet with parchment paper.
5. Roll teaspoonful of dough into small balls, about 1-inch in diameter. Place on prepared sheet.
6. Smash cookie slightly then press a pistachio in the center. Bake 12-15 minutes or until the edges are lightly browned.
7. Transfer to wire rack to cool completely. Store in airtight container. Serving size is 3 cookies.

Nutrition Facts Per Serving

Calories 108 Total Carbs 5g Net Carbs 3g Protein 4g Fat 8g Sugar 3g Fiber 2g

Rosemary Potato Chips

Prep time: 10 minutes, Cook time: 20 minutes, Serves: 6

Ingredients:

2 medium red potatoes, unpeeled cut in 1/16-inch slices	cream 2 tbsp. fresh rosemary, chopped fine
1 ¼ cup fat-free sour	

What you'll need from store cupboard:

1 tbsp. olive oil	Nonstick cooking spray
¼ tsp garlic salt	
1/8 tsp black pepper	

Instructions:

1. Heat oven to 450 degrees. Spray 2 baking sheets with cooking spray.
2. In a small bowl, combine rosemary, garlic salt, and pepper.
3. Pat potatoes dry with paper towels. Arrange in single layer on prepared pans, spray with cooking spray.
4. Bake 10 minutes. Flip over, brush with oil and sprinkle with herb mixture.
5. Bake 5-10 minutes more until golden brown. Cool before serving.
6. Serving size is about 10 chips with 3 tablespoons sour cream for dipping.

Nutrition Facts Per Serving

Calories 83 Total Carbs 14g Net Carbs 12g Protein 2g Fat 3g Sugar 1g Fiber 2g

Tangy Almond Shortbread Cookies

Prep time: 5 minutes, Cook time: 15 minutes, Serves: 8

Ingredients:

6 tbsp. margarine

1 tsp freshly grated lemon zest

What you'll need from store cupboard:

2 cup almond flour	Nonstick cooking spray
1/3 cup Splenda	

Instructions:

1. In a small saucepan, melt margarine over medium heat.
2. Stir in flour, Splenda, and zest until thoroughly combined.
3. Form dough into a "log", wrap with plastic wrap and chill in the freezer for 30 minutes, or the refrigerator for 2 hours.
4. Heat oven to 350 degrees. Spray a cookie sheet with cooking spray.
5. Use a sharp knife to slice dough in ½-inch thick cookies. Place on prepared cookie sheet. Bake 15 minutes or until golden brown and firm.
6. Cool completely before serving. Serving size is 2 cookies.

Nutrition Facts Per Serving

Calories 254 Total Carbs 13g Net Carbs 10g Protein 5g Fat 20g Sugar 9g Fiber 3g

Chapter 7 - Salads Recipe

Asian Style Slaw

Prep time: 5 minutes, chill time: 2 hours, Serves: 8

Ingredients:
1 lb. bag coleslaw mix
5 scallions, sliced

What you'll need from store cupboard:
1 cup sunflower seeds
1 cup almonds, sliced
3 oz. ramen noodles, broken into small
pieces
¾ cup vegetable oil
½ cup Splenda
1/3 cup vinegar

Instructions:
1. In a large bowl, combine coleslaw, sunflower seeds, almonds, and scallions.
2. Whisk together the oil, vinegar and Splenda in a large measuring cup. Pour over salad, and stir to combine.
3. Stir in ramen noodles, cover and chill 2 hours.

Nutrition Facts Per Serving
Calories 354 Total Carbs 24g Net Carbs 21g Protein 5g Fat 26g Sugar 10g Fiber 3g

Asparagus & Bacon Salad

Prep time: 5 minutes, Cook time: 5 minutes, Serves: 1

Ingredients:
1 hard-boiled egg, peeled and sliced
1 2/3 cups asparagus, chopped
2 slices bacon, cooked crisp and crumbled

What you'll need from store cupboard:
1 tsp extra virgin olive oil
1 tsp red wine vinegar
½ tsp Dijon mustard
Pinch salt and pepper, to taste

Instructions:
1. Bring a pot of water to a boil. Add the asparagus and cook 2-3 minutes or until tender-crisp. Drain and add cold water to stop the cooking process.
2. In a small bowl, whisk together, mustard, oil, vinegar, and salt and pepper to taste.
3. Place the asparagus on a plate, top with egg and bacon. Drizzle with vinaigrette and serve.

Nutrition Facts Per Serving
Calories 356 Total Carbs 10g Net Carbs 5g Protein 25g Fat 25g Sugar 5g Fiber 5g

Autumn Slaw

Prep time: 15 minutes, chill time: 2 hours, Serves: 8

Ingredients:
10 cup cabbage, shredded
½ red onion, diced fine
¾ cup fresh Italian parsley, chopped

What you'll need from store cupboard:
¾ cup almonds, slice & toasted
¾ cup dried cranberries
1/3 cup vegetable oil
¼ cup apple cider vinegar
2 tbsp. sugar free maple syrup
4 tsp Dijon mustard
½ teaspoon salt
Salt & pepper, to taste

Instructions:
1. In a large bowl, whisk together vinegar, oil, syrup, Dijon, and ½ teaspoon salt. Add the onion and stir to combine. Let rest 10 minutes, or cover and refrigerate until ready to use.
2. After 10 minutes, add remaining Ingredients to the dressing mixture and toss to coat. Taste and season with salt and pepper if needed. Cover and chill 2 hours before serving.

Nutrition Facts Per Serving
Calories 133 Total Carbs 12g net Carbs 8g Protein 2g Fat 9g Sugar 5g Fiber 4g

Cantaloupe & Prosciutto Salad

Total time: 15 minutes, Serves: 4

Ingredients:
6 mozzarella balls, quartered
1 medium cantaloupe, peeled and cut into small cubes
4 oz. prosciutto, chopped
1 tbsp. fresh lime
juice
1 tbsp. fresh mint, chopped

What you'll need from store cupboard
2 tbsp. extra virgin olive oil
1 tsp honey

Instructions:
1. In a large bowl, whisk together oil, lime juice, honey, and mint. Season with salt and pepper to taste.
2. Add the cantaloupe and mozzarella and toss to combine. Arrange the mixture on a serving plate and add prosciutto. Serve.

Nutrition Facts Per Serving
Calories 240 Total Carbs 6g Protein 18g Fat 16g Sugar 4g Fiber 0g

Avocado & Citrus Shrimp Salad

Prep time: 10 minutes, Cook time: 5 minutes, Serves: 4

Ingredients:

1 lb. medium shrimp, peeled and deveined, remove tails
8 cup salad greens

1 lemon
1 avocado, diced
1 shallot, diced fine

What you'll need from store cupboard:

½ cup almonds, sliced and toasted
1 tbsp. olive oil

Salt and freshly ground black pepper

Instructions:

1. Cut the lemon in half and squeeze the juice, from both halves, into a small bowl, set aside. Slice the lemon into thin wedges.
2. Heat the oil in a skillet over medium heat. Add lemon wedges and let cook, about 1 minute, to infuse the oil with the lemons.
3. Add the shrimp and cook, stirring frequently, until shrimp turn pink. Discard the lemon wedges and let cool.
4. Place the salad greens in a large bowl. Add the shrimp, with the juices from the pan, and toss to coat. Add remaining Ingredients and toss to combine. Serve.

Nutrition Facts Per Serving

Calories 425 Total Carbs 17 Net Carbs 8g Protein 35 Fat 26 Sugar 2 Fiber 9

Southwest Chicken Salad

Prep time: 10 minutes, Serves: 6

Ingredients:

2 cups chicken, cooked and shredded
1 small red bell

pepper, diced fine
¼ cup red onion, diced fine

What you'll need from store cupboard:

1/4 cup reduced-fat mayonnaise
1 ½ tsp ground cumin

1 tsp garlic powder
1/2 tsp coriander
Salt and pepper to taste

Instructions:

1. Combine all Ingredients in a large bowl and mix to thoroughly combine. Taste and adjust seasonings as desired. Cover and chill until ready to serve.

Nutrition Facts Per Serving

Calories 117 Total Carbs 4g Net Carbs 0g Protein 14g Fat 5g Sugar 2g Fiber 0g

Baked "Potato" Salad

Prep time: 15 minutes, Cook time: 15 minutes, Serves: 8

Ingredients:

2 lb. cauliflower, separated into small florets
6-8 slices bacon, chopped and fried crisp

6 boiled eggs, cooled, peeled, and chopped
1 cup sharp cheddar cheese, grated
½ cup green onion, sliced

What you'll need from store cupboard:

1 cup reduced-fat mayonnaise
2 tsp yellow mustard
1 ½ tsp onion

powder, divided
Salt and fresh-ground black pepper to taste

Instructions:

1. Place cauliflower in a vegetable steamer, or a pot with a steamer insert, and steam 5-6 minutes.
2. Drain the cauliflower and set aside.
3. In a small bowl, whisk together mayonnaise, mustard, 1 teaspoon onion powder, salt, and pepper.
4. Pat cauliflower dry with paper towels and place in a large mixing bowl. Add eggs, salt, pepper, remaining ½ teaspoon onion powder, then dressing. Mix gently to combine Ingredients together.
5. Fold in the bacon, cheese, and green onion. Serve warm or cover and chill before serving.

Nutrition Facts Per Serving

Calories 247 Total Carbs 8g Net Carbs 5g Protein 17g Fat 17g Sugar 3g Fiber 3g

Chopped Veggie Salad

Total time: 15 minutes, Serves: 4

Ingredients:

1 cucumber, chopped
1 pint cherry tomatoes, cut in half
3 radishes, chopped

1 yellow bell pepper chopped
½ cup fresh parsley, chopped

What you'll need from store cupboard:

3 tbsp. lemon juice
1 tbsp. olive oil

Salt to taste

Instructions:

1. Place all Ingredients in a large bowl and toss to combine. Serve immediately, or cover and chill until ready to serve.

Nutrition Facts Per Serving

Calories 70 Total Carbs 9g Net Carbs 7g Protein 2g Fat 4g Sugar 5g Fiber 2g

Broccoli & Bacon Salad

Prep time: 10 minutes, Serves: 4
Ingredients:

2 cups broccoli, separated into florets	¼ cup low-fat Greek yogurt
4 slices bacon, chopped and cooked crisp	1/8 cup red onion, diced fine
½ cup cheddar cheese, cubed	1/8 cup almonds, sliced

What you'll need from store cupboard:

¼ cup reduced-fat mayonnaise	1 tbsp. granulated sugar substitute
1 tbsp. lemon juice	¼ tsp salt
1 tbsp. apple cider vinegar	¼ tsp pepper

Instructions:
1. In a large bowl, combine broccoli, onion, cheese, bacon, and almonds.
2. In a small bowl, whisk remaining Ingredients together till combined.
3. Pour dressing over broccoli mixture and stir. Cover and chill at least 1 hour before serving.

Nutrition Facts Per Serving
Calories 217 Total Carbs 12g Net Carbs 10g Protein 11g Fat 14g Sugar 6g Fiber 2g

Broccoli & Mushroom Salad

Total time: 10 minutes, Serves: 4
Ingredients:

4 sun-dried tomatoes, cut in half	florets
	1 cup mushrooms, sliced
3 cup torn leaf lettuce	1/3 cup radishes, sliced
1 ½ cup broccoli	

What you'll need from store cupboard:

2 tbsp. water	bouillon granules
1 tbsp. balsamic vinegar	¼ tsp parsley
	¼ tsp dry mustard
1 tsp vegetable oil	1/8 tsp cayenne pepper
¼ tsp chicken	

Instructions:
1. Place tomatoes in a small bowl and pour boiling water over, just enough to cover. Let stand 5 minutes, drain.
2. Chop tomatoes and place in a large bowl. Add lettuce, broccoli, mushrooms, and radishes.
3. In a jar with a tight fitting lid, add remaining Ingredients and shake well. Pour over salad and toss to coat. Serve.

Nutrition Facts Per Serving
Calories 54, Total Carbs 9g Net Carbs 7g Protein 3g Fat 2g Sugar 2g Fiber 2g

Festive Holiday Salad

Prep time: 10 minutes, chill time: 1 hour, Serves: 8
Ingredients:

1 head broccoli, separated into florets	thin
	2 cup cherry tomatoes, halved
1 head cauliflower, separated into florets	½ cup fat free sour cream
1 red onion, sliced	

What you'll need from store cupboard:
1 cup lite mayonnaise
1 tbsp. Splenda

Instructions:
1. In a large bowl combine vegetables.
2. In a small bowl, whisk together mayonnaise, sour cream and Splenda. Pour over vegetables and toss to mix.
3. Cover and refrigerate at least 1 hour before serving.

Nutrition Facts Per Serving
Calories 152 Total Carbs 12g Net Carbs 10g Protein 2g Fat 10g Sugar 5g Fiber 2g

Creamy Crab Slaw

Prep time: 10 minutes, chill time: 1 hour, Serves: 4
Ingredients:

½ lb. cabbage, shredded	2 hard-boiled eggs, chopped
½ lb. red cabbage, shredded	Juice of 1/2 lemon

What you'll need from store cupboard:

2 6 oz. cans crabmeat, drained	1 tsp celery seeds
	Salt & pepper, to taste
½ cup lite mayonnaise	

Instructions:
1. In a large bowl, combine both kinds of cabbage.
2. In a small bowl, combine mayonnaise, lemon juice, and celery seeds. Add to cabbage and toss to coat.
3. Add crab and eggs and toss to mix, season with salt and pepper. Cover and refrigerate 1 hour before serving.

Nutrition Facts Per Serving
Calories 380 Total Carbs 25g Net Carbs 17g Protein 18g Fat 24g Sugar 13g Fiber 8g

Caprese Salad

Total time: 10 minutes, Serves: 4
Ingredients:

3 medium tomatoes, cut into strips
cut into 8 slices ¼ cup fresh basil,
2 (1-oz.) slices sliced thin
mozzarella cheese,

What you'll need from store cupboard:

2 tsp extra-virgin 1/8 tsp salt
olive oil Pinch black pepper

Instructions:

1. Place tomatoes and cheese on serving plates. Sprinkle with salt and pepper. Drizzle oil over and top with basil. Serve.

Nutrition Facts Per Serving

Calories 77 Total Carbs 4g Protein 5g Fat 5g Sugar 2g Fiber 1g

Shrimp & Avocado Salad

Prep time: 20 minutes, Cook time: 5 minutes,
Serves: 4
Ingredients:

½ lb. raw shrimp, chopped
peeled and deveined 1/4 cucumber,
3 cups romaine julienned
lettuce, chopped 2 tbsp. green onions,
1 cup napa cabbage, diced fine
chopped 2 tbsp. fresh cilantro,
1 avocado, pit diced
removed and sliced 1 tsp fresh ginger,
¼ cup red cabbage, diced fine

What you'll need from store cupboard:

2 tbsp. coconut oil spice
1 tbsp. sesame seeds Fat-free Ranch
1 tsp Chinese five dressing

Instructions:

1. Toast sesame seeds in a medium skillet over medium heat. Shake the skillet to prevent them from burning. Cook until they start to brown, about 2 minutes. Set aside.
2. Add the coconut oil to the skillet. Pat the shrimp dry and sprinkle with the five spice. Add to hot oil. Cook 2 minutes per side, or until they turn pink. Set aside.
3. Arrange lettuce and cabbage on a serving platter. Top with green onions, cucumber, and cilantro. Add shrimp and avocado.
4. Drizzle with desired amount of dressing and sprinkle sesame seeds over top. Serve.

Nutrition Facts Per Serving

Calories 306 Total Carbs 20g Net Carbs 15g Protein 15g Fat 19g Sugar 4g Fiber 5g

Celery Apple Salad

Prep time: 5 minutes, Total time: 15 minutes,
Serves: 4
Ingredients:

2 green onions, diced sliced thin
2 Medjool dates, 2 cup celery, sliced
pitted & diced fine ½ cup celery leaves,
1 honey crisp apple, diced

What you'll need from store cupboard:

1/4 cup walnuts, chopped
Maple Shallot Vinaigrette, (chapter 16)

Instructions:

1. Heat oven to 375 degrees. Place walnuts on a cookie sheet and bake 10 minutes, stirring every few minutes, to toast.
2. In a large bowl, combine all Ingredients and toss to mix.
3. Drizzle vinaigrette over and toss to coat. Serve immediately.

Nutrition Facts Per Serving

Calories 171 Total Carbs 25g Net Carbs 21g Protein 3g Fat 8g Sugar 15g Fiber 4g

Chicken Guacamole Salad

Prep time: 10 minutes, Cook time: 20 minutes,
Serves: 6
Ingredients:

1 lb. chicken breast, 1/3 cup onion, diced
boneless & skinless 3 tbsp. cilantro, diced
2 avocados 2 tbsp. fresh lime
1-2 jalapeno peppers, juice
seeded & diced

What you'll need from store cupboard:

2 cloves garlic, diced Salt & pepper, to
1 tbsp. olive oil taste

Instructions:

1. Heat oven to 400 degrees. Line a baking sheet with foil.
2. Season chicken with salt and pepper and place on prepared pan. Bake 20 minutes, or until chicken is cooked through. Let cool completely.
3. Once chicken has cooled, shred or dice and add to a large bowl. Add remaining Ingredients and mix well, mashing the avocado as you mix it in. Taste and season with salt and pepper as desired. Serve immediately.

Nutrition Facts Per Serving

Calories 324 Total Carbs 12g Net Carbs 5g Protein 23g Fat 22g Sugar 1g Fiber 7g

Grilled Vegetable & Noodle Salad

Prep time: 15 minutes, Cook time: 10 minutes, Serves: 4

Ingredients:

2 ears corn-on-the-cob, husked	1/3 cup fresh basil, diced
1 red onion, cut in ½-inch thick slices	1/3 cup feta cheese, crumbled
1 tomato, diced fine	

What you'll need from store cupboard:

1 recipe Homemade Noodles, (chapter 15) cook & drain	Vinaigrette, (chapter 16)
4 tbsp. Herb	Nonstick cooking spray

Instructions:

1. Heat grill to medium heat. Spray rack with cooking spray.
2. Place corn and onions on the grill and cook, turning when needed, until lightly charred and tender, about 10 minutes.
3. Cut corn off the cob and place in a medium bowl. Chop the onion and add to the corn.
4. Stir in noodles, tomatoes, basil, and vinaigrette, toss to mix. Sprinkle cheese over top and serve.

Nutrition Facts Per Serving

Calories 330 Total Carbs 19g Net Carbs 16g Protein 10g Fat 9g Sugar 5g Fiber 3g

Layered Salad

Prep time: 10 minutes, Serves: 10

Ingredients:

6 slices bacon, chopped and cooked crisp	thawed
	1 cup sharp cheddar cheese, grated
2 tomatoes, diced	1/4 cup red onion, diced fine
2 stalks celery, sliced	
1 head romaine lettuce, diced	What you'll need from the store cupboard
1 red bell pepper, diced	1 cup fat-free ranch dressing
1 cup frozen peas,	

Instructions:

1. Use a 9x13- inch glass baking dish and layer half the lettuce, pepper, celery, tomatoes, peas, onion, cheese, bacon, and dressing. Repeat. Serve or cover and chill until ready to serve.

Nutrition Facts Per Serving

Calories 130 Total Carbs 14g Net Carbs 12g Protein 6g Fat 6g Sugar 5g Fiber 2g

Pomegranate & Brussels Sprouts Salad

Prep time: 10 minutes, Total time: 10 minutes, serves; 6

Ingredients:

3 slices bacon, cooked crisp & crumbled	sprouts, shredded
	3 cup kale, shredded
3 cup Brussels	1 ½ cup pomegranate seeds

What you'll need from store cupboard:

½ cup almonds, toasted & chopped
¼ cup reduced fat parmesan cheese, grated
Citrus Vinaigrette, (chapter 16)

Instructions:

1. Combine all Ingredients in a large bowl.
2. Drizzle vinaigrette over salad, and toss to coat well. Serve garnished with more cheese if desired.

Nutrition Facts Per Serving

Calories 256 Total Carbs 15g Net Carbs 10g Protein 9g Fat 18g Sugar 5g Fiber 5g

Healthy Taco Salad

Prep time: 15 minutes, Cook time: 10 minutes, Serves: 4

Ingredients:

2 whole Romaine hearts, chopped	3 oz. grape tomatoes, halved
1 lb. lean ground beef	½ cup cheddar cheese, cubed
1 whole avocado, cubed	2 tbsp. sliced red onion

What you'll need from store cupboard:

1/2 batch Tangy Mexican Salad Dressing (chapter 16)	1 tsp ground cumin
	Salt and pepper to taste

Instructions:

1. Cook ground beef in a skillet over medium heat. Break the beef up into little pieces as it cooks. Add seasonings and stir to combine. Drain grease and let cool for about 5 minutes.
2. To assemble the salad, place all Ingredients into a large bowl. Toss to mix then add dressing and toss. Top with reduced-fat sour cream and/or salsa if desired.

Nutrition Facts Per Serving

Calories 449 Total Carbs 9g Net Carbs 4g Protein 40g Fat 22g Sugar 3g Fiber 5g

Strawberry & Avocado Salad

Total time: 10 minutes, Serves: 6
Ingredients:
6 oz. baby spinach sliced
2 avocados, chopped ¼ cup feta cheese,
1 cup strawberries, crumbled
What you'll need from store cupboard:
Creamy Poppy Seed Dressing (chapter 16)
¼ cup almonds, sliced
Instructions:
1. Add spinach, berries, avocado, nuts and cheese to a large bowl and toss to combine.
2. Pour ½ recipe of Creamy Poppy Seed Dressing over salad and toss to coat. Add more dressing if desired. Serve.

Nutrition Facts Per Serving
Calories 253 Total Carbs 19g Net Carbs 13g
Protein 4g Fat 19g Sugar 9g Fiber 6g

Lobster Roll Salad with Bacon Vinaigrette

Prep time: 10 minutes, Cook time: 35 minutes, Serves: 6
Ingredients:
6 slices bacon 2 cups romaine
2 whole grain lettuce, torn
ciabatta rolls, halved 1 cup seeded
horizontally cucumber, diced
3 medium tomatoes, 1 cup red sweet
cut into wedges peppers, diced
2 (8 oz.) spiny 2 tablespoons shallot,
lobster tails, fresh or diced fine
frozen (thawed) 2 tablespoons fresh
2 cups fresh baby chives, diced fine
spinach
What you'll need from store cupboard:
2 cloves garlic, diced fine
3 tbsp. white wine vinegar
3 tbsp. olive oil, divided
Instructions:
1. Heat a grill to medium heat, or medium heat charcoals.
2. Rinse lobster and pat dry. Butterfly lobster tails. Place on the grill, cover and cook 25 – 30 minutes, or until meat is opaque.
3. Remove lobster and let cool.
4. In a small bowl, whisk together 2 tablespoons olive oil and garlic. Brush the cut sides of the rolls with oil mixture. Place on grill, cut side down, and cook until crisp, about 2 minutes. Transfer to cutting board.
5. While lobster is cooking, chop bacon and cook in a medium skillet until crisp. Transfer to paper towels. Reserve 1 tablespoon bacon grease.
6. To make the vinaigrette: combine reserved bacon grease, vinegar, shallot, remaining 1 tablespoons oil and chives in a glass jar with an air-tight lid. Screw on the lid and shake to combine.
7. Remove the lobster from the shells and cut into 1 ½-inch pieces. Cut rolls into 1-inch cubes.
8. To assemble salad: in a large bowl, combine spinach, romaine, tomatoes, cucumber, peppers, lobster, and bread cubes. Toss to combine. Transfer to serving platter and drizzle with vinaigrette. Sprinkle bacon over top and serve.

Nutrition Facts Per Serving
Calories 255 Total Carbs 18g Net Carbs 16g
Protein 20g Fat 11g Sugar 3g Fiber 2g

Mustard "Potato" Salad

Prep time: 15 minutes, Cook time: 5 minutes, Serves: 8
Ingredients:
2 pounds cauliflower, and diced
separated into small ½ cup celery, diced
florets ¼ cup red onion,
1 boiled egg, peeled diced
What you'll need from store cupboard:
¼ cup light 1 tbsp. Dijon mustard
mayonnaise ¼ tsp celery seed
1 tbsp. pickle relish ¼ tsp black pepper
Instructions:
1. Place cauliflower in a vegetable steamer and cook 5 minutes, or until almost tender. Drain and let cool.
2. In a small bowl, whisk together mayonnaise, relish, mustard, celery seed and pepper.
3. Once cauliflower is cooled off pat dry and place in a large bowl. Add egg, celery and onion.
4. Pour dressing over vegetables and mix, gently, to combine. Cover and chill at least 2 hours before serving.

Nutrition Facts Per Serving
Calories 71 Total Carbs 9g Net Carbs 6g
Protein 3g Fat 3g Sugar 4g Fiber 3g

Harvest Salad

Prep time: 15 minutes, Cook time: 25 minutes, Serves: 6

Ingredients:

10 oz. kale, deboned and chopped
1 ½ cup blackberries
½ butternut squash, cubed
¼ cup goat cheese, crumbled

What you'll need from store cupboard:

Maple Mustard Salad Dressing (chapter 16)
1 cup raw pecans
1/3 cup raw pumpkin seeds
¼ cup dried cranberries
3 1/2 tbsp. olive oil
1 ½ tbsp. sugar free maple syrup
3/8 tsp salt, divided
Pepper, to taste
Nonstick cooking spray

Instructions:

1. Heat oven to 400 degrees. Spray a baking sheet with cooking spray.
2. Spread squash on the prepared pan, add 1 ½ tablespoons oil, 1/8 teaspoon salt, and pepper to squash and stir to coat the squash evenly. Bake 20-25 minutes.
3. Place kale in a large bowl. Add 2 tablespoons oil and ½ teaspoon salt and massage it into the kale with your hands for 3-4 minutes.
4. Spray a clean baking sheet with cooking spray. In a medium bowl, stir together pecans, pumpkin seeds, and maple syrup until nuts are coated. Pour onto prepared pan and bake 8-10 minutes, these can be baked at the same time as the squash.
5. To assemble the salad: place all of the Ingredients in a large bowl. Pour dressing over and toss to coat. Serve.

Nutrition Facts Per Serving

Calories 436 Total Carbs 24g Net Carbs 17g Protein 9g Fat 37g Sugar 5g Fiber 7g

Watermelon & Arugula Salad

Prep time: 10 minutes, chill time: 1 hour Serves: 6

Ingredients:

4 cups watermelon, cut in 1-inch cubes
3 cup arugula
1 lemon, zested
½ cup feta cheese, crumbled
¼ cup fresh mint, chopped
1 tbsp. fresh lemon juice

What you'll need from store cupboard:

3 tbsp. olive oil
Fresh ground black
pepper
Salt to taste

Instructions:

1. Combine oil, zest, juice and mint in a large bowl. Stir together.
2. Add watermelon and gently toss to coat. Add remaining Ingredients and toss to combine. Taste and adjust seasoning as desired.
3. Cover and chill at least 1 hour before serving.

Nutrition Facts Per Serving

Calories 148 Total Carbs 10g Net Carbs 9g Protein 4g Fat 11g Sugar 7g Fiber 1g

Pickled Cucumber & Onion Salad

Total time: 10 minutes, Serves: 2

Ingredients:

½ cucumber, peeled and sliced
¼ cup red onion, sliced thin

What you'll need from store cupboard:

1 tbsp. olive oil
1 tbsp. white vinegar
1 tsp dill

Instructions:

1. Place all Ingredients in a medium bowl and toss to combine. Serve.

Nutrition Facts Per Serving

Calories 79 Total Carbs 4g Net Carbs 3g Protein 1g Fat 7g Sugar 2g Fiber 1g

Pecan Pear Salad

Total time: 15 minutes, Serves: 8

Ingredients:

10 oz. mixed greens
3 pears, chopped
½ cup blue cheese, crumbled

What you'll need from store cupboard:

2 cup pecan halves
1 cup dried cranberries
½ cup olive oil
6 tbsp. champagne vinegar
2 tbsp. Dijon mustard
¼ tsp salt

Instructions:

1. In a large bowl combine greens, pears, cranberries and pecans.
2. Whisk remaining Ingredients, except blue cheese, together in a small bowl Pour over salad and toss to coat. Serve topped with blue cheese crumbles.

Nutrition Facts Per Serving

Calories 325 Total Carbs 20g Net Carbs 14g Protein 5g Fat 26g Sugar 10g Fiber 6g

Warm Portobello Salad

Prep time: 5 minutes, Cook time: 10 minutes, Serves: 4

Ingredients:

6 cup mixed salad greens	mushrooms, sliced
1 cup Portobello	1 green onion, sliced

What you'll need from store cupboard:

Walnut or Warm Bacon Vinaigrette (chapter 16)	1 tbsp. olive oil
	1/8 tsp ground black pepper

Instructions:

1. Heat oil in a nonstick skillet over med-high heat. Add mushrooms and cook, stirring occasionally, 10 minutes, or until they are tender. Stir in onions and reduce heat to low.
2. Place salad greens on serving plates, top with mushrooms and sprinkle with pepper. Drizzle lightly with your choice of vinaigrette.

Nutrition Facts Per Serving

Calories 81 Total Carbs 9g Protein 4g Fat 4g Sugar 0g Fiber 0g

Asian Noodle Salad

Prep time: 30 minutes, Serves: 4

Ingredients:

2 carrots, sliced thin	1 bag tofu Shirataki
2 radish, sliced thin	Fettuccini noodles
1 English cucumber, sliced thin	¼ cup lime juice
1 mango, julienned	¼ cup fresh basil, chopped
1 bell pepper, julienned	¼ cup fresh cilantro, chopped
1 small serrano pepper, seeded and sliced thin	2 tbsp. fresh mint, chopped

What you'll need from store cupboard:

2 tbsp. rice vinegar	peanuts finely chopped
2 tbsp. sweet chili sauce	1 tbsp. Splenda
2 tbsp. roasted	½ tsp sesame oil

Instructions:

1. Pickle the vegetables: In a large bowl, place radish, cucumbers, and carrots. Add vinegar, coconut sugar, and lime juice and stir to coat the vegetables. Cover and chill 15 – 20 minutes.
2. Prep the noodles: remove the noodles from the package and rinse under cold water. Cut into smaller pieces. Pat dry with paper towels.

3. To assemble the salad. Remove the vegetables from the marinade, reserving marinade, and place in a large mixing bowl. Add noodles, mango, bell pepper, chili, and herbs.
4. In a small bowl, combine 2 tablespoons marinade with the chili sauce and sesame oil. Pour over salad and toss to coat. Top with peanuts and serve.

Nutrition Facts Per Serving

Calories 158 Total Carbs 30g Net Carbs 24g Protein 4g Fat 4g Sugar 19g Fiber 6g

Zucchini "Pasta" Salad

Prep time: 45 minutes, chill time: 1 hour, Serves: 5

Ingredients:

5 oz. zucchini, spiralized	crumbled
1 avocado, peeled and sliced	¼ cup tomatoes, diced
1/3 cup feta cheese,	¼ cup black olives, diced

What you'll need from store cupboard:

1/3 cup Green Goddess Salad Dressing	1 tsp basil
1 tsp olive oil	Salt and pepper to taste

Instructions:

1. Place zucchini on paper towel lined cutting board. Sprinkle with a little bit of salt and let sit for 30 minutes to remove excess water. Squeeze gently.
2. Add oil to medium skillet and heat over med-high heat. Add zucchini and cook, stirring frequently, until soft, about 3 – 4 minutes.
3. Transfer zucchini to a large bowl and add remaining Ingredients, except for the avocado. Cover and chill for 1 hour.
4. Serve topped with avocado.

Nutrition Facts Per Serving

Calories 200 Total Carbs 7g Net Carbs 4g Protein 3g Fat 18g Sugar 2g Fiber 3g

Summer Corn Salad

Prep time: 10 minutes, chill time: 2 hours, Serves: 8

Ingredients:

2 avocados, cut into 1/2-inch cubes
1 pint cherry tomatoes, cut in half
2 cups fresh corn kernels, cooked
½ cup red onion, diced fine
¼ cup cilantro, chopped
1 tbsp. fresh lime juice
½ tsp lime zest

What you'll need from store cupboard:

2 tbsp. olive oil
¼ tsp salt
¼ tsp pepper

Instructions:

1. In a large bowl, combine corn, avocado, tomatoes, and onion.
2. In a small bowl, whisk together remaining Ingredients until combined. Pour over salad and toss to coat.
3. Cover and chill 2 hours. Serve.

Nutrition Facts Per Serving

Calories 239 Total Carbs 20g Net Carbs 13g Protein 4g Fat 18g Sugar 4g Fiber 7g

Holiday Apple & Cranberry Salad

Total time: 15 minutes, Serves: 10

Ingredients:

12 oz. salad greens
3 Honeycrisp apples, sliced thin
1/2 lemon
½ cup blue cheese, crumbled

What you'll need from store cupboard:

Apple Cider Vinaigrette (chapter 16)
1 cup pecan halves, toasted
¾ cup dried cranberries

Instructions:

1. Put the apple slices in a large plastic bag and squeeze the half lemon over them. Close the bag and shake to coat.
2. In a large bowl, layer greens, apples, pecans, cranberries, and blue cheese. Just before serving, drizzle with enough vinaigrette to dress the salad. Toss to coat all Ingredients evenly.

Nutrition Facts Per Serving

Calories 291 Total Carbs 19g Net Carbs 15g Protein 5g Fat 23g Sugar 13g Fiber 4g

Chapter 8 - Desserts Recipe

Strawberry Cheesecake

Prep time: 15 minutes, Cook time: 15 minutes, Serves: 12

Ingredients:

3 cups medium-size fresh strawberries, halved
2 1/2 packages fat-free cream cheese, soft
1 cup skim milk
1/3 cup margarine, melted

What you'll need from store cupboard:

2 cups graham cracker crumbs
¾ cup + 2 tbsp. sugar substitute
¼ cup low-sugar strawberry spread
1 envelope unflavored gelatin
1 tbsp. lemon juice
2 tsp vanilla extract
Nonstick cooking spray

Instructions:

1. Heat oven to 350 degrees. Spray a 9-inch springform pan with cooking spray.
2. In a medium bowl, combine cracker crumbs and margarine, stirring to combine. Press on bottom and up sides of prepared pan. Bake 8 minutes, let cool.
3. Add milk to a small sauce pan and sprinkle gelatin over top, let stand 1 minutes. Cook over low heat, stirring constantly until gelatin dissolves, about 2 minutes. Let cool slightly.
4. In a large bowl, beat cream cheese until smooth and creamy. Slowly add lemon juice and vanilla, beat well.
5. Slowly beat in gelatin mixture, beating until smooth. Add ¾ cup sugar and beat just until blended. Pour into crust, cover and chill 3 hours.
6. In a medium saucepan, combine berries, 2 tablespoons sugar, and strawberry spread. Cook over med-low heat, stirring constantly, until spread melts and berries are coated. Spoon over cheesecake.
7. To serve, loosen cheese cake from side of pan and remove. Cut into wedges.

Nutrition Facts Per Serving

Calories 368 Total Carbs 30g Net Carbs 28g Protein 6g Fat 23g Sugar 20g Fiber 2g

Cappuccino Mousse

Prep time: 5 minutes, chill time: 1 hour,
Serves: 8
Ingredients:
2 cup low fat cream
cheese, soft
1 cup half-n-half
½ cup almond milk,

unsweetened
1/4 cup strong
brewed coffee, cooled
completely

What you'll need from store cupboard:
1-2 tsp coffee extract
1 tsp vanilla liquid sweetener
Whole coffee beans for garnish

Instructions:
1. In a large bowl, beat cream cheese and coffee on high speed until smooth. Add milk, 1 teaspoon coffee extract and liquid sweetener. Beat until smooth and thoroughly combined.
2. Pour in half-n-half and continue beating until mixture resembles the texture of mousse.
3. Spoon into dessert glasses or ramekins, cover and chill at least 1 hour before serving. Garnish with a coffee bean and serve.

Nutrition Facts Per Serving
Calories 98 Total Carbs 5g Protein 9g Fat 5g
Sugar 0g Fiber 0g

Apple Pear & Pecan Dessert Squares

Prep time: 10 minutes, Cook time: 25 minutes,
serves; 24
Ingredients:
1 Granny Smith
apple, sliced, leave
peel on
1 Red Delicious
apple, sliced, leave
peel on
1 ripe pear, sliced,

leave peel on
3 eggs
½ cup plain fat-free
yogurt
1 tbsp. lemon juice
1 tbsp. margarine

What you'll need from store cupboard:
1 package spice cake
mix
1 ¼ cup water,
divided
½ cup pecan pieces
1 tbsp. Splenda

1 tsp cinnamon
½ tsp vanilla
¼ tsp nutmeg
Nonstick cooking
spray

Instructions:
1. Heat oven to 350°F. Spray jelly-roll pan with nonstick cooking spray.

2. In a large bowl, beat cake mix, 1 cup water, eggs and yogurt until smooth. Pour into prepared pan and bake 20 minutes or it passes the toothpick test. Cool completely.
3. In a large nonstick skillet, over med-high heat, toast the pecans, stirring, about 2 minutes or until lightly browned. Remove to a plate.
4. Add the remaining ¼ cup water, sliced fruit, juice and spices to the skillet. Bring to a boil. Reduce heat to medium and cook 3 minutes or until fruit is tender crisp.
5. Remove from heat and stir in Splenda, margarine, vanilla, and pecans. Spoon evenly over cooled cake. Slice into 24 squares and serve.

Nutrition Facts Per Serving
Calories 130 Total Carbs 20g Net Carbs 19g
Protein 2g Fat 5g Sugar 10g Fiber 1g

Cream Cheese Pound Cake

Prep time: 10 minutes, Cook time: 35 minutes,
Serves: 14
Ingredients:
4 eggs
3 ½ oz. cream

cheese, soft
4 tbsp. butter, soft

What you'll need from store cupboard:
1 ¼ cup almond flour
¾ cup Splenda
1 tsp baking powder
1 tsp of vanilla

¼ tsp of salt
Butter flavored
cooking spray

Instructions:
1. Heat oven to 350 degrees. Spray an 8-inch loaf pan with cooking spray.
2. In a medium bowl, combine flour, baking powder, and salt.
3. In a large bowl, beat butter and Splenda until light and fluffy. And cream cheese and vanilla and beat well.
4. Add the eggs, one at a time, beating after each one. Stir in the dry Ingredients until thoroughly combined.
5. Pour into prepared pan and bake 30-40 minutes or cake passes the toothpick test. Let cool 10 minutes in the pan, then invert onto serving plate. Slice and serve.

Nutrition Facts Per Serving
Calories 202 Total Carbs 15g Net Carbs 14g
Protein 5g Fat 13g Sugar 13g Fiber 1g

Broiled Stone Fruit

Prep time: 5 minutes, Cook time: 5 minutes, Serves: 2
Ingredients:

1 peach	2 tbsp. sugar free
1 nectarine	whipped topping

What you'll need from store cupboard:
1 tbsp. Splenda brown sugar
Nonstick cooking spray

Instructions:
1. Heat oven to broil. Line a shallow baking dish with foil and spray with cooking spray.
2. Cut the peach and nectarine in half and remove pits. Place cut side down in prepared dish. Broil 3 minutes.
3. Turn fruit over and sprinkle with Splenda brown sugar. Broil another 2-3 minutes.
4. Transfer 1 of each fruit to a dessert bowl and top with 1 tablespoon of whipped topping. Serve.

Nutrition Facts Per Serving
Calories 101 Total Carbs 22g Net Carbs 20g Protein 1g Fat 1g Sugar 19g Fiber 2g

Blueberry Lemon "Cup" Cakes

Prep time: 5 minutes, Cook time: 10 minutes, Serves: 5
Ingredients:

4 eggs	½ cup blueberries
½ cup coconut milk	2 tbsp. lemon zest

What you'll need from store cupboard:

½ cup + 1 tsp coconut flour	1 tsp baking soda
¼ cup Splenda	½ tsp lemon extract
¼ cup coconut oil, melted	¼ tsp stevia extract
	Pinch salt

Instructions:
1. In a small bowl, toss berries in the 1 teaspoon of flour.
2. In a large bowl, stir together remaining flour, Splenda, baking soda, salt, and zest.
3. Add the remaining Ingredients and mix well. Fold in the blueberries.
4. Divide batter evenly into 5 coffee cups. Microwave, one at a time, for 90 seconds, or until they pass the toothpick test.

Nutritional Facts Per Serving
Calories 263 Total Carbs 14g Net Carbs 12g Protein 5g Fat 20g Sugar 12g Fiber 2g

Peach Custard Tart

Prep time: 5 minutes, Cook time: 40 minutes, Serves: 8
Ingredients:

12 oz. frozen unsweetened peach slices, thaw and drain	1 cup skim milk
	4 tbsp. cold margarine, cut into pieces
2 eggs, separated	

What you'll need from store cupboard:

1 cup flour	1 tsp vanilla
3 tbsp. Splenda	¼ tsp + 1/8 tsp salt,
2-3 tbsp. cold water	divided
¼ tsp nutmeg	

Instructions:
1. Heat oven to 400 degrees.
2. In a medium bowl, stir together flour and ¼ teaspoon salt. With a pastry blender, cut in margarine until mixture resembles coarse crumbs. Stir in cold water, a tablespoon at a time, just until moistened. Shape into a disc.
3. On a lightly floured surface, roll out dough to an 11-inch circle. Place in bottom of a 9-inch tart pan with a removable bottom. Turn the edge under and pierce the sides and bottom with a fork.
4. In a small bowl, beat 1 egg white with a fork, discard the other or save for another use. Lightly brush crust with egg. Place the tart pan on a baking sheet and bake 10 minutes. Cool.
5. In a large bowl, whisk together egg yolks, Splenda, vanilla, nutmeg, and 1/8 teaspoon salt until combined.
6. Pour milk in a glass measuring cup and microwave on high for 1 minute. Do not boil. Whisk milk into egg mixture until blended.
7. Arrange peaches on the bottom of the crust and pour egg mixture over the top. Bake 25-30 minutes, or until set. Cool to room temperature. Cover and chill at least 2 hours before serving.

Nutritional Facts Per Serving
Calories 180 Total Carbs 22g Net Carbs 21g Protein 5g Fat 7g Sugar 9g Fiber 1g

Blueberry No Bake Cheesecake

Prep time: 5 minutes, chill time; 3 hours, Serves: 8

Ingredients:

16 oz. fat free cream cheese, softened	topping, thawed
	¾ cup blueberries
1 cup sugar free frozen whipped	1 tbsp. margarine, melted

What you'll need from store cupboard:

8 zwieback toasts	1 envelope
1 cup boiling water	unflavored gelatin
1/3 cup Splenda	1 tsp vanilla

Instructions:

1. Place the toasts and margarine in a food processor. Pulse until mixture resembles coarse crumbs. Press on the bottom of a 9-inch springform pan.
2. Place gelatin in a medium bowl and add boiling water. Stir until gelatin dissolved completely.
3. In a large bowl, beat cream cheese, Splenda, and vanilla on medium speed until well blended. Beat in whipped topping. Add gelatin, in a steady stream, while beating on low speed. Increase speed to medium and beat 4 minutes or until smooth and creamy.
4. Gently fold in berries and spread over crust. Cover and chill 3 hours or until set.

Nutrition Facts Per Serving

Calories 316 Total Carbs 20g Protein 6g Fat 23g Sugar 10g Fiber 0g

Apricot Soufflé

Prep time: 5 minutes, cook time; 30 minutes, serves; 6

Ingredients:

4 egg whites	1/3 cup dried
3 egg yolks, beaten	apricots, diced fine
3 tbsp. margarine	¼ cup warm water
What you'll need from store cupboard	2 tbsp. flour
	¼ tsp cream of tartar
¾ cup sugar free apricot fruit spread	1/8 tsp salt

Instructions:

1. Heat oven to 325 degrees.
2. In a medium saucepan, over medium heat, melt margarine. Stir in flour and cook, stirring, until bubbly.
3. Stir together the fruit spread and water in a small bowl and add it to the saucepan with the apricots. Cook,

stirring, 3 minutes or until mixture thickens.

4. Remove from heat and whisk in egg yolks. Let cool to room temperature, stirring occasionally.
5. In a medium bowl, beat egg whites, salt, and cream of tartar on high speed until stiff peaks form. Gently fold into cooled apricot mixture.
6. Spoon into a 1 1/2 –quart soufflé dish. Bake 30 minutes, or until puffed and golden brown. Serve immediately.

Nutrition Facts Per Serving

Calories 116 Total Carbs 7g Protein 4g Fat 8g Sugar 1g Fiber 0g

Autumn Skillet Cake

Prep time: 10 minutes, Cook time: 30 minutes, Serves: 10

Ingredients:

3 eggs, room temperature	soft
	3 tbsp. fat free sour cream
1 cup of fresh cranberries	2 tbsp. butter, melted
4 oz. cream cheese,	

What you'll need from store cupboard:

2 cup of almond flour, sifted	1 tsp pumpkin spice
	1 tsp ginger
¾ cup Splenda	¼ tsp nutmeg
¾ cup pumpkin puree	¼ tsp salt
1 ½ tbsp. baking powder	Nonstick cooking spray
2 tsp cinnamon	

Instructions:

1. Heat oven to 350 degrees. Spray a 9-inch cast iron skillet or cake pan with cooking spray.
2. In a large bowl, beat Splenda, butter and cream cheese until thoroughly combined. Add eggs, one at a time, beating after each.
3. Add pumpkin and spices and combine. Add the dry Ingredients and mix well. Stir in the sour cream. Pour into prepared pan.
4. Sprinkle cranberries over the batter and with the back of a spoon, push them half-way into the batter. Bake 30 minutes or the cake passes the toothpick test. Cool completely before serving.

Nutrition Facts Per Serving

Calories 280 Total Carbs 23g Net Carbs 20g Protein 7g Fat 17g Sugar 16g Fiber 3g

Peanut Butter Pie

Prep time: 10 minutes, chill time: 4 hours, Serves: 8

Ingredients:

1 ½ cup skim milk
1 1/2 cup frozen fat-free whipped topping, thawed and divided
1 small pkg. sugar-
free instant vanilla pudding mix
1 (1 ½ oz.) pkg. sugar-free peanut butter cups, chopped

What you'll need from store cupboard:

1 (9-inch) reduced-fat graham cracker pie crust
1/3 cup reduced-fat peanut butter
½ tsp vanilla

Instructions:

1. In a large bowl, whisk together milk and pudding mix until it thickens. Whisk in peanut butter, vanilla, and 1 cup whip cream. Fold in peanut butter cups.
2. Pour into pie crust and spread remaining whip cream over top. Cover and chill at least 4 hours before serving.

Nutrition Facts Per Serving

Calories 191 Total Carbs 27g Protein 4g Fat 6g Sugar 6g Fiber 0g

Chocolate Cherry Cake Roll

Prep time: 10 minutes, Cook time: 15 minutes, Serves: 10

Ingredients:

10 maraschino cherries, drained and patted dry
4 eggs, room temperature
1 cup sugar-free Cool
Whip, thawed
⅔ cup maraschino cherries, chop, drain and pat dry
½ cup cream cheese, soft

What you'll need from store cupboard:

⅓ cup flour
½ cup Splenda for baking
¼ cup unsweetened cocoa powder
1 tablespoon sugar-free hot fudge ice
cream topping
¼ tsp baking soda
¼ tsp salt
Unsweetened cocoa powder
Nonstick cooking spray

Instructions:

1. Heat oven to 375 degrees. Spray a large sheet baking pan with cooking spray. Line bottom with parchment paper, spray and flour the paper.
2. In a small bowl, stir together flour, ¼ cup cocoa, baking soda, and salt.
3. In a large bowl, beat eggs on high speed for 5 minutes,

4. Gradually add sweetener and continue beating until mixture is thick and lemon-colored.
5. Fold in dry Ingredients. Spread evenly into prepared pan. Bake 15 minutes or top springs back when touched lightly.
6. Place a clean towel on a cutting board and sprinkle with cocoa powder. Turn cake onto towel and carefully remove parchment paper.
7. Starting at a short end, roll up towel. Cool on a wire rack for 1 hour.
8. Prepare the filling: in a small bowl, beat cream cheese until smooth. Add ½ cup whipped topping, beat on low until combined. Fold in another ½ cup whipped topping. Fold in the chopped cherries.
9. Unroll cake and remove the towel. Spread the filling to within 1 inch of the edges. Reroll cake and trim the ends. Cover and chill at least 2 hours or overnight.
10. To serve, warm up the fudge topping and drizzle over cake, garnish with whole cherries, then slice and serve.

Nutrition Facts Per Serving

Calories 163 Total Carbs 25g Protein 5g Fat 3g Sugar 12g Fiber 0g

Strawberry Sorbet

Prep time: 5 minutes, chill time: 4 hours, Serves: 4

Ingredients:

10 oz. strawberries, frozen

What you'll need from store cupboard:

2 cups water
¼ cup honey

Instructions:

1. Place strawberries, water, and honey in a blender and process until smooth and creamy.
2. Pour mixture into ice cream maker and process according to instructions.
3. Transfer to a plastic container with an airtight lid and freeze 4 hours before serving.

Nutrition Facts Per Serving

Calories 38g Total Carbs 9g Net Carbs 7g Protein 0g Fat 0g Sugar 7g Fiber 2g

Baked Maple Custard

Prep time: 5 minutes, cook time; 1 hour 15 minutes, serves; 6

Ingredients:

2 ½ cup half-and-half	2 tbsp. sugar free
½ cup egg substitute	maple syrup
What you'll need	2 tsp vanilla
from store cupboard	Dash nutmeg
3 cup boiling water	Nonstick cooking
¼ cup Splenda	spray

Instructions:

1. Heat oven to 325°degrees. Lightly spray 6 custard cups or ramekins with cooking spray.
2. In a large bowl, whisk together half-n-half, egg substitute, Splenda, vanilla, and nutmeg. Pour evenly into prepared custard cups. Place cups in a 13x9-inch baking dish.
3. Pour boiling water around, being careful not to splash it into, the cups. Bake 1 hour 15 minutes, centers will not be completely set.
4. Remove cups from pan and cool completely. Cover and chill overnight.
5. Just before serving, drizzle with the maple syrup.

Nutrition Facts Per Serving

Calories 190 Total Carbs 15g Protein 5g Fat 12g Sugar 8g Fiber 0g

Tiramisu

Prep time: 20 minutes, chill time: 4 hours, Serves: 15

Ingredients:

2 (8 oz.) pkgs.	2 (3 oz.) pkgs
reduced-fat cream	ladyfingers, split
cheese, soft	¼ cup skim milk
2 cup fat-free sour	2 tbsp. coffee liqueur
cream	

What you'll need from store cupboard:

⅔ cup Splenda	2 tbsp. unsweetened
½ cup strong brewed	cocoa powder, sifted
coffee	½ tsp vanilla

Instructions:

1. In a large bowl, combine sour cream, cream cheese, sugar substitute, milk, and vanilla. Beat on high until smooth.
2. In a small bowl stir together coffee and liqueur.
3. Place one package of lady fingers, cut side up, in a 2-quart baking dish. Brush with ½ the coffee mixture. Spread ½ the

cheese mixture over top. Repeat layers.

4. Sprinkle cocoa powder over top. Cover and chill 4 hours or overnight. Cut into squares to serve.

Nutrition Facts Per Serving

Calories 208 Total Carbs 24g Protein 6g Fat 8g Sugar 14g Fiber 0g

Cheesecake

Prep time: 25 minutes, Cook time: 10 minutes, Serves: 16

Ingredients:

3 (8 oz.) pkgs. fat-free cream cheese, soft	½ cup semisweet chocolate, melted and cooled
1 cup fat-free sour cream	2 tbsp. margarine, melted
¾ cup skim milk	

What you'll need from store cupboard:

½ cup graham crackers, finely crushed	unflavored gelatin
	2 tsp vanilla
1/3 cup Splenda	Chocolate curls
1 envelope	(optional)

Instructions:

1. In a medium bowl, stir together cracker crumbs and margarine until moistened. Press evenly on the bottom of an 8-inch springform pan. Cover and chill.
2. In a small sauce pot, add milk and sprinkle gelatin over top, let stand 5 minutes. Heat to low heat, and stir until gelatin dissolve. Remove from heat and let cool 15 minutes.
3. In a large bowl, beat cream cheese until smooth. Beat in sour cream, sugar, and vanilla. Slowly beat in gelatin mixture.
4. Divide cheese mixture in half. Slowly stir the melted chocolate into one half.
5. Spread half the chocolate mixture evenly over chilled crust. Spoon half the white cheese mix over chocolate in small dollops. Using a butter knife, swirl the two layers together. Repeat with remaining fillings. Cover and chill 6 hours, or until set.
6. To serve, loosen cheesecake from side of pan with a small knife, remove side of pan. Cut into wedges and garnish with chocolate curls if desired.

Nutrition Facts Per Serving

Calories 240 Total Carbs 14g Protein 5g Fat 18g Sugar 9g Fiber 0g

Dark Chocolate Coffee Cupcakes

Prep time: 10 minutes, Cook time: 20 minutes, Serves: 24

Ingredients:

2 eggs	cream
½ cup fat free sour	½ cup butter, melted

What you'll need from store cupboard:

2 cup Splenda	chocolate
1 cup almond flour, sifted	½ cup coconut flour
1 cup strong coffee, room temperature	3 tsp of baking powder
4 oz. unsweetened	½ tsp-salt

Instructions:

1. Heat oven to 350 degrees. Line two 12 cup muffin tins with cupcake liners.
2. Melt the chocolate in a double broiler, set aside and allow to cool.
3. Combine the Splenda, almond and coconut flours, baking powder and sea-salt.
4. In a small bowl, combine the coffee, sour cream and butter.
5. Add the butter mixture to the dry Ingredients and beat on low speed until thoroughly combined.
6. Add the eggs, one at a time, beating after each one. Fold in the chocolate until well blended.
7. Spoon into prepared pans and bake 20-25 minutes or they pass the toothpick test. Cool completely before serving.

Nutrition Facts Per Serving

Calories 173 Total Carbs 20g Net Carbs 19g Protein 2g Fat 9g Sugar 16g Fiber 1g

Blackberry Crostata

Prep time: 10 minutes, Cook time: 20 minutes, Serves: 6

Ingredients:

1 9-inch pie crust, unbaked	Juice and zest of 1 lemon
2 cup fresh blackberries	2 tbsp. butter, soft

What you'll need from store cupboard:

3 tbsp. Splenda, divided	2 tbsp. cornstarch

Instructions:

1. Heat oven to 425 degrees. Line a large baking sheet with parchment paper and unroll pie crust in pan.
2. In a medium bowl, combine blackberries,

2 tablespoons Splenda, lemon juice and zest, and cornstarch. Spoon onto crust leaving a 2-inch edge. Fold and crimp the edges.
3. Dot the berries with 1 tablespoon butter. Brush the crust edge with remaining butter and sprinkle crust and fruit with remaining Splenda.
4. Bake 20-22 minutes or until golden brown. Cool before cutting and serving.

Nutrition Facts Per Serving

Calories 206 Total Carbs 24g Net Carbs 21g Protein 2g Fat 11g Sugar 9g Fiber 3g

German Chocolate Cake Bars

Prep time: 10 minutes, Cook time: 5 minutes, Serves: 20

Instructions:

2 cup unsweetened coconut flakes	¾ cup chopped pecans
1 cup coconut milk, divided	¾ cup dark baking chocolate, chopped

What you'll need from store cupboard:

1 ½ cup almond flour cracker crumbs (chapter 4)	substitute
	½ cup coconut oil
½ cup + 2 tbsp. powdered sugar	Nonstick cooking spray

Instructions:

1. Spray an 8x8-inch baking dish with cooking spray.
2. In a large bowl, combine the coconut, ½ cup sugar substitute, cracker crumbs and pecan, stir to combine.
3. In a medium sauce pan, combine ½ cup milk and oil, cook over medium heat until oil is melted and mixture is heated through. Pour over coconut mixture and stir to combine. Press evenly in prepared baking dish and chill 1-2 hours.
4. In a clean saucepan, place the chocolate and remaining milk over med-low heat. Cook, stirring constantly, until chocolate is melted and mixture is smooth. Add the 2 tablespoons sugar substitute and stir to combine.
5. Pour chocolate over the coconut layer and chill 1 hour, or until set. Cut into squares to serve.

Nutrition Facts Per Serving

Calories 245 Total Carbs 12g Net Carbs 9g Protein 3g Fat 19g Sugar 7g Fiber 3g

Coconut Milk Shakes

Prep time: 5 minutes, blend time: 5 minutes, Serves: 2

Ingredients:

1 ½ cup vanilla ice cream

½ cup coconut milk, unsweetened

What you'll need from store cupboard:

2 ½ tbsp. coconut flakes

1 tsp unsweetened cocoa

Instructions:

1. Heat oven to 350 degrees.
2. Place coconut on a baking sheet and bake, 2-3 minutes, stirring often, until coconut is toasted.
3. Place ice cream, milk, 2 tablespoons coconut, and cocoa in a blender and process until smooth.
4. Pour into glasses and garnish with remaining toasted coconut. Serve immediately.

Nutrition Facts Per Serving

Calories 323 Total Carbs 23g Net Carbs 19g Protein 3g Fat 24g Sugar 18g Fiber 4g

Blackberry Soufflés

Prep time: 15 minutes, Cook time: 30 minutes, Serves: 4

Ingredients:

12 oz. blackberries

4 egg whites

What you'll need from store cupboard:

1/3 cup Splenda   powdered sugar

1 tbsp. water   Nonstick cooking

1 tbsp. Swerve   spray

Instructions:

1. Heat oven to 375 degrees. Spray 4 1-cup ramekins with cooking spray.
2. In a small saucepan, over med-high heat, combine blackberries and 1 tablespoon water, bring to a boil. Reduce heat and simmer until berries are soft. Add Splenda and stir over medium heat until Splenda dissolves, without boiling.
3. Bring back to boiling, reduce heat and simmer 5 minutes. Remove from heat and cool 5 minutes.
4. Place a fine meshed sieve over a small bowl and push the berry mixture through it using the back of a spoon. Discard the seeds. Cover and chill 15 minutes.
5. In a large bowl, beat egg whites until soft peaks form. Gently fold in berry mixture.

Spoon evenly into prepared ramekins and place them on a baking sheet.

6. Bake 12 minutes, or until puffed and light brown. Dust with powdered Swerve and serve immediately.

Nutrition Facts Per Serving

Calories 141 Total Carbs 26g Net Carbs 21g Protein 5g Fat 0g Sugar 20g Fiber 5g

Caramel Pecan Pie

Prep time: 5 minutes, Cook time: 35 minutes, serves 8

Ingredients:

1 cup pecans, chopped	1/3 cup margarine, melted
¾ cup almond milk, unsweetened	1 tbsp. margarine, cold

What you'll need from store cupboard:

2 cup almond flour	¾ tsp sea salt
½ cup + 2 tablespoons Splenda for baking	½ tsp vanilla
	½ tsp maple syrup, sugar free
1 tsp vanilla	Nonstick cooking
1 tsp Arrowroot powder	spray

Instructions:

1. Heat oven to 350 degrees. Spray a 9-inch pie pan with cooking spray.
2. In a medium bowl, combine flour, melted margarine, 2 tablespoons Splenda, and vanilla. Mix to thoroughly combine Ingredients. Press on bottom and sides of prepared pie pan. Bake 12 -15 minutes, or until edges start to brown. Set aside.
3. In a small sauce pan, combine milk, remaining Splenda, arrowroot, salt, ½ teaspoon vanilla, and syrup. Cook over medium heat until it starts to boil, stirring constantly. Keep cooking until it turns a gold color and starts to thicken, about 2-3 minutes. Remove from heat and let cool. Stir in ½ the pecans.
4. Pour the filling in the crust and top with remaining pecans. Bake about 15 minutes, or until filling starts to bubble. Cool completely before serving.

Nutrition Facts Per Serving

Calories 375 Total Carbs 20g Net Carbs 15g Protein 7g Fat 30g Sugar 14g Fiber 5g

Chocolate Orange Bread Pudding

Prep time: 10 minutes, cook time; 35 minutes, serves; 8

Ingredients:

4 cups French baguette cubes	3 eggs, lightly beaten
1 ½ cups skim milk	1-2 tsp orange zest, grated

What you'll need from store cupboard

¼ cup Splenda	3 tbsp. unsweetened cocoa powder
¼ cup sugar-free chocolate ice cream topping	1 tsp vanilla
	¾ tsp cinnamon

Instructions:

1. Heat oven to 350°F.
2. In medium bowl, stir together Splenda and cocoa. Stir in milk, eggs, zest, vanilla, and cinnamon until well blended.
3. Place bread cubes in an 8-inch square baking dish. Pour milk mixture evenly over the top.
4. Bake 35 minutes or until a knife inserted in the center comes out clean. Cool 5-10 minutes.
5. Spoon into dessert dishes and drizzle lightly with ice cream topping. Serve.

Nutrition Facts Per Serving

Calories 139 Total Carbs 23g Net Carbs 22g Protein 6g Fat 2g Sugar 9g Fiber 1g

Chocolate Torte

Prep time: 15 minutes, Cook time: 35 minutes, serves; 12

Ingredients:

5 eggs, separated, room temperature
¾ cup margarine, sliced

What you'll need from store cupboard:

1 pkg. semisweet chocolate chips	¼ tsp cream of tartar
½ cup Splenda	Nonstick cooking spray

Instructions:

1. Heat oven to 350 degrees. Spray a 6-7-inch springform pan with cooking spray.
2. In a microwave safe bowl, melt chocolate chips and margarine, in 30 second intervals.
3. In a large bowl, beat egg yolks till thick and lemon colored. Beat in chocolate.
4. In a separate large bowl, with clean beaters, beat egg whites and cream of tartar till foamy. Beat in Splenda, 1 tablespoon at a time, till sugar is dissolved, continue beating till stiff glossy peaks form.

5. Fold ¼ of egg whites into chocolate mixture, then fold in the rest. Transfer to prepared pan. Bake 30-35 minutes, or center is set. Let cool completely before removing side of pan and serving.

Nutrition Facts Per Serving

Calories 181 Total Carbs 10g Protein 3g Fat 14g Sugar 10g Fiber 0g

Sticky Ginger Cake

Prep time: 10 minutes, Cook time: 30 minutes, Serves: 16

Ingredients:

2 eggs, beaten	2 tsp fresh ginger, grated
1 cup buttermilk	
2 tbsp. butter	

What you'll need from store cupboard:

1 cup flour	1 tsp ginger
¼ cup + 1 tbsp. honey	1 tsp cinnamon
¼ cup + 1 tbsp. molasses	½ tsp allspice
¼ cup Splenda brown sugar	¼ tsp salt
1 tbsp. water	Nonstick cooking spray
1 tsp baking soda	Swerve confections sugar, for dusting

Instructions:

1. Heat oven to 400 degrees. Spray an 8-inch square pan with cooking spray.
2. In a saucepan over medium heat, stir together ¼ honey, ¼ cup molasses, Splenda, butter and grated ginger until butter is melted. Remove from heat and let cool 5 minutes.
3. In a medium bowl, stir together the dry Ingredients.
4. In a small bowl, beat the eggs and buttermilk together. Whisk into the molasses mixture until combined. Add to dry Ingredients and mix well. Pour into prepared pan.
5. Bake 25 minutes. Use a skewer to poke holes every inch across the top of the cake.
6. In a small bowl mix remaining honey, molasses and water together. Brush over hot cake. Cool completely and dust lightly with confectioner's sugar before serving.

Nutrition Facts Per Serving

Calories 102 Total Carbs 18g Protein 2g Fat 2g Sugar 11g Fiber 0g

Lemon Meringue Ice Cream

Prep time: 5 minutes, Cook time: 15 minutes, serves; 8

Ingredients:

4 eggs, separated
2 cans coconut milk, refrigerated for 24 hours

6 tbsp. fresh lemon juice
Zest of 2 lemons

What you'll need from store cupboard:

2 ½ tbsp. liquid stevia

1 tbsp. vanilla
1 tsp cream of tartar

Instructions:

1. Heat oven to 325 degrees.
2. In a medium bowl, beat the egg whites and cream of tartar on high speed until soft peaks from. Add 1 ½ tablespoons of stevia and continue beating on high until stiff peaks from.
3. Spread the meringue in a small baking dish and bake 15 minutes, or until the top is golden brown. Remove from oven and let cool completely.
4. Turn the canned coconut milk upside down and open. Drain off the water, save it for another use later. Scoop the cream into a large bowl. Add the egg yolks, juice, zest, remaining tablespoon of stevia, and vanilla and beat until Ingredients are thoroughly combined.
5. Pour into an ice cream maker and freeze according to directions.
6. In a liter sized plastic container, spread a layer of ice cream to cover the bottom. Top with a layer of meringue. Repeat layers. Place an airtight cover on the container and freeze at least 3 hours before serving.

Nutritional Facts Per Serving

Calories 152 Total Carbs 3g Protein 4g Fat 14g Sugar 1g Fiber 0g

Cinnamon Bread Pudding

Prep time: 10 minutes, Cook time: 45 minutes, Serves: 6

Ingredients:

4 cups day-old French or Italian bread, cut into ¾-inch cubes
2 cups skim milk

2 egg whites
1 egg
4 tbsp. margarine, sliced

What you'll need from store cupboard:

5 tsp Splenda
1 ½ tsp cinnamon

¼ tsp salt
1/8 tsp ground cloves

Instructions:

1. Heat oven to 350 degrees.
2. In a medium sauce pan, heat milk and margarine to simmering. Remove from heat and stir till margarine is completely melted. Let cool 10 minutes.
3. In a large bowl, beat egg and egg whites until foamy. Add Splenda, spices and salt. Beat until combined, then add in cooled milk and bread.
4. Transfer mixture to a 1 ½ quart baking dish. Place on rack of roasting pan and add 1 inch of hot water to roaster.
5. Bake until pudding is set and knife inserted in center comes out clean, about 40 – 45 minutes.

Nutrition Facts Per Serving

Calories 362 Total Carbs 25g Net Carbs 23g Protein 14g Fat 10g Sugar 10g Fiber 2g

Apple Crisp

Prep time: 20 minutes, Cook time: 30 minutes, Serves: 8

Ingredients:

5 cups Granny Smith apples, peeled and sliced

3 tablespoons margarine

What you'll need from store cupboard:

½ cup rolled oats
¼ cup + 2 tbsp. Splenda
3 tbsp. flour

1 tsp lemon juice
¾ teaspoon apple pie spice, divided

Instructions:

1. Heat oven to 375.
2. In a large bowl, combine apples, 2 tablespoons Splenda, lemon juice, and ½ teaspoon apple pie spice. Mix to thoroughly coat apples.
3. Place apples in a 2-quart square baking pan.
4. In a medium bowl, combine oats, flour, ¼ Splenda, and remaining apple pie spice. With a pastry knife, cut in butter until mixture resembles coarse crumbs. Sprinkle evenly over apples.
5. Bake 30 – 35 minutes, or until apples are tender and topping is golden brown. Serve warm.

Nutrition Facts Per Serving

Calories 153 Total Carbs 27g Net Carbs 23g Protein 1g Fat 5g Sugar 18g Fiber 4g

Coconut Cream Pie

Prep time: 5 minutes, Cook time: 10 minutes, Serves: 8
Ingredients:

2 cup raw coconut, grated and divided
2 cans coconut milk, full fat and refrigerated for 24 hours
½ cup raw coconut, grated and toasted
2 tbsp. margarine, melted

What you'll need from store cupboard:

1 cup Splenda
½ cup macadamia
nuts
¼ cup almond flour

Instructions:

1. Heat oven to 350 degrees.
2. Add the nuts to a food processor and pulse until finely ground. Add flour, ½ cup Splenda, and 1 cup grated coconut. Pulse until Ingredients are finely ground and resemble cracker crumbs.
3. Add the margarine and pulse until mixture starts to stick together. Press on the bottom and sides of a 9-inch pie pan. Bake 10 minutes or until golden brown. Cool
4. Turn the canned coconut upside down and open. Pour off the water and scoop the cream into a large bowl. Add remaining ½ cup Splenda and beat on high until stiff peaks form.
5. Fold in remaining 1 cup coconut and pour into crust. Cover and chill at least 2 hours. Sprinkle with toasted coconut, slice, and serve.

Nutritional Facts Per Serving
Calories 329 Total Carbs 15g Net Carbs 4g Protein 4g Fat 23g Sugar 4g Fiber 11g

No-Bake Chocolate Swirl No Bake Lemon Tart

Prep time: 10 minutes, chill time: 2 hours, Serves: 8
Ingredients:

½ cup margarine, soft
1/3 cup + 3 tbsp. fresh lemon juice, divided
1/3 cup almond milk,
unsweetened
4 ½ tbsp. margarine, melted
3-4 tbsp. lemon zest, grated fine

What you'll need from store cupboard:

1 cup almond flour
¾ cup coconut,
grated fine
¼ cup + 3 tbsp.

Splenda
2 ½ tsp vanilla, divided
2 tsp lemon extract
¼ teaspoon salt

Instructions:

1. Spray a 9-inch tart pan with cooking spray.
2. In a medium bowl combine, flour, coconut, 3 tablespoons lemon juice, 2 tablespoons Splenda, melted margarine, 1 ½ teaspoons vanilla, and a pinch of salt until thoroughly combined. Dump into prepared pan and press evenly on bottom and halfway up sides. Cover and chill until ready to use.
3. In a medium bowl, beat the soft margarine until fluffy. Add remaining Ingredients and beat until mixture is smooth. Taste and add more lemon juice or Splenda if desired.
4. Pour the filling into the crust. Cover and chill until filling is set, about 2 hours.

Nutritional Facts Per Serving
Calories 317 Total Carbs 17g Net Carbs 15g Protein 3g Fat 25g Sugar 13g Fiber 2g

Coconutty Pudding Clouds

Prep time: 5 minutes, Serves: 4
Ingredients:

2 cup of heavy whipping cream
½ cup of reduced-fat cream cheese, soft
½ cup hazelnuts,
ground
4 tbsp. unsweetened coconut flakes, toasted

What you'll need from store cupboard:

2 tbsp. stevia, divided
½ tsp of vanilla
½ tsp of hazelnut
extract
½ tsp of cacao powder, unsweetened

Instructions:

1. In a medium bowl, beat cream, vanilla, and 1 tablespoon stevia until soft peaks form.
2. In another mixing bowl, beat cream cheese, cocoa, remaining stevia, and hazelnut extract until smooth.
3. In 4 glasses, place ground nuts on the bottom, add a layer of the cream cheese mixture, then the whip cream, and top with toasted coconut. Serve immediately.

Nutrition Facts Per Serving
Calories 396 Total Carbs 12g Net Carbs 11g Protein 6g Fat 35g Sugar 9g Fiber 1g

Gingerbread Soufflés

Prep time: 15 minutes, Cook time: 25 minutes, Serves: 10

Ingredients:

6 eggs, separated
1 cup skim milk
1 cup fat free

whipped topping
2 tbsp. butter, soft

What you'll need from store cupboard:

½ cup Splenda
1/3 cup molasses
¼ cup flour
2 tsp pumpkin pie spice
2 tsp vanilla

1 tsp ginger
¼ tsp salt
1/8 tsp cream of tartar
Butter flavored cooking spray

Instructions:

1. Heat oven to 350 degrees. Spray 10 ramekins with cooking spray and sprinkle with Splenda to coat, shaking out excess. Place on a large baking sheet.
2. In a large saucepan, over medium heat, whisk together milk, Splenda, flour and salt until smooth. Bring to a boil, whisking constantly. Pour into a large bowl and whisk in molasses, butter, vanilla, and spices. Let cool 15 minutes.
3. Once spiced mixture has cooled, whisk in egg yolks.
4. In a large bowl, beat egg whites and cream of tartar on high speed until stiff peaks form. Fold into spiced mixture, a third at a time, until blended completely. Spoon into ramekins.
5. Bake 25 minutes until puffed and set. Serve immediately with a dollop of whipped topping.

Nutrition Facts Per Serving
Calories 170 Total Carbs 24g Protein 4g Fat 5g Sugar 18g Fiber 0g

Mini Key Lime Tarts

Prep time: 5 minutes, Cook time: 10 minutes, Serves: 8

Ingredients:

4 sheets phyllo dough*
¾ cup skim milk
¾ cup fat-free whipped topping, thawed
½ cup egg substitute
½ cup fat free sour cream

6 tbsp. fresh lime juice
What you'll need from store cupboard
2 tbsp. cornstarch
½ cup Splenda
Butter-flavored cooking spray

Instructions:

1. In a medium saucepan, combine milk, juice, and cornstarch. Cook, stirring, over medium heat 2-3 minutes or until thickened. Remove from heat.
2. Add egg substitute and whisk 30 seconds to allow it to cook. Stir in sour cream and Splenda. Cover and chill until completely cool.
3. Heat oven to 350 degrees. Spray 8 muffin cups with cooking spray.
4. Lay 1 sheet of the phyllo on a cutting board and lightly spray it with cooking spray. Repeat this with the remaining sheets so they are stacked on top of each other.
5. Cut the phyllo into 8 squares and gently place them in the prepared muffin cups, pressing firmly on the bottom and sides. Bake 8-10 minutes or until golden brown. Remove them from the pan and let cool.
6. To serve: spoon the lime mixture evenly into the 8 cups and top with whipped topping. Garnish with fresh lime slices if desired.

Nutrition Facts Per Serving
Calories 82 Total Carbs 13g Net Carbs 12g Protein 3g Fat 1g Sugar 10g Fiber 1g

Sangria Jello Cups

Prep time: 10 minutes, chill time: 4 hours, Serves: 6

Ingredients:

1 cup raspberries
1 cup green grapes, halved

What you'll need from store cupboard:

1 pkg. lemon gelatin, sugar free
1 pkg. raspberry gelatin, sugar free
11 oz. mandarin

oranges, drain
1 ½ cup boiling water
1 cup cold water
1 cup white wine

Instructions:

1. Place both gelatins in a large bowl and add boiling water. Stir to dissolve. Let rest 10 minutes.
2. Stir in cold water and wine, cover and refrigerate 45 minutes, or until partially set.
3. Fold in oranges, raspberries and grapes. Spoon evenly into 6 wine glasses. Cover and refrigerate 4 hours or until set.

Nutrition Facts Per Serving
Calories 88 Total Carbs 11g Net Carbs 9g Protein 3g Fat 0g Sugar 8g Fiber 2g

Moist Butter Cake

Prep time: 15 minutes, Cook time: 30 minutes, Serves: 14

Ingredients:

3 eggs
¾ cup margarine, divided

½ cup fat free sour cream

What you'll need from store cupboard:

2 cup almond flour, packed
1 cup Splenda, divided
1 tsp baking powder

2 tbsp. water
1 tbsp. + 1 tsp vanilla, divided
Butter flavored cooking spray

Instructions:

1. Heat oven to 350 degrees. Spray a Bundt cake pan generously with cooking spray.
2. In a large bowl, whisk together flour, sour cream, ½ cup margarine, 3 eggs, 2/3 cup Splenda, baking powder, and 1 teaspoon vanilla until thoroughly combined.
3. Pour into prepared pan and bake 30-35 minutes, or it passes the toothpick test. Remove from oven.
4. Melt ¼ cup margarine in a small saucepan over medium heat. Whisk in 1/3 cup Splenda, tablespoon vanilla, and water. Continue to stir until Splenda is completely dissolved.
5. Use a skewer to poke several small holes in top of cake. Pour syrup mixture evenly over cake making sure all the holes are filled. Swirl the pan a couple of minutes until the syrup is absorbed into the cake.
6. Let cool 1 hour. Invert onto serving plate, slice and serve.

Nutrition Facts Per Serving
Calories 259 Total Carbs 18g Net Carbs 16g Protein 4g Fat 17g Sugar 15g Fiber 2g

Peach Ice Cream

Prep time: 15 minutes, chill time: 4 hours, Serves: 32

Ingredients:

4 peaches, peel and chop
8 oz. fat free whipped topping

2 cup skim milk
¼ cup fresh lemon juice

What you'll need from store cupboard:

2-12 oz. cans fat free evaporated milk

14 oz. can sweetened condensed milk

3.4 oz. pkg. sugar free instant vanilla pudding mix
½ cup Splenda

1 tsp vanilla
½ tsp almond extract
1/8 tsp salt

Instructions:

1. In a large bowl, beat milk and pudding mix on low speed 2 minutes. Beat in remaining Ingredients, except whipped topping until thoroughly combined. Fold in whipped topping.
2. Freeze in ice cream maker according to manufacturer's directions, this may take 2 batches. Transfer to freezer containers and freeze 4 hours before serving. Serving size is ½ cup.

Nutrition Facts Per Serving
Calories 106 Total Carbs 19g Protein 3g Fat 1g Sugar 15g Fiber 0g

Watermelon Ice

Prep time: 5 minutes, chill time; 8 hours, serves; 8

Ingredients:

5 cup cubed watermelon, remove seeds
½ cup light cranberry juice cocktail

What you'll need from store cupboard
½ cup Splenda
1 envelope unflavored gelatin

Instructions:

1. Place watermelon in a food processor and pulse until almost smooth.
2. In a small saucepan, over low heat, stir together Splenda and gelatin. Slowly add juice. Cook, stirring, until gelatin dissolves.
3. Add to watermelon and process until combined.
4. Pour into an 8-inch square dish, cover and freeze 5 hours, or until firm.
5. Break watermelon mixture into chunks. Freeze another 3 hours.
6. To serve; scrape and stir mixture with a fork to create an icy texture. Spoon into dessert dishes and serve.

Nutrition Facts Per Serving
Calories 94 Total Carbs 20g Protein 1g Fat 0g Sugar 18g Fiber 0g

Pineapple Frozen Yogurt

**Prep time: 5 minutes, chill time: 1 hour,
Serves: 4**
Ingredients:
½ cup half-and-half   fat yogurt
½ cup plain reduced-   ¼ cup egg substitute
What you'll need from store cupboard:
¾ cup crushed pineapple, in juice
¼ cup Splenda
Instructions:
1. In a medium bowl, beat egg substitute until thick and cream colored. Add remaining Ingredients and mix to thoroughly combine. Cover and chill completely, if using an ice cream maker. Once chilled add to ice cream maker and freeze according to manufacturer's directions.
2. Or, you can pour the mixture into a shallow glass baking dish and freeze. Stir and scrape the mixture, every 10 minutes, with a rubber spatula until it reaches desired consistency, about 1 hour.

Nutrition Facts Per Serving
Calories 145 Total Carbs 20g Protein 5g Fat 4g Sugar 17g Fiber 0g

Pumpkin Ice Cream with Candied Pecans

**Prep time: 20 minutes, chill time: 1 hour,
Serves: 8**
Ingredients:
2 eggs   unsweetened, divided
2 cup almond milk,   1 cup half-n-half
What you'll need from store cupboard:
1 cup pumpkin   ¾ cup Candied
1 envelope   Pecans, (chapter 6)
unflavored gelatin   2 tsp pumpkin pie
¾ cup Splenda   spice
Instructions:
1. Pour one cup almond milk into a small bowl. Sprinkle gelatin on top. Allow to sit for about 5 minutes.
2. In a medium saucepan, whisk together Splenda and the eggs. Whisk in pumpkin and pumpkin spice. Whisk in gelatin.
3. Bring the mixture just to a simmer, then remove from heat. Allow to cool about 5 minutes at room temperature, then refrigerate, uncovered for 45 minutes,

stirring occasionally. Do not cool too long or the mixture will set.
4. Remove pumpkin mixture from the refrigerator and whisk in half-n-half and remaining cup of almond milk. Pour into an ice-cream freezer and freeze according to manufactures instructions.
5. When ice cream reaches the desired consistency, transfer to a freezer-safe container with a lid. Stir in candied pecans, cover, and place container in the freezer to further harden the ice cream.

Nutrition Facts Per Serving
Calories 254 Total Carbs 26g Net Carbs 24g Protein 5g Fat 13g Sugar 22g Fiber 2g

Raspberry & Dark Chocolate Mini Soufflés

**Prep time: 10 minutes, Cook time: 10 minutes,
Serves: 6**
Ingredients:
1 cup fresh raspberries
4 egg whites
What you'll need from store cupboard:
½ oz. dark chocolate,   6 tsp Splenda
chopped   1 tsp margarine, soft
Instructions:
1. Heat oven to 400 degrees. Use the margarine to grease 6 small ramekins.
2. Puree the raspberries in a blender or food processor and press through a fine sieve to get all of the seeds out. Add 1 tablespoons Splenda and set aside.
3. Beat egg whites until thickened and start adding the remaining Splenda, gradually, until the mixture forms stiff glossy peaks.
4. Gently fold ⅓ of the egg whites into the raspberry puree. Once mixed, fold the raspberry puree mixture into the remaining egg whites and fold gently until there are no streaks of pink left.
5. Spoon the raspberry mixture into the ramekins filling them half full. Divide the chocolate between the ramekins and then fill to the top with soufflé mixture. Place ramekins on a baking sheet. Bake for 9 minutes until golden brown and puffed up. Serve immediately.

Nutrition Facts Per Serving
Calories 60 Total Carbs 8g Net Carbs 7g Protein 3g Fat 1g Sugar 6g Fiber 1g

Raspberry Lemon Cheesecake Squares

Prep time: 5 minutes, Cook time: 40 minutes, serves; 12

Ingredients:

2 cups raspberries
1 cup fat-free sour cream
¾ cup fat-free cream cheese, softened
½ cup egg substitute
2 tbsp. lemon juice
2 tsp lemon zest, divided

What you'll need from store cupboard:

½ cup + 3 tbsp. Splenda
1 tsp vanilla
Nonstick cooking spray

Instructions:

1. Heat oven to 350°F. Spray 8-inch square baking pan with cooking spray.
2. In a large bowl, beat cream cheese, ½ cup Splenda, and vanilla on high speed until smooth. Add juice, 1 teaspoon zest, and egg substitute. Beat until thoroughly combined. Pour into prepared pan.
3. Bake 40 minutes or until firm to the touch. Remove from oven and cool completely.
4. In a small bowl, stir together the sour cream and 1 tablespoon Splenda until smooth. Spoon evenly over cooled cheesecake. Cover and refrigerate overnight.
5. 30 minutes before serving, toss the berries and remaining 2 tablespoons Splenda in small bowl. Let sit. Just before serving, stir in the remaining zest and spoon the berry mixture over the top of the cheesecake. Cut into 12 bars and serve.

Nutrition Facts Per Serving

Calories 144 Total Carbs 18g Net Carbs 17g Protein 3g Fat 5g Sugar 14g Fiber 1g

Pomegranate Panna Cotta

Prep time: 15 minutes, chill time: 4 hours, Serves: 8

Ingredients:

2 ½ cup heavy cream
½ cup skim milk
8 tbsp. pomegranate seeds
½ vanilla pod

What you'll need from store cupboard:

1 envelope plain gelatin
¼ cup Splenda

Instructions:

1. Pour milk in a small, wide bowl and sprinkle gelatin over. Let set for 10 minutes.
2. Scrape the seeds from the vanilla pod into a heavy bottomed sauce pan, add the pod too. Add cream and Splenda and bring to a simmer over medium heat, stirring frequently. Remove from heat and stir in gelatin mixture.
3. Pour the mixture through a fine mesh sieve, then divide evenly between 8 4-oz. ramekins or jars. Cover and refrigerate at least 4 hours or overnight.
4. Serve topped with 1 tablespoon of pomegranate seeds.

Nutrition Facts Per Serving

Calories 250 Total Carbs 10g Net Carbs 7g Protein 3g Fat 15g Sugar 7g Fiber 3g

Toffee Apple Mini Pies

Prep time: 20 minutes, Cook time: 25 minutes, Serves: 12

Ingredients:

2 9-inch pie crusts, soft
2 cup Gala apples, diced fine
1 egg, beaten
1 tbsp. butter, cut in 12 cubes
1 ½ tsp fresh lemon juice

What you'll need from store cupboard:

2 tbsp. toffee bits
1 tbsp. Splenda
½ tsp cinnamon
Nonstick cooking spray

Instructions:

1. Heat oven to 375 degrees. Spray a cookie sheet with cooking spray.
2. In a medium bowl, stir together apples, toffee, Splenda, lemon juice, and cinnamon.
3. Roll pie crusts, one at a time, out on a lightly floured surface. Use a 3-inch round cookie cutter to cut 12 circles from each crust. Place 12 on prepared pan.
4. Brush the dough with half the egg. Spoon 1 tablespoon of the apple mixture on each round, leaving ½- inch edge. Top with pat of butter. Place second dough round on top and seal edges closed with a fork. Brush with remaining egg.
5. Bake 25 minutes, or until golden brown. Serve warm.

Nutrition Facts Per Serving

Calories 154 Total Carbs 17g Net Carbs 16g Protein 1g Fat 9g Sugar 6g Fiber 1g

Mini Bread Puddings

Prep time: 5 minutes, Cook time: 35 minutes, Serves: 12

Ingredients:

6 slices cinnamon bread, cut into cubes	What you'll need from store cupboard
1 ¼ cup skim milk	1/3 cup Splenda
½ cup egg substitute	1 tsp vanilla
1 tbsp. margarine, melted	1/8 tsp salt
	1/8 tsp nutmeg

Instructions:

1. Heat oven to 350°F. Line 12 medium-size muffin cups with paper baking cups.
2. In a large bowl, stir together milk, egg substitute, Splenda, vanilla, salt and nutmeg until combined. Add bread cubes and stir until moistened. Let rest 15 minutes.
3. Spoon evenly into prepared baking cups. Drizzle margarine evenly over the tops. Bake 30-35 minutes or until puffed and golden brown. Remove from oven and let cool completely.

Nutrition Facts Per Serving
Calories 105 Total Carbs 16 Net Carbs 15g Protein 4g Fat 2g Sugar 9g Fiber 1g

Raspberry Peach Cobbler

Prep time: 15 minutes, Cook time: 40 minutes, Serves: 8

Ingredients:

1 ¼ lbs. peaches, peeled and sliced	buttermilk
2 cups fresh raspberries	2 tbsp. cold margarine, cut into pieces
½ cup low-fat	1 tsp lemon zest

What you'll need from store cupboard:

¾ cup + 2 tbsp. flour, divided	½ tsp baking soda
4 tbsp. + 2 tsp Splenda, divided	1/8 tsp salt
½ tsp baking powder	Nonstick cooking spray

Instructions:

1. Heat oven to 425 degrees. Spray an 11×7-inch baking dish with cooking spray.
2. In a large bowl, stir together 2 tablespoons Splenda and 2 tablespoons flour. Add the fruit and zest and toss to coat. Pour into prepared baking dish. Bake 15 minutes, or until fruit is bubbling around the edges.
3. In a medium bowl, combine remaining flour, 2 tablespoons Splenda, baking powder, baking soda, and salt. Cut in margarine with pastry cutter until it resembles coarse crumbs. Stir in the buttermilk just until moistened.
4. Remove the fruit from the oven and top with dollops of buttermilk mixture. Sprinkle the remaining 2 teaspoons of Splenda over the top and bake 18-20 minutes or top is lightly browned. Serve warm.

Nutrition Facts Per Serving
Calories 130 Total Carbs 22g Net Carbs 19g Protein 2g Fat 3g Sugar 10g Fiber 3g

Raspberry Almond Clafoutis

Prep time: 10 minutes, Cook time: 1 hour, Serves: 8

Ingredients:

1 pint raspberries, rinse and pat dry	unsweetened
	¼ cup half-n-half
3 eggs	4 tbsp. margarine
¾ cup almond milk,	

What you'll need from store cupboard:

½ cup almond flour	½ tsp baking powder
1/3 cup Splenda	¼ tsp allspice
¼ cup almonds, sliced	¼ tsp almond extract
1 tbsp. coconut flour	Nonstick cooking spray
1 ½ tsp vanilla	

Instructions:

1. Heat oven to 350 degrees. Spray a 9-inch pie dish with cooking spray and place on a baking sheet.
2. Place the berries, in a single layer, in the pie dish.
3. In a medium bowl, stir together the flours, baking powder, and allspice.
4. Add the margarine to a small saucepan and melt over low heat. Once melted, remove from heat and whisk in Splenda until smooth.
5. Pour the margarine into a large bowl and whisk in eggs, one at a time. Add extracts and dry Ingredients. Stir in the almond milk and half-n-half, batter will be thin.
6. Pour over the raspberries and top with almonds. Bake 50-60 minutes, or center is set and top is lightly browned. Cool to room temperature before serving.

Nutrition Facts Per Serving
Calories 273 Total Carbs 19g Net Carbs 13g Protein 7g Fat 19g Sugar 11g Fiber 6g

Carrot Cupcakes

Prep time: 10 minutes, Cook time: 35 minutes, Serves: 12

Ingredients:

2 cup carrots, grated   2 eggs
1 cup low fat cream   1-2 tsp skim milk
cheese, soft

What you'll need from store cupboard:

½ cup coconut oil,   2 tsp vanilla, divided
melted   1 tsp baking powder
¼ cup coconut flour   1 tsp cinnamon
¼ cup Splenda   Nonstick cooking
¼ cup honey   spray

Instructions:

1. Heat oven to 350 degrees. Lightly spray a muffin pan with cooking spray, or use paper liners.
2. In a large bowl, stir together the flour, baking powder, and cinnamon.
3. Add the carrots, eggs, oil, Splenda, and vanilla to a food processor. Process until Ingredients are combined but carrots still have some large chunks remaining. Add to dry Ingredients and stir to combine.
4. Pour evenly into prepared pan, filling cups 2/3 full. Bake 30-35 minutes, or until cupcakes pass the toothpick test. Remove from oven and let cool.
5. In a medium bowl, beat cream cheese, honey, and vanilla on high speed until smooth. Add milk, one teaspoon at a time, beating after each addition, until frosting is creamy enough to spread easily.
6. Once cupcakes have cooled, spread each one with about 2 tablespoons of frosting. Chill until ready to serve.

Nutritional Facts Per Serving

Calories 160 Total Carbs 13g Net Carbs 12g Protein 4g Fat 10g Sugar 11g Fiber 1g

Café Mocha Torte

Prep time: 15 minutes, Cook time: 25 minutes, Serves: 14

Ingredients:

8 eggs
1 cup margarine, cut into cubes

What you'll need from store cupboard:

1 lb. bittersweet   room temperature
chocolate, chopped   Nonstick cooking
¼ cup brewed coffee,   spray

Instructions:

1. Heat oven to 325 degrees. Spray an 8-inch springform pan with cooking spray. Line bottom of sides with parchment paper and spray again. Wrap the outside with a double layer of foil and place in 9x13-inch baking dish. Put a small saucepan of water on to boil.
2. In a large bowl, beat the eggs on med speed until doubled in volume, about 5 minutes.
3. Place the chocolate, margarine and coffee into microwave safe bowl and microwave on high, until chocolate is melted and mixture is smooth, stir every 30 seconds.
4. Fold 1/3 of the eggs into chocolate mixture until almost combined. Add the remaining eggs, 1/3 at a time and fold until combined.
5. Pour into prepared pan. Pour boiling water around the springform pan until it reaches halfway up the sides. Bake 22-25 minutes, or until cake has risen slightly and edges are just beginning to set.
6. Remove from water bath and let cool completely. Cover with plastic wrap and chill 6 hours or overnight. About 30 minutes before serving, run a knife around the edges and remove the side of the pan. Slice and serve.

Nutrition Facts Per Serving

Calories 260 Total Carbs 12g Net Carbs 11g Protein 5g Fat 21g Sugar 11g Fiber 1g

Sweet Potato Crème Brule

Prep time: 10 minutes, Cook time: 1 hour 5 minutes, Serves: 12

Ingredients:

7 egg yolks

1 ¼ cup sweet potato, bake, peel & mash

2 cup half-n-half

1 tbsp. fresh lemon juice

What you'll need from store cupboard:

¾ cup Splenda

¼ cup + 1/3 cup Splenda brown sugar

3 tsp vanilla

Butter flavored cooking spray

Instructions:

1. Heat oven to 325 degrees. Spray a 10-inch metal quiche dish with cooking spray.
2. In a medium bowl, combine sweet potato, ¼ cup Splenda brown sugar, and lemon juice. Spoon into prepared dish.
3. In a 2-quart saucepan, whisk together half-n-half, Splenda, egg yolks, and vanilla. Cook over med-low heat 15 minutes, stirring frequently, until hot, do not boil. Pour over sweet potato mixture.
4. Place dish in a shallow pan and put in the oven. Pour enough boiling water to cover half way up the sides of the dish. Bake 1 hour or until a knife inserted in the center comes out clean. Cool on rack. Cover and refrigerate 8 hours or overnight.
5. Heat oven to broil. Sprinkle custard with 1/3 cup Splenda brown sugar and place dish on a baking sheet. Broil 3-5 minutes or until sugar has melted. Cool 5 minutes before serving.

Nutrition Facts Per Serving

Calories 193 Total Carbs 24g Protein 3g Fat 7g Sugar 21g Fiber 0g

Tropical Fruit Tart

Prep time: 10 minutes, Cook time: 10 minutes, Serves: 8

Ingredients:

1 mango, peeled, pitted and sliced thin

1 banana, sliced thin

2 egg whites

What you'll need from store cupboard:

15 ¼ oz. can pineapple chunks in juice, undrained

3 ½ oz. can sweetened flaked coconut

1 cup cornflakes,

crushed

3 teaspoons Splenda

2 tsp cornstarch

1 tsp coconut extract

Nonstick cooking spray

Instructions:

1. Heat oven to 425 degrees. Spray a 9-inch springform pan with cooking spray.
2. In a medium bowl, combine cornflakes, coconut, and egg whites. Toss until blended. Press firmly over the bottom and ½-inch up the sides of the prepared pan. Bake 8 minutes or until edges start to brown. Cool completely.
3. Drain the juice from the pineapple into a small saucepan. Add cornstarch and stir until smooth. Bring to boil over high heat and let cook 1 minute, stirring constantly. Remove from heat and cool completely. Once cooled stir in Splenda and coconut extract.
4. In a medium bowl, combine pineapple, mango, and banana. Spoon over crust and drizzle with pineapple juice mixture. Cover and chill at least 2 hours before serving.

Nutrition Facts Per Serving

Calories 120 Total Carbs 19g Net Carbs 17g Protein 2g Fat 4g Sugar 13g Fiber 2g

Chapter 9 - Soups and Stews Recipe

Guinness Beef Stew with Cauliflower Mash

Prep time: 10 minutes, Cook time: 8 hours, Serves: 4

Ingredients:

2 lb. beef round steak, cut into 1-inch cubes
1 large head cauliflower, separated into florets
5 sprigs fresh thyme
1 medium carrot, cut into 1/2-inch pieces
1 stick of celery, cut into 1/2-inch pieces
1 cup yellow onion, cut into large pieces
2/3 cup Guinness
1 tbsp. margarine

What you'll need from store cupboard:

2 cups low sodium beef broth
2 tbsp. arrowroot starch
1 tbsp. + 1 tsp garlic, diced fine
2 tsp olive oil
Sea salt & pepper to taste

Instructions:

1. Add oil to a large nonstick skillet and heat over med-high heat. Add beef and sear on all sides. Transfer to crock pot.
2. Add thyme, Guinness, carrot, onion, celery, garlic, and broth. Set to low and cook 6-8 hours, or 4-5 on high.
3. One hour before the stew is ready, mix arrowroot with 1 ½ tablespoons water and stir into stew.
4. For the mash: bring 2 cups water to a boil in a large pot and add cauliflower. Cover and cook 10 -12 minutes, or until cauliflower is soft.
5. Drain. Add salt, pepper, 1 teaspoon garlic, and margarine. Use an immersion blender and process until it resembles mashed potatoes.
6. To serve: ladle stew in a bowl and spoon about ¼ cup of the mash on top. Garnish with fresh thyme, parsley, and cracked pepper if desired.

Nutrition Facts Per Serving

Calories 563 Total Carbs 17g Net Carbs 11g Protein 75g Fat 28g Sugar 7g Fiber 6g

Chicken Pappardelle

Preparation time: 15 minutes, Cook time: 15 minutes, Serves: 4

Ingredients:

¾ lb. chicken breast, sliced lengthwise into 1/8-inch strips
1 small onion, sliced thin
8 cup spinach, chopped fine
4 cup low sodium chicken broth
1 cup fresh basil

What you'll need from store cupboard:

2 quarts water
¼ cup reduced fat parmesan cheese, divided
6 cloves garlic, diced
1 tbsp. walnuts, chopped
¼ tsp cinnamon
¼ tsp paprika
¼ tsp red pepper flakes
Salt
Olive oil cooking spray

Instructions:

1. Bring 2 quarts water to a simmer in a medium pot.
2. Lightly spray a medium skillet with cooking spray and place over med-high heat. Add the garlic and cook until golden brown. Add the cinnamon, paprika, red pepper flakes, basil leaves, and onion. Cook until the onion has softened, about 2 minutes.
3. Add the spinach and cook until it has wilted and softened, another 2 minutes. Add the broth, bring to a simmer, cover, and cook until tender, about 5 minutes.
4. Add a pinch of salt to the now-simmering water. Turn off the heat and add the chicken and stir so that all the strips are separated. Cook just until the strips have turned white; they will be half-cooked. Using a slotted spoon, transfer the strips to a plate to cool.
5. Check the spinach mixture; cook it until most of the broth has evaporated Stir in half the cheese and season with salt to taste. Add the chicken, toss to coat, and continue to cook until the chicken strips have cooked through, about 90 seconds. Spoon the mixture onto four plates, top with the remaining cheese and serve.

Nutrition Facts Per Serving

Calories 174 Total Carbs 7g Net Carbs 5g Protein 24g Fat 5g Sugar 2g Fiber 2g

African Christmas Stew

Prep time: 15 minutes, cook time; 1 hour 40 minutes, serves; 6

Ingredients:

3 ½ lbs. chicken, whole pieces with bones in
6 Roma tomatoes
2 scallions, diced
white and green parts
1 onion, sliced thin
1 cup carrots, sliced

What you'll need from store cupboard:

2 cups water
1/8 cup vegetable oil
3 tbsp. parsley
2 cloves garlic, diced fine
1 tbsp. paprika
1 ½ tsp thyme
¼ tsp curry powder
1 bay leaf
Salt and pepper, to taste

Instructions:

1. Season chicken with salt and pepper on both sides.
2. Place the tomatoes, onion, and scallions in a food processor and pulse until pureed.
3. In a large soup pot, heat the oil over medium heat. Add chicken and brown on both sides.
4. Pour the tomato mixture over the chicken and add the remaining Ingredients. Bring to a low boil.
5. Reduce heat to low, cover, and simmer 60-90 minutes until the chicken is cooked through and the carrots are tender. Discard bay leaf before serving. Serve as is or over cauliflower rice.

Nutrition Facts Per Serving

Calories 480 Total Carbs 9g Net Carbs 7g Protein 78g Fat 13g Sugar 5g Fiber 2g

Asian Meatball Soup

Prep time: 15 minutes, Cook time: 5 hours, serves; 4

Ingredients:

½ lb. ground pork
4 cup mustard greens, torn
4 scallions, sliced thin
2 tsp fresh ginger, peeled and grated fine

What you'll need from store cupboard:

4 cup low sodium chicken broth
2 tbsp. soy sauce
1 tbsp. vegetable oil
2 cloves garlic, diced fine
1 tsp peppercorns, crushed
1 tsp fish sauce
¾ tsp red pepper flakes,
½ tsp cumin seeds,

chopped coarse
Sea salt and black
pepper

Instructions:

1. In a large bowl, combine pork, garlic, ginger, and spices. Season with salt and pepper. Use your hands to combine all Ingredients thoroughly.
2. Heat oil in a large skillet over medium heat. Form pork into 1-inch balls and cook in oil till brown on all sides. Use a slotted spoon to transfer the meatballs to a crock pot.
3. Add remaining Ingredients and stir. Cover and cook on low 4-5 hours or until meatballs are cooked through. Serve.

Nutrition Facts Per Serving

Calories 156 Total Carbs 7g Net Carbs 5g Protein 19g Fat 6g Sugar 2g Fiber 2g

Bacon & Cabbage Soup

Prep time: 15 minutes, Cook time: 6 hours, Serves: 6

Ingredients:

6 bacon strips, cut into 1-inch pieces
3 cup cauliflower, separated into florets
2 cup cabbage, sliced thin
2 celery stalks, peeled and diced
1 onion, diced
1 carrot, peeled and diced

What you'll need from store cupboard:

5 cup low sodium chicken broth
2 cloves garlic, diced
fine
¼ tsp thyme

Instructions:

1. Cook bacon in a large skillet over med-high heat until almost crisp. Remove from skillet and place on paper towels to drain.
2. Add the celery, garlic, and onion to the skillet and cook, stirring frequently, about 5 minutes. Use a slotted spoon to transfer to the crock pot.
3. Add the bacon, broth, cabbage, carrot, and thyme to the crock pot. Cover and cook on low 4-5 hours or until the carrots are tender.
4. Add the cauliflower and cook until tender, about 1-2 hours. Serve.

Nutrition Facts Per Serving

Calories 148 Total Carbs 8g Net Carbs 5g Protein 10g Fat 8g Sugar 3g Fiber 3g

Beef & Lentil Soup

Prep time: 10 minutes, Cook time: 7 hours, serves; 8

Ingredients:

1 ½ lbs. beef stew meat	1 cup onion, diced
	½ cup celery, diced

What you'll need from store cupboard:

6 cup water	2 tsp salt
½ cup lentils	1 tsp olive oil
2 cloves garlic, diced	Fresh ground black pepper
2 bay leaves	

Instructions:

1. In a large skillet over med-high heat, heat oil. Add beef and brown on all sides. Use a slotted spoon to transfer the meat to a crock pot.
2. Add remaining Ingredients, cover and cook on low 6-7 hours or until beef is tender. Discard bay leaves before serving.

Nutrition Facts Per Serving

Calories 213 Total Carbs 9g Net Carbs 5g Protein 29g Fat 6g Sugar 1g Fiber 4g

Beef Burgundy & Mushroom Stew

Prep time: 15 minutes, Cook time: 8 hours, Serves: 4

Ingredients:

1 lb. sirloin steak, cut into bite size pieces	1 cup mushrooms, sliced
2 carrots, peeled and cut into 1-inch pieces	¾ cup pearl onions, thawed if frozen

What you'll need from store cupboard:

1 cup Burgundy wine	1 bay leaf
½ cup low sodium beef broth	1 tsp marjoram
3 cloves garlic, diced	½ tsp salt
2 tbsp. olive oil	½ tsp thyme
	¼ tsp pepper

Instructions:

1. Heat the oil in a large skillet over med-high heat. Add steak and brown on all sides. Transfer to a crock pot.
2. Add remaining Ingredients and stir to combine. Cover and cook on low 7-8 hours or until steak is tender and vegetables are cooked through. Discard the bay leaf before serving.

Nutrition Facts Per Serving

Calories 353 Total Carbs 8g Net Carbs 7g Protein 36g Fat 14g Sugar 3g Fiber 1g

Cioppino

Prep time: 20 minutes, Cook time: 45 minutes, Serves: 6

Ingredients:

20 hard shelled clams	3 stalks celery, sliced thin
20 shelled mussels	
1 lb. red snapper	2 onions, diced fine
1 lb. very large shrimp, deveined, shell-on	1 yellow pepper, seeded and diced
1 lb. large sea scallops, muscles removed from side if attached	¼ cup fresh parsley, chopped
	¼ cup fresh basil, chopped

What you'll need from store cupboard:

1 can whole plum tomatoes, drained and chopped, reserve juice	¼ cup light olive oil
	8 cloves garlic, diced fine
1 ½ cup dry white wine	2 tbsp. tomato paste
	2 tbsp. Splenda
1 cup bottled clam juice	2 bay leaves
	1 ½ tsp salt
1 cup low sodium chicken broth	1 tsp black pepper
	1 tsp oregano

Instructions:

1. Add onion, oil, garlic, bay leaves, oregano, salt and pepper to a large pot and cook over medium heat until onions are soft.
2. Stir in celery, bell pepper, and tomato paste and cook, stirring, 1 minute. Add wine and bring to a boil, cook until liquid is reduced by half, about 5-6 minutes.
3. Stir in tomatoes, reserved juice, clam juice, broth and Splenda. Reduce heat and simmer, covered 30 minutes.
4. Add the clams and mussels and cook until they open. Transfer opened clams and mussels to a bowl as soon as they open. Discard any that do not open.
5. Season fish, shrimp and scallops with salt and pepper and add to the pot. Simmer covered 3 minutes or just until shrimp start to turn pink. If shrimp cooks before the fish, remove it to a bowl.
6. Turn off heat and discard bay leaves. Return all cooked seafood back to the pot and add parsley. Serve warm garnished with chopped basil.

Nutrition Facts Per Serving

Calories 514 Total Carbs 26g Net Carbs 23g Protein 62g Fat 13g Sugar 13g Fiber 3g

Beef Vegetable Soup

Prep time: 15 minutes, Cook time: 7 hours, Serves: 6

Ingredients:

1 lb. lean ground beef, cooked and drained	medium sized florets
	1 tomato, diced
2 stalks celery, sliced	½ onion, diced
1 large head of cauliflower, separated	1 cup carrots, sliced thick
	1 cup corn kernels

What you'll need from store cupboard:

4 cup water	sauce
1 ¾ cup low sodium beef broth	½ cup white cooking wine
1 ½ cup tomato	1 tbsp. parsley

Instructions:

1. Place everything but the cauliflower in a crock pot. Cover and cook on low 5-6 hours or until vegetables are almost tender.
2. Add the cauliflower and cook another 60 minutes. Serve.

Nutrition Facts Per Serving

Calories 254 Total Carbs 20g Net Carbs 14g Protein 29g Fat 6g Sugar 9g Fiber 6g

Beef Zoodle Stew

Prep time: 15 minutes, cook time; 1 hour 25 minutes, Serves: 6

Ingredients:

1 lb. beef stew meat	3 carrots, peeled and diced
4 large zucchinis, spiralize	½ red onion, diced
3 celery stalks, diced	

What you'll need from store cupboard:

14oz. can tomatoes, diced	1 tsp thyme
4 cup low-sodium beef broth	½ tsp cayenne pepper
2 cloves garlic, diced fine	¼ tsp red pepper flakes
1-2 bay leaves	Salt and pepper, to taste
3 tbsp. Worcestershire sauce	Freshly chopped parsley, to garnish
2 tbsp. olive oil	

Instructions:

1. Heat oil in a large saucepan over medium heat. Add beef and cook until brown on all sides. Remove from pan and set aside.
2. Add the garlic to the pan and cook 30 seconds. Then stir in onion and red pepper flakes. Cook 1 minute and add the celery and carrots. Sweat the vegetables for 2 minutes, stirring occasionally.
3. Add the beef back to the pan with the Worcestershire, thyme, and cayenne pepper and stir. Season with salt and pepper to taste. Add the broth, tomatoes, and bay leaves and bring to a boil.
4. Reduce heat, cover and let simmer 40 minutes. Remove the cover and cook 35 minutes more or until stew thickens.
5. Divide the zucchini noodles evenly among four bowls. Ladle stew evenly over zucchini and let set for a few minutes to cook the zucchini. Top with fresh parsley and serve.

Nutrition Facts Per Serving

Calories 225 Total Carbs 13g Net Carbs 10g Protein 29g Fat 6g Sugar 8g Fiber 3g

Chipotle Chicken & Corn Soup

Prep time: 15 minutes, Cook time: 30 minutes, Serves: 8

Ingredients:

1 onion, diced	cooked and cut in cubes
2 chipotle peppers in adobo sauce, diced	½ cup fat free sour cream
3 cup corn kernels	
2 cup chicken breast,	¼ cup cilantro, diced

What you'll need from store cupboard:

2 14 ½ oz. cans fire roasted tomatoes, diced	4 cloves garlic, diced
	1 tbsp. sunflower oil
4 cup low sodium chicken broth	2 tsp adobo sauce
	1 tsp cumin
	¼ tsp pepper

Instructions:

1. Heat oil in a large pot over med-high heat. Add onion and cook until tender, about 3-5 minutes. Add garlic and cook 1 minute more.
2. Add broth, tomatoes, corn, chipotle peppers, adobo sauce, and seasonings. Bring to a boil. Reduce heat and simmer 20 minutes.
3. Stir in chicken and cook until heated through. Serve garnished with sour cream and cilantro.

Nutrition Facts Per Serving

Calories 145 Total Carbs 20g Net Carbs 16g Protein 10g Fat 3g Sugar 6g Fiber 4g

Beer Cheese & Chicken Soup

Prep time: 15 minutes, cook time; 5 hours 30 minutes, Serves: 6-8
Ingredients:

6 slices bacon, cut into 1 inch pieces
1 lb. chicken breast, cut into bite size pieces
2 cup half-and-half
1 cup cheddar cheese, grated
1 cup light beer
4 tbsp. margarine

What you'll need from store cupboard:

1 cup low sodium chicken broth
¼ cup flour
2 tsp garlic powder
1 tsp cayenne pepper
1 tsp smoked paprika
1 tsp salt
1 tsp black pepper, coarsely ground
1 tsp Worcestershire sauce

Instructions:

1. Cook bacon in a medium skillet, over med-high heat until almost crisp. Remove with a slotted spoon and add to crock pot.
2. Add chicken to the skillet and cook until no longer pink. Add it to the bacon along with the broth, beer, and Worcestershire. Cover and cook on low 4 hours.
3. Melt margarine in a small saucepan over medium heat. Add flour and spices and whisk until smooth. Whisk in half-n-half and continue stirring until thoroughly combined. Stir into chicken mixture in crock pot.
4. Add the cheese and stir well. Cook another 60-90 minutes or until cheese has completely melted and soup has thickened. Serve.

Nutrition Facts Per Serving
Calories 453 Total Carbs 9g Protein 32g Fat 30g Sugar 0g Fiber 0g

Clam & Bacon Soup

Prep time: 20 minutes, Cook time: 20 minutes, Serves: 8
Ingredients:

10-12 large clams, in the shell
4 slices bacon, chopped and cooked
almost crisp
3 cups cauliflower, separated into florets
½ cup onion, diced

What you'll need from store cupboard:

6 cup water
1 tsp Worcestershire sauce

Instructions:

1. Scrub clams and rinse under cold running water. Place in a large pot and add water.

Bring to a simmer over med-high heat. Cover and cook until clams open, about 8-10 minutes. Transfer clams to bowl to cool.
2. Cook onion in the same pan used for the bacon, 2-3 minutes. Stir to scrape up the brown bits on the bottom of the pan.
3. When clams are cool enough to touch, remove the meat from the shells and chop it.
4. Bring the clam liquid to a boil. Add cauliflower and cook until almost tender, about 5 minutes.
5. Stir in the bacon, Worcestershire sauce and clams. Season with salt and pepper to taste and cook until everything is heated through. Serve immediately.

Nutrition Facts Per Serving
Calories 105 Total Carbs 4g Protein 7g Fat 7g Sugar 2g Fiber 1g

Crab & Cauliflower Bisque

Prep time: 20 minutes, Cook time: 30 minutes, Serves: 8
Ingredients:

1 lb. lump crabmeat, cooked and shells removed
1 medium head cauliflower, separated into very small florets
1 white onion, diced fine
1 cup celery, diced fine
1 cup carrots, diced fine
1 cup half-n-half
1 tbsp. sherry
4 tbsp. margarine

What you'll need from store cupboard:

6 cup chicken broth
1½ tsp coarse salt
1 tsp white pepper

Instructions:

1. In a large saucepan, over med-high heat, melt margarine. Add celery, onion, and carrot. Cook, stirring frequently, until vegetables are tender.
2. Add in cauliflower, broth, salt, and pepper, and cook until soup starts to boil. Reduce heat to medium and cook 15 minutes, or until cauliflower is tender.
3. Pour into a blender and add cream and sherry. Process until combined and soup is smooth. Pour back into the saucepan.
4. Fold in crab and heat through. Serve.

Nutrition Facts Per Serving
Calories 201 Total Carbs 10g Net Carbs 7g Protein 14g Fat 11g Sugar 4g Fiber 3g

Salmon Dill Soup

Prep time: 5 minutes, Cook time: 30 minutes, Serves: 4

Ingredients:

4 skinless salmon fillets, cut into pieces	peeled and diced ½ cup heavy cream
1 green onion, diced fine	2 tbsp. fresh dill, diced
1 daikon radish,	2 tbsp. margarine

What you'll need from store cupboard:

4 cups seafood stock or vegetable broth	½ cup white wine Salt and black pepper

Instructions:

1. In a large saucepan, melt margarine over med-high heat. Add onions and sauté for 1-2 minutes.
2. Add wine and cook until liquid is reduced by half.
3. Add the radish and broth. Cook until radish is tender, about 15 minutes. Add salmon, cream and dill and cook another 5-8 minutes until salmon is flaky. Salt and pepper to taste.

Nutrition Facts Per Serving
Calories 537 Total Carbs 8g Net Carbs 7g Protein 46g Fat 33g Sugar 2g Fiber 1g

Cajun Seafood Stew

Prep time: 20 minutes, Cook time: 40 minutes, Serves: 8

Ingredients:

6 live blue crabs	1 ½ large yellow onions, diced
2 lb. medium shrimp, peeled, deveined and tails removed	1 green bell pepper, diced
1 lb. jumbo lump crabmeat	1/3 cup parsley, diced fine
5 scallions, diced	¼ cup fresh lemon juice
4 stalks celery, diced	

What you'll need from store cupboard:

8 cup low sodium vegetable broth	1 tbsp. Worcestershire sauce
6 cloves garlic, diced fine	2 bay leaves
½ cup olive oil	½ tsp cayenne
½ cup flour	Salt & pepper to taste

Instructions:

1. Prepare crabs, working with one at a time. Remove and discard legs. Remove and save the claws. Discard the underside, the triangular section, and pull the body away from the shell.

Remove gills and organs and rinse thoroughly. Place clean crabs in a bowl, cover and refrigerate till ready to use.

2. Heat oil in a large stock pot over med-high heat. Whisk in flour and cook, stirring constantly, until you have a dark roux. Add vegetables and cook, stirring frequently, until vegetables are soft, about 10-12 minutes.
3. Add the cleaned crabs, broth, Worcestershire and spices and bring to a boil. Reduce heat, cover and simmer 15-20 minutes.
4. Add remaining seafood and cook until shrimp turn pink, 3-5 minutes. Stir in parsley, lemon juice and scallions. Serve.

Nutrition Facts Per Serving
Calories 442 Total Carbs 17g Protein 54g Fat 19g Sugar 3g Fiber 1g

Chipotle Bacon & Chicken Chowder

Prep time: 5 minutes, Cook time: 30 minutes, Serves: 6

Ingredients:

1 ½ lbs. chicken breast, boneless, skinless & cut in 1-inch pieces	3 cup half-n-half
	4 chipotle peppers in adobo sauce, diced fine
½ lb. bacon, chopped	2 tbsp. cilantro, diced

What you'll need from store cupboard:

6 cup low sodium chicken broth	½ tsp onion powder
1 tsp salt	½ tsp garlic powder
	½ tsp pepper

Instructions:

1. Place a large saucepan over med-high heat. Add bacon and cook until crisp. Transfer to a paper towel lined plate.
2. Add the chicken and cook until browned on all sides.
3. Add the broth and seasonings and simmer for 10 to 15 minutes, or until the chicken is cooked through. Stir in the half-n-half and chipotles and simmer 5 minutes more. Serve topped with the bacon and cilantro.

Nutrition Facts Per Serving
Calories 496 Total Carbs 7g Net Carbs 6g Protein 46g Fat 32g Sugar 0g Fiber 1g

Chicken & Pepper Stew

Prep time: 15 minutes, Cook time: 4 hours, Serves: 4

Ingredients:

2 small onions, quartered	½ cup yellow pepper, diced
1 ½ cup chicken, cut into 1-inch pieces	½ cup red pepper, diced
1 cup broccoli florets	½ cup mushrooms, diced
½ cup green bell pepper, diced	2 tbsp. margarine

What you'll need from store cupboard:

4 cup low sodium chicken broth	1 tsp rosemary
1/8 cup water	1 tsp corn starch
4 cloves garlic, diced fine	½ tsp thyme
	Salt and pepper to taste

Instructions:

1. Heat 1 tablespoon margarine in large skillet over medium heat. Add chicken and cook till no longer pink. Remove from skillet and add to crock pot.
2. Add remaining tablespoon of margarine to skillet along with onions and garlic. Sauté until onions begin to soften. Add to chicken.
3. Add the broth, vegetables and seasonings to the crock pot. Cover and cook on high 2-3 hours till chicken is cooked through and vegetables are tender.
4. Stir the corn starch into the 1/8 cup of water and stir into the stew. Cook another 60 minutes, or until thickened.

Nutrition Facts Per Serving

Calories 207 Total Carbs 15g Net Carbs 12g Protein 20g Fat 8g Sugar 6g Fiber 3g

Chorizo & Corn Chowder

Prep time: 15 minutes, Cook time: 4 ½ hours, Serves: 4

Ingredients:

1 onion, diced	2 cup cauliflower, separate in small florets
1 fennel bulb, cut in ¼-inch pieces	
6 sprigs fresh thyme	1 ½ cup corn, frozen
3 oz. cured chorizo	½ cup half-n-half

What you'll need from store cupboard:

4 cup low sodium chicken broth	2 tbsp. flour
2 cloves garlic, diced fine	Salt & pepper, to taste

Instructions:

1. Place cauliflower, onion, fennel, corn, garlic, and half the chorizo in a crock pot. Stir in flour and ½ teaspoon each salt and pepper.
2. Pour in the broth and thyme and stir to combine. Cover and cook on high heat 4 ½ hours, or until vegetables are tender.
3. Ten minutes before serving, add remaining chorizo to a hot skillet and cook over med-high heat until browned and crisp, about 3 minutes.
4. Discard the thyme and stir in half-n-half. Ladle into bowls and garnish with chorizo.

Nutrition Facts Per Serving

Calories 206 Total Carbs 26g Net Carbs 21g Protein 12g Fat 7g Sugar 5g Fiber 5g

Creamy Sweet Potato & Cauliflower Bisque

Prep time: 10 minutes, Cook time: 20 minutes, Serves: 4

Ingredients:

1 head cauliflower, separated into large florets	1 onion, diced fine
	1 cup skim milk
1 large sweet potato, peeled and cut into cubes	1/3 block of low fat cream cheese, cut into cubes
	1 tsp margarine

What you'll need from store cupboard:

2 cup low sodium vegetable broth	1/8 tsp red pepper flakes
2 cloves garlic, peeled	Salt and pepper to taste
½ tsp rosemary	

Instructions:

1. Melt margarine in a large sauce pan over med-high heat. Add onion, and cook until soft, 2-3 minutes.
2. Add remaining vegetables, broth and seasonings and bring to a boil. Reduce heat to low and cook until potato is soft, 12-15 minutes.
3. Stir in the milk and cream cheese until cheese has melted. Use an immersion blender and process until smooth. Taste and add salt and pepper if needed. Serve.

Nutrition Facts Per Serving

Calories 125 Total Carbs 23g Net Carbs 18g Protein 9g Fat 0g Sugar 10g Fiber 5g

Tuscan Sausage Soup

Prep time: 15 minutes, Cook time: 15 minutes, Serves: 8

Ingredients:

1 lb. pork sausage, cooked	grated and cooked
2 cup half-n-half	½ cup onion, diced
1 ½ cup cauliflower,	¼ cup margarine

What you'll need from store cupboard:

1 cup chicken broth	1 tsp salt
4 cloves garlic, diced fine	½ tsp black pepper

Instructions:

1. In a large saucepan, over medium heat, melt margarine. Add onion and garlic, cook, stirring occasionally, 1-2 minutes.
2. Pour in the broth and cream. Bring to a boil stirring constantly.
3. Add sausage and cauliflower and season with salt and pepper. Heat through and serve.

Nutrition Facts Per Serving

Calories 336 Total Carbs 5g Net Carbs 4g Protein 14g Fat 29g Sugar 1g Fiber 1g

Cheesy Ham & Broccoli Soup

Prep time: 10 minutes, cook time; 6 hours, serves; 8

Ingredients:

2 cup broccoli florets	into small cubes
2 cup cheddar cheese, grated	2 stalks celery, peeled and diced
1 ½ cup ham, cut	1 onion, diced

What you'll need from store cupboard:

8 cup low sodium vegetable broth	1 bay leaf
2 tbsp. olive oil	¼ tsp salt
	1/8 tsp black pepper

Instructions:

1. Heat the oil in a medium skillet over med-high heat. Add the onion and celery and cook, stirring frequently, about 5 minutes.
2. Add the broth, ham, celery mixture, and seasonings to a crock pot. Cover and cook on low 3-4 hours.
3. Add the broccoli and cook another 1-2 hours or until broccoli starts to get tender. Stir in cheese and cook until completely melted. Discard bay leaf and serve.

Nutrition Facts Per Serving

Calories 214 Total Carbs 8g Net Carbs 7g Protein 12g Fat 15g Sugar 2g Fiber 1g

Beef & Sweet Potato Stew

Prep time: 20 minutes, Cook time: 1 hour 10 minutes, Serves: 6

Ingredients:

2 lb. top sirloin steak, diced	2 stalks celery, diced
	1 red onion, diced
1 ½ lbs. sweet potato, peeled and cut in ½-inch cubes	1 carrot, peeled and diced
½ lb. cremini mushrooms, quartered	2 tbsp. fresh parsley, chopped
	4 sprigs fresh thyme

What you'll need from store cupboard:

4 cup low sodium beef broth	2 tbsp. tomato paste
½ cup dry red wine	2 tbsp. olive oil
¼ cup flour	2 bay leaves
3 cloves garlic, diced	Salt and pepper, to taste

Instructions:

1. Heat oil in a large stockpot over medium heat. Season steak with salt and pepper and add to pot. Cook, stirring occasionally, until brown on all sides. Remove from pot and set aside.
2. Add onion, carrot, and celery. Cook, stirring occasionally, 3-4 minutes or until tender.
3. Add garlic and mushrooms and cook another 3-4 minutes. Whisk in flour and tomato paste and cook until lightly browned, about 1 minute.
4. Stir in wine, scraping up any browned bits from the bottom of the pot. Add the broth, thyme, bay leaves and steak. Bring to a boil, reduce heat and simmer about 30 minutes, or until steak is tender.
5. Add sweet potato and cook 20 minutes or until potatoes are tender and stew has thickened. Discard bay leaves and thyme sprigs. Stir in parsley and serve.

Nutrition Facts Per Serving

Calories 421 Total Carbs 14g Net Carbs 12g Protein 51g Fat 15g Sugar 4g Fiber 2g

Chunky Chicken Noodle Soup

Prep time: 10 minutes, cook time 35 minutes, Serves: 8
Ingredients:

2 lbs. chicken thighs, boneless and skinless
2 carrots, sliced
2 celery stalks, sliced
2 tsp fresh ginger, grated

What you'll need from store cupboard:

8 cup low sodium chicken broth
2 cup homemade pasta, (chapter 15)
1 tbsp. garlic, diced
fine
1 tbsp. chicken bouillon
Salt and pepper, to taste

Instructions:

1. Place chicken and 1 cup broth in a large soup pot over medium heat. Bring to a simmer and cook until chicken is done, about 20 minutes. Transfer chicken to a bowl and shred using 2 forks.
2. Add the carrots, celery, garlic, ginger, and bouillon to the pot and stir well. Add in remaining broth and bring back to a boil. Reduce heat and simmer until vegetables are tender, about 15 minutes.
3. Add pasta and cook another 5 minutes for fresh pasta, or 7 for dried. Add the chicken to the soup and salt and pepper to taste. Serve.

Nutrition Facts Per Serving
Calories 210 Total Carbs 15g Net Carbs 12g Protein 23g Fat 7g Sugar 7g Fiber 3g

Creamy Chicken & Cauliflower Rice Soup

Prep time: 20 minutes, Cook time: 5 hours, Serves: 6
Ingredients:

2 carrots, peeled and diced
2 stalks celery, peeled and diced
1/2 onion, diced
2 cup skim milk
2 cups cauliflower, riced
1 cup chicken, cooked and shredded
3 tbsp. Margarine

What you'll need from store cupboard:

4 cup low sodium chicken broth
5 cloves garlic, diced
½ tsp rosemary
½ tsp thyme
½ tsp parsley
1 bay leaf

Instructions:

1. Melt margarine in a large skillet over medium heat. Add carrots, celery, onion

and garlic. Cook, stirring frequently, about 5 minutes. Place in crock pot.
2. Add chicken broth and seasonings. Cover and cook on low 4 hours.
3. Add in the chicken, milk and cauliflower rice. Cook another 60 minutes or until cauliflower is tender. Discard bay leaf before serving.

Nutrition Facts Per Serving
Calories 151 Total Carbs 10g Net Carbs 8g Protein 12g Fat 6g Sugar 6g Fiber 2g

Southwest Chicken Soup

Prep time: 10 minutes, Cook time: 3 hours 35 minutes, Serves: 8
Ingredients:

2 lbs. boneless skinless chicken breasts
1 onion, diced
1 green pepper, diced
6 oz. reduced fat cream cheese
½ cup half-n-half
1 tbsp. margarine

What you'll need from store cupboard:

2 (10 oz.) cans diced tomatoes with green chilies
3 ½ cup low sodium chicken broth, divided
3 cloves garlic, diced fine
1 packet of taco seasoning
Salt and pepper to taste

Instructions:

1. Place chicken in a crock pot with 1 cup broth. Cover and cook on high 3 hours. Season with salt and pepper.
2. When chicken is cooked through remove from crock pot and shred.
3. In a large saucepan, heat butter over medium heat until melted. Add green pepper, onion, and garlic and cook until onion is translucent.
4. Use a spoon to smoosh the cream cheese into the veggies so it will melt and Ingredients will come together easily.
5. Once the cream cheese is melted, add the remaining Ingredients. Simmer on low heat for 20 minutes.
6. Add chicken, cover and simmer another 10 minutes. Serve garnished with grated cheese, chopped cilantro, or a dollop of sour cream if desired.

Nutrition Facts Per Serving
Calories 336 Total Carbs 8g Net Carbs 7g Protein 37g Fat 17g Sugar 3g Fiber 1g

Curried Chicken Soup

Prep time: 15 minutes, Cook time: 20 minutes, Serves: 12

Ingredients:

2 carrots, diced
2 stalks celery, diced
1 onion, diced
3 cup chicken, cooked and cut in
¼ cup margarine, cubed
cubes
2 cups cauliflower, grated
1 cup half-n-half

What you'll need from store cupboard:

4 ½ cup low sodium vegetable broth
2 12 oz. can fat free evaporated milk
¾ cup + 2 tbsp. flour
1 tsp salt
1 tsp curry powder

Instructions:

1. Melt butter in a large pot over medium heat. Add carrots, celery, and onion and cook 2 minutes.
2. Stir in flour until well blended. Stir in seasonings. Slowly add milk and half-n-half. Bring to a boil, cook, stirring, 2 minutes or until thickened.
3. Slowly stir in broth. Add chicken and cauliflower and bring back to boil. Reduce heat and simmer 10 minutes, or until vegetable are tender. Serve.

Nutrition Facts Per Serving

Calories 204 Total Carbs 17g Protein 17g Fat 7g Sugar 8g Fiber 1g

Easy Seafood Chowder

Prep time: 5 minutes, Cook time: 25 minutes, Serves: 4

Ingredients:

1 ½ lbs. frozen mixed seafood, thaw and cut into bite-sized pieces
3 celery stalks, diced
1 ½ cups onion, diced
½ cup half-n-half
4-5 tbsp. fresh dill, chopped

What you'll need from store cupboard:

2 ½ cup low sodium chicken broth
1 ½ cup white wine
1 ½ tbsp. olive oil
1 ½ tbsp. corn starch
1 ½ tbsp. cold water
1 ½ tsp garlic, diced fine
Salt and pepper

Instructions:

1. Heat oil in a large soup pot over medium heat. Add onion and celery and cook until softened, about 5-7 minutes. Stir in garlic and cook for another 30 seconds.
2. Add wine to the pot and bring to a low boil, cooking until most of the liquid has disappeared.
3. Combine the corn starch and water in a small bowl and stir until dissolved. Add cornstarch mixture and chicken broth to the pan. Simmer for 7-10 minutes or until thickened, stirring occasionally.
4. Season the soup to taste with salt and pepper then add the seafood and dill to the pot. Simmer until seafood is cooked through, about 3-7 minutes. Stir in half-n-half and cook just until heated through. Serve garnished with more fresh dill if desired.

Nutrition Facts Per Serving

Calories 353 Total Carbs 16g Net Carbs 15g Protein 27g Fat 10g Sugar 3g Fiber 1g

Mexican Beef Stew

Prep time: 15 minutes, Cook time: 1 hours 30 minutes, Serves: 6

Ingredients:

1 ½ lb. beef round steak, cut into ½-inch pieces
1 ¾ cup tomatoes, diced
1 cup carrots, sliced
1 cup onion, diced
¼ cup sweet red pepper, diced
1 jalapeno, seeded and diced
2 tbsp. cilantro, diced

What you'll need from store cupboard:

1 ¾ cup low sodium beef broth
1 clove garlic, diced
2 tbsp. flour
2 tbsp. water
1 tbsp. vegetable oil
1 ½ tsp chili powder
½ tsp salt

Instructions:

1. Heat the oil in a large pot over med-high heat. Add the steak and cook until brown on all sides.
2. Add the broth, carrots, onion, red pepper, jalapeno, garlic, and seasonings and bring to a low boil. Reduce heat to low, cover and simmer 45 minutes, stirring occasionally.
3. Add the tomatoes and continue cooking 15 minutes.
4. Stir the flour and water together in a measuring up until smooth. Add to stew with the cilantro and continue cooking another 20-30 minutes or until stew has thickened. Serve.

Nutrition Facts Per Serving

Calories 312 Total Carbs 9g Net Carbs 7g Protein 39g Fat 13g Sugar 4g Fiber 2g

French Onion Soup

Prep time: 10 minutes, Cook time: 4 hours, Serves: 6-8

Ingredients:

2 large white onions, thinly sliced	cheese, grated
2 cups gruyere	1 tbsp. margarine

What you'll need from store cupboard:

6 cups low-sodium beef broth	1 bay leaf
1 clove garlic, diced fine	½ tsp salt
	½ tsp thyme
	¼ tsp pepper

Instructions:

1. Place all Ingredients, except cheese, in the crock pot. Stir well to mix. Cover and cook on high 3-4 hours, or low 6-8 hours.
2. Remove bay leaf.
3. Heat broiler. Ladle soup into ovenproof bowls and top with cheese. Place bowls on baking sheet and broil until cheese is melted and starting to brown. Serve immediately.

Nutrition Facts Per Serving

Calories 219 Total Carbs 5g Protein 16g Fat 15g Sugar 2g Fiber 0g

Hearty Bell Pepper Stew

Prep time: 20 minutes, Cook time: 4 hours, Serves: 8

Ingredients:

1 lb. hot Italian sausage	3 cup green pepper, diced
1 lb. lean ground sirloin	3 cup onion, diced
3 ½ cup tomatoes, diced	1 cup cauliflower, grated

What you'll need from store cupboard:

4 cup low sodium beef broth	4 cloves garlic, diced fine
1 cup tomato sauce	1 tsp basil
2 tbsp. olive oil	½ tsp oregano

Instructions:

1. Heat the oil in a large skillet over med-high heat. Add in both kinds of meat and cook, breaking it up with a spoon, until no longer pink on the outside. Remove the meat with a slotted spoon and place in crock pot.
2. Add the green pepper, onion and garlic to the skillet. Cook, stirring frequently, about 5 minutes. Remove the vegetables

with a slotted spoon and add to the meat mixture.
3. Add in the broth, tomatoes, tomato sauce and seasonings. Cover and cook on high 2-3 hours.
4. Add the cauliflower and cook another 60 minutes or until cauliflower is tender.

Nutrition Facts Per Serving

Calories 312 Total Carbs 14g Net Carbs 11g Protein 19g Fat 20g Sugar 8g Fiber 3g

Irish Stew

Prep time: 15 minutes, Cook time: 1 ½ hours, Serves: 8

Ingredients:

1 ½ lbs. lamb stew meat	3 onions, diced
4 carrots, cut in 1-inch pieces	2 potatoes, peel and cube
	1 cup peas

What you'll need from store cupboard:

4 cup low sodium beef broth	1 tsp salt
1/3 cup + 1 tbsp. flour	1 tsp thyme
3 cloves garlic, diced	½ tsp Worcestershire sauce
2 tbsp. water	½ tsp pepper

Instructions:

1. Place 1/3 cup flour in a Ziploc bag. Add lamb, a few pieces at a time, and shake to coat.
2. Heat oil in a large pot over medium heat. Add lamb, in batches, and cook until brown on all sides. Transfer to plate.
3. Add onions to the pot and cook until tender. Add garlic and cook 1 minute more.
4. Stir in broth, scraping brown bits from the bottom of the pot. Add the lamb back to the pot. Bring to a boil. Reduce heat, cover, and simmer 1 hour or until lamb is tender.
5. Add potatoes and carrots, cover and cook 20 minutes. Stir in peas and cook until vegetables are tender.
6. Add the Worcestershire and seasonings and stir to mix. Whisk together the water and remaining tablespoon of flour until smooth, stir into the stew and bring back to a boil. Cook, stirring, 2 minutes until thickened. Serve

Nutrition Facts Per Serving

Calories 324 Total Carbs 23g Net Carbs 19g Protein 30g Fat 12g Sugar 5g Fiber 4g

Italian Sausage Soup

Prep time: 10 minutes, Cook time: 7 hours, Serves: 6

Ingredients:

1 lb. ground pork	2 cups fresh kale, chopped
¾ lb. tiny red new potatoes, each cut into 8 pieces	1 large onion, chopped

What you'll need from store cupboard:

4 cups reduced-sodium chicken broth	1 tsp oregano
1 (12 oz.) can fat-free evaporated milk	¼ tsp salt
2 cloves garlic, diced fine	¼ to ½ teaspoon crushed red pepper
2 tbsp. cornstarch	Crushed red pepper (optional)

Instructions:

1. In a large skillet, over medium heat, cook pork, onion, and garlic until meat is browned, drain fat.
2. Return to skillet and add seasonings. Cook another minute.
3. Transfer to crock pot. Add broth and potatoes. Cover and cook on low 6-8 hours, or high 3-4 hours.
4. If crock pot is on low, switch to high. In a small bowl, whisk the cornstarch and milk together until smooth. Add to crock pot with the kale. Cook another 30-60 minutes or until soup starts to bubble around the edges. Serve garnished with more red pepper flakes if desired.

Nutrition Facts Per Serving

Calories 209 Total Carbs 18g Net Carbs 17g Protein 27g Fat 3g Sugar 7g Fiber 1g

Italian Veggie Soup

Prep time: 15 minutes, cook time; 5 hours, serves; 8

Ingredients:

4 cups cabbage, chopped	2 cup fresh spinach, chopped
2 celery stalks, diced	1 cup carrots, diced
2 green bell peppers, diced	1 cup green beans, cut in 1-inch pieces
1 small onion, diced	

What you'll need from store cupboard:

28 oz. can low sodium tomatoes, diced	2 tbsp. tomato paste
6 cup low sodium vegetable broth	1 tbsp. parsley
	1 tbsp. basil
	2 cloves garlic, diced fine

2 bay leaves	seasoning
1 ½ tsp Italian	Pepper to taste

Instructions:

1. Place all the vegetables in a large crock pot.
2. Add canned tomatoes, broth, tomato paste, bay leaves, Italian seasoning, and pepper and stir to combine.
3. Cover and cook on high for 5 hours. Add parsley, basil and spinach and cook for 5 minutes more.

Nutrition Facts Per Serving

Calories 85 Total Carbs 20g Net Carbs 15g Protein 3g Fat 1g Sugar 10g Fiber 5g

Roasted Mushroom & Cauliflower Soup

Prep time: 15 minutes, Cook time: 30 minutes, Serves: 4

Ingredients:

1 small (600g) cauliflower, trimmed, chopped	1 leek, halved lengthways, thinly sliced
5 cup mushrooms, sliced	½ cup flat-leaf parsley, chopped

What you'll need from store cupboard:

4 cup low sodium chicken broth	3 tsp curry powder
4 tbsp. olive oil	Nonstick cooking spray

Instructions:

1. Heat oven to 425 degrees.
2. Spray two large baking sheets with cooking spray. Place cauliflower in one pan and mushrooms in the other. Drizzle each with 1 ½ tablespoons oil and sprinkle with 1 ½ teaspoons curry powder.
3. Place cauliflower on the top rack of oven and mushrooms below, cook 20-25 minutes or until vegetables are tender.
4. In a large saucepan, heat remaining oil over medium heat. Add leek, cook 5 minutes, stirring occasionally, until soft. Add broth and bring to a boil. Add roasted vegetables and return to boil.
5. Remove from heat, use an immersion blender, and process until almost smooth. Stir in parsley and adjust seasonings to taste. Serve.

Nutrition Facts Per Serving

Calories 187 Total Carbs 11g Net Carbs 8g Protein 7g Fat 15g Sugar 4g Fiber 3g

Harvest Vegetable Soup

Prep time: 25 minutes, Cook time: 50 minutes, Serves: 12

Ingredients:

3 carrots, halved and slice thin
2 green onions, slice thin
2 tart apples, peeled and diced
2 turnips, peeled and diced
2 parsnips, peeled
and sliced
1 onion, diced
3 cup potato, peeled and cubed
2 cup butternut squash, peeled and cubed
1 tbsp. margarine

What you'll need from store cupboard:

7 cup low sodium vegetable broth
1 tbsp. olive oil
1 clove garlic, diced
1 bay leaf
½ tsp basil
¼ tsp thyme
¼ tsp pepper

Instructions:

1. Heat margarine and oil in a large soup pot over medium heat. Add carrots, celery, and onion and cook until tender, about 10 minutes. Add garlic and cook 1 minute more.
2. Add broth, potatoes, squash, apple, turnips, parsnips, and bay leaf, stir to combine. Bring to a boil. Reduce heat and simmer 20 minutes.
3. Stir in seasonings and cook 15 minutes, or until all the vegetables are tender. Discard bay leaf and serve.

Nutrition Facts Per Serving
Calories 118 Total Carbs 24g Net Carbs 20g Protein 2g Fat 2g Sugar 9g Fiber 4g

Korean Beef Soup

Prep time: 15 minutes, Cook time: 4 hours, Serves: 8

Ingredients:

1 pound of beef, cut into cubes
1 Korean white radish, peeled and
diced
1 cup green onions, diced

What you'll need from store cupboard:

1 gallon water
3 tbsp. soy sauce
1 tbsp. oil
1 tbsp. Sesame seeds, toasted
2 cloves garlic, diced fine
1 tsp salt
1 tsp pepper

Instructions:

1. Set crock pot to high and pour the water in to start heating.

2. In a small bowl, combine green onions, soy sauce, oil, sesame seeds, garlic, salt, and pepper. Divide evenly between two Ziploc bags.
3. Place the meat in one bag and the radish in the other. Let set for 1 hour.
4. Turn the crock pot down to low and add the contents of the meat bag. Let cook 1 hour, then add the contents of the radish bag. Cook another 3-4 hours.

Nutrition Facts Per Serving
Calories 120 Total Carbs 3g Net Carbs 2g Protein 18g Fat 4g Sugar 0g Fiber 1g

Pork Posole

Prep time: 5 minutes, Cook time: 25 minutes, Serves: 6

Ingredients:

1 yellow onion, diced fine
1 ½ cup pork, cook & shred
1 fresh lime, cut in wedges
½ bunch cilantro, chopped

What you'll need from store cupboard:

15 oz. can hominy, drain
4 oz. can green chilies, diced
3 oz. tomato paste
3 cup low sodium chicken broth
2 cup water
2 tbsp. vegetable oil
2 tbsp. flour
2 tbsp. chili powder
¾ tsp salt
½ tsp cumin
½ tsp garlic powder
¼ tsp cayenne pepper

Instructions:

1. Heat oil in a large pot over medium heat. Add onion and cook 3-5 minutes, or until it softens.
2. Add the flour and chili powder and cook 2 minutes more, stirring continuously.
3. Add water, tomato paste, and seasonings. Whisk mixture until tomato paste dissolves. Bring to a simmer and let thicken, about 2-3 minutes.
4. Stir in broth, pork, chilies, and hominy and cook until heated through, about 10 minutes.
5. Ladle into bowls and garnish with a lime wedge and chopped cilantro.

Nutrition Facts Per Serving
Calories 234 Total Carbs 33g Net Carbs 24g Protein 11g Fat 8g Sugar 12g Fiber 9g

Sausage & Pepper Soup

Prep time: 5 minutes, Cook time: 1 hour, Serves: 6

Ingredients:

2 lbs. pork sausage
10 oz. raw spinach
1 medium bell pepper, diced

What you'll need from store cupboard:

4 cups low sodium beef broth
1 can tomatoes w/ jalapenos
1 tbsp. olive oil
1 tbsp. chili powder
1 tbsp. cumin
1 tsp onion powder
1 tsp garlic powder
1 tsp Italian seasoning
3/4 tsp kosher salt

Instructions:

1. In a large pot, over medium heat, heat oil until hot. Add sausage and cook until browned. Drain fat.
2. Add bell pepper and stir. Season with salt and pepper.
3. Add tomatoes and stir. Place spinach on top and cover. Once spinach wilts, add spices and broth and stir to combine.
4. Reduce heat to medium-low. Cover and cook 30 minutes, stirring occasionally.
5. Remove lid and let simmer another 15 minutes. Serve.

Nutrition Facts Per Serving

Calories 580 Total Carbs 5g Net Carbs 3g Protein 34g Fat 46g Sugar 2g Fiber 2g

Spicy Shrimp Soup

Prep time: 10 minutes, Cook time: 25 minutes, Serves: 6

Ingredients:

1 lb. shrimp, peel & devein
1 onion, diced

What you'll need from store cupboard:

8 oz. green chilies, diced
4 cup low sodium chicken broth
1 cup flour
1 cup water
3 cloves garlic, diced
3 tbsp. olive oil
1 tbsp. Worcestershire sauce
1 tsp cumin

Instructions:

1. Heat oil in a large saucepan over med-high heat. Add onion and cook until soft, about 3-5 minutes. Add garlic and cook 1 minute more.
2. Stir in broth, chilies, Worcestershire, and cumin and bring to a simmer. Let simmer 8-10 minutes.
3. In a small bowl, whisk together water and flour until smooth.
4. Add shrimp to the pot and stir in the flour mixture. Continue cooking, stirring, 2-3 minutes until shrimp are cooked through and mixture has thickened. Serve.

Nutrition Facts Per Serving

Calories 305 Total Carbs 33g Net Carbs 22g Protein 23g Fat 10g Sugar 17g Fiber 11g

Tomato Soup with Seafood

Prep time: 20 minutes, Cook time: 45 minutes, Serves: 8

Ingredients:

1 lb. medium shrimp, peel and devein
½ lb. cod, cut in pieces
1 onions, diced
1 red bell pepper, diced
1 green pepper, diced
1 cup cauliflower, separated into small florets
3 tbsp. fresh parsley, diced fine

What you'll need from store cupboard:

15 oz. tomato sauce
14 ½ oz. can tomatoes, diced and juice
1 quart vegetable broth
3 cloves garlic, diced
fine
1 tbsp. olive oil
½ tsp oregano
¼ tsp basil
¼ tsp pepper
1 pinch salt
1 bay leaf

Instructions:

1. Heat oil in large soup pot over med-high heat. Add onion and bell peppers and cook, stirring occasionally, 3-5 minutes, or until they start to get soft.
2. Add the garlic and cook 1 minute more. Transfer vegetables to a food processor along with canned tomatoes. Process until smooth. Pour back into soup pot and add tomato sauce, broth and seasoning.
3. Bring to a boil. Reduce heat and simmer 15-20 minutes, or until soup starts to thicken and is reduced.
4. Add the fish and shrimp and cook just until fish is cooked through and shrimp turn pink. Stir in parsley and discard bay leaf before serving.

Nutrition Facts Per Serving

Calories 174 Total Carbs 10g Net Carbs 8g Protein 24g Fat 4g Sugar 6g Fiber 2g

Smoky Lentil & Leek Soup

Prep time: 10 minutes, Cook time: 2 hours, Serves: 4

Ingredients:

4 slices bacon, chopped
1 leek, discard dark green part, wash and chop
What you'll need

from store cupboard
3 cup low sodium chicken broth
1 cup red lentils
2 cloves garlic, diced

Instructions:

1. Place a medium saucepan over med-high heat and add bacon. Cook until almost crisp, 2-3 minutes. Add leek and garlic and cook until leek starts to get soft, 3 minutes. Transfer to crock pot.
2. Add remaining Ingredients and stir to combine. Cover and cook on high 2 hours. When the lentils are soft, the soup is done. Serve.

Nutrition Facts Per Serving

Calories 299 Total Carbs 33g Net Carbs 18g Protein 21g Fat 8g Sugar 2g Fiber 15g

Steak & Broccoli Soup

Prep time: 20 minutes, Cook time: 6 hours, serves; 8

Ingredients:

1 lb. sirloin steak, cut into bite size pieces
4 cup broccoli florets
4 cup spinach, torn

3 celery stalks, diced
2 carrots, cut into 1 inch pieces
1 yellow onion, diced

What you'll need from store cupboard:

6 cup low sodium beef broth
4 cloves garlic, diced
1 tbsp. olive oil

1 bay leaf
1 tsp salt
1 tsp cayenne pepper
½ tsp black pepper

Instructions:

1. Heat oil in a large skillet over med-high heat. Brown meat on all sides. Remove from skillet with a slotted spoon and place in crock pot.
2. Add remaining Ingredients, except for the broccoli and spinach. Cover and cook on low 3-4 hours or until the carrots are almost tender.
3. Add broccoli and spinach and continue cooking another 1-2 hours, or until steak is tender and vegetables are cooked through. Discard the bay leaf before serving.

Nutrition Facts Per Serving

Calories 183 Total Carbs 8g Net Carbs 6g Protein 23g Fat 7g Sugar 3g Fiber 2g

Turkey & Bacon Chowder

Prep time: 15 minutes, Cook time: 35 minutes, Serves: 8

Ingredients:

6 slices bacon, cut in 1-inch pieces
4 cups cooked turkey meat, shredded
1 large shallot, peeled and diced
1 ½ cups sweet potato, peeled and

diced
½ cup celery, diced
½ cup half-n-half
½ cup sharp cheddar cheese, grated
1 tbsp. fresh thyme leaves, chopped

What you'll need from store cupboard:

8 cups turkey (or chicken) broth
1 tsp dried parsley
1 tsp xanthan gum

½ tsp liquid smoke
Salt & pepper to taste

Instructions:

1. Place bacon in a large saucepan and cook over medium heat until it is almost crisp.
2. After cooking bacon, reserve ¼ cup. Add shallots and celery to remaining bacon in the pan and cook until soft, about 5 minutes.
3. Add the broth, cream, and cheese, whisking until cheese is melted and the mixture is almost smooth.
4. Add in potato, turkey, parsley, and liquid smoke. Simmer 20 minutes, or until potatoes are soft.
5. Whisk in xanthan gum and cook another 5 minutes until slightly thickened.
6. Stir in thyme and season to taste with salt and pepper. Serve, garnish with more fresh thyme if desired.

Nutrition Facts Per Serving

Calories 231 Total Carbs 12g Net Carbs 9g Protein 27g Fat 9g Sugar 3g Fiber 3g

Tangy Asparagus Bisque

Prep time: 10 minutes, Cook time: 20 minutes, Serves: 4

Ingredients:

2 lbs. fresh asparagus, remove the bottom and cut into small pieces
1 yellow onion, diced

1 small lemon, zest and juice
1 tsp fresh thyme, diced fine

What you'll need from store cupboard:

4 cup low sodium vegetable broth
3 tbsp. olive oil
3 cloves garlic, diced

fine
Salt & pepper, to taste

Instructions:
1. Heat oil in a large saucepan over med-high heat. Add asparagus and onion and cook, stirring occasionally, until nicely browned, about 5 minutes. Add garlic and cook 1 minute more.
2. Stir in remaining Ingredients and bring to a boil. Reduce heat, and simmer 12-15 minutes or until asparagus is soft.
3. Use an immersion blender and process until smooth. Salt and pepper to taste and serve.

Nutrition Facts Per Serving
Calories 169 Total Carbs 17g Net carbs 11g Protein 6g Fat 11g Sugar 7g Fiber 6g

Vegetable Noodle Soup

Prep time: 15 minutes, Cook time: 35 minutes, Serves: 4
Ingredients:

3-4 stalks kale, washed & torn	1 onion, sliced
3 stalks celery, diced	1 tbsp. fresh thyme, diced
3 carrots, peel & dice	

What you'll need from store cupboard:

2 14 oz. cans tomatoes, crushed	½ cup reduced fat parmesan cheese
2 ½ cup water	1 tbsp. olive oil
1 cup Homemade Noodles, (chapter 15)	2 cloves garlic, diced
	1 ½ tsp. salt
	½ tsp. pepper

Instructions:
1. Heat the oil in a large saucepan over med-high heat. Add the onion, cooking until caramelized, about 8 minutes.
2. Reduce heat and add carrots, celery, garlic and seasonings and cook 6 minutes.
3. Stir in tomatoes and water, use a wooden spoon and scrape up brown bits from the bottom of the pan. Simmer 20 minutes, or until vegetables are tender.
4. Add the noodles and cook another 3-4 minutes. Ladle into bowls and sprinkle with parmesan cheese.

Nutrition Facts Per Serving
Calories 216 Total Carbs 20g Net Carbs 15g Protein 11g Fat 11g Sugar 9g Fiber 5g

White Bean & Chicken Soup

Prep time: 20 minutes, Cook time: 2 hours, Serves: 12
Ingredients:

2 lbs. chicken breasts, boneless, skinless, cut in cubes	thin
3 carrots, sliced	1 onion, diced
2 stalks celery, slice	¼ cup fresh parsley, diced

What you'll need from store cupboard:

½ lb. baby lima beans, dried	2 cup water
½ lb. great northern beans, dried	1 clove garlic, diced
	2 tbsp. sunflower oil, divided
4 cup low sodium chicken broth	1 tsp salt, divided
	½ tsp pepper

Instructions:
1. Sort the beans and discard any discolored ones. Rinse under cold water and add to a large pot. Add enough water to cover beans by 2 inches. Place over med-high heat and bring to a boil, cook 2 minutes. Remove from heat, cover, and let stand 2-4 hours or until beans have softened.
2. Drain and rinse beans, transfer to a large bowl.
3. Sprinkle chicken with ½ teaspoon salt. Heat 1 tablespoon oil in the large pot over med-high heat and add chicken. Cook until no longer pink. Transfer to a bowl and drain fat.
4. Heat remaining tablespoon of oil in the pot and add onion. Cook until tender. Add carrots and celery, and garlic and cook 1-2 minutes.
5. Stir in broth, water, pepper, beans and chicken and bring to a boil. Reduce heat, cover and simmer 2 hours, or until beans are tender. Stir in parsley and remaining salt and serve.

Nutrition Facts Per Serving
Calories 237 Total Carbs 18g Net Carbs 13g Protein 29g Fat 5g Sugar 2g Fiber 5g

Smoky Pumpkin Soup

Prep time: 20 minutes, Cook time: 40 minutes, Serves: 6
Ingredients:

10 slices bacon, diced   1 onion, diced
2 lb. fresh pumpkin,   ½ cup half-n-half
peel, remove seeds &   1 tsp margarine
cube

What you'll need from store cupboard:
2 pint low sodium chicken broth
1 tbsp. tomato puree

Instructions:

1. Melt the margarine in large heavy pot over med-high heat. Add onion, bacon and pumpkin. Cook 2-3 minutes, stirring occasionally. Reduce heat and cook 6-8 minutes. Transfer about 2 tablespoons of bacon to a paper towel line plate for later.
2. Stir in tomato puree, broth and cream. Bring to a simmer. Reduce heat to low and cook 30 minutes, or until pumpkin is soft.
3. Use an immersion blender to process soup until smooth. Taste and season as needed. Ladle into bowls and sprinkle with reserved bacon. Serve.

Nutrition Facts Per Serving
Calories 260 Total Carbs 16g Net Carbs 11g
Protein 15g Fat 15g Sugar 6g Fiber 5g

South American Fish Stew

Prep time: 10 minutes, Cook time: 25 minutes, Serves: 6
Ingredients:

2 lbs. tilapia fillets,   1 large onion, diced
cut into bite-sized   1/8 cup fresh
pieces   cilantro, diced
3 bell peppers, cut   4 tbsp. fresh lime
into 2-inch strips   juice

What you'll need from store cupboard:
14 oz. can tomatoes,   1 ½ tbsp. cumin
diced and drained   1 ½ tbsp. paprika
14 oz. can coconut   1 tbsp. olive oil
milk   1 ½ tsp salt
3-4 cloves garlic,   1 ½ tsp pepper
diced fine

Instructions:

1. In a large bowl combine lime juice, cumin, paprika, garlic, salt and pepper. Add fish and stir to coat. Cover and refrigerate at least 20 minutes, or overnight.

2. Heat oil in a large sauce pot over med-high heat. Add onion and cook until they start to soften, about 3 minutes. Add peppers, tomatoes, and fish and stir to combine. Add coconut milk and stir in.
3. Reduce heat to low, cover, and cook 20 minutes, stirring occasionally. Stir in the cilantro for the last 5 minutes of cooking time. Serve.

Nutrition Facts Per Serving
Calories 347 Total Carbs 15g Net Carbs 12g
Protein 31g Fat 19g Sugar 8g Fiber 3g

Spicy Tomato Chicken Soup

Prep time: 15 minutes, Cook time: 3 hours, serves; 6
Ingredients:

1 ½ lbs. chicken   2 cup tomatoes,
breasts, boneless,   diced
skinless and cut into   ½ cup green chilies,
bite size pieces   diced
1 onion, diced

What you'll need from store cupboard:
4 cup low sodium   1 tbsp. olive oil
chicken broth   1 tbsp. cumin
3 cloves garlic, diced   2 tsp paprika
1 ½ tbsp. chili   2 tsp salt
powder

Instructions:

1. Season chicken with salt. Heat oil in a large skillet over medium heat. Add chicken and cook until no longer pink. Remove from skillet and place in crock pot.
2. Add the tomatoes, onions, green chilies and garlic to a blender or food processor and pulse until smooth. Pour over chicken.
3. Add the broth and seasonings. Cover and cook on high 2-3 hours until chicken is cooked through and the soup has thickened slightly. Serve.

Nutrition Facts Per Serving
Calories 276 Total Carbs 7g Net Carbs 5g
Protein 35g Fat 11g Sugar 4g Fiber 2g

Slow Cooker Poblano Soup

Prep time: 10 minutes, Cook time: 35 minutes, Serves: 8

Ingredients:

1 ½ lbs. chicken breast, cut into large pieces
3 Poblano peppers, chopped
1 cup onion, diced
1 cup cauliflower, diced
¼ cup cilantro diced
¼ cup reduced fat cream cheese, cubed

What you'll need from store cupboard:

2 ½ cups water
½ cup navy beans, soak in hot water 1 hour
5 cloves garlic, diced
fine
1-2 tsp salt
1 tsp coriander
1 tsp cumin

Instructions:

1. Place all Ingredients, except cream cheese, into a crock pot. Cover and cook on high 4-5 hours, or until chicken is cooked through.
2. Remove chicken and let cool slightly. With an immersion blender, puree the soup until almost smooth.
3. Add the cream cheese and stir until melted. Shred the chicken and add it back to the soup. Let cook just until heated through. Serve.

Nutrition Facts Per Serving

Calories 211 Total Carbs 13g Net Carbs 9g Protein 29g Fat 5g Sugar 3g Fiber 4g

Chapter 10 - Poultry Recipe

Creamy Italian Chicken & Pasta

Prep time: 10 minutes, Cook time: 20 minutes, Serves: 4

Ingredients:

2 chicken breasts, cut in 1-inch pieces
1 cup half-n-half
1 cup baby spinach
¼ cup fresh basil, diced finely
¼ cup sun-dried tomatoes

What you'll need from store cupboard:

½ recipe of homemade pasta, (chapter 14) cook and drain
½ cup dry white wine
¼ cup reduced fat parmesan cheese
1 tbsp. olive oil
1 tsp flour
1 tsp lemon juice
½ tsp Dijon mustard
¼ tsp garlic powder
¼ tsp Italian seasoning
¼ tsp smoked paprika
Salt & pepper, to taste

Instructions:

1. Heat oil in a large skillet over med-high heat. Add chicken and seasonings. Cook, stirring frequently, until chicken is no longer pink, about 5 minutes. Transfer to a plate.
2. Add broth, Dijon, flour and lemon juice to the skillet. Stir until combined and cook until mixture starts to bubble.
3. Add the sun-dried tomatoes and half-n-half to the pan. Let it simmer for 2 minutes.
4. Add chicken back to the pan. Cook for another few minutes until the chicken is cooked through.
5. Stir in the basil and spinach. Let it cook for a minute or so until spinach wilts. Taste and season with extra salt & pepper if needed.
6. Add pasta and toss to coat. Serve immediately with parmesan cheese sprinkled over the top.

Nutrition Facts Per Serving

Calories 316 Total Carbs 12g Net Carbs 10g Protein 25g Fat 16g Sugar 3g Fiber 2g

Honey Garlic Chicken

Prep time: 5 minutes, Cook time: 6 hours, Serves: 6

Ingredients:

6 chicken thighs

What you'll need from store cupboard:

2 tbsp. sugar free ketchup

2 tbsp. honey

2 tbsp. lite soy sauce

3 cloves garlic, diced fine

Instructions:

1. Add everything, except chicken, to the crock pot. Stir to combine.
2. Lay chicken, skin side up, in a single layer. Cover and cook on low 6 hours, or high for 3 hours.
3. Place chicken in a baking dish and broil 2-3 minutes to caramelize the outside. Serve.

Nutrition Facts Per Serving

Calories 57 Total Carbs 7g Protein 4g Fat 2g Sugar 6g Fiber 0g

Hot Chicken Salad Casserole

Prep time: 15 minutes, Cook time: 30 minutes, Serves: 6

Ingredients:

3 cup chicken breast, cooked and cut into cubes

6 oz. container plain low-fat yogurt

1 cup celery, diced

1 cup yellow or red sweet pepper, diced

¾ cup cheddar cheese, grated

¼ cup green onions, diced

What you'll need from store cupboard:

1 can reduced-fat and reduced-sodium condensed cream of chicken soup

½ cup cornflakes, crushed

¼ cup almonds, sliced

1 tbsp. lemon juice

¼ teaspoon ground black pepper

Instructions:

1. Heat oven to 400 degrees.
2. In a large bowl, combine chicken, celery, red pepper, cheese, soup, yogurt, onions, lemon juice, and black pepper, stir to combine. Transfer to 2-quart baking dish.
3. In a small bowl stir the cornflakes and almonds together. Sprinkle evenly over chicken mixture.
4. Bake 30 minutes or until heated through. Let rest 10 minutes before serving.

Nutrition Facts Per Serving

Calories 238 Total Carbs 9g Net Carbs 8g Protein 27g Fat 10g Sugar 3g Fiber 1g

Cajun Chicken & Pasta

Prep time: 15 minutes, Cook time: 20 minutes, Serves: 4

Ingredients:

3 chicken breasts, boneless, skinless, cut in 1-inch pieces

4 Roma tomatoes, diced

1 green bell pepper, sliced

1 red bell pepper, sliced

½ red onion, sliced

1 cup half-n-half

2 tbsp. margarine

¼ cup fresh parsley, diced

What you'll need from store cupboard:

½ recipe homemade pasta, (chapter 14), cook and drain

2 cup low sodium chicken broth

½ cups white wine

2 tbsp. olive oil

3 tsp Cajun spice mix

3 cloves garlic, diced fine

Cayenne pepper, to taste

Freshly ground black pepper, to taste

Salt, to taste

Instructions:

1. Place chicken in a bowl and sprinkle with 1 ½ teaspoons Cajun spice, toss to coat.
2. Heat 1 tablespoon oil and 1 tablespoon margarine in a large cast iron skillet over high heat. add chicken, cooking in 2 batches, cook until brown on one side, about 1 minute, flip and brown the other side. Transfer to a plate with a slotted spoon.
3. Add remaining oil and margarine to the pan. Add peppers, onion, and garlic. Sprinkle remaining Cajun spice over vegetables and salt to taste. Cook, stirring occasionally, until vegetables start to turn black, 3-5 minutes. Add tomatoes and cook another 30 seconds. Transfer vegetables to a bowl with a slotted spoon.
4. Add wine and broth to the pan and cook, stirring to scrape up brown bits from the bottom, 3-5 minutes. Reduce heat to med-low and add half-n-half, stirring constantly. Cook until sauce starts to thicken. Taste and season with cayenne, pepper and salt, it should be spicy.
5. Add chicken and vegetables to the sauce and cook 1-2 minutes until hot. Stir in pasta and parsley and serve.

Nutrition Facts Per Serving

Calories 475 Total Carbs 21g Net Carbs 17g Protein 38g Fat 25g Sugar 10g Fiber 4g

Arroz Con Pollo

Prep time: 10 minutes, Cook time: 25 minutes, Serves: 4

Ingredients:

1 onion, diced	grated
1 red pepper, diced	1 cup peas, thaw
2 cup chicken breast, cooked and cubed	2 tbsp. cilantro, diced
1 cup cauliflower,	½ tsp lemon zest

What you'll need from store cupboard:

14 ½ oz. low sodium chicken broth	1 clove garlic, diced
¼ cup black olives, sliced	2 tsp olive oil
	¼ tsp salt
¼ cup sherry	¼ tsp cayenne pepper

Instructions:

1. Heat oil in a large skillet over med-high heat. Add pepper, onion and garlic and cook 1 minute. Add the cauliflower and cook, stirring frequently, until light brown, 4-5 minutes.
2. Stir in broth, sherry, zest and seasonings. Bring to a boil. Reduce heat, cover and simmer 15 minutes.
3. Stir in the chicken, peas and olives. Cover and simmer another 3-6 minutes or until heated through. Serve garnished with cilantro.

Nutrition Facts Per Serving
Calories 161 Total Carbs 13g Net Carbs 9g Protein 14g Fat 5g Sugar 5g Fiber 4g

Balsamic Chicken & Vegetable Skillet

Prep time: 10 minutes, Cook time: 20 minutes, Serves: 4

Ingredients:

1 lb. chicken breasts, cut in 1-inch cubes	1 cup baby Bella mushrooms, sliced
1 cup cherry tomatoes, halved	1 tbsp. fresh basil, diced
1 cup broccoli florets	

What you'll need from store cupboard:

1/2 recipe homemade pasta, cooked and drain well (chapter 14)	2 tbsp. olive oil, divided
	1 tsp pepper
	½ tsp garlic powder
½ cup low sodium chicken broth	½ tsp salt
3 tbsp. balsamic vinegar	½ tsp red pepper flakes

Instructions:

1. Heat oil in a large, deep skillet over med-high heat. Add chicken and cook until browned on all sides, 8-10 minutes.
2. Add vegetables, basil, broth, and seasonings. Cover, reduce heat to medium and cook 5 minutes, or vegetables are tender.
3. Uncover and stir in cooked pasta and vinegar. Cook until heated through, 3-4 minutes. Serve.

Nutrition Facts Per Serving
Calories 386 Total Carbs 11g Net Carbs 8g Protein 43g Fat 18g Sugar 5g Fiber 3g

Middle East Chicken Skewers

Prep time: 20 minutes, Cook time: 15 minutes, Serves: 6

Ingredients:

2 ½ lbs. chicken thighs, boneless, skinless, cut in large pieces	wedges
	Zest & juice of 1 lemon
	1 cup plain Greek yogurt
1 red onion, cut in	

What you'll need from store cupboard:

5 cloves garlic, diced	½ tsp pepper
2 tbsp. olive oil	½ tsp cumin
2 tsp paprika	1/8 tsp cinnamon
1 ¾ tsp salt	Nonstick cooking spray
1 tsp red pepper flakes	

Instructions:

1. In a medium bowl, combine the yogurt, olive oil, paprika, cumin, cinnamon, red pepper flakes, lemon zest, lemon juice, salt, pepper and garlic.
2. Thread the chicken onto metal skewers, folding if the pieces are long and thin, alternating occasionally with the red onions. Place the kebabs on a baking sheet lined with aluminum foil. Spoon or brush the marinade all over the meat, coating well. Cover and refrigerate at least eight hours or overnight.
3. Heat the grill to medium-high heat. Spray the rack with cooking spray. Grill the kebabs until golden brown and cooked through, turning skewers occasionally, 10 to 15 minutes. Transfer the skewers to a platter and serve.

Nutrition Facts Per Serving
Calories 474 Total Carbs 14g Net Carbs 13g Protein 64g Fat 18g Sugar 12g Fiber 1g

Asian Roasted Duck Legs

Prep time: 10 minutes, Cook time: 90 minutes, Serves: 4

Ingredients:

4 duck legs
3 plum tomatoes, diced
1 red chili, deseeded and sliced
½ small Savoy cabbage, quartered
2 tsp fresh ginger, grated

What you'll need from store cupboard:

3 cloves garlic, sliced
2 tbsp. soy sauce
2 tbsp. honey
1 tsp five-spice powder

Instructions:

1. Heat oven to 350 degrees.
2. Place the duck in a large skillet over low heat and cook until brown on all sides and most of the fat is rendered, about 10 minutes. Transfer duck to a deep baking dish. Drain off all but 2 tablespoons of the fat.
3. Add ginger, garlic, and chili to the skillet and cook 2 minutes until soft. Add soy sauce, tomatoes and 2 tablespoons water and bring to a boil.
4. Rub the duck with the five spice seasoning. Pour the sauce over the duck and drizzle with the honey. Cover with foil and bake 1 hour. Add the cabbage for the last 10 minutes.

Nutrition Facts Per Serving

Calories 211 Total Carbs 19g Net Carbs 16g Protein 25g Fat 5g Sugar 14g Fiber 3g

BBQ Chicken & Noodles

Prep time: 10 minutes, Cook time: 25 minutes, Serves: 4

Ingredients:

4 slices bacon, diced
1 chicken breast, boneless, skinless, cut into 1-inch pieces
1 onion, diced
1 cup low fat cheddar cheese, grated
½ cup skim milk

What you'll need from store cupboard:

14 ½ oz. can tomatoes, diced
2 cup low sodium chicken broth
¼ cup barbecue sauce, (chapter 16)
2 cloves garlic, diced
fine
¼ tsp red pepper flakes
Homemade noodles, (chapter 15)
Salt and pepper, to taste

Instructions:

1. Place a large pot over med-high heat.

Add bacon and cook until crispy. Drain fat, reserving 1 tablespoon.
2. Stir in chicken and cook until browned on all sides, 3-5 minutes.
3. Add garlic and onion and cook, stirring often, until onions are translucent, 3-4 minutes.
4. Stir in broth, tomatoes, milk, and seasonings. Bring to boil, cover, reduce heat and simmer 10 minutes.
5. Stir in barbecue sauce, noodle, and cheese and cook until noodles are done and cheese has melted, 2-3 minutes. Serve.

Nutrition Facts Per Serving

Calories 331 Total Carbs 18g Net Carbs 15g Protein 34g Fat 13g Sugar 10g Fiber 3g

Cheesy Chicken & Spinach

Prep time: 10 minutes, Cook time: 45 minutes, Serves: 6

Ingredients:

3 chicken breasts, boneless, skinless and halved lengthwise
6 oz. low fat cream
cheese, soft
2 cup baby spinach
1 cup mozzarella cheese, grated

What you'll need from store cupboard:

2 tbsp. olive oil, divided
3 cloves garlic, diced fine
1 tsp Italian seasoning
Nonstick cooking spray

Instructions:

1. Heat oven to 350 degrees. Spray a 9x13-inch glass baking dish with cooking spray.
2. Lay chicken breast cutlets in baking dish. Drizzle 1 tablespoon oil over chicken. Sprinkle evenly with garlic and Italian seasoning. Spread cream cheese over the top of chicken.
3. Heat remaining tablespoon of oil in a small skillet over medium heat. Add spinach and cook until spinach wilts, about 3 minutes. Place evenly over cream cheese layer. Sprinkle mozzarella over top.
4. Bake 35-40 minutes, or until chicken is cooked through. Serve.

Nutrition Facts Per Serving

Calories 363 Total Carbs 3g Protein 31g Fat 25g Sugar 0g Fiber 0g

Cheesy Chicken & "Potato" Casserole

Prep time: 10 minutes, Cook time: 40 minutes, Serves: 6

Ingredients:

4 slices bacon, cooked and crumbled
3 cups cauliflower
3 cups chicken, cooked and chopped
3 cups broccoli florets
2 cups reduced fat cheddar cheese, grated
1 cup fat free sour cream

4 tbsp. margarine, soft
What you'll need from store cupboard
1 tsp salt
½ tsp black pepper
½ tsp garlic powder
½ tsp paprika
Nonstick cooking spray

Instructions:

1. In a large saucepan add 4-5 cups of water and bring to a boil. Add the cauliflower and cook about 4-5 minutes, or until it is tender drain well. Repeat with broccoli.
2. Heat oven to 350 degrees. Spray a baking dish with cooking spray.
3. In a medium bowl, mash the cauliflower with the margarine, sour cream and seasonings. Add remaining Ingredients, saving ½ the cheese, and mix well.
4. Spread mixture in prepared baking dish and sprinkle remaining cheese on top. Bake 20-25 minutes, or until heated through and cheese has melted. Serve.

Nutrition Facts Per Serving

Calories 346 Total Carbs 10g Net Carbs 8g Protein 28g Fat 15g Sugar 4g Fiber 2g

Cheesy Stuffed Chicken

Prep time: 15 minutes, Cook time: 20 minutes, Serves: 4

Ingredients:

1 lb. chicken breasts, boneless and butterflied
2 cups fresh spinach, chopped

4 oz. low fat cream cheese, soft
¼ cup mozzarella cheese, grated

What you'll need from store cupboard:

¼ cup reduced fat Parmesan cheese
1 tbsp. garlic, diced fine
1 tbsp. olive oil
1 tsp chili powder

1 tsp Italian seasoning
¾ tsp black pepper, divided
½ tsp salt

Instructions:

1. In a medium bowl, combine spinach, cream cheese, parmesan, mozzarella, garlic, ½ teaspoon salt and ½ teaspoon pepper, stir to combine.
2. In a small bowl, stir together the chili powder, Italian seasoning, salt, and pepper, use it to season both sides of the chicken. Spoon ¼ of the cheese mixture into the middle of the chicken and fold over to seal it inside.
3. Heat oil in a large skillet over med-high heat. Add the chicken, cover and cook 9-10 minutes per side, or until cooked through. Serve.

Nutrition Facts Per Serving

Calories 256 Total Carbs 2g Net Carbs 1g Protein 29g Fat 14g Sugar 0g Fiber 1g

Jalapeno Turkey Burgers

Prep time: 5 minutes, Cook time: 10 minutes, Serves: 4

Ingredients:

1 lb. lean ground turkey
4 slices pepper Jack cheese
2 jalapeno peppers, seeded and diced

4 tbsp. lettuce, shredded
4 tbsp. fat free sour cream
2 tbsp. cilantro, diced
2 tbsp. light beer

What you'll need from store cupboard:

4 low carb hamburger buns
2 cloves garlic, diced
4 tbsp. salsa
½ tsp pepper
¼ tsp hot pepper

sauce
¼ tsp salt
¼ tsp cayenne pepper
Nonstick cooking spray.

Instructions:

1. Heat grill to medium heat. Spray the grill rack with cooking spray.
2. In a large bowl, combine jalapenos, cilantro, beer, pepper sauce, garlic, pepper, salt, and cayenne. Crumble turkey over mixture and combine thoroughly. Shape into 4 patties.
3. Place the burgers on the grill and cook 3-5 minutes per side, or until meat thermometer reaches 165 degrees. Top each with slice of cheese, cover, and cook until cheese melts.
4. Place patties on buns and top with salsa, sour cream and lettuce.

Nutrition Facts Per Serving

Calories 389 Total Carbs 20g Net Carbs 14g Protein 38g Fat 19g Sugar 4g Fiber 6g

Chicken Stuffed with Mushrooms

Prep time: 15 minutes, Cook time: 3 hours, Serves: 4

Ingredients:

4 thin chicken breasts, boneless and skinless

What you'll need from store cupboard:

1 small can mushrooms, drain and slice	wine
	1 tbsp. cornstarch
½ cup + 2 tbsp. low sodium chicken broth	½ tsp sage
	½ tsp garlic powder
½ cup fine bread crumbs	¼ tsp marjoram
	Salt & pepper to taste
1 tbsp. dry white	

Instructions:

1. Place chicken between 2 sheets of plastic wrap and pound to 1/8-inch thick, working from the center to the edges.
2. In a small bowl, combine mushrooms, bread crumbs, 2 tablespoons broth and seasonings. Spoon one fourth stuffing mix onto short end of chicken breast. Fold long sides in and roll up. Secure with toothpick.
3. Place chicken in crock pot and add the ½ cup broth. Cover and cook on high 3 hours, or until chicken is cooked through. Transfer chicken to a plate and tent with foil to keep warm.
4. Strain cooking liquid through a sieve into a small saucepan. Place over medium heat. In a small bowl, whisk together the wine and cornstarch. Add to the saucepan and cook, stirring constantly, until sauce is bubbly and thick. Cook 2 minutes more. Spoon sauce over chicken and serve.

Nutrition Facts Per Serving

Calories 181 Total Carbs 13g Net Carbs 12g Protein 28g Fat 2g Sugar 1g Fiber 1g

Roasted Duck Legs with Balsamic Mushrooms

Prep time: 15 minutes, Cook time: 1 hour, Serves: 4

Ingredients:

4 bone-in, skin-on duck legs	into thick slices
	1 green onion, sliced thin
1/2 lb. cremini mushrooms, remove stems and cut caps	1 small shallot, sliced thin
3-4 fresh thyme sprigs, crushed	lightly

What you'll need from store cupboard:

5 Tbs. extra-virgin olive oil	½ tsp fresh thyme, chopped
5 Tbs. balsamic vinegar	Kosher salt and freshly ground pepper
2 cloves garlic, sliced thin	

Instructions:

1. Rinse duck and pat dry with paper towels.
2. In a shallow glass bowl, large enough to hold the duck, combine 3 tablespoons oil, 3 tablespoons vinegar, garlic, shallot, thyme sprigs, ½ teaspoon salt and some pepper. Add the duck, turning to coat. Cover and chill 3-4 hours turning legs once or twice.
3. Remove the duck from the marinade. Pour the marinade into a saucepan and bring to a boil over high heat. Remove from heat.
4. Place a footed rack on the bottom of a large pot, tall enough that the duck legs can stand 2 inches from the bottom. Add about 1 inch of water. Place the duck, skin side up on the rack. Cover and bring to a boil over med-high heat. Let steam until the skin is translucent, about 20 minutes.
5. While duck is steaming, heat the oven to 450 degrees. Line a roasting pan large enough to hold the duck with foil. Place a flat rack in the pan.
6. When the duck is ready, transfer it skin side up to the prepared rack. Brush the skin with the glaze and roast, until skin is brown and crisp, about 20 minutes. Remove from oven and glaze the duck again. Let rest for 5 minutes.
7. In a large skillet, over med-high heat, heat the remaining oil. Add mushrooms and green onions and cook, stirring frequently about 2 minutes. Add the remaining vinegar, chopped thyme, salt and pepper to taste. Cook until mushrooms are soft and most of the liquid has evaporated.
8. To serve, place duck leg on a plate and spoon mushrooms over.

Nutrition Facts Per Serving

Calories 374 Total Carbs 4g Net Carbs 3g Protein 26g Fat 28g Sugar 1g Fiber 1g

Chicken & Shrimp Satay

Prep time: 20 minutes, Cook time: 10 minutes, Serves: 6

Ingredients:

¾ lb. chicken tenders, cut into cubes
¾ lb. shrimp, peeled and deveined
4 green onions diced
¼ cup onion, diced
2 tbsp. margarine, divided
1 tbsp. + ¾ tsp lemon juice
1 tbsp. ¾ tsp lime juice
1 tbsp. fresh parsley, diced fine

What you'll need from store cupboard:

2/3 cup low sodium chicken broth
½ cup white wine
¼ cup reduced fat chunky peanut butter
2 cloves garlic, diced fine
2 ¼ tsp Splenda brown sugar
¼ tsp salt
¼ tsp basil
¼ tsp thyme
¼ tsp rosemary
1/8 tsp cayenne pepper
Nonstick cooking spray

Instructions:

1. Skewer shrimp and chicken on 12 skewers. Place in a large shallow baking dish.
2. In 1 tablespoon margarine in a small skillet over medium heat. Add green onions and cook until starting to soften. Add garlic and cook 1 more minute.
3. Stir in parsley, wine, 1 tablespoon lemon juice, and 1 tablespoon lime juice. Remove from heat and cool 5 minutes. Pour over skewers, turning to coat. Cover and refrigerate 4 hours or overnight.
4. Heat grill to medium. Spray the grill rack with cooking spray.
5. Heat remaining tablespoon of margarine in a small sauce pan over medium heat. Add onion and cook until tender. Stir in broth, peanut butter, Splenda brown sugar, lemon juice, lime juice, salt and seasonings. Cook, stirring until blended. Remove from heat.
6. Place skewers on the grill, discarding the marinade. Cook 7-8 minutes, turning often, or until shrimp are pink and chicken is cooked through. Brush with sauce during the last minute of cooking. Serve remaining sauce for dipping.

Nutrition Facts Per Serving

Calories 297 Total Carbs 9g Net Carbs 8g Protein 32g Fat 13g Sugar 3g Fiber 1g

Turkey Stuffed Poblano Peppers

Prep time: 15 minutes, Cook time: 40 minutes, Serves: 2

Ingredients:

2 Poblano peppers, halved lengthwise, cores and seeds removed
1 lb. ground turkey
½ cup low-fat cheddar cheese, grated
1 green onion, diced
1 tbsp. cilantro, chopped

What you'll need from store cupboard:

8 oz. can tomato sauce
1 tbsp. olive oil
1 tsp oregano
1 tsp paprika
1 tsp ground cumin
½ tsp onion powder
½ tsp garlic paste or minced garlic
Salt and pepper

Instructions:

1. Heat oven to 350 degrees.
2. Use tongs to roast the skin of the peppers over an open flame until charred and blistered all over. Or place on a cookie sheet under the broiler until skin is charred.
3. Place peppers in a plastic bag to steam for 15 minutes.
4. In a small bowl, stir together tomato sauce, oregano, paprika, and cumin
5. Heat oil in a large skillet over medium heat. Add turkey, onion powder, and garlic paste. Cook, stirring frequently, until meat has browned. Stir in 2 tablespoons of the sauce and season with salt and pepper.
6. Pour remaining sauce in the bottom of a baking dish.
7. With a butter knife, scrape the charred skin off the peppers, and place on sauce in dish.
8. Divide turkey mixture evenly over the peppers, sprinkle with cheese. Cover and bake 20 minutes.
9. Remove the foil, and bake until cheese starts to brown, about 5-7 minutes. Serve garnished with chopped green onion and cilantro.

Nutrition Facts Per Serving

Calories 665 Total Carbs 12g Net Carbs 9g Protein 71g Fat 36g Sugar 8g Fiber 3g

Chicken Marsala

Prep time: 10 minutes, Cook time: 25 minutes, Serves: 4

Ingredients:

4 boneless chicken breasts	sliced
½ lb. mushrooms,	1 tbsp. margarine

What you'll need from store cupboard:

1 cup Marsala wine	Pinch of white pepper
¼ cup flour	Pinch of oregano
1 tbsp. oil	Pinch of basil

Instructions:

1. On a shallow plate, combine flour and seasonings.
2. Dredge the chicken in the flour mixture to coat both sides.
3. In a large skillet, over medium heat, heat oil until hot. Add chicken and cook until brown on both sides, about 15 minutes. Transfer chicken to a plate.
4. Reduce heat to low and add mushrooms and ¼ cup of the wine. Cook about 5 minutes. Scrape bottom of pan to loosen any flour. Stir in reserved flour mixture and the remaining wine.
5. Simmer until mixture starts to thicken, stirring constantly. Add the chicken back to the pan and cook an additional 5 minutes. Serve.

Nutrition Facts Per Serving
Calories 327 Total Carbs 9g Net Carbs 8g Protein 21g Fat 14g Sugar 1g Fiber 1g

Chicken Tuscany

Prep time: 10 minutes, Cook time: 15 minutes, Serves: 4

Ingredients:

1½ lbs. chicken breasts, boneless, skinless and sliced thin	1 cup spinach, chopped 1 cup half-n-half

What you'll need from store cupboard:

½ cup reduced fat parmesan cheese	tomatoes
½ cup low sodium chicken broth	2 tbsp. olive oil
½ cup sun dried	1 tsp Italian seasoning
	1 tsp garlic powder

Instructions:

1. Heat oil in a large skillet over med-high heat. Add chicken and cook 3-5 minutes per side, or until browned and cooked through. Transfer to a plate.
2. Add half-n-half, broth, cheese and

seasonings to the pan. Whisk constantly until sauce starts to thicken. Add spinach and tomatoes and cook, stirring frequently, until spinach starts to wilt, about 2-3 minutes.
3. Add chicken back to the pan and cook just long enough to heat through.

Nutrition Facts Per Serving
Calories 462 Total Carbs 6g Net Carbs 5g Protein 55g Fat 23g Sugar 0g Fiber 1g

Hawaiian Chicken

Prep time: 15 minutes, Cook time: 3 hours, Serves: 8

Ingredients:

8 chicken thighs, bone-in and skin-on	1 red onion, diced
1 red bell pepper, diced	2 tbsp. fresh parsley, chopped
	2 tbsp. margarine

What you'll need from store cupboard:

8 oz. can pineapple chunks	sauce
8 oz. can crushed pineapple	2 tbsp. apple cider vinegar
1 cup pineapple juice	2 tbsp. honey
½ cup low sodium chicken broth	2 tbsp. cornstarch
¼ cup Splenda brown sugar	1 tsp garlic powder
	1 tsp Sriracha
¼ cup water	½ tsp ginger
3 tbsp. light soy	½ tsp sesame seeds
	Salt & pepper to taste

Instructions:

1. Season chicken with salt and pepper.
2. Melt butter in a large skillet over medium heat. Add chicken, skin side down, and sear both side until golden brown. Add chicken to the crock pot.
3. In a large bowl, combine pineapple juice, broth, Splenda, soy sauce, honey, vinegar, Sriracha, garlic powder, and ginger. Pour over chicken.
4. Top with kinds of pineapple. Cover and cook on high 2 hours. Baste the chicken occasionally.
5. Mix the cornstarch and water together until smooth. Stir into chicken and add the pepper and onion, cook another 60 minutes, or until sauce has thickened. Serve garnished with parsley and sesame seeds.

Nutrition Facts Per Serving
Calories 296 Total Carbs 24g Protein 17g Fat 13g Sugar 18g Fiber 1g

Chicken Zucchini Patties with Salsa

Prep time: 10 minutes, Cook time: 10 minutes, Serves: 8

Ingredients:

2 cup chicken breast, cooked, divided
1 zucchini, cut in ¾-inch pieces
¼ cup cilantro, diced

What you'll need from store cupboard:

1/3 cup bread crumbs
1/3 cup lite mayonnaise
2 tsp olive oil
½ tsp salt
¼ tsp pepper
Roasted Tomato Salsa, (chapter 16)

Instructions:

1. Place 1 ½ cups chicken and zucchini into a food processor. Cover and process until coarsely chopped. Add bread crumbs, mayonnaise, pepper, cilantro, remaining chicken, and salt. Cover and pulse until chunky.
2. Heat oil in a large skillet over med-high heat. Shape chicken mixture into 8 patties and cook 4 minutes per side, or until golden brown. Serve topped with salsa.

Nutrition Facts Per Serving

Calories 146 Total Carbs 10g Net Carbs 8g Protein 12g Fat 7g Sugar 5g Fiber 2g

Turkey Meatballs with Spaghetti Squash

Prep time: 15 minutes, Cook time: 35 minutes, Serves: 4

Ingredients:

1 lb. lean ground turkey
1 lb. spaghetti squash, halved and seeds removed
2 egg whites
1/3 cup green onions, diced fine
¼ cup onion, diced fine
2 ½ tbsp. flat leaf parsley, diced fine
1 tbsp. fresh basil, diced fine

What you'll need from store cupboard:

14 oz. can no-salt-added tomatoes, crushed
1/3 cup soft whole wheat bread crumbs
¼ cup low sodium chicken broth
1 tsp garlic powder
1 tsp thyme
1 tsp oregano
½ tsp red pepper flakes
½ tsp whole fennel seeds

Instructions:

1. In a small bowl, combine bread crumbs, onion, garlic, parsley, pepper flakes, thyme, and fennel.
2. In a large bowl, combine turkey and egg whites. Add bread crumb mixture and mix well. Cover and chill 10 minutes. Heat the oven to broil.
3. Place the squash, cut side down, in a glass baking dish. Add 3-4 tablespoons of water and microwave on high 10-12 minutes, or until fork tender.
4. Make 20 meatballs from the turkey mixture and place on a baking sheet. Broil 4-5 minutes, turn and cook 4 more minutes.
5. In a large skillet, combine tomatoes and broth and bring to a simmer over low heat. Add meatballs, oregano, basil, and green onions. Cook, stirring occasionally, 10 minutes or until heated through.
6. Use a fork to scrape the squash into "strands" and arrange on a serving platter. Top with meatballs and sauce and serve.

Nutrition Facts Per Serving

Calories 253 Total Carbs 15g Net Carbs 13g Protein 27g Fat 9g Sugar 4g Fiber 2g

Ranch Chicken Casserole

Prep time: 5 minutes, Cook time: 30 minutes, Serves: 8

Ingredients:

2 cup chicken, cooked & diced
½ lb. bacon, cooked & diced
4 eggs
1 cup reduced fat cheddar cheese, grated
½ cup half-n-half

What you'll need from store cupboard:

½ cup fat free Ranch dressing
Nonstick cooking spray

Instructions:

1. Heat oven to 350 degrees. Lightly spray an 8x8-inch or 11x7-inch pan with cooking spray.
2. Spread chicken and bacon in the bottom of prepared pan. Top with cheese.
3. Whisk together eggs, half-n-half, and ranch dressing. Pour on top of chicken mixture.
4. Bake, uncovered, for 30 to 35 minutes.

Nutrition Facts Per Serving

Calories 413 Total Carbs 2g Protein 38g Fat 27g Sugar 1g Fiber 0g

Roast Turkey & Rosemary Gravy

Prep time: 20 minutes, Cook time: 1 ¾ hours,
Serves: 18

Ingredients:

6 lb. turkey breast, bone in	white parts only
2 apples, sliced	3 tbsp. margarine
1 ½ cup leek, sliced,	2 tsp fresh rosemary, diced, divided

What you'll need from store cupboard:

2 ¼ cup low sodium chicken broth	¼ cup flour
	1 tbsp. sunflower oil

Instructions:
1. Heat oven to 325 degrees.
2. Place apples and leeks in the bottom of a large roasting pan, and pour in 1 cup of broth. Place turkey on top.
3. In a small bowl, combine oil and 1 ½ teaspoons rosemary. Loosen skin over turkey and rub rosemary mixture over the turkey. Secure skin to underside of turkey with toothpicks.
4. Bake 1 ¾-2 ¼ hours, basting every 30 minutes, until turkey is cooked through. If turkey starts to get too brown, cover with foil.
5. Once turkey is done, cover and let rest 15 minutes before slicing. Discard apples and leeks. Save ¼ cup cooking liquid.
6. Melt margarine in a small saucepan over medium heat. Add flour and remaining rosemary and cook, stirring, until combined. Skim fat off the reserved cooking liquid and add to saucepan with remaining broth. Bring to a boil, cook, stirring, 1 minute until thickened. Serve with turkey.

Nutrition Facts Per Serving
Calories 306 Total Carbs 6g Net Carbs 5g
Protein 33g Fat 14g Sugar 3g Fiber 1g

Chutney Turkey Burgers

Prep time: 10 minutes, Cook time: 15 minutes,
Serves: 4

Ingredients:

1 lb. lean ground turkey	½ cup chutney, divided
16 baby spinach leaves	¼ cup fresh parsley, diced
4 slices red onion	2 tsp lime juice
2 green onions, diced	

What you'll need from store cupboard:

8 Flourless Burger	Buns, (chapter 14)
1 tbsp. Dijon mustard	Nonstick cooking spray.
½ tsp salt	
¼ tsp pepper	

Instructions:
1. Heat grill to med-high heat. Spray rack with cooking spray.
2. In a small bowl, combine ¼ cup chutney, mustard, and lime juice.
3. In a large bowl, combine parsley, green onions, salt, pepper, and remaining chutney. Crumble turkey over mixture and mix well. Shape into 4 patties.
4. Place burgers on the grill and cook 5-7 minutes per side, or meat thermometer reaches 165 degrees.
5. Serve on buns with spinach leaves, sliced onions and reserved chutney mixture.

Nutrition Facts Per Serving
Calories 275 Total Carbs 15g Net Carbs 13g
Protein 28g Fat 11g Sugar 2g Fiber 2g

Chicken & Spinach Pasta Skillet

Prep time: 10 minutes, Cook time: 15 minutes,
Serves: 4

Ingredients:

1 lb. chicken, boneless, skinless, cut into 1-inch pieces	chopped
	1 lemon, juiced and zested
10 cup fresh spinach,	

What you'll need from store cupboard:

½ recipe homemade pasta, (chapter 14) cook and drain	parmesan cheese, divided
½ cup dry white wine	2 tbsp. extra-virgin olive oil
4 cloves garlic, diced fine	½ tsp salt
4 tbsp. reduced fat	¼ tsp ground pepper

Instructions:
1. Heat oil in a large, deep skillet over med-high heat. Add chicken, salt and pepper. Cook, stirring occasionally, until just cooked through, 5-7 minutes.
2. Add garlic and cook, stirring, until fragrant, about 1 minute.
3. Stir in wine, lemon juice and zest; bring to a simmer. Remove from heat. Stir in spinach and pasta. Cover and let stand until the spinach is just wilted. Divide among 4 plates and top each serving with 1 tablespoon Parmesan.

Nutrition Facts Per Serving
Calories 415 Total Carbs 12g Net Carbs 9g
Protein 40g Fat 19g Sugar 4g Fiber 3g

Creamy Chicken Tenders

Prep time; 5 minutes, Cook time: 15 minutes, Serves: 4

Ingredients:

1 lb. chicken breast tenders
1 cup half-n-half
4 tbsp. margarine

What you'll need from store cupboard:

2 tsp garlic powder
2 tsp chili powder

Instructions:

1. In a small bowl, stir together seasonings with a little salt if desired. Sprinkle over chicken to coat.
2. Heat 2 tablespoons margarine in a large skillet over medium heat. Cook chicken until no longer pink, 3-4 minutes per side. Transfer to a plate.
3. Add half-n-half and stir, scraping up the brown bits from the bottom of the skillet, and cook until it starts to boil. Reduce heat to med-low and simmer until sauce is reduced by half. Stir in remaining margarine and add chicken back to sauce to heat through. Serve.

Nutrition Facts Per Serving

Calories 281 Total Carbs 3g Protein 24g Fat 19g Sugar 0g Fiber 0g

Creamy Turkey & Peas with Noodles

Prep time: 10 minutes, Cook time: 15 minutes, Serves: 4

Ingredients:

1 lb. lean ground turkey
1 lemon, juice and zest
1 ½ cup skim milk
1 cup low fat sharp
cheddar cheese, grated
1 cup peas, frozen
¼ cup fresh parsley, diced
1 tbsp. margarine

What you'll need from store cupboard:

Homemade noodles, (chapter 14)
½ cup low sodium chicken broth
3 tbsp. flour
1 tbsp. olive oil
3 cloves garlic, diced
fine
½ tsp ground mustard
Pinch of nutmeg
Salt and pepper, to taste

Instructions:

1. Heat oil in a large skillet over med-high heat. Add turkey and season with salt and pepper. Cook, breaking up with a spatula, until no longer pink. Add garlic and cook 1 minute more.
2. Add the margarine and flour, and cook, stirring, 2 minutes until combined.
3. Stir in the broth and milk. Bring to a low boil, reduce heat to low and simmer until mixture starts to thicken.
4. Add the cheese and cook, stirring until it melts and combines into the sauce. Add the seasonings and peas, simmer 5 minutes, stirring occasionally.
5. Add the noodles and lemon juice and cook another 2 minutes. Serve garnished with lemon zest and parsley.

Nutrition Facts Per Serving

Calories 427 Total Carbs 18g Net Carbs 16g Protein 40g Fat 22g Sugar 7g Fiber 2g

Spicy Lettuce Wraps

Prep time: 10 minutes, Cook time: 5 minutes, Serves: 6

Ingredients:

12 Romaine lettuce leaves
1 lb. ground chicken
1/3 cup green onions,
slice thin
2 tsp fresh ginger, grated

What you'll need from store cupboard:

1/3 cup water chestnuts, diced fine
1/3 cup peanuts, chopped
2 cloves garlic, diced fine
3 tbsp. lite soy sauce
1 tbsp. cornstarch
1 tbsp. peanut oil
¼ tsp red pepper flakes

Instructions:

1. In a large bowl, combine chicken, ginger, garlic, and pepper flakes.
2. In a small bowl, stir together cornstarch and soy sauce until smooth.
3. Heat oil in a large skillet over med-high heat, Add chicken and cook, stirring, 2-3 minutes, or chicken is cooked through.
4. Stir in soy sauce and cook, stirring, until mixture starts to thicken, about 30 seconds. Add water chestnuts, green onions, and peanuts and heat through.
5. Lay lettuce leaves out on a work surface. Divide filling evenly over them and roll up. Filling can also be made ahead of time and reheated as needed. Serve warm with Chinese hot mustard for dipping, (chapter 16).

Nutrition Facts Per Serving

Calories 234 Total Carbs 13g Net Carbs 12g Protein 26g Fat 12g Sugar 6g Fiber 1g

Crunchy Grilled Chicken

Prep time: 15 minutes, Cook time: 10 minutes, Serves: 8

Ingredients:

8 chicken breast halves, boneless and skinless
1 cup fat free sour cream
¼ cup lemon juice
Butter flavored spray, refrigerated

What you'll need from store cupboard:

2 cup stuffing mix, crushed
4 tsp Worcestershire sauce
2 tsp paprika
1 tsp celery salt
1/8 tsp garlic powder
Nonstick cooking spray

Instructions:

1. In a large Ziploc bag combine sour cream, lemon juice, Worcestershire, and seasonings. Add chicken, seal, and turn to coat. Refrigerate 1-4 hours.
2. Heat grill to medium heat. Spray rack with cooking spray.
3. Place stuffing crumbs in a shallow dish. Coat both sides of chicken with crumbs and spritz with butter spray.
4. Place on grill and cook 4-7 minutes per side, or until chicken is cooked through. Serve.

Nutrition Facts Per Serving

Calories 230 Total Carbs 22g Net Carbs 21g Protein 25g Fat 3g Sugar 4g Fiber 1g

Orange Chicken

Prep time: 15 minutes, Cook time: 20 minutes, Serves: 6

Ingredients:

1 ½ lbs. chicken breast, cut into ½-inch pieces
1 medium orange,
zest then cut in half
½ inch fresh ginger, peel and grate

What you'll need from store cupboard:

1 cup pork rinds
½ cup coconut flour
2 cloves garlic, peeled
4 tbsp. coconut oil,
divided
2 tbsp. Swerve confectioners
1 tsp black pepper
1 tsp salt

Instructions:

1. Add the pork rinds, coconut flour and pepper to a food processor. Pulse until the mixture becomes a fine powder. Dump into a medium bowl.
2. Season the chicken with salt and pepper.
3. Heat 2 tablespoons oil in a large skillet over med-high heat. Add the chicken to the pork rind mixture and toss to coat. Add to skillet and cook, 2-3 minutes per side, or until browned. This will need to be done in batches. Transfer to paper towel lined plate.
4. Add remaining oil to a small sauce pan and heat over med-high heat. Add swerve and stir to combine. Once the swerve has dissolved, lower the heat to medium and add zest, garlic, ginger, and the juice from half the orange. Stir and bring to a simmer, stirring occasionally. Remove from heat when it thickens and becomes glossy.
5. Place the chicken on serving plate. Pour the orange glaze over it, sprinkle with sesame seeds and serve.

Nutrition Facts Per Serving

Calories 377 Total Carbs 10g Net Carbs 9g Protein 37g Fat 23g Sugar 8g Fiber 1g

Curried Chicken & Apples

Prep time: 15 minutes, Cook time: 30 minutes, Serves: 4

Ingredients:

1 lb. chicken breasts, boneless, skinless, cut in 1-inch cubes
2 tart apples, peel and slice
1 sweet onion, cut in
half and slice
1 jalapeno, seeded and diced
2 tbsp. cilantro, diced
½ tsp ginger, grated

What you'll need from store cupboard:

14 ½ oz. tomatoes, diced and drained
½ cup water
3 cloves garlic, diced
2 tbsp. sunflower oil
1 tsp salt
1 tsp coriander
½ tsp turmeric
¼ tsp cayenne pepper

Instructions:

1. Heat oil in a large skillet over med-high heat. Add chicken and onion, and cook until onion is tender. Add garlic and cook 1 more minute.
2. Add apples, water and seasonings and stir to combine. Bring to a boil. Reduce heat and simmer 12-15 minutes, or until chicken is cooked through, stirring occasionally.
3. Stir in tomatoes, jalapeno, and cilantro and serve.

Nutrition Facts Per Serving

Calories 371 Total Carbs 23g Net Carbs 18g Protein 34g Fat 16g Sugar 15g Fiber 5g

Korean Chicken

Prep time: 15 minutes, Cook time: 3-4 hours, Serves: 6

Ingredients:

2 lbs. chicken thighs, boneless and skinless
2 tbsp. fresh ginger, grated

What you'll need from store cupboard:

4 cloves garlic, diced fine	2 tbsp. toasted sesame oil
¼ cup lite soy sauce	2 tsp cornstarch
¼ cup honey	Pinch of red pepper flakes
2 tbsp. Korean chili paste	

Instructions:

1. Add the soy sauce, honey, chili paste, sesame oil, ginger, garlic and pepper flakes to the crock pot, stir to combine. Add the chicken and turn to coat in the sauce.
2. Cover and cook on low 3–4 hours or till chicken is cooked through.
3. When the chicken is cooked, transfer it to a plate.
4. Pour the sauce into a medium saucepan. Whisk the cornstarch and ¼ cup cold water until smooth. Add it to the sauce. Cook over medium heat, stirring constantly, about 5 minutes, or until sauce is thick and glossy.
5. Use 2 forks and shred the chicken. Add it to the sauce and stir to coat. Serve.

Nutrition Facts Per Serving

Calories 397 Total Carbs 18g Protein 44g Fat 16g Sugar 13g Fiber 0g

Turkey & Mushroom Casserole

Prep time: 15 minutes, Cook time: 50 minutes, Serves: 8

Ingredients:

1 lb. cremini mushrooms, washed and sliced	and cut in bite size pieces
1 onion, diced	2 cup reduced fat Mozzarella, grated, divided
6 cup cauliflower, grated	1 cup fat free sour cream
4 cup turkey, cooked	

What you'll need from store cupboard:

½ cup lite mayonnaise	2 tbsp. Dijon mustard
¼ cup reduced fat parmesan cheese	1 ½ tsp thyme
2 tbsp. olive oil, divided	1 ½ tsp poultry seasoning
	Salt and fresh-ground black pepper to taste

Nonstick cooking   spray

Instructions:

1. Heat oven to 375 degrees. Spray a 9x13-inch baking dish with cooking spray.
2. In a medium bowl, stir together sour cream, mayonnaise, mustard, ½ teaspoon each thyme and poultry seasoning, 1 cup of the mozzarella, and parmesan cheese.
3. Heat 2 teaspoons oil in a large skillet over med-high heat. Add mushrooms and sauté until they start to brown and all liquid is evaporated. Transfer them to the prepared baking dish.
4. Add 2 more teaspoons oil to the skillet along with the onion and sauté until soft and they start to brown. Add the onions to the mushrooms.
5. Add another 2 teaspoons oil to the skillet with the cauliflower. Cook, stirring frequently, until it starts to get soft, about 3-4 minutes. Add the remaining thyme and poultry seasoning and cook 1 more minute.
6. Season with salt and pepper and add to baking dish. Place the turkey over the vegetables and stir everything together.
7. Spread the sauce mixture over the top and stir to combine. Sprinkle the remaining mozzarella over the top and bake 40 minutes, or until bubbly and cheese is golden brown. Let cool 5 minutes, then cut and serve.

Nutrition Facts Per Serving

Calories 351 Total Carbs 13g Net Carbs 10g Protein 37g Fat 16g Sugar 5g Fiber 3g

Chicken Cordon Bleu

Prep time: 20 minutes, Cook time: 25 minutes, Serves: 8

Ingredients:

8 chicken breast halves, boneless and skinless	cheese, grated
	2/3 cup skim milk
8 slices ham	½ cup fat free sour cream
1 ½ cup mozzarella	

What you'll need from store cupboard:

1 can low fat condensed cream of chicken soup	1 tsp paprika
	½ tsp pepper
1 cup corn flakes, crushed	½ tsp garlic powder
	¼ tsp salt
1 tsp lemon juice	Nonstick cooking spray

Instructions:

1. Heat oven to 350 degrees. Spray a 13x9-inch baking dish with cooking spray.
2. Flatten chicken to ¼-inch thick. Sprinkle with pepper and top with slice of ham and 3 tablespoons of cheese down the middle. Roll up, tuck ends under and secure with a toothpick.
3. Pour milk into a shallow bowl. In a separate shallow bowl, combine corn flakes and seasonings. Dip chicken in milk then roll in corn flake mixture and place in prepared dish.
4. Bake 25-30 minutes or until chicken is cooked through.
5. In a small saucepan, whisk together soup, sour cream, and lemon juice until combined. Cook over medium heat until hot.
6. Remove toothpicks from chicken and place on plates, top with sauce and serve.

Nutrition Facts Per Serving
Calories 382 Total Carbs 9g Net Carbs 8g Protein 50g Fat 14g Sugar 2g Fiber 1g

Mediterranean Grilled Chicken

Prep time: 5 minutes, Cook time: 10 minutes, Serves: 4

Ingredients:
4 chicken breasts, boneless, skinless

What you'll need from store cupboard:

6 oz. pesto	vinegar
¼ cup olive oil	2 tsp garlic, diced
¼ cup lemon juice	fine
2 tbsp. red wine	

Instructions:

1. In a large freezer bag or a container mix together the olive oil, lemon juice, red wine vinegar, minced garlic and pesto. Add chicken and toss to coat. Place in refrigerator and marinate for 6 to 8 hours.
2. Heat grill to med-high. Cook chicken, 3-4 minutes per side, or until cooked through. Or, you can bake it in a 400 degree oven until no longer pink, about 30 minutes. Serve.

Nutrition Facts Per Serving
Calories 378 Total Carbs 2g Protein 36g Fat 25g Sugar 2g Fiber 0g

Lemon Chicken

Prep time: 10 minutes, Cook time: 10 minutes, Serves: 4

Ingredients:

3 large boneless, skinless chicken breasts, cut into strips	pepper, cut into 2 inch strips
	¼ cup snow peas
¼ cup red bell pepper, cut into 2 inch strips	¼ cup fresh lemon juice
	1 tsp fresh ginger, peeled and diced fine
¼ cup green bell	

What you'll need from store cupboard:

¼ cup + 1 tbsp. low sodium soy sauce, divided	1 tbsp. Splenda
	1 tbsp. vegetable oil
¼ cup low-fat, low-sodium chicken broth	2 cloves garlic, diced fine
	2 tsp cornstarch

Instructions:

1. In a medium bowl, whisk together 1 teaspoon cornstarch and 1 tablespoon soy sauce. Add chicken, cover and chill about 10 minutes.
2. In a separate medium mixing bowl, stir together lemon juice, ¼ cup soy sauce, broth, ginger, garlic, Splenda, and remaining cornstarch until thoroughly combined.
3. Heat oil in a large skillet over med-high heat. Add chicken and cook, stirring frequently, 3-4 minutes or just until chicken is no longer pink.
4. Add sauce, peppers and peas. Cook 2 more minutes or until sauce thickens and vegetables are tender-crisp. Serve.

Nutrition Facts Per Serving
Calories 242 Total Carbs 9g Net Carbs 8g Protein 27g Fat 10g Sugar 5g Fiber 1g

Creole Chicken

Prep time: 15 minutes, Cook time: 25 minutes, Serves: 2

Ingredients:

2 chicken breast halves, boneless and skinless	1/3 cup green bell pepper, julienned
	¼ cup celery, diced
1 cup cauliflower rice, cooked	¼ cup onion, diced

What you'll need from store cupboard:

14 ½ oz. stewed tomatoes, diced	1 tsp chili powder
	½ tsp thyme
1 tsp sunflower oil	1/8 tsp pepper

Instructions:

1. Heat oil in a small skillet over medium heat. Add chicken and cook 5-6 minutes per side or cooked through. Transfer to plate and keep warm.
2. Add the pepper, celery, onion, tomatoes, and seasonings. Bring to a boil. Reduce heat, cover, and simmer 10 minutes or until vegetables start to soften.
3. Add chicken back to pan to heat through. Serve over cauliflower rice.

Nutrition Facts Per Serving

Calories 362 Total Carbs 14g Net Carbs 10g Protein 45g Fat 14g Sugar 8g Fiber 4g

Crispy Italian Chicken with Zucchini

Prep time: 5 minutes, Cook time: 20 minutes, Serves: 4

Ingredients:

4 thin chicken breasts, boneless and skinless	sliced
	8 tbsp. margarine, divided
2 medium zucchini,	

What you'll need from store cupboard:

½ cup Italian bread crumbs	parmesan, grated
	¼ cup flour
½ cup + 1 tbsp. reduced fat	2 cloves garlic, diced fine

Instructions:

1. Melt 4 tablespoons margarine in a shallow glass dish in the microwave. In another shallow dish, combine bread crumbs, flour, and ½ cup parmesan.
2. Melt 2 tablespoons margarine in a large skillet over medium heat. Dip chicken in the melted butter, then bread crumbs to coat and add to skillet. Cook 3-4 minutes per side until crispy and chicken is cooked through. Transfer to paper towel lined plate.
3. Add remaining 2 tablespoons butter to the skillet and when melted add garlic. Cook 1 minute. Add zucchini and cook, stirring occasionally, until tender, about 5-8 minutes.
4. Salt and pepper to taste and add 1 tablespoon parmesan. Add chicken back to skillet just to heat through. Serve.

Nutrition Facts Per Serving

Calories 457 Total Carbs 20g Net Carbs 18g Protein 33g Fat 27g Sugar 3g Fiber 2g

French Onion Chicken & Vegetables

Prep time: 10 minutes, Cook time: 4 hours, Serves: 10

Ingredients:

1 lb. chicken breasts, boneless and skinless, cut in 1-inch pieces	quartered
	½ lb. mushrooms, halved
	½ cup sweet onion, sliced
1 lb. green beans, trim	1 tsp lemon zest
1 lb. red potatoes,	

What you'll need from store cupboard:

2 14 ½ oz. cans low sodium chicken broth	sauce
	½ tsp lemon pepper
2 tbsp. onion soup mix	½ tsp salt
	½ tsp pepper
1 tbsp. sunflower oil	¼ tsp garlic powder
2 tsp Worcestershire	

Instructions:

1. Sprinkle chicken with lemon pepper.
2. Heat oil in a large skillet over medium heat. Cook chicken 4-5 minutes or until brown on all sides.
3. Layer the green beans, potatoes, mushrooms, and onion in the crock pot.
4. In a small bowl, combine remaining Ingredients and pour over vegetables. Top with chicken.
5. Cover and cook on low heat 4-5 hours or until vegetables are tender. Serve.

Nutrition Facts Per Serving

Calories 256 Total Carbs 15g Net Carbs 12g Protein 30g Fat 8g Sugar 2g Fiber 3g

Healthy Turkey Chili

Prep time: 10 minutes, Cook time: 45 minutes, Serves: 4

Ingredients:

1 lb. lean ground turkey	diced
	1 onion, diced
2 carrots, peeled and diced	1 zucchini, diced
	1 red pepper, diced
2 stalks of celery,	

What you'll need from store cupboard:

14 oz. can tomato sauce	fine
	1 tbsp. chili powder
1 can black beans, drained and rinsed	1 tbsp. olive oil
	2 tsp salt
1 can kidney beans, drained and rinsed	1 tsp pepper
	1 tsp cumin
3 cups water	1 tsp coriander
3 garlic cloves, diced	1 bay leaf

Instructions:

1. Heat oil in a heavy bottom soup pot over med-high heat. Add turkey and onion and cook until no longer pink, 5-10 minutes.
2. Add the vegetables and cook, stirring occasionally, 5 minutes. Add the garlic and spices and cook, stirring, 2 minutes.
3. Add the remaining Ingredients and bring to a boil. Reduce heat to low and simmer 30

Nutrition Facts Per Serving
Calories 218 Total Carbs 14g Net Carbs 10g Protein 25g Fat 9g Sugar 6g Fiber 4g

Mediterranean Stuffed Chicken

Prep time: 25 minutes, Cook time: 45 minutes, Serves: 6

Ingredients:

6 chicken breast halves, boneless and skinless	thin
	1 cup feta cheese, crumbled
10 oz. spinach, thaw and squeeze dry	½ cup sun dried tomatoes
4 green onions, slice	

What you'll need from store cupboard:

1 cup boiling water	¼ tsp salt
1 clove garlic, diced	¼ tsp pepper
¼ cup Greek olives, diced	Nonstick cooking spray

Instructions:

1. Heat oven to 350 degrees. Spray 13x9-inch baking dish with cooking spray.
2. Place tomatoes in a bowl and add boiling water. Let set for 5 minutes.
3. In a medium bowl, combine spinach, cheese, onions, olive and garlic. Drain the tomatoes and chop, add to spinach mixture.
4. Flatten chicken to ¼-inch thick and sprinkle with salt and pepper.
5. Spread spinach mixture over chicken and roll up, secure with toothpicks. Place in prepared dish and cover with foil.
6. Bake 30 minutes. Uncover, and bake 15-20 minutes, or until chicken is cooked through. Remove toothpicks before serving.

Nutrition Facts Per Serving
Calories 221 Total Carbs 6g Net Carbs 4g Protein 27g Fat 10g Sugar 1g Fiber 2g

Pecan Chicken Enchiladas

Prep time: 20 minutes, Cook time: 45 minutes, Serves: 12

Ingredients:

1 onion, diced	4 oz. low fat cream cheese
4 cup chicken breast, cooked and cubed	½ cup reduced fat cheddar cheese, grated
1 cup fat free sour cream	
1 cup skim milk	2 tbsp. cilantro, diced

What you'll need from store cupboard:

12 6-inch flour tortillas, warm	diced
	1 tbsp. water
1 can low fat condensed cream of chicken soup	1 tsp cumin
	¼ tsp pepper
	1/8 tsp salt
¼ cup pecans, toasted	Nonstick cooking spray
2 tbsp. green chilies,	

Instructions:

1. Heat oven to 350 degrees. Spray a 13x9-inch baking dish with cooking spray.
2. Spray a nonstick skillet with cooking spray and place over medium heat. Add onion and cook until tender.
3. In a large bowl, beat cream cheese, water, cumin, salt, and pepper until smooth. Stir in the onion, chicken, and pecans.
4. Spoon 1/3 cup chicken mixture down the middle of each tortilla. Roll up and place, seam side down, in prepared baking dish.
5. In a medium bowl, combine soup, sour cream, milk, and chilies and pour over enchiladas.
6. Cover with foil and bake 40 minutes. Uncover and sprinkle cheese over top and bake another 5 minutes until cheese is melted. Sprinkle with cilantro and serve.

Nutrition Facts Per Serving
Calories 320 Total Carbs 27g Net Carbs 25g Protein 21g Fat 13g Sugar 4g Fiber 2g

Sweet & Sour Chicken

Prep time: 5 minutes, Cook time: 10 minutes, Serves: 4

Ingredients:

1 ½ lbs. chicken thighs, boneless, skinless and cut into 1 inch pieces
1 red bell pepper, cut into ¾ inch pieces

What you'll need from store cupboard:

8 oz. can pineapple tidbits, drained
¾ cup sweet and sour sauce
2 tbsp. vegetable oil

Instructions:

1. Heat oil in a large skillet over medium heat. Add chicken and cook until no longer pink, about 5-6 minutes.
2. Add the pepper and sauce and cook until pepper is tender, 3-4 minutes.
3. Stir in the pineapple and cook until hot, about 2 minutes. Serve over cauliflower rice (chapter 15).

Nutrition Facts Per Serving

Calories 483 Total Carbs 22g Protein 50g Fat 19g Sugar 18g Fiber 0g

Turkey Sloppy Joes

Prep time: 15 minutes, Cook time: 4 hours, Serves: 8

Ingredients:

1 lb. lean ground turkey
1 onion, diced
½ cup celery, diced
¼ cup green bell pepper, diced

What you'll need from store cupboard:

8 Flourless Burger Buns, (chapter 14)
1 can no salt added condensed tomato soup
½ cup ketchup, (chapter 14)
2 tbsp. yellow mustard
1 tbsp. Splenda brown sugar
¼ tsp pepper

Instructions:

1. In a large saucepan, over medium heat, cook turkey, onion, celery, and green pepper until turkey is no longer pink. Transfer to crock pot.
2. Add remaining Ingredients and stir to combine. Cover, and cook on low heat 4 hours. Stir well and serve on buns.

Nutrition Facts Per Serving

Calories 197 Total Carbs 12g Net Carbs 11g Protein 17g Fat 8g Sugar 8g Fiber 1g

Spiced Chicken Breasts with Peach Pepper Relish

Prep time: 20 minutes, Cook time: 15 minutes, Serves: 4

Ingredients:

4 chicken breast halves, boneless and skinless

What you'll need from store cupboard:

¼ cup sugar free peach preserves
2 tbsp. lemon juice
½ tsp salt
¼ tsp cinnamon
¼ tsp cloves
¼ tsp nutmeg
¼ tsp red pepper flakes
Peach Pepper Relish, (chapter 16)
Nonstick cooking spray

Instructions:

1. Heat grill to medium heat. Spray rack with cooking spray.
2. In a small bowl combine, salt, cinnamon, cloves, and nutmeg. Rub the chicken with the spice mixture.
3. In a separate bowl, stir together the preserves, lemon juice, and pepper flakes.
4. Place chicken on the grill, cover, and cook 6-8 minutes per side. Baste every few minutes with the preserve mixture. Serve topped with relish.

Nutrition Facts Per Serving

Calories 239 Total Carbs 14g Net Carbs 12g Protein 35g Fat 5g Sugar 8g Fiber 2g

Slow Cooker Lemon Chicken with Gravy

Prep time: 15 minutes, Cook time: 3 hours, Serves: 4

Ingredients:

1 lb. chicken tenderloins
3 tbsp. fresh lemon juice
3 tbsp. margarine, cubed
2 tbsp. fresh parsley, diced
2 tbsp. fresh thyme, diced
1 tbsp. lemon zest

What you'll need from store cupboard:

¼ cup low sodium chicken broth
2 cloves garlic, sliced
2 tsp cornstarch
2 tsp water
½ tsp salt
½ tsp white pepper

Instructions:

1. Add the broth, lemon juice, margarine, zest, garlic, salt and pepper to the crock pot, stir to combine. Add chicken, cover and cook on low heat 2 ½ hours.
2. Add the parsley and thyme and cook 30 minutes more, or chicken is cooked through.
3. Remove chicken to a plate and keep warm. Pour cooking liquid into a small saucepan and place over medium heat.
4. Stir water and cornstarch together until smooth. Add to sauce pan and bring to a boil. Cook, stirring, 2 minutes or until thickened. Serve with chicken.

Nutrition Facts Per Serving
Calories 303 Total Carbs 2g Protein 33g Fat 17g Sugar 0g Fiber 0g

South of the Border Chicken Casserole

Prep time: 15 minutes, Cook time: 30 minutes, Serves: 10
Ingredients:

1 lb. chicken breast, cooked and shredded	cheese, grated
1 red bell pepper, diced	½ cup fat free sour cream
1 onion, diced	¼ cup half-n-half
1 cup pepper Jack	2 tbsp. cilantro, diced fine

What you'll need from store cupboard:

1 cup salsa	2 tsp oregano
2 tbsp. olive oil	2 tsp salt
1 tbsp. chili powder	1 tsp pepper
1 tbsp. cumin	

Instructions:

1. Heat oven to 350 degrees.
2. Heat the oil in a large skillet over med-high heat. Add the pepper, onion, salt and pepper and cook until soft.
3. In a large bowl, stir together chili powder, cumin, and oregano. Add sour cream, salsa, veggies, and chicken and mix well.
4. Pour mixture into a 9x13-inch baking dish. Pour the half-n-half evenly over the top and sprinkle with the cheese. Bake 30 minutes, or until heated through and cheese is starting to brown. Serve garnished with cilantro.

Nutrition Facts Per Serving
Calories 240 Total Carbs 8g Net Carb 7g Protein 20g Fat 14g Sugar 3g Fiber 1g

Seared Duck Breast with Red Wine & Figs

Prep time: 15 minutes, Cook time: 35 minutes, Serves: 6
Ingredients:
2 duck breasts, with skin still on
¼ onion, diced
1 sprig fresh rosemary

What you'll need from store cupboard:

½ cup red wine	½ clove garlic, diced
1 tbsp. sugar free fig preserves	1/8 tsp Splenda
½ tbsp. red wine vinegar	Salt & pepper, to taste
	1 pinch sugar

Instructions:

1. Heat the oven to 450 degrees. Sprinkle the duck breasts with Splenda, salt and pepper.
2. Place a cast iron skillet over med-high heat. Place the duck breasts in the pan skin side down. Cook for 3 minutes, moving them around to make sure the skin doesn't burn.
3. Flip the breasts over and place the pan in the oven. Cook for 5 minutes. Then remove the breasts, and set aside.
4. Return the skillet to the stove medium heat. Add the onions and cook for 10 minutes. Add the garlic and cook for 1 minute more.
5. Add the wine, vinegar, fig preserves, and herb sprig. Cook, stirring occasionally, for 15 minutes. Then strain the sauce into a small saucepan.
6. With five minutes left in cooking the sauce, place the duck breasts back into the oven to warm.
7. Slice the duck into 1/2-inch thick pieces, and spoon on some of the sauce. Serve.

Nutrition Facts Per Serving
Calories 180 Total Carbs 4g Protein 18g Fat 7g Sugar 3g Fiber 0g

Southwest Turkey Lasagna

Prep time: 20 minutes, Cook time: 20 minutes, Serves: 8

Ingredients:

1 lb. lean ground turkey	8 oz. fat free cream cheese
1 onion, diced	1 cup Mexican cheese blend, grated
1 green bell pepper, diced	½ cup fat free sour cream
1 red pepper, diced	

What you'll need from store cupboard:

6 8-inch low carb whole wheat tortillas	16)
10 oz. enchilada sauce	1 tsp chili powder
½ cup salsa, (chapter	Nonstick cooking spray

Instructions:

1. Heat oven to 400 degrees. Spray a 13x9-inch baking dish with cooking spray.
2. In a large skillet, over medium heat, cook turkey, onion, and peppers until turkey is no longer pink. Drain fat.
3. Stir in cream cheese and chili powder.
4. Pour enchilada sauce into a shallow dish. Dip tortillas in sauce to coat. Place two tortillas in prepared dish. Spread with ½ the turkey mixture and sprinkle 1/3 of the cheese over turkey. Repeat layer. Top with remaining tortillas and cheese.
5. Cover with foil and bake 20-25 minutes, or until heated through. This can also be frozen up to 3 months.
6. Let rest 10 minutes before cutting. Serve topped with salsa and sour cream.

Nutrition Facts Per Serving

Calories 369 Total Carbs 36g Net Carbs 17g Protein 27g Fat 22g Sugar 4g Fiber 19g

Turkey Stuffed Peppers

Prep time: 10 minutes, Cook time: 55 minutes, Serves: 8

Ingredients:

1 lb. lean ground turkey	1 ½ cup mozzarella cheese
4 green bell peppers, halved and ribs and seeds removed	1 cup cauliflower, grated
1 onion, diced	1 cup mushrooms, diced

What you'll need from store cupboard:

3 cups spaghetti sauce, (chapter 16)	fine
3 cloves garlic, diced	2 tbsp. olive oil

Instructions:

1. Heat the oil in a large skillet over med-high heat. Add the garlic, mushrooms, and onion. Add the turkey, cook, breaking up the turkey with a spatula, until turkey is cooked through, about 10 minutes.
2. Stir in the cauliflower, and cook, stirring frequently, 3-5 minutes. Add the spaghetti sauce and 1 cup mozzarella. Stir to combine and remove from heat.
3. Heat oven to 350 degrees. Place bell peppers in a large baking dish, skin side down. Fill the insides with the turkey mixture, place any extra filling around the peppers. Top each pepper with remaining mozzarella. Bake 40-45 minutes or the peppers are tender. Serve immediately.

Nutrition Facts Per Serving

Calories 214 Total Carbs 14g Net Carbs 10g Protein 20g Fat 11g Sugar 9g Fiber 4g

Teriyaki Turkey Bowls

Prep time: 10 minutes, Cook time: 15 minutes, Serves: 4

Ingredients:

1 lb. lean ground turkey

1 medium head cauliflower, separated into small florets

What you'll need from store cupboard:

1 cup water, divided	1 ½ tbsp. cornstarch
¼ cup + 1 tbsp. soy sauce	1 tsp crushed red pepper flakes
2 tbsp. Hoisin sauce	1 tsp garlic powder
2 tbsp. honey	Salt

Instructions:

1. In a medium nonstick skillet, cook turkey over med-high heat until brown.
2. In a medium saucepan, combine ¾ cup water, ¼ cup soy sauce, hoisin, pepper flakes, honey, and garlic powder and cook over medium heat, stirring occasionally, until it starts to bubble.
3. In a small bowl whisk together ¼ cup water and cornstarch and add to the saucepan. Bring mixture to a full boil, stirring occasionally. Once it starts to boil, remove from heat and the turkey. Stir to combine.
4. Place the cauliflower florets in a food processor and pulse until it resembles rice.
5. Spray a nonstick skillet with cooking spray and add the cauliflower and 1 tablespoon soy sauce and cook until cauliflower starts to get soft, about 5-7 minutes.
6. To serve, spoon cauliflower evenly into four bowls, top with turkey mixture and garnish with

Nutrition Facts Per Serving

Calories 267 Total Carbs 24g Net Carbs 20g Protein 26g Fat 9g Sugar 15g Fiber 4g

Thai Turkey Stir Fry

Prep time: 5 minutes, Cook time: 15 minutes, Serves: 6

Ingredients:

1 1/2 lb. lean ground turkey	1 red bell pepper, cut in thin strips
1-2 cups Thai basil, chopped	2 tbsp. fresh lime juice
1 onion, cut in slivers	

What you'll need from store cupboard:

2-3 large cloves garlic, peeled and sliced	1 tbsp. fish sauce
	1 tbsp. Sriracha Sauce
1 tbsp. + 1 tsp peanut oil	1 tbsp. soy sauce
	1 tbsp. honey

Instructions:

1. In a small bowl, whisk together lime juice, fish sauce, Sriracha, soy sauce, and honey.
2. Place a large wok or heavy skillet over high heat. Once the pan gets hot, add 1 tablespoon oil and let it get hot. Add garlic and cook just until fragrant, about 30 seconds. Remove the garlic and discard.
3. Add the onion and bell pepper and cook, stirring frequently 1-2 minutes, or until they start to get soft, transfer to a bowl.
4. Add the remaining oil, if it's needed and cook the turkey, breaking it up as it cooks, until it starts to brown and liquid has evaporated.
5. Add the vegetables back to the pan along with the basil and cook another minute more. Stir in sauce until all Ingredients are mixed well. Cook, stirring 2 minutes, or until most of the sauce is absorbed. Serve immediately.

Nutrition Facts Per Serving

Calories 214 Total Carbs 7g Net Carbs 6g Protein 23g Fat 11g Sugar 5g Fiber 1g

Peppered Duck Breasts with Grilled Plums

Prep time: 10 minutes, Cook time: 20 minutes, Serves: 6

Ingredients:

4 (12-14 oz.) boneless Muscovy duck breast halves, trim off excess fat

6 firm purple plums, halved, pitted

4 tsp fresh thyme, chopped.

What you'll need from store cupboard:

1 tbsp. extra-virgin olive oil

2 tsp fresh ground

black pepper, divided

1 ½ tsp salt, divided

½ tsp Splenda

Instructions:

1. Heat grill to med-high heat.
2. With a sharp knife, score skin of duck in crisscross pattern, being careful not to cut the meat. Sprinkle both sides with 1 teaspoon thyme, 1 teaspoon pepper and 1 teaspoon salt. Cover and chill.
3. In a large bowl, toss plums with olive oil, Splenda, 1 teaspoon thyme, remaining pepper, and ½ teaspoon salt.
4. Place plums, cut side down, on grill and cook until grill marks appear and plums start to soften, about 4 minutes. Flip over and grill another 4 minutes, until soft but they still retain their shape. Transfer to bowl and cover with foil.
5. Heat two large skillets over med-high heat. Add 2 breasts per pan, skin side down. Cook until skin is crisp and most of the fat is rendered off, about 7 minutes. Flip over and cook to desired doneness, duck should be served rare, so about 6-8 minutes.
6. Transfer duck to a cutting board and let rest 5 minutes. Slice the duck in thin slices and arrange on plates. Place 2 plum halves alongside the duck. Drizzle juice from the bowl over the duck and sprinkle with remaining thyme. Serve.

Nutrition Facts Per Serving

Calories 346 Total Carbs 9g Net Carbs 8g Protein 50g Fat 12g Sugar 7g Fiber 1g

Spicy Grilled Turkey Breast

Prep time: 15 minutes, Cook time: 1 ½ hours, Serves: 14

Ingredients:

5 lb. turkey breast, bone in

What you'll need from store cupboard:

1 cup low sodium chicken broth

¼ cup vinegar

¼ cup jalapeno pepper jelly

2 tbsp. Splenda brown sugar

2 tbsp. olive oil

1 tbsp. salt

2 tsp cinnamon

1 tsp cayenne pepper

½ tsp ground mustard

Nonstick cooking spray

Instructions:

1. Heat grill to medium heat. Spray rack with cooking spray. Place a drip pan on the grill for indirect heat.
2. In a small bowl, combine Splenda brown sugar with seasonings.
3. Carefully loosen the skin on the turkey from both sides with your fingers. Spread half the spice mix on the turkey. Secure the skin to the underneath with toothpicks and spread remaining spice mix on the outside.
4. Place the turkey over the drip pan and grill 30 minutes.
5. In a small saucepan, over medium heat, combine broth, vinegar, jelly, and oil. Cook and stir 2 minutes until jelly is completely melted. Reserve ½ cup of the mixture.
6. Baste turkey with some of the jelly mixture. Cook 1-1 ½ hours, basting every 15 minutes, until done, when thermometer reaches 170 degrees.
7. Cover and let rest 10 minutes. Discard the skin. Brush with reserved jelly mixture and slice and serve.

Nutrition Facts Per Serving

Calories 314 Total Carbs 5g Protein 35g Fat 14g Sugar 5g Fiber 0g

Turkey Noodle Casserole

Prep time: 15 minutes, Cook time: 45 minutes, Serves: 4

Ingredients:

2 cup turkey breast, cooked and cubed	1 cup fat free cottage cheese
10 oz. spinach, thaw and squeeze dry	¾ cup mozzarella cheese, grated

What you'll need from store cupboard:

Homemade Noodles, (chapter 15)	1/8 tsp garlic salt
1 can low fat condensed cream of chicken soup	1/8 tsp rosemary
	1/8 tsp paprika
	Nonstick cooking spray

Instructions:

1. Heat oven to 350 degrees. Spray a 2-quart casserole dish with cooking spray.
2. In a large bowl combine turkey, soup, and seasonings.
3. In a separate bowl combine spinach, cottage cheese, and half the mozzarella cheese.
4. Place ½ the noodles in the prepared dish. Add half the turkey mixture and half the spinach mixture. Repeat.
5. Cover with foil and bake 35 minutes. Uncover and sprinkle remaining cheese over top. Bake 10-15 minutes longer until edges are lightly browned.
6. Let rest 5 minutes before sprinkling with paprika. Serve.

Nutrition Facts Per Serving

Calories 267 Total Carbs 12g Net Carbs 10g Protein 26g Fat 8g Sugar 4g Fiber 2g

Turkey & Pepper Skillet

Prep time: 5 minutes, Cook time: 25 minutes, Serves: 4

Ingredients:

4 turkey cutlets, ¼-inch thick	tomatoes, fire-roasted
1 red bell pepper, cut into strips	2 tbsp. extra-virgin olive oil, divided
1 yellow bell pepper, cut into strips	2 tsp red wine vinegar
½ large sweet onion, sliced	1 tsp salt, divided
What you'll need from store cupboard	½ teaspoon Italian seasoning
14 oz. can crushed	¼ teaspoon black pepper

Instructions:

1. Season turkey with ½ teaspoon salt. Heat 1 tablespoon oil in a large skillet over med-high heat. Add turkey, 2 cutlets at a time, and cook 1-3 minutes, then flip and cook until done, 1-2 more minutes. Transfer to a plate and keep warm while you cook the other 2 cutlets.
2. Add the onion, peppers, and remaining salt to the skillet. Cover and cook, stirring frequently, until vegetables are soft, about 5-7 minutes.
3. Add seasoning and pepper, and cook, stirring, 30 seconds. Add vinegar, and cook, stirring, until liquid has almost evaporated completely. Add tomatoes and bring to a simmer, stirring frequently.
4. Add the turkey back to the skillet, reduce heat to med-low, and cook, turning cutlets to coat with sauce, 1-2 minutes. Serve garnished with fresh chopped basil if desired.

Nutrition Facts Per Serving

Calories 245 Total Carbs 14g Net Carbs 19g Protein 31g Fat 9g Sugar 9g Fiber 4g

Turkey Roulade

Prep time: 20 minutes, Cook time: 40 minutes, serves; 8

Ingredients:

4 8 oz. turkey cutlets	1 cup mushrooms, diced
5 oz. spinach, thaw and squeeze dry	½ cup onion, diced fine
1 egg, beaten	
1 cup tart apple, peel and dice	2 tbsp. lemon juice
	2 tsp lemon zest

What you'll need from store cupboard:

½ cup bread crumbs	1/8 tsp nutmeg
2 tsp olive oil	Nonstick cooking spray
¾ tsp salt, divided	
¼ tsp pepper	

Instructions:

1. Heat oven to 375 degrees. Spray 11x7-inch baking pan with cooking spray.
2. Heat oil in a large skillet over med-high heat. Add apple, mushrooms, and onion and cook until tender.
3. Remove from heat and stir in spinach, juice, zest, nutmeg, and ¼ teaspoon salt.
4. Cut the cutlets down the center to within ½ inch of the bottom. Open them so they lay flat and flatten to ¼-inch thickness. Sprinkle with salt and pepper.
5. Spread spinach mixture over cutlets leaving 1 inch around the edges. Roll up and tie closed with butcher string.
6. Place bread crumbs in a shallow dish. Dip each roulade in the egg then roll in bread crumbs. Place seam side down in prepared dish.
7. Bake 40-45 minutes or until turkey is cooked through. Let stand 5 minutes. Cut away the string and serve.

Nutrition Facts Per Serving
Calories 262 Total Carbs 10g Net Carbs 8g Protein 36g Fat 8g Sugar 4g Fiber 2g

Zesty Chicken & Asparagus Pasta

Prep time: 10 minutes, Cook time: 15 minutes, Serves: 4

Ingredients:

2 chicken breasts, boneless, skinless, cut in 1-inch pieces	½ cup half-n-half
	½ cup mozzarella cheese, grated
1 lb. asparagus, trim ends and cut in 2-inch pieces	Juice and zest of one lemon
	3 tbsp. margarine

What you'll need from store cupboard:

½ recipe homemade pasta, (chapter 14) cook and drain	fine
	1 tsp garlic powder
2/3 cup reduced fat parmesan cheese	½ tsp oregano
	½ tsp oregano
1½ tbsp. olive oil	¼ tsp thyme
1½ tbsp. garlic, diced	Salt and black pepper, to taste

Instructions:

1. Heat oil in a large skillet, over med-high heat. Add the chicken and salt and pepper to taste. Stir in oregano and cook 5 minutes, stirring occasionally until chicken is cooked through. Add 1 teaspoon diced garlic and cook 1 minute more. Transfer to plate.
2. Add margarine to the skillet and let melt. Add remaining garlic and asparagus and cook 1 minute, or until asparagus starts to turn bright green.
3. Whisk in the remaining Ingredients. Cook, stirring frequently, until cheese melts and sauce thickens. Add the pasta and chicken, toss to coat and cook until heated through. Serve garnished with more parmesan cheese and chopped parsley if desired.

Nutrition Facts Per Serving
Calories 455 Total Carbs 15g Net Carbs 11g Protein 36g Fat 29g Sugar 6g Fiber 4g

Turkey Enchiladas

Prep time: 15 minutes, Cook time: 35 minutes, Serves: 8

Ingredients:

3 cup turkey, cooked and cut in pieces
1 onion, diced
1 bell pepper, diced
1 cup fat free sour cream
1 cup reduced fat cheddar cheese, grated

What you'll need from store cupboard:

8 6-inch flour tortillas
14 ½ oz. low sodium chicken broth
¾ cup salsa
3 tbsp. flour
2 tsp olive oil
1 ¼ tsp coriander
¼ tsp pepper
Nonstick cooking spray

Instructions:

1. Spray a large saucepan with cooking spray and heat oil over med-high heat. Add onion and bell pepper and cook until tender.
2. Sprinkle with flour, coriander and pepper and stir until blended. Slowly stir in broth. Bring to a boil and cook, stirring, 2 minutes or until thickened.
3. Remove from heat and stir in sour cream and ¾ cup cheese.
4. Heat oven to 350 degrees. Spray a 13x9-inch pan with cooking spray.
5. In a large bowl, combine turkey, salsa, and 1 cup of cheese mixture. Spoon 1/3 cup mixture down middle of each tortilla and roll up. Place seam side down in prepared dish.
6. Pour remaining cheese mixture over top of enchiladas. Cover and bake 20 minutes. Uncover and sprinkle with remaining cheese. Bake another 5-10 minutes until cheese is melted and starts to brown.

Nutrition Facts Per Serving

Calories 304 Total Carbs 29g Net Carbs 27g Protein 23g Fat 10g Sugar 5g Fiber 2g

Chapter 11 - Fish and Seafood Recipe

Cajun Catfish

Prep time: 5 minutes, Cook time: 15 minutes, Serves: 4

Ingredients:

4 (8 oz.) catfish fillets

What you'll need from store cupboard:

2 tbsp. olive oil
2 tsp garlic salt
2 tsp thyme
2 tsp paprika
½ tsp cayenne
pepper
½ tsp red hot sauce
¼ tsp black pepper
Nonstick cooking spray

Instructions:

1. Heat oven to 450 degrees. Spray a 9x13-inch baking dish with cooking spray.
2. In a small bowl whisk together everything but catfish. Brush both sides of fillets, using all the spice mix.
3. Bake 10-13 minutes or until fish flakes easily with a fork. Serve.

Nutrition Facts Per Serving

Calories 366 Total Carbs 0g Protein 35g Fat 24g Sugar 0g Fiber 0g

Cajun Flounder & Tomatoes

Prep time: 10 minutes, Cook time: 15 minutes, Serves: 4

Ingredients:

4 flounder fillets
2 ½ cups tomatoes, diced
¾ cup onion, diced
¾ cup green bell pepper, diced

What you'll need from store cupboard:

2 cloves garlic, diced fine
1 tbsp. Cajun
seasoning
1 tsp olive oil

Instructions:

1. Heat oil in a large skillet over med-high heat. Add onion and garlic and cook 2 minutes, or until soft. Add tomatoes, peppers and spices, and cook 2-3 minutes until tomatoes soften.
2. Lay fish over top. Cover, reduce heat to medium and cook, 5-8 minutes, or until fish flakes easily with a fork. Transfer fish to serving plates and top with sauce.

Nutrition Facts Per Serving

Calories 194 Total Carbs 8g Net Carbs 6g Protein 32g Fat 3g Sugar 5g Fiber 2g

Baked Salmon with Garlic Parmesan Topping

Prep time: 5 minutes, Cook time: 20 minutes, Serves: 4

Ingredients:

1 lb. wild caught salmon filets
2 tbsp. margarine

What you'll need from store cupboard:

¼ cup reduced fat parmesan cheese, grated
¼ cup light mayonnaise
2-3 cloves garlic, diced
2 tbsp. parsley
Salt and pepper

Instructions:

1. Heat oven to 350 and line a baking pan with parchment paper.
2. Place salmon on pan and season with salt and pepper.
3. In a medium skillet, over medium heat, melt butter. Add garlic and cook, stirring 1 minute.
4. Reduce heat to low and add remaining Ingredients. Stir until everything is melted and combined.
5. Spread evenly over salmon and bake 15 minutes for thawed fish or 20 for frozen. Salmon is done when it flakes easily with a fork. Serve.

Nutrition Facts Per Serving

Calories 408 Total Carbs 4g Protein 41g Fat 24g Sugar 1g Fiber 0g

Pan Seared Trout & Salsa

Prep time: 5 minutes, Cook time: 10 minutes, Serves: 6

Ingredients:

6 6 oz. trout filets
6 lemon slices

What you'll need from store cupboard:

4 tbsp. olive oil
¾ tsp salt
½ tsp pepper
Italian-Style Salsa, (chapter 16)

Instructions:

1. Sprinkle filets with salt and pepper.
2. Heat oil in a large nonstick skillet over med-high heat. Cook trout, 3 filets at a time, 2-3 minutes per side, or fish flakes easily with a fork. Repeat with remaining filets.
3. Serve topped with salsa and a slice of lemon.

Nutrition Facts Per Serving

Calories 320 Total Carbs 2g Protein 30g Fat 21g Sugar 1g Fiber 0g

Jambalaya

Prep time: 10 minutes, Cook time: 40 minutes, Serves: 6

Ingredients:

1 lb. raw shrimp, peel & devein
14 oz. Andouille sausage, cut into 1-inch pieces
1 medium cauliflower, riced
4 stalks celery, diced
½ white onion, diced
½ red bell pepper, diced
4 tbsp. margarine

What you'll need from store cupboard:

2 cups low sodium chicken broth
½ can tomatoes & green chilies
3 cloves garlic, diced fine
2 tsp garlic powder
2 tsp Old Bay
1 ½ tsp onion powder
1 tsp thyme
1 tsp oregano
1 tsp basil
1/2 tsp cayenne pepper

Instructions:

1. Place large stock pot over med-high heat.
2. In a small bowl, stir together garlic powder, onion powder, thyme, oregano, basil, Old Bay, and cayenne until combined.
3. Add 2 tablespoons margarine to the stock pot and let melt.
4. Add the riced cauliflower with 2 teaspoons of the spice mixture. Cook, stirring frequently, about 5 minutes. Transfer to a bowl.
5. Add the remaining margarine to the stock pot and melt. Then add the sausage and cook 5 minutes, stirring to brown all sides.
6. Add onion, celery, and pepper and stir to combine. Cook about 3 minutes until vegetables start to get soft.
7. Add the garlic and cook, stirring, 1 minute. Add the cauliflower and combine then add half the spice mixture and tomatoes, simmer 2-3 minutes.
8. Pour in the broth and bring to a boil, cook 8-10 minutes.
9. Season shrimp with remaining spice mixture and add to the pot, cook 3-4 minutes just until shrimp turn pink. Serve.

Nutrition Facts Per Serving

Calories 428 Total Carbs 13g Net Carbs 10g Protein 33g Fat 27g Sugar 4g Fiber 3g

Baked Seafood Casserole

Prep time: 20 minutes, Cook time: 30 minutes, serves 6

Ingredients:

12 oz. shrimp, peeled and deveined

12 oz. cod, cut into 1-inch squares

2 medium leeks, white part only, cut into matchstick pieces

2 stalks celery, diced

1 cup half-n-half

4 tbsp. margarine

What you'll need from store cupboard:

1 cup dry white wine

1 cup water

½ cup reduced fat parmesan cheese, grated

¼ cup super fine almond flour

2 small bay leaves whole

2 ½ tsp Old Bay Seasoning

½ tsp xanthan gum

¼ tsp sea salt

Instructions:

1. Heat oven to 400 degrees.
2. Poach the seafood: In a large, heavy pot, combine wine, water, bay leaves, and ½ teaspoon Old bay. Bring just to boiling over med-high heat. Reduce heat to low and simmer 3 minutes.
3. Add shrimp and cook until they start to turn pink. Transfer to a bowl. Repeat for cod.
4. Turn heat back to med-high heat and continue simmering poaching liquid until it is reduced to about 1 cup. Remove from heat, strain and save for later.
5. In a separate large sauce pan melt 2 tablespoons margarine over med-high heat. Add leeks and celery and season with salt. Cook, stirring occasionally, until vegetables are soft.
6. In an 8-inch square baking dish, layer vegetables and seafood.
7. In the same saucepan you used for the vegetables, melt 1 tablespoon of margarine. Stir in xanthan gum and stir to coat. After xanthan is coated gradually stir in reserved poaching liquid. Bring to a simmer scraping up the browned bits on the bottom of the pan.
8. When sauce starts to thicken, stir in half-n-half. Bring back to a simmer and cook, stirring frequently, until the sauce has the same texture as gravy. Taste and adjust seasoning as desired. Pour over seafood in the baking dish.
9. In a food processor, or blender, combine the almond flour, parmesan, 2 teaspoons Old Bay, and 1 tablespoon margarine. Process until thoroughly combined. Sprinkle over casserole and bake 20 minutes or until topping is brown and crisp. Serve.

Nutrition Facts Per Serving

Calories 344 Total Carbs 9g Net Carbs 8g Protein 30g Fat 17g Sugar 2g Fiber 1g

Monterey Crab Quiche

Prep time: 20 minutes, Cook time: 45 minutes, Serves: 16

Ingredients:

½ lb. lump crab meat

8 egg whites, dived

4 eggs

2 cup low fat cottage cheese

2 cup Monterey Jack cheese, grated

½ cup onion, diced

1 tbsp. margarine

2 9-inch pie crusts

What you'll need from store cupboard:

2 4 oz. cans green chilies, chopped

1/3 cup flour

2 cloves garlic, diced

fine

¾ tsp baking powder

¼ tsp salt

Instructions:

1. Heat oven to 400 degrees.
2. Melt margarine in a small skillet over med-low heat. Add onion and cook until tender. Add garlic and cook 1 minute more.
3. In a large bowl, combine 6 egg whites, eggs, cottage cheese, 1 ½ cups cheese, chilies, crab, flour, baking powder, onion mixture, and salt.
4. In a separate large bowl, beat remaining egg whites until stiff peaks form. Fold into crab mixture. Pour into pie crusts.
5. Bake 10 minutes, reduce heat to 350 degrees and bake 30 minutes. Sprinkle with remaining cheese and bake 5 minutes more, or a knife inserted in centers comes out clean.
6. Let cool 10 minutes before slicing and serving.

Nutrition Facts Per Serving

Calories 251 Total Carbs 22g Net Carbs 18g Protein 14g Fat 13g Sugar 7g Fiber 4g

Spanish Halibut

Prep time: 10 minutes, Cook time: 40 minutes, Serves: 6

Ingredients:

6 6 oz. halibut filets, pat dry

6 thick slices tomato

1 onion, sliced thin

1 cup mushrooms, sliced thin

4 ½ tsp margarine

What you'll need from store cupboard:

½ cup bread crumbs

¼ cup white wine

2 tbsp. pimientos, diced

1 tbsp. olive oil

1 ¼ tsp salt

¼ tsp mace

¼ tsp cayenne pepper

¼ tsp black pepper

Instructions:

1. Heat oven to 350 degrees. Brush the bottom of 13x9-inch baking dish with the oil.
2. Place the onion and pimiento on the bottom of prepared dish.
3. In a small bowl, combine seasonings and sprinkle on both sides of the halibut.
4. Place halibut in the baking dish. Top each filet with a slice of tomato then sprinkle with mushrooms and green onions. Pour wine over all.
5. Melt margarine in a skillet over medium heat. Add bread crumbs and cook, stirring, until light brown. Sprinkle over fish.
6. Cover with foil and bake 20 minutes. Uncover and bake 20-25 minutes longer or fish flakes easily with fork. Serve.

Nutrition Facts Per Serving

Calories 205 Total Carbs 13g Net Carbs 11g Protein 22g Fat 6g Sugar 4g Fiber 2g

Seafood Enchiladas

Prep time: 20 minutes, Cook time: 1 hour, Serves: 8

Ingredients:

1¼ lb. medium shrimp, raw, peel & devein

8 oz. fresh halibut, cod, tilapia, or sea bass

2 poblano peppers, stemmed, seeded, & diced

1 red bell pepper, diced

1 onion, diced

1 cup light sour cream

¾ cup skim milk

½ cup reduced fat cream cheese, soft

½ cup green onions, sliced thin

What you'll need from store cupboard:

8 (6") low-carb whole wheat flour tortillas

5 cups water

2 cloves garlic, diced fine

2 tbsp. flour

2 tsp sunflower oil

¼ tsp salt

¼ tsp black pepper

Nonstick cooking spray

Instructions:

1. Rinse shrimp and fish then pat dry with paper towels.
2. Heat oven to 350 degrees. Spry a 3-quart rectangular baking dish with cooking spray.
3. Add water to a large saucepan and bring to boiling over med-high heat. Add shrimp and cook until shrimp turn pink, 1-3 minutes. Drain, rinse with cold water, and chop.
4. Place a steamer insert into a deep skillet with a tight fitting lid. Add water to just below the insert and bring to a boil. Place fish in the insert, cover and steam 4-6 minutes, or until fish flakes easily with a fork.
5. Flake the fish into bite-size pieces and set aside.
6. Heat oil in a large nonstick skillet over medium heat. Add bell pepper, poblanos, and onion. Cook 5-10 minutes, or until vegetables are tender. Stir in garlic and 1 minute more. Remove from heat and add shrimp and fish.
7. Wrap tortillas in foil, making sure it's tight, and place in the oven until heated through, about 10 minutes.
8. In a medium bowl, beat cream cheese until smooth. Beat in sour cream, ¼ teaspoon salt and pepper. Slowly beat in the milk until smooth. Stir ½ cup sauce into the fish and shrimp mixture.
9. To assemble, spoon shrimp mixture on one side of the tortillas and roll up. Place, seam side down, in prepare baking dish. Pour remaining sauce over the top.
10. Cover with foil, and bake 35 minutes, or until heated through. Let rest 5 minutes before serving. Garnish with chopped green onions.

Nutrition Facts Per Serving

Calories 458 Total Carbs 38g Net Carbs 17g Protein 34g Fat 17g Sugar 4g Fiber 21g

BBQ Oysters with Bacon

Prep time: 20 mins, Cook time: 10 mins, Serves: 2

Ingredients:

1 dozen fresh oysters, shucked and left on the half shell	bacon, cut into thin strips
3 slices thick cut	Juice of ½ lemon

What you'll need from store cupboard:

1/3 cup sugar-free ketchup (chapter 16)	Dash of hot sauce
¼ cup Worcestershire sauce	Lime wedges for garnish
1 tsp horseradish	Rock salt

Instructions:

1. Heat oven to broil. Line a shallow baking dish with rock salt. Place the oysters snugly into the salt.
2. In a large bowl, combine remaining Ingredients and mix well.
3. Add a dash of Worcestershire to each oyster then top with bacon mixture. Cook 10 minutes, or until bacon is crisp. Serve with lime wedges.

Nutrition Facts Per Serving
Calories 234 Total Carbs 10g Protein 13g Fat 13g Sugar 9g Fiber 0g

Fisherman's Pie

Prep time: 15 minutes, Cook time: 25 minutes, Serves: 4

Ingredients:

12 shrimp, peel & devein	cauliflower puree, (chapter 14)
8 oz. cod, cut in 1-inch pieces	½ cup onion, diced
4 oz. salmon, cut in 1-inch pieces	¼ cup heavy cream
1 slice bacon	2 tbsp. butter
4 cup cheesy	1 tbsp. fresh parsley, diced

What you'll need from store cupboard:

1 cup low sodium vegetable broth	¼ tsp celery salt
½ cup dry white wine	Salt & pepper, to taste
1 clove garlic, diced fine	Nonstick cooking spray

Instructions:

1. Heat oven to 400 degrees. Spray a large casserole dish, or 4 small ones with cooking spray.
2. Melt butter in a medium saucepan over medium heat. Add onion and cook until soft. Add the garlic and cook 1 minute more.
3. Pour in the wine and broth and cook 5 minutes.
4. Stir in cream, bacon, and celery salt and simmer 5 minutes, until bacon is cooked through and most of the fat has rendered off. Remove the slice of bacon, chop it up and add it back to the pot.
5. Add the seafood, parsley, salt, and pepper to taste and simmer 2-3 minutes. Transfer mixture to prepared casserole dish.
6. Place the cauliflower in a large Ziploc bag, or pastry bag, and snip off one corner. Pipe the cauliflower in small rosettes to cover the top. Bake 8-10 minutes, or until heated through and top is lightly browned, you may need to broil it for 1-2 minutes to reach the browned color. Serve.

Nutrition Facts Per Serving
Calories 338 Total Carbs 10g Net Carbs 7g Protein 38g Fat 14g Sugar 3g Fiber 3g

Cajun Shrimp & Roasted Vegetables

Prep time: 5 minutes, Cook time: 15 minutes, Serves: 4

Ingredients:

1 lb. large shrimp, peeled and deveined	½ bunch asparagus, cut into thirds
2 zucchini, sliced	2 red bell pepper, cut into chunks
2 yellow squash, sliced	

What you'll need from store cupboard:

2 tbsp. olive oil	Salt & pepper, to taste
2 tbsp. Cajun Seasoning	

Instructions:

1. Heat oven to 400 degrees.
2. Combine shrimp and vegetables in a large bowl. Add oil and seasoning and toss to coat.
3. Spread evenly in a large baking sheet and bake 15-20 minutes, or until vegetables are tender. Serve.

Nutrition Facts Per Serving
Calories 251 Total Carbs 13g Net Carbs 9g Protein 30g Fat 9g Sugar 6g Fiber 4g

Cilantro Lime Grilled Shrimp

Prep time: 5 minutes, Cook time: 5 minutes, Serves: 6

Ingredients:

1 ½ lbs. large shrimp raw, peeled, deveined with tails on
Juice and zest of 1

lime
2 tbsp. fresh cilantro chopped

What you'll need from store cupboard:

¼ cup olive oil
2 cloves garlic, diced fine
1 tsp smoked paprika

¼ tsp cumin
1/2 teaspoon salt
¼ tsp cayenne pepper

Instructions:

1. Place the shrimp in a large Ziploc bag.
2. Mix remaining Ingredients in a small bowl and pour over shrimp. Let marinate 20-30 minutes.
3. Heat up the grill. Skewer the shrimp and cook 2-3 minutes, per side, just until they turn pick. Be careful not to overcook them. Serve garnished with cilantro.

Nutrition Facts Per Serving

Calories 317 Total Carbs 4g Protein 39g Fat 15g Sugar 0g Fiber 0g

Blackened Shrimp

Prep time: 5 minutes, Cook time: 5 minutes, Serves: 4

Ingredients:

1 ½ lbs. shrimp, peel & devein
4 lime wedges

4 tbsp. cilantro, chopped

What you'll need from store cupboard:

4 cloves garlic, diced
1 tbsp. chili powder
1 tbsp. paprika
1 tbsp. olive oil
2 tsp Splenda brown sugar

1 tsp cumin
1 tsp oregano
1 tsp garlic powder
1 tsp salt
½ tsp pepper

Instructions:

1. In a small bowl combine seasonings and Splenda brown sugar.
2. Heat oil in a skillet over med-high heat. Add shrimp, in a single layer, and cook 1-2 minutes per side.
3. Add seasonings, and cook, stirring, 30 seconds. Serve garnished with cilantro and a lime wedge.

Nutrition Facts Per Serving

Calories 252 Total Carbs 7g Net Carbs 6g Protein 39g Fat 7g Sugar 2g Fiber 1g

Coconut Shrimp

Prep time: 15 minutes, Cook time: 20 minutes, Serves: 6

Ingredients:

2 lbs. jumbo shrimp, peel & devein & pat dry
2 eggs

What you'll need from store cupboard:

¾ cup unsweetened coconut
¾ cup coconut flour
½ cup sunflower oil
1 tbsp. Creole seasoning

2 tsp Splenda
1 tsp salt
½ tsp garlic powder
Sriracha Dipping Sauce, (chapter 16)

Instructions:

1. Heat oil in a pot over med-high heat, you need about 3 inches of oil.
2. In a medium bowl, combine coconut, flour, Creole seasoning, salt, garlic powder, and Splenda.
3. In a small bowl beat the eggs.
4. Dip shrimp in the eggs then the coconut mixture to coat. Cook, 1/3 of the shrimp at a time, 2-3 minutes, or until golden brown. Transfer to paper towel lined plate.
5. Serve hot with Sriracha dipping sauce, or your favorite dipping sauce.

Nutrition Facts Per Serving

Calories 316 Total Carbs 10g Net Carbs 7g Protein 29g Fat 17g Sugar 6g Fiber 3g

Grilled Tuna Steaks

Prep time: 5 minutes, Cook time: 10 minutes, Serves: 6

Ingredients:

6 6 oz. tuna steaks
3 tbsp. fresh basil, diced

What you'll need from store cupboard:

4 ½ tsp olive oil
¾ tsp salt
¼ tsp pepper

Nonstick cooking spray

Instructions:

1. Heat grill to medium heat. Spray rack with cooking spray.
2. Drizzle both sides of the tuna with oil. Sprinkle with basil, salt and pepper.
3. Place on grill and cook 5 minutes per side, tuna should be slightly pink in the center. Serve.

Nutrition Facts Per Serving

Calories 343 Total Carbs 0g Protein 51g Fat 14g Sugar 0g Fiber 0g

Crab Cakes

Prep time: 10 minutes, Cook time: 10 minutes, Serves: 8 (2 crab cakes per serving)
Ingredients:

1 lb. lump blue crabmeat	1 tbsp. fresh parsley, chopped fine
1 tbsp. red bell pepper, diced fine	2 eggs
1 tbsp. green bell pepper, diced fine	¼ tsp fresh lemon juice

What you'll need from store cupboard:

¼ cup + 1 tbsp. lite mayonnaise	powder
¼ cup Dijon mustard	1 tbsp.
2 tbsp. sunflower oil	Worcestershire sauce
1 tbsp. baking	1 ½ tsp Old Bay

Instructions:

1. In a small bowl, whisk together ¼ cup mayonnaise, Dijon mustard, Worcestershire, and lemon juice until combined. Cover and chill until ready to serve.
2. In a large bowl, mix crab, bell peppers, parsley, eggs, 1 tablespoon mayonnaise, baking powder, and Old Bay seasoning until Ingredients are combined.
3. Heat oil in a large skillet over med-high heat. Once oil is hot, drop 2 tablespoons crab mixture into hot skillet. They will be loose but as the egg cooks they will hold together.
4. Cook 2 minutes or until firm, then flip and cook another minutes. Transfer to serving plate. Serve with mustard dipping sauce.

Nutrition Facts Per Serving
Calories 96 Total Carbs 3g Protein 12g Fat 4g Sugar 1g Fiber 0g

Crab Frittata

Prep time: 10 minutes, Cook time: 50 minutes, Serves: 4
Ingredients:

4 eggs	1 cup half-n-half
2 cups lump crabmeat	1 cup green onions, diced

What you'll need from store cupboard:

1 cup reduced fat parmesan cheese, grated	1 tsp smoked paprika
1 tsp salt	1 tsp Italian seasoning
1 tsp pepper	Nonstick cooking spray

Instructions:

1. Heat oven to 350 degrees. Spray an 8-inch springform pan, or pie plate with cooking spray.
2. In a large bowl, whisk together the eggs and half-n-half. Add seasonings and parmesan cheese, stir to mix.
3. Stir in the onions and crab meat. Pour into prepared pan and bake 35-40 minutes, or eggs are set and top is lightly browned.
4. Let cool 10 minutes, then slice and serve warm or at room temperature.

Nutrition Facts Per Serving
Calories 276 Total Carbs 5g Net Carbs 4g Protein 25g Fat 17g Sugar 1g Fiber 1g

Shrimp in Coconut Curry

Prep time: 10 minutes, Cook time: 25 minutes, Serves: 4
Ingredients:

1 lb. extra-large shrimp, peel & devein	2 tbsp. fresh lemon juice
1 onion, diced fine	1 tbsp. fresh ginger, grated
1 ¾ cup coconut milk, unsweetened	

What you'll need from store cupboard:

14.5 oz. can tomatoes, diced	1 tsp curry powder
3 cloves garlic, diced fine	1 tsp salt, or to taste
1 tbsp. coconut oil	½ tsp turmeric
2 tsp coriander	¾ tsp black pepper
	¼ tsp cayenne

Instructions:

1. In a medium bowl combine lemon juice, ¼ teaspoon salt, ¼ teaspoon pepper and the cayenne pepper. Add shrimp and toss to coat. Cover and refrigerate at least 10 minutes.
2. Heat the oil in a large, deep, skillet over med-high heat. Add onion and cook until it starts to soften, about 2-3 minutes. Add remaining seasonings and cook 1 minute more.
3. Add tomatoes with juices and coconut milk, stir and bring to boil. Cook, stirring occasionally, 5 minutes.
4. Add shrimp and marinade and cook till shrimp turn pink about 2-3 minutes. Serve.

Nutrition Facts Per Serving
Calories 448 total Carbs 12g Net carbs 9g Protein 29g fat 30g Sugar 5g fiber 3g

Crock Pot Fish & Tomatoes

Prep time: 10 mins, Cook time: 2 hours 30 mins, Serves: 4

Ingredients:

1 lb. cod   1 small onion, diced
1 bell pepper, diced

What you'll need from store cupboard:

15 oz. can tomatoes,   fine
diced   ½ tsp basil
1/3 cup low-sodium   ½ tsp oregano
vegetable broth   ½ tsp salt
1 clove garlic, diced   ¼ tsp pepper

Instructions:

1. Place the onion, bell pepper, tomatoes, and garlic in the crock pot. Stir to mix.
2. Place fish on top. Sprinkle with herbs and seasonings. Pour broth over top.
3. Cover and cook on high 1-2 hours, or low 2-4 hours.

Nutrition Facts Per Serving

Calories 165 Total Carbs 11g Net Carbs 8g Protein 28g Fat 1g Sugar 6g Fiber 3g

Crunchy Lemon Shrimp

Prep time: 5 minutes, Cook time: 10 minutes, Serves: 4

Ingredients:

1 lb. raw shrimp,   chopped
peeled and deveined   2 tbsp. lemon juice,
2 tbsp. Italian   divided
parsley, roughly

What you'll need from store cupboard:

⅔ cup panko bread   divided
crumbs   Salt and pepper, to
2½ tbsp. olive oil,   taste

Instructions:

1. Heat oven to 400 degrees.
2. Place the shrimp evenly in a baking dish and sprinkle with salt and pepper. Drizzle on 1 tablespoon lemon juice and 1 tablespoon of olive oil. Set aside.
3. In a medium bowl, combine parsley, remaining lemon juice, bread crumbs, remaining olive oil, and ¼ tsp each of salt and pepper. Layer the panko mixture evenly on top of the shrimp.
4. Bake 8-10 minutes or until shrimp are cooked through and the panko is golden brown.

Nutrition Facts Per Serving

Calories 283 Total Carbs 15g Net Carbs 14g Protein 28g Fat 12g Sugar 1g Fiber 1g

Dill Smoked Salmon over Noodles

Prep time: 10 minutes, Cook time: 10 minutes, Serves: 4

Ingredients:

6 oz. smoked salmon,   ¼ cup half-n-half
chopped   3 tbsp. margarine
Juice from 1/2 a   2 tbsp. fresh dill,
lemon   diced

What you'll need from store cupboard:

Homemade noodles,   1 tbsp. olive oil
chapter 14   2 cloves garlic, diced
½ cup low sodium   fine
chicken broth   Salt & pepper, to
½ cup dry white wine   taste

Instructions:

1. Heat oil and margarine in a large skillet over med-high heat. Add garlic and cook 30 seconds.
2. Add broth, wine, and lemon juice. Cook until sauce is reduced by half, about 4 minutes.
3. Stir in the half-n-half and noodles and cook 2 minutes, or until noodles are done.
4. Stir in the salmon and salt and pepper to taste. Serve garnished with the fresh dill.

Nutrition Facts Per Serving

Calories 273 Total Carbs 4g Protein 14g Fat 21g Sugar 0g Fiber 0g

Shrimp & Artichoke Skillet

Prep time: 5 minutes, Cook time: 10 minutes, Serves: 4

Ingredients:

1 ½ cups shrimp,   2 12 oz. jars
peel & devein   artichoke hearts,
2 shallots, diced   drain & rinse
1 tbsp. margarine   2 cups white wine
What you'll need   2 cloves garlic, diced
from store cupboard   fine

Instructions:

1. Melt margarine in a large skillet over med-high heat. Add shallot and garlic and cook until they start to brown, stirring frequently.
2. Add artichokes and cook 5 minutes. Reduce heat and add wine. Cook 3 minutes, stirring occasionally.
3. Add the shrimp and cook just until they turn pink. Serve.

Nutrition Facts Per Serving

Calories 487 Total Carbs 26g Net Carbs 17g Protein 64g Fat 5g Sugar 3g Fiber 9g

Paella

Prep time: 25 minutes, Cook time: 35 minutes, Serves: 6

Ingredients:

1 lb. chicken thighs, skinless & boneless	1 medium head cauliflower, grated
1 lb. medium shrimp, raw, peel & devein	1 yellow onion, diced fine
1 dozen mussels, cleaned	1 green bell pepper, sliced into strips
2 chorizo sausages, cut into pieces	1 cup frozen peas

What you'll need from store cupboard:

15 oz. can tomatoes, diced, drain well	2 tsp salt
2 tbsp. extra-virgin olive oil	1 tsp saffron
	½ tsp pepper
2 tsp garlic, diced fine	¼ tsp paprika
	Nonstick cooking spray

Instructions:

1. Heat the oven to broil. Spray a baking dish with cooking spray.
2. Sprinkle salt and pepper on both sides of the chicken and place in baking dish. Bake, about 4 minutes per side, until no longer pink in the middle. Let cool completely.
3. Heat 1 tablespoon of the oil in a medium skillet over medium heat. Add onion, pepper, and garlic. Cook, about 4-5 minutes, stirring frequently, until peppers start to get soft. Transfer to a bowl.
4. Add chorizo to the skillet and cook 2 minutes, stirring frequently. Drain off the fat and add to the vegetables.
5. Once the chicken has cooled, cut into small pieces and add it to the vegetables.
6. In a large saucepot, over medium heat, add the remaining oil. Once it is hot, add the cauliflower and seasonings. Cook 8-10 minutes, until cauliflower is almost tender, stirring frequently.
7. Add the mussels and shrimp and cook until mussels open and shrimp start to turn pink.
8. Add the mixture in the bowl with the tomatoes and peas and stir to combine everything together. Cook another 5 minutes until everything is heated through and all of the mussels have opened. Serve.

Nutrition Facts Per Serving

Calories 423 Total Carbs 21g Net Carbs 15g Protein 46g Fat 18g Sugar 9g Fiber 6g

Seafood Gumbo

Prep time: 5 minutes, Cook time: 3 hours 10 minutes, Serves: 10

Ingredients:

1 ½ lb. raw medium shrimp, peel & devein	10 oz. package frozen cut okra, thawed
½ lb. lump crabmeat	1 cup onion, diced
½ lb. Andouille sausage, cut into ½-inch pieces	1 cup green bell pepper, diced
	½ cup celery, diced

What you'll need from store cupboard:

15 oz. tomatoes, diced	fine
4 cups low sodium beef broth	1 tbsp. white vinegar
2 cups water	1 tbsp. coconut aminos
½ cup cassava flour	1 tbsp. hot sauce
1/3 cup + 1 tbsp. avocado oil	1 1/2 - 2 tsp salt
2 bay leaves	1 tsp Cajun seasoning
1 clove garlic, diced	¼ tsp thyme

Instructions:

1. In a stock pot, heat the avocado oil over med-low heat. Sprinkle in flour and whisk constantly until a smooth paste forms. Continue cooking and whisking, until the roux turns a deep amber color, don't let it burn. This will take about 30 minutes but is the secret to a great gumbo.
2. When roux reaches the amber color, add celery, onion, bell pepper, and garlic. Stir to combine then add sausage. Whisk in 1 cup water and bring to a simmer over medium heat. Cook 15 minutes, or until vegetables start to soften. If too much liquid evaporates add the second cup of water.
3. In a medium saucepan bring broth to a boil. If the second cup of water wasn't used yet, add it here. Stir the hot broth into sausage mixture and whisk well.
4. Stir in aminos, salt, hot sauce, Cajun seasoning, bay leaves, thyme, and tomatoes. Let simmer over med-low heat 2 hours.
5. Heat the remaining tablespoon of oil in a skillet. Add okra and vinegar and cook over medium heat 15 minutes, or until okra is soft and sticky. Stir into gumbo with the shrimp and crab. Reduce heat to low and simmer another 45 minutes. Serve.

Nutrition Facts Per Serving

Calories 254 Total Carbs 13g Net Carbs 10g Protein 28g Fat 10g Sugar 3g Fiber 3g

Crispy Baked Flounder with Green Beans

Prep time: 10 minutes, Cook time: 20 minutes, serves 4

Ingredients:

1 lb. flounder	4 tbsp. margarine
2 cups green beans	8 basil leaves

What you'll need from store cupboard:

1 ¾ oz. pork rinds	Salt and pepper to
½ cup reduced fat	taste
parmesan cheese	Nonstick cooking
3 cloves garlic	spray

Instructions:

1. Heat oven to 350 degrees. Spray a baking dish with cooking spray.
2. Steam green beans until they are almost tender, about 15 minutes, less if you use frozen or canned beans. Lay green beans in the prepared dish.
3. Place the fish filets over the green beans and season with salt and pepper.
4. Place the garlic, basil, pork rinds, and parmesan in a food processor and pulse until mixture resembles crumbs. Sprinkle over fish. Cut margarine into small pieces and place on top.
5. Bake 15-20 minutes or until fish flakes easily with a fork. Serve.

Nutrition Facts Per Serving

Calories 358 Total Carbs 5g Protein 39g Fat 20g Sugar 1g fiber 2g

Garlic Shrimp with Sun Dried Tomatoes

Prep time: 10 minutes, Cook time: 30 minutes, Serves: 4

Ingredients:

½ lb. shrimp, peeled and deveined	tomatoes
4 oz. sun-dried	1 cup half-n-half

What you'll need from store cupboard:

1 cup reduced fat	¼ tsp salt
parmesan cheese	¼ tsp paprika
4 cloves garlic, diced fine	¼ teaspoon crushed red pepper
2 tbsp. olive oil	½ recipe homemade
1 teaspoon dried basil	pasta, cook and drain, (chapter 14)

Instructions:

1. Heat oil in a large skillet over medium heat. Add garlic and tomatoes and cook 1 minute.

2. Add shrimp, sprinkle with salt and paprika, and cook about 2 minutes.
3. Add half-n-half, basil, and crushed red pepper and bring to boil. Reduce heat to simmer. Whisk the parmesan cheese into the hot cream and stir to melt cheese, on low heat.
4. Remove from heat. Add pasta and stir to coat. Serve.

Nutrition Facts Per Serving

Calories 353 Total Carbs 23g Net Carbs 20g Protein 37g Fat 22g Sugar 3g Fiber 3g

Sweet & Spicy Seafood Pasta

Prep time: 10 minutes, Cook time: 10 minutes, Serves: 4

Ingredients:

¼ lb. shrimp, peel & devein	strips
	Juice of 1 lemon
¼ lb. scallops	½ cup fresh
6 oz. Chilean sea bass, cut in 1/2-inch pieces	pineapple, diced
	½ cup flat-leaf parsley, diced
½ white onion, cut in	

What you'll need from store cupboard:

1½ cup white wine	1½ tbsp. salt
¼ cup extra virgin olive oil	¾ tsp red pepper flakes
3 cloves garlic, diced fine	½ recipe Homemade Pasta, (chapter 15)

Instructions:

1. Heat the oil in a large pot over high heat. Add the onion and cook until soft, stirring constantly, about 1 minute.
2. Add the garlic, shrimp, scallops, sea bass and salt. Stir and cook for about another minute.
3. Add the pasta to the pot and toss, making sure each strand is coated with oil. Reduce the heat to medium and add wine, lemon juice and pineapple and continue tossing until the pasta and fish are fully cooked, about 8 minutes.
4. Remove from heat and stir in the parsley and red pepper flakes. Serve immediately.

Nutrition Facts Per Serving

Calories 334 Total Carbs 13g Net Carbs 11g Protein 25g Fat 21g Sugar 6g Fiber 2g

Maple Glazed Salmon

Prep time: 5 minutes, Cook time: 25 minutes, Serves: 8

Ingredients:
3 lb. salmon

What you'll need from store cupboard:

½ cup sugar free maple syrup	2 tbsp. paprika
3 tbsp. Dijon mustard	1 ½ tbsp. Splenda brown sugar
2 tbsp. chili powder	1 ½ tsp salt

Instructions:
1. Heat oven to 375 degrees. Line a large baking sheet with foil, you need enough to fold foil, and seal over the fish.
2. In a small bowl, stir together mustard, chili powder, smoked paprika, Splenda, and salt.
3. Place the salmon on the foil and using the back of a spoon, spread with the mustard paste.
4. Pull the foil up and over the salmon, being careful to not lay the foil on the salmon as the paste will stick to it, and pinch the foil closed like a packet.
5. Bake for 14-15 minutes. Remove from the oven and carefully open the foil, avoiding the escaping steam.
6. Turn oven to broil. Drizzle the salmon with the maple syrup. Broil 2-3 minutes. Serve.

Nutrition Facts Per Serving
Calories 248 Total Carbs 4g Net Carbs 3g Protein 33g Fat 11g Sugar 2g Fiber 1g

Seafood Medley over Pasta

Prep time: 5 minutes, Cook time: 20 minutes, Serves: 6

Ingredients:

24 oz. seafood mix, thaw	¼ cup fresh parsley, diced
1 lemon, cut in wedges	1 onion, diced

What you'll need from store cupboard:

28 oz. can petite tomatoes, diced	fine
2½ cup low-sodium chicken broth	2 tbsp. olive oil
	1 tsp paprika
2/3 cup dry white wine	¼ tsp salt and
	¼ tsp black pepper
4 cloves garlic, diced	1 recipe Homemade Pasta, (chapter 15)

Instructions:

1. Heat oil in a large, deep skillet over med-high heat. Add garlic and cook until fragrant, about 1 minute.
2. Add wine and simmer until most of the liquid has evaporated. Increase heat to high and stir in tomatoes, broth, and seasonings, bring to a boil.
3. Add the pasta, reduce heat to med-low and cook until pasta is tender, about 7-9 minutes, stirring occasionally.
4. Add seafood and cook 3-4 minutes or all of it is cooked. Serve garnished with parsley and a lemon wedge.

Nutrition Facts Per Serving
Calories 358 Total Carbs 24g Net Carbs 19g Protein 35g Fat 11g Sugar 11g Fiber 5g

Shrimp Pasta in Red Pepper Sauce

Prep time; 10 minutes, Cook time: 20 minutes, Serves: 4

Ingredients:

¾ lb. shrimp, cooked	8 oz. snow peas, steamed
3 red bell peppers, chopped	2 tbsp. margarine
1 onion, diced	

What you'll need from store cupboard:

1 cup low sodium chicken broth	¼ tsp pepper
½ tsp salt	1 recipe Homemade Pasta, cook & drain, (chapter 15)
½ tsp chicken bouillon	

Instructions:

1. Melt margarine in a large skillet over med-high heat. Add onions and cook, stirring frequently, until translucent.
2. Add the peppers, broth, bouillon, salt and pepper and bring to a simmer. Cover, reduce heat, and cook 5-10 minutes, or until peppers are soft.
3. Add mixture to a blender and process until smooth. Pour it back into the pan.
4. Add the shrimp and cook until heated through. Stir in the pasta and snow peas and mix well. Serve.

Nutrition Facts Per Serving
Calories 387 Total Carbs 27g Net Carbs 21g Protein 40g Fat 14g Sugar 14g Fiber 6g

Lobster Chowder

Prep time: 10 minutes, Cook time: 25 minutes, Serves: 4

Ingredients:

1 small onion, diced fine	separated in medium florets
1 quart skim milk	¼ cup bacon, cut into small pieces
2 cups lobster meat, cooked	2 tbsp. margarine
2 cups cauliflower,	

What you'll need from store cupboard:

2 cups water	Salt to taste

Instructions:

1. Melt margarine in a large saucepan over med-high heat. Add bacon and cook, stirring occasionally, 3-4 minutes. Add onion and salt and cook until onions are soft, about 5-7 minutes.
2. Add water and cauliflower and bring to a boil. Cook 8-10 minutes, or until cauliflower is tender.
3. Stir in milk and lobster and cook until heated through, 3-4 minutes. Serve.

Nutrition Facts Per Serving

Calories 280 Total Carbs 17g Net carbs 15g Protein 27g Fat 10g Sugar 14g fiber 2g

Maple Orange Salmon

Prep time: 5 minutes, Cook time: 20 minutes, Serves: 4

Ingredients:

1 ½ lb. salmon fillet
1 tbsp. orange juice

What you'll need from store cupboard:

2 tbsp. sugar free maple syrup	2 tsp garlic, diced fine
2 tbsp. grainy Dijon mustard	Nonstick cooking spray

Instructions:

1. Heat oven to 375 degrees. Spray baking dish with cooking spray and lay salmon in dish, skin side down.
2. In a small mixing bowl, whisk together orange juice, syrup, mustard, and garlic. Pour sauce over fish and cover with foil.
3. Bake 15 minutes. Uncover, and bake another 5 minutes until top of fish is caramelized and fish flakes easily with a fork.

Nutrition Facts Per Serving

Calories 247 Total Carbs 6g Protein 33g Fat 11g Sugar 1g Fiber 0g

Tangy Orange Roughy

Prep time: 5 minutes, Cook time: 15 minutes, Serves: 4

Ingredients:

4 orange roughy filets
¼ cup fresh lemon juice

What you'll need from store cupboard:

¼ cup reduced sodium soy sauce	½ tsp lemon pepper
1 tbsp. Splenda	Nonstick cooking spray
½ tsp ginger	

Instructions:

1. In a large Ziploc bag combine lemon juice, soy sauce, Splenda, and ginger. Add fish, seal, and turn to coat. Refrigerate 30 minutes.
2. Heat oven to 350 degrees. Spray a large baking sheet with cooking spray.
3. Place filets on prepared pan and sprinkle with lemon pepper. Bake 12-15 minutes, or until fish flakes easily with fork.

Nutrition Facts Per Serving

Calories 239 Total Carbs 4g Net Carbs 3g Protein 25g Fat 12g Sugar 4g Fiber 1g

Shrimp with Pumpkin Risotto

Prep time: 5 minutes, Cook time: 15 minutes, Serves: 3

Ingredients:

½ lb. raw shrimp, peel & devein	grated
	¼ cup half-n-half
2 cups cauliflower,	2 tbsp. margarine

What you'll need from store cupboard:

½ cup low sodium vegetable broth	2 cloves garlic, diced fine
¼ cup pumpkin puree	¼ tsp sage
¼ cup reduced fat parmesan cheese	¼ tsp salt
	¼ tsp pepper

Instructions:

1. Melt margarine in a large skillet over med-high heat. Add garlic and cook 1-2 minutes.
2. Add the broth, pumpkin, and half-n-half and whisk until smooth.
3. Add cauliflower and parmesan and cook 5 minutes, or until cauliflower is tender. Stir in shrimp and cook until they turn pink. Season with salt and pepper and serve.

Nutrition Facts Per Serving

Calories 236 Total Carbs 9g Net Carbs 7g Protein 21g Fat 13g Sugar 3g Fiber 2g

Red Clam Sauce & Pasta

Prep time: 10 minutes, Cook time: 3 hours, Serves: 4
Ingredients:
1 onion, diced
¼ cup fresh parsley, diced
What you'll need from store cupboard:

2 6 ½ oz. cans clams, chopped, undrained	1 tbsp. sunflower oil
14 ½ oz. tomatoes, diced, undrained	1 tsp Splenda
	1 tsp basil
6 oz. tomato paste	½ tsp thyme
2 cloves garlic, diced	½ recipe Homemade
1 bay leaf	Pasta, cook & drain (chapter 15)

Instructions:
1. Heat oil in a small skillet over med-high heat. Add onion and cook until tender, Add garlic and cook 1 minute more. Transfer to crock pot.
2. Add remaining Ingredients, except pasta, cover and cook on low 3-4 hours.
3. Discard bay leaf and serve over cooked pasta.

Nutrition Facts Per Serving
Calories 223 Total Carbs 32g Net Carbs 27g Protein 12g Fat 6g Sugar 15g Fiber 5g

Mediterranean Shrimp Pasta

Prep time: 15 minutes, Cook time: 20 minutes, Serves: 4
Ingredients:

1 lb. med. shrimp, peel & devein	½ cup sun dried tomatoes
1 lb. asparagus, trimmed & cut in 1-inch pieces	½ cup green onions, sliced thin

What you'll need from store cupboard:

½ recipe Homemade Pasta, (chapter 15) cook & drain	2 tbsp. clam juice
8 oz. tomato sauce	2 tbsp. apple juice, unsweetened
1 cup boiling water	1 tbsp. olive oil
2 cloves garlic, diced	1 tsp curry powder
	¼ tsp pepper

Instructions:
1. Place tomatoes in a small bowl and pour boiling water over top. Let stand 5 minutes, drain.
2. In a small bowl combine tomato sauce, clam juice, apple juice, and seasonings.
3. Heat oil in a large skillet over med-high heat. Add asparagus and cook 2 minutes.

Add green onions and garlic and cook 1 more minute.
4. Stir in shrimp. Cook, stirring, 3 minutes or until shrimp turn pink. Stir in the tomato mixture and sun dried tomatoes and heat through. Add the pasta and cook just until everything is hot. Serve.

Nutrition Facts Per Serving
Calories 296 Total Carbs 20g Net Carbs 15g Protein 37g Fat 9g Sugar 9g Fiber 5g

Seafood & Broccoli Pasta

Prep time: 10 minutes, Cook time: 15 minutes, Serves: 6
Ingredients:

1 lb. shrimp, peel & devein	steamed
	2 6.5 oz. cans clams, chopped
1 lb. sea scallops, pat dry	1 cup half-n-half
1 lb. broccoli florets,	½ cup margarine

What you'll need from store cupboard:

1 cup clam juice	3 tbsp. flour
6 cloves garlic, diced fine	1 recipe Homemade Pasta, cook & drain, (chapter 15)
4 tbsp. reduced fat parmesan	

Instructions:
1. Melt margarine in a large pot over medium heat. Add garlic and cook 2 minutes, stirring frequently.
2. Add shrimp and scallops and cook 5 minutes or until shrimp turn pink. Stir in the clams, clam juice, and half-n-half and bring to a low boil.
3. Stir in the flour and cook, stirring, until sauce has thickened. Add the broccoli and heat through. Serve over cooked pasta garnished with parmesan cheese.

Nutrition Facts Per Serving
Calories 519 Total Carbs 28g Net Carbs 23g Protein 50g Fat 23g Sugar 7g Fiber 5g

Italian Steamed Mussels

Prep time: 10 minutes, Cook time: 10 minutes, Serves: 4

Ingredients:

2 lbs. mussels, cleaned

2 plum tomatoes, peeled, seeded and diced

1 cup onion, diced

2 tbsp. fresh parsley, diced

What you'll need from store cupboard:

¼ cup dry white wine

3 cloves garlic, diced fine

3 tbsp. olive oil

2 tbsp. fresh breadcrumbs

¼ teaspoon crushed red pepper flakes

Instructions:

1. Heat oil in a large sauce pot over medium heat. Add the onions and cook until soft, about 2-3 minutes. Add garlic and cook 1 minute more.
2. Stir in wine, tomatoes, and pepper flakes. Bring to a boil, stirring occasionally. Add the mussels and cook 3-4 minutes, or until all the mussels have opened. Discard any mussels that do not open.
3. Once mussels open, transfer them to a serving bowl. Add bread crumbs to the sauce and continue to cook, stirring frequently, until mixture thickens. Stir in parsley and pour evenly over mussels. Serve.

Nutrition Facts Per Serving

Calories 340 Total Carbs 18g Net Carbs 16g Protein 29g Fat 16g Sugar 4g Fiber 2g

Salmon Milano

Prep time: 10 minutes, Cook time: 20 minutes, Serves: 6

Ingredients:

2 ½ lb. salmon filet

2 tomatoes, sliced

½ cup margarine

What you'll need from store cupboard:

½ cup basil pesto

Instructions:

1. Heat the oven to 400 degrees. Line a 9x15-inch baking sheet with foil, making sure it covers the sides. Place another large piece of foil onto the baking sheet and place the salmon filet on top of it.
2. Place the pesto and margarine in blender or food processor and pulse until smooth. Spread evenly over salmon. Place tomato slices on top.

3. Wrap the foil around the salmon, tenting around the top to prevent foil from touching the salmon as much as possible. Bake 15-25 minutes, or salmon flakes easily with a fork. Serve.

Nutrition Facts Per Serving

Calories 444 Total Carbs 2g Protein 55g Fat 24g Sugar 1g Fiber 0g

Margarita Grilled Salmon

Prep time: 5 minutes, cook time 15 minutes, Serves: 8

Ingredients:

2-3 lb. salmon, with skin

2 limes, sliced thin

1 lime, juiced and zested

1 avocado

What you'll need from store cupboard:

3 tbsp. lite mayonnaise

1 tsp olive oil

1 tsp tequila

1 tsp salt

1 clove garlic

Nonstick cooking spray

Instructions:

1. In a small bowl, combine the lime zest, juice, tequila, olive oil and salt.
2. Spray the skin side of the fish with cooking spray. Lay on a large cookie sheet and cover with the marinade. Let sit for 30 minutes.
3. Spray the grill with cooking spray and then heat to medium high. Cook skin side down and close the grill. Cook for 10 - 15 minutes depending on the thickness of your fish.
4. Place the avocado, mayonnaise and garlic in a blender or food processor and pulse until smooth and combined. Serve along with the fish.

Nutrition Facts Per Serving

Calories 413 Total Carbs 7g Protein 45g Fat 23g Sugar 1g Fiber 3g

Tuna Carbonara

Prep time: 5 minutes, Cook time: 25 minutes, Serves: 4

Ingredients:

½ lb. tuna fillet, cut in pieces

2 eggs

4 tbsp. fresh parsley, diced

What you'll need from store cupboard:

½ recipe Homemade Pasta, cook & drain, (chapter 15)

½ cup reduced fat parmesan cheese

2 cloves garlic, peeled

2 tbsp. extra virgin olive oil

Salt & pepper, to taste

Instructions:

1. In a small bowl, beat the eggs, parmesan and a dash of pepper.
2. Heat the oil in a large skillet over med-high heat. Add garlic and cook until browned. Add the tuna and cook 2-3 minutes, or until tuna is almost cooked through. Discard the garlic.
3. Add the pasta and reduce heat. Stir in egg mixture and cook, stirring constantly, 2 minutes. If the sauce is too thick, thin with water, a little bit at a time, until it has a creamy texture.
4. Salt and pepper to taste and serve garnished with parsley.

Nutrition Facts Per Serving

Calories 409 Total Carbs 7g Net Carbs 6g Protein 25g Fat 30g Sugar 3g Fiber 1g

Chapter 12 - Vegetable Mains Recipe

Cauliflower Mushroom Risotto

Prep time: 10 minutes, Cook time: 30 minutes, Serves: 2

Ingredients:

1 medium head cauliflower, grated

8 oz. Porcini mushrooms, sliced

1 yellow onion, diced fine

What you'll need from store cupboard:

2 cup low sodium vegetable broth

2 tsp garlic, diced fine

2 tsp white wine

vinegar

Salt & pepper, to taste

Olive oil cooking spray

Instructions:

1. Heat oven to 350 degrees. Line a baking sheet with foil.
2. Place the mushrooms on the prepared pan and spray with cooking spray. Sprinkle with salt and toss to coat. Bake 10-12 minutes, or until golden brown and the mushrooms start to crisp.
3. Spray a large skillet with cooking spray and place over med-high heat. Add onion and cook, stirring frequently, until translucent, about 3-4 minutes. Add garlic and cook 2 minutes, until golden.
4. Add the cauliflower and cook 1 minute, stirring.
5. Place the broth in a saucepan and bring to a simmer. Add to the skillet, ¼ cup at a time, mixing well after each addition.
6. Stir in vinegar. Reduce heat to low and let simmer, 4-5 minutes, or until most of the liquid has evaporated.
7. Spoon cauliflower mixture onto plates, or in bowls, and top with mushrooms. Serve.

Nutrition Facts Per Serving

Calories 134 Total Carbs 22g Protein 10g Fat 0g Sugar 5g Fiber 2g

Asian Fried Eggplant

Prep time: 10 minutes, Cook time: 40 minutes, Serves: 4

Ingredients:

1 large eggplant, sliced into fourths
3 green onions, diced, green tips only
1 tsp fresh ginger, peeled & diced fine

What you'll need from store cupboard:

¼ cup + 1 tsp cornstarch	1 tbsp. vegetable oil
	1 tbsp. fish sauce
1 ½ tbsp. soy sauce	2 tsp Splenda
1 ½ tbsp. sesame oil	¼ tsp salt

Instructions:

1. Place eggplant on paper towels and sprinkle both sides with salt. Let for 1 hour to remove excess moisture. Pat dry with more paper towels.
2. In a small bowl, whisk together soy sauce, sesame oil, fish sauce, Splenda, and 1 teaspoon cornstarch.
3. Coat both sides of the eggplant with the ¼ cup cornstarch, use more if needed.
4. Heat oil in a large skillet, over med-high heat. Add ½ the ginger and 1 green onion, then lay 2 slices of eggplant on top. Use ½ the sauce mixture to lightly coat both sides of the eggplant. Cook 8-10 minutes per side. Repeat.
5. Serve garnished with remaining green onions.

Nutrition Facts Per Serving
Calories 155 Total Carbs 18g Net Carbs 13g Protein 2g Fat 9g Sugar 6g Fiber 5g

Garden Vegetable Pasta

Prep time: 10 minutes, Cook time: 30 minutes, Serves: 6

Ingredients:

2 lbs. fresh cherry tomatoes, halved	chopped
2 zucchini, chopped	½ cup mozzarella cheese, grated
2 ears corn, cut kernels off the cob	½ cup fresh basil, sliced thin
1 yellow squash,	

What you'll need from store cupboard:

Homemade Pasta, cook & drain, (chapter 15)	2 cloves garlic crushed
5 tbsp. olive oil, divided	Crushed red pepper flakes, to taste
	Salt, to taste

Instructions:

1. Heat 3 tablespoons oil in a large skillet over medium heat. Add garlic and tomatoes. Cover, reduce heat to low, and cook 15 minutes, stirring frequently.
2. In a separate skillet, heat remaining oil over med-high heat. Add zucchini, squash, and corn. Reduce heat to medium, and cook until vegetables are tender. Sprinkle with salt.
3. Heat oven to 400 degrees.
4. In a large bowl combine tomato mixture, vegetables, and pasta, toss to mix. Pour into a 9x13-inch baking dish and top with cheese. Bake 10 minutes, or until cheese melts and begins to brown. Serve.

Nutrition Facts Per Serving
Calories 347 Total Carbs 31g Net Carbs 24g Protein 21g Fat 18g Sugar 13g Fiber 7g

Tex Mex Veggie Bake

Prep time: 10 minutes, Cook time: 35 minutes, Serves: 8

Ingredients:

2 cup cauliflower, grated	grated
	1 cup reduced fat Mexican cheese blend, grated
1 cup fat free sour cream	
1 cup reduced fat cheddar cheese,	½ cup red onion, diced

What you'll need from store cupboard:

11 oz. can Mexicorn, drain	1 cup black beans, rinsed
10 oz. tomatoes & green chilies	1 cup salsa
	¼ tsp pepper
2 ¼ oz. black olives, drain	Nonstick cooking spray

Instructions:

1. Heat oven to 350 degrees. Spray a 2 ½-quart baking dish with cooking spray.
2. In a large bowl, combine beans, corn, tomatoes, salsa, sour cream, cheddar cheese, pepper, and cauliflower. Transfer to baking dish. Sprinkle with onion and olives.
3. Bake 30 minutes. Sprinkle with Mexican blend cheese and bake another 5-10 minutes, or until cheese is melted and casserole is heated through. Let rest 10 minutes before serving.

Nutrition Facts Per Serving
Calories 266 Total Carbs 33g Net Carbs 27g Protein 16g Fat 8g Sugar 8g Fiber 6g

Butternut Fritters

Prep time: 15 minutes, Cook time: 15 minutes, Serves: 6
Ingredients:
5 cup butternut squash, grated
2 large eggs
1 tbsp. fresh sage, diced fine
What you'll need from store cupboard:
2/3 cup flour   Salt and pepper, to
2 tbsp. olive oil   taste
Instructions:
1. Heat oil in a large skillet over med-high heat.
2. In a large bowl, combine squash, eggs, sage and salt and pepper to taste. Fold in flour.
3. Drop ¼ cup mixture into skillet, keeping fritters at least 1 inch apart. Cook till golden brown on both sides, about 2 minutes per side.
4. Transfer to paper towel lined plate. Repeat. Serve immediately with your favorite dipping sauce.

Nutrition Facts Per Serving
Calories 164 Total Carbs 24g Net Carbs 21g Protein 4g Fat 6g Sugar 3g Fiber 3g

Roasted Cauliflower with Tomatoes

Prep time: 15 minutes, Cook time: 45 minutes, Serves: 4
Ingredients:
1 large head   3 scallions, sliced
cauliflower, separated   1 onion, diced fine
in florets
What you'll need from store cupboard:
15 oz. can petite   vinegar
tomatoes, diced   1 tbsp. balsamic
4 cloves garlic, diced   vinegar
fine   3 tsp Splenda
4 tbsp. olive oil,   1 tsp salt
divided   1 tsp pepper
1 tbsp. red wine   ½ tsp chili powder
Instructions:
1. Heat oven to 400 degrees.
2. Place cauliflower on a large baking sheet and drizzle with 2 tablespoons of oil. Sprinkle with salt and pepper, to taste. Use hands to rub oil and seasoning into florets then lay in single layer. Roast until fork tender.
3. Heat 1 tablespoon oil in a large skillet

over med-low heat. Add onion and cook until soft.
4. Stir in tomatoes, with juice, Splenda, both vinegars, and the teaspoon of salt. Bring to a boil, reduce heat and simmer 20-25 minutes. For a smooth sauce, use an immersion blender to process until smooth, or leave it chunky.
5. In a separate skillet, heat remaining oil over med-low heat and saute garlic 1-2 minutes. Stir in tomato sauce, and increase heat to medium. Cook, stirring frequently, 5 minutes. Add chili powder and cauliflower and toss to coat. Serve garnished with scallions.

Nutrition Facts Per Serving
Calories 107 Total Carbs 23g Net Carbs 16g Protein 6g Fat 0g Sugar 12g Fiber 7g

Crust Less Broccoli Quiche

Prep time: 10 minutes, Cook time: 1 hour, Serves: 6
Ingredients:
3 large eggs   cheese, grated
2 cups broccoli   2/3 cup unsweetened
florets, chopped   almond milk
1 small onion, diced   ½ cup feta cheese,
1 cup cheddar   crumbled
What you'll need from store cupboard:
1 tbsp. extra virgin   ¼ tsp black pepper
olive oil   Nonstick cooking
½ tsp sea salt   spray
Instructions:
1. Heat oven to 350 degrees. Spray a 9-inch baking dish with cooking spray.
2. Heat the oil in a large skillet over medium heat. Add onion and cook 4-5 minutes, until onions are translucent.
3. Add broccoli and stir to combine. Cook until broccoli turns a bright green, about 2 minutes. Transfer to a bowl.
4. In a small bowl, whisk together almond milk, egg, salt, and pepper. Pour over the broccoli. Add the cheddar cheese and stir the Ingredients together. Pour into the prepared baking dish.
5. Sprinkle the feta cheese over the top and bake 45 minutes to 1 hour, or until eggs are set in the middle and top is lightly browned. Serve.

Nutrition Facts Per Serving
Calories 182 Total Carbs 5g Net Carbs 4g Protein 10g Fat 14g Sugar 2g Fiber 1g

Chili Relleno Casserole

Prep time: 5 minutes, **Cook time:** 35 minutes, **Serves:** 8

Ingredients:

3 eggs	3/4 cup half-n-half
1 cup Monterey jack pepper cheese, grated	½ cup cheddar cheese, grated

What you'll need from store cupboard:

2 (7 oz.) cans whole green chilies, drain well	½ tsp salt Nonstick cooking spray

Instructions:

1. Heat oven to 350 degrees. Spray an 8-inch baking pan with cooking spray.
2. Slice each chili down one long side and lay flat.
3. Arrange half the chilies in the prepared baking pan, skin side down, in single layer.
4. Sprinkle with the pepper cheese and top with remaining chilies, skin side up.
5. In a small bowl, beat eggs, salt, and half-n-half. Pour over chilies. Top with cheddar cheese.
6. Bake 35 minutes, or until top is golden brown. Let rest 10 minutes before serving.

Nutrition Facts Per Serving
Calories 295 Total Carbs 36g Net Carbs 22g Protein 13g Fat 13g Sugar 21g Fiber 14g

Eggplant-Zucchini Parmesan

Prep time: 10 minutes, **Cook time:** 2 hours, **Serves:** 6

Ingredients:

1 medium eggplant, peeled and cut into 1-inch cubes	cut into 1-inch pieces
1 medium zucchini,	1 medium onion, cut into thin wedges

What you'll need from store cupboard:
1½ cups purchased light spaghetti sauce
2/3 cup reduced fat parmesan cheese, grated

Instructions:

1. Place the vegetables, spaghetti sauce and 1/3 cup parmesan in the crock pot. Stir to combine. Cover and cook on high 2 – 2 1/2 hours, or on low 4-5 hours.
2. Sprinkle remaining parmesan on top before serving.

Nutrition Facts Per Serving
Calories 81 Total Carbs 12g Net Carbs 7g Protein 5g Fat 2g Sugar 7g Fiber 5g

Creamy Pasta with Peas

Prep time: 10 minutes, **Cook time:** 10 minutes, **Serves:** 4

Ingredients:

4 tomatoes, deseeded & diced	1 cup peas, thawed
4 oz. fat free cream cheese, cut in cubes	½ cup skim milk
	4 tbsp. fresh parsley, diced

What you'll need from store cupboard:

½ recipe Homemade Pasta, cook & drain, (chapter 15)	3 tbsp. olive oil
	1 tsp oregano
4 cloves garlic, diced fine	1 tsp basil
	½ tsp garlic salt

Instructions:

1. Heat oil in a large skillet over medium heat. Add garlic and tomatoes, cook 3-4 minutes, stirring frequently.
2. Add peas, milk, cream cheese, and seasonings. Cook, stirring, 5 minutes, or until cream cheese has melted.
3. Add pasta and toss to coat. Serve garnished with parsley.

Nutrition Facts Per Serving
Calories 332 Total Carbs 19g Net Carbs 14g Protein 14g Fat 23g Sugar 10g Fiber 5g

Grilled Portobello & Zucchini Burger

Prep time: 5 minutes, **Cook time:** 10 minutes, **Serves:** 2

Ingredients:

2 large portabella mushroom caps	2 slices low fat cheese
½ small zucchini, sliced	Spinach

What you'll need from store cupboard:
2 100% whole wheat sandwich thins
2 tsp roasted red bell peppers
2 tsp olive oil

Instructions:

1. Heat grill, or charcoal, to med-high heat.
2. Lightly brush mushroom caps with olive oil. Grill mushroom caps and zucchini slices until tender, about 3-4 minutes per side.
3. Place on sandwich thin. Top with sliced cheese, roasted red bell pepper, and spinach. Serve.

Nutrition Facts Per Serving
Calories 177 Total Carbs 26g Protein 15g Fat 3g Sugar 3g Fiber 8g

Faux Chow Mein

Prep time: 10 minutes, Cook time: 20 minutes, Serves: 4

Ingredients:

1 large spaghetti squash, halved and seeds removed	1 onion, diced fine
	2 cup Cole slaw mix
	2 tsp fresh ginger, grated
3 stalks celery, sliced diagonally	

What you'll need from store cupboard:

¼ cup Tamari	2 tbsp. olive oil
3 cloves garlic, diced fine	1 tbsp. Splenda
	¼ tsp pepper
3-4 tbsp. water	

Instructions:

1. Place squash, cut side down, in shallow glass dish and add water. Microwave on high 8-10 minutes, or until squash is soft. Use a fork to scoop out the squash into a bowl.
2. In a small bowl, whisk together Tamari, garlic, sugar, ginger and pepper.
3. Heat oil in large skillet over med-high heat. Add onion and celery and cook, stirring frequently, 3-4 minutes. Add Cole slaw and cook until heated through, about 1 minute.
4. Add the squash and sauce mixture and stir well. Cook 2 minutes, stirring frequently. Serve.

Nutrition Facts Per Serving
Calories 129 Total Carbs 13g Net Carbs 11g Protein 3g Fat 7g Sugar 6g Fiber 2g

Florentine Pizza

Prep time: 15 minutes, Cook time: 20 minutes, Serves: 2

Ingredients:

1 3/4 cup grated mozzarella cheese	2 tbsp. reduced fat parmesan cheese, grated
½ cup frozen spinach, thaw	
1 egg	2 tbsp. cream cheese, soft

What you'll need from store cupboard:

¾ cup almond flour	seasoning
¼ cup light Alfredo sauce	¼ tsp red pepper flakes
½ tsp Italian	Pinch of salt

Instructions:

1. Heat oven to 400 degrees.
2. Squeeze all the excess water out of the spinach.

3. In a glass bowl, combine mozzarella and almond flour. Stir in cream cheese. Microwave 1 minute on high, then stir. If the mixture is not melted, microwave another 30 seconds.
4. Stir in the egg, seasoning, and salt. Mix well. Place dough on a piece of parchment paper and press into a 10-inch circle.
5. Place directly on the oven rack and bake 8-10 minutes or until lightly browned.
6. Remove the crust and spread with the Alfredo sauce, then add spinach, parmesan and red pepper flakes evenly over top. Bake another 8-10 minutes. Slice and serve.

Nutrition Facts Per Serving
Calories 441 Total Carbs 14g Net Carbs 9g Protein 24g Fat 35g Sugar 4g Fiber 5g

Pizza Stuffed Portobello's

Prep time: 5 minutes, Cook time: 10 minutes, Serves: 4

Ingredients:

8 Portobello mushrooms, stems removed	tomatoes, sliced
	½ cup crushed tomatoes
1 cup mozzarella cheese, grated	½ cup fresh basil, chopped
1 cup cherry	

What you'll need from store cupboard:

2 tbsp. balsamic vinegar	flakes
	½ tbsp. garlic powder
1 tbsp. olive oil	¼ tsp pepper
1 tbsp. oregano	Pinch salt
1 tbsp. red pepper	

Instructions:

1. Heat oven to broil. Line a baking sheet with foil.
2. Place mushrooms, stem side down, on foil and drizzle with oil. Sprinkle with garlic powder, salt and pepper. Broil for 5 minutes.
3. Flip mushrooms over and top with crushed tomatoes, oregano, parsley, pepper flakes, cheese and sliced tomatoes. Broil another 5 minutes.
4. Top with basil and drizzle with balsamic. Serve.

Nutrition Facts Per Serving
Calories 113 Total Carbs 11g Net Carbs 7g Protein 9g Fat 5g Sugar 3g Fiber 4g

Fiesta Casserole

Prep time: 15 minutes, Cook time: 30 minutes, Serves: 12

Ingredients:

1 head cauliflower, grated	seeded and diced fine
1 red bell pepper, diced fine	½ white onion, diced fine
1 green bell pepper, diced fine	1½ cups cheddar cheese, grated
1 jalapeno pepper,	1 tsp cilantro, diced fine

What you'll need from store cupboard:

½ cup salsa	Nonstick cooking spray
3 tbsp. water	
1 tsp chili powder	

Instructions:

1. Heat oven to 350 degrees. Spray a 7x11x2-inch baking pan with cooking spray.
2. In a large skillet, over medium heat, cook onions and peppers until soft, about 5 minutes. Add cilantro and chili powder and stir.
3. Place the cauliflower and water in a glass bowl and microwave on high for 3 minutes. Stir in 1 cup cheese and the salsa.
4. Stir the pepper mixture into the cauliflower and combine. Spread in prepared pan. Sprinkle the remaining cheese over the top and bake 30-35 minutes.
5. Let rest 5 minutes before cutting into 12 squares and serving.

Nutrition Facts Per Serving

Calories 74 Total Carbs 4g Net Carbs 3g Protein 4g Fat 5g Sugar 2g Fiber 1g

Zucchini Fritters

Prep time: 40 minutes, Cook time: 10 minutes, Serves: 4

Ingredients:

3 zucchini, grated	crumbled
2 eggs	¼ cup fresh dill, chopped
1 onion, diced	
¾ cups feta cheese,	1 tbsp. margarine

What you'll need from store cupboard:

½ cup flour	Pepper to taste
1 tsp salt	Oil for frying

Instructions:

1. Place zucchini in a large colander and sprinkle with the salt. Toss with fingers and let sit 30 minutes. Squeeze with back of spoon to remove the excess water. Place the zucchini between paper towels and squeeze again. Place in large bowl and let dry.
2. Melt margarine in a large skillet over med-high heat. Add onion and cook until soft, about 5 minutes. Add to zucchini along with the feta and dill and mix well.
3. In a small bowl, whisk together the flour and eggs. Pour over zucchini and mix well.
4. Add oil to the skillet to equal ½-inch and heat over med-high heat until very hot. Drop golf ball sized scoops of zucchini mixture into oil and flatten into a patty. Cook until golden brown on both sides. Transfer to paper towel line plate.
5. Serve with Garlic Dipping Sauce, (chapter 16), or sauce of your choice.

Nutrition Facts Per Serving

Calories 253 Total Carbs 21g Net Carbs 18g Protein 10g Fat 15g Sugar 5g Fiber 3g

Chapter 13 - Pork Lamb and Beef Recipe

Chestnut Stuffed Pork Roast

Prep time: 15 minutes, Cook time: 1 hour 35 minutes, Serves: 15

Ingredients:

5 lb. pork loin roast, boneless, double tied
½ lb. ground pork
½ cup celery, diced fine
½ cup onion, diced fine
2 tbsp. fresh parsley, diced, divided
1 tbsp. margarine

What you'll need from store cupboard:

15 oz. can chestnuts, drained
2 cup low sodium chicken broth
3 tbsp. flour
2 tbsp. brandy,
divided
½ tsp salt
½ tsp pepper
1/8 tsp allspice
Salt & black pepper, to taste

Instructions:

1. Heat oven to 350 degrees.
2. Untie roast, open and pound lightly to even thickness.
3. Melt margarine in a skillet over med-high heat. Add celery and onion and cook until soft.
4. In a large bowl, combine ground pork, 1 tablespoon parsley, 1 tablespoon brandy and seasonings. Mix in celery and onion. Spread over roast.
5. Lay a row of chestnuts down the center. Roll meat around filling and tie securely with butcher string. Roast in oven 1 ½ hours or until meat thermometer reaches 145 degrees. Remove and let rest 10 minutes.
6. Measure out 2 tablespoons of drippings, discard the rest, into a saucepan. Place over medium heat and whisk in flour until smooth. Add broth and cook, stirring, until mixture thickens. Chop remaining chestnuts and add to gravy along with remaining brandy and parsley. Season with salt and pepper if desired. Slice the roast and serve topped with gravy.

Nutrition Facts Per Serving

Calories 416 Total Carbs 15g Protein 48g Fat 16g Sugar 0g Fiber 0g

Beef Tenderloin Steaks with Brandied Mushrooms

Prep time: 10 minutes, Cook time: 20 minutes, Serves: 4

Ingredients:

4 beef tenderloin steaks, about ¾ inch thick
3 ½ cups Portobello mushrooms, sliced
1 tbsp. margarine

What you'll need from store cupboard:

½ cup brandy, divided
1 tsp balsamic vinegar
½ tsp salt
½ tsp coarsely
ground pepper
½ tsp instant coffee granules
Nonstick cooking spray

Instructions:

1. Heat oven to 200 degrees.
2. Salt and pepper both sides of the steaks and let sit 15 minutes.
3. In a small bowl, mix together coffee, vinegar, all but 1 tablespoon brandy, salt and pepper.
4. Spray a large skillet with cooking spray and place over med-high heat.
5. Spray the mushrooms with cooking spray and add to the hot pan. Cook 5 minutes or until most of the liquid is absorbed. Transfer the mushrooms to a bowl.
6. Add the steaks to the skillet and cook 3 minutes per side. Reduce heat to med-low and cook 2 more minutes or to desired doneness. Place on dinner plates, cover with foil and place in oven.
7. Add the brandy mixture to the skillet and bring to a boil. Boil 1 minute, or until reduced to about ¼ cup liquid. Stir in mushrooms and cook 1-2 minutes, or most of the liquid has evaporated.
8. Remove from heat and stir in remaining 1 tablespoon brandy and the margarine.
9. Spoon evenly over steaks and serve immediately.

Nutrition Facts Per Serving

Calories 350 Total Carbs 1g Protein 44g Fat 12g Sugar 0g Fiber 0g

Hearty Beef Chili

Prep time: 15 minutes, Cook time: 1 hour, Serves: 4

Ingredients:

1 lb. lean ground beef
1 large bell pepper, diced
1 cup onion, diced

What you'll need from store cupboard:

4 oz. can green chilies, diced	fine
1 cup tomato sauce	2 tsp chili powder
1 cup low sodium beef broth	1 tsp salt
1 tbsp. tomato paste	1 tsp Worcestershire
2 cloves garlic, diced	1 tsp cumin
	½ tsp celery salt
	¼ tsp pepper

Instructions:

1. Heat a large pan over med-high heat. Add beef, onions, bell pepper and garlic and cook, stirring occasionally, until beef is no longer pink. Drain fat.
2. Add remaining Ingredients and bring to a simmer. Reduce heat to med-low and simmer 30 minutes to an hour. Taste and adjust seasonings if needed. Serve.

Nutrition Facts Per Serving

Calories 355 Total Carbs 30g Net Carbs 20g Protein 40g Fat 9g Sugar 18g Fiber 10g

Herb Crusted Baked Ham

Prep time: 5 minutes, Cook time: 1 hour 15 minutes, Serves: 8

Ingredients:

5 lb. smoked ham, bone-in
2 tbsp. fresh rosemary, diced

What you'll need from store cupboard:

1 cup yellow mustard	2 tbsp. garlic, diced
½ cup lite mayonnaise	fine
	Pepper, to taste

Instructions:

1. Heat oven to 300 degrees.
2. Place ham in a roasting pan, fat side up.
3. In a small bowl, combine all Ingredients and spread over ham.
4. Pour ½ cup water in the bottom of the roaster and bake 1 hour 15 minutes. Let rest 10 minutes before slicing and serving.

Nutrition Facts Per Serving

Calories 327 Total Carbs 10g Net Carbs 7g Protein 22g Fat 22g Sugar 0g Fiber 3g

Pork Chops with Creamy Marsala Sauce

Prep time: 10 minutes, Cook time: 20 minutes, Serves: 4

Ingredients:

4 thin boneless pork loin chops, (about 1 pound), trimmed	and slice thin
	1 cup low-fat milk
4 thin slices prosciutto, (2 ounces), chopped	3 tsp fresh oregano, chopped fine
	3 tsp fresh chives, chopped fine
1 small onion, halve	

What you'll need from store cupboard:

½ cup Marsala, (see Note), divided	olive oil
	¼ tsp kosher salt
¼ cup flour	¼ tsp freshly ground
2 tsp cornstarch	pepper
2 tsp extra-virgin	

Instructions:

1. Mix 2 tablespoons of the wine with cornstarch, set aside.
2. Place flour in a shallow dish. Sprinkle chops with salt and pepper then coat in flour.
3. Heat oil in nonstick skillet over med-high heat. Once it gets hot, reduce heat to medium and add pork. Cook until browned on both sides, 2 minutes per side. Transfer to a plate.
4. Add prosciutto to the pan and cook, stirring constantly, about 1 minute, until browned. Add onion and cook, stirring frequently, 2-3 minutes until it starts to get soft.
5. Add remaining wine, oregano, and 1 ½ teaspoons chives to the pan and bring to a boil. Add milk and cornstarch mix and adjust heat to make sure mixture stays at a simmer. Stir occasionally until sauce has thickened and reduced slightly, about 4-6 minutes.
6. Add pork chops to the sauce, turning to coat, and cook until heated through. Serve topped with sauce and garnished with remaining chives.

Nutrition Facts Per Serving

Calories 499 Total Carbs 14g Net Carbs 13g Protein 32g Fat 32g Sugar 5g Fiber 1g

Alfredo Sausage & Vegetables

Prep time: 10 minutes, Cook time: 15 minutes, Serves: 6

Ingredients:

1 pkg. smoked sausage, cut in ¼-inch slices	½ cup red bell pepper, cut in matchsticks
1 cup half-and-half	½ cup peas, frozen
½ cup zucchini, cut in matchsticks	¼ cup margarine
½ cup carrots, cut in matchsticks	¼ cup onion, diced
	2 tbsp. fresh parsley, diced

What you'll need from store cupboard:

½ recipe Homemade Pasta, cook & drain, (chapter 15)	1 clove garlic, diced fine
1/3 cup reduced fat parmesan cheese	Salt & pepper, to taste

Instructions:

1. Melt margarine in a large skillet over medium heat. Add onion and garlic and cook, stirring occasionally, 3-4 minutes or until onion is soft.
2. Increase heat to med-high. Add sausage, zucchini, carrots, and red pepper. Cook, stirring frequently, 5-6 minutes, or until carrots are tender crisp.
3. Stir in peas and half-n-half, cook 1-2 minutes until heated through. Stir in cheese, parsley, salt, and pepper. Add pasta nd toss to mix. Serve.

Nutrition Facts Per Serving
Calories 283 Total Carbs 18g Net Carbs 14g Protein 21g Fat 15g Sugar 8g Fiber 4g

Beef & Veggie Quesadillas

Prep time: 15 minutes, Cook time: 10 minutes, Serves: 4

Ingredients:

¾ lb. lean ground beef	1 carrot, grated
2 tomatoes, seeded and diced	¾ cup mushrooms, diced
1 onion, diced	½ cup mozzarella cheese, grated
1 zucchini, grated	¼ cup cilantro, diced

What you'll need from store cupboard:

4 8-inch whole wheat tortillas, warmed	¼ tsp hot pepper sauce
2 cloves garlic, diced	Nonstick cooking spray
2 tsp chili powder	
¼ tsp salt	

Instructions:

1. Heat oven to 400 degrees. Spray a large baking sheet with cooking spray.
2. Cook beef and onions in a large nonstick skillet over medium heat, until beef is no longer pink, drain fat. Transfer to a bowl and keep warm.
3. Add the mushrooms, zucchini, carrot, garlic, chili powder, salt and pepper sauce to the skillet and cook until vegetables are tender.
4. Stir in the tomatoes, cilantro and beef.
5. Lay the tortillas on the prepared pan. Cover half of each with beef mixture, and top with cheese. Fold other half over filling. Bake 5 minutes. Flip over and bake 5-6 minute more or until cheese has melted. Cut into wedges and serve.

Nutrition Facts Per Serving
Calories 319 Total Carbs 31g Net Carbs 26g Protein 33g Fat 7g Sugar 5g Fiber 5g

Bacon & Cauliflower Casserole

Prep time: 15 minutes, Cook time: 20 minutes, Serves: 6

Ingredients:

6 slices bacon, cooked and crumbled, divided	2 cup cheddar cheese, grated and divided
3 scallions, sliced thin, divided	1 cup fat free sour cream
5 cup cauliflower	

What you'll need from store cupboard:

½ tsp salt
¼ tsp fresh cracked pepper
Nonstick cooking spray

Instructions:

1. Heat oven to 350 degrees. Spray casserole dish with cooking spray.
2. Steam cauliflower until just tender.
3. In a large bowl, combine cauliflower, sour cream, half the bacon, half the scallions and half the cheese. Stir in salt and pepper. Place in prepared baking dish and sprinkle remaining cheese over top.
4. Bake 18-20 minutes until heated through. Sprinkle remaining scallions and bacon over top and serve.

Nutrition Facts Per Serving
Calories 332 Total Carbs 15g Net Carbs 11g Protein 21g Fat 20g Sugar 6g Fiber 4g

Asian Beef Bowls

Prep time: 15 minutes, Cook time: 15 minutes, Serves: 4

Ingredients:

1 lb. lean ground beef
1 bunch green onions, sliced
¼ cup fresh ginger, grated

What you'll need from store cupboard:

Cauliflower Rice, (chapter 15)
¼ cup toasted sesame oil
5 cloves garlic, diced
fine
2 tbsp. light soy sauce
2 tsp sesame seeds

Instructions:

1. Heat oil in a large, cast iron skillet over high heat. Add all but 2 tablespoons, of the onions and cook until soft and starting to brown, about 5 minutes.
2. Add beef, and cook, breaking up with a spatula, until no longer pink. About 8 minutes.
3. Add remaining Ingredients and simmer 2-3 minutes, stirring frequently. Serve over hot cauliflower rice garnished with sesame seeds and reserved green onions.

Nutrition Facts Per Serving

Calories 383 Total Carbs 24g Net Carbs 22g Protein 40g Fat 21g Sugar 11g Fiber 2g

BBQ Pork Tacos

Prep time: 20 minutes, Cook time: 6 hours, Serves: 16

Ingredients:

2 lb. pork shoulder, trim off excess fat
2 onions, diced fine
2 cups cabbages, shredded

What you'll need from store cupboard:

16 (6-inch) low carb whole wheat tortillas
4 chipotle peppers in adobo sauce, pureed
1 cup light barbecue
sauce
2 cloves garlic, diced fine
1 ½ tsp paprika

Instructions:

1. In a medium bowl, whisk together garlic, barbecue sauce and chipotles, cover and chill.
2. Place pork in the crock pot. Cover and cook on low 8-10 hours, or on high 4-6 hours.
3. Transfer pork to a cutting board. Use two forks and shred the pork, discarding the fat. Place pork back in the crock pot. Sprinkle with paprika then pour the barbecue sauce over mixture.
4. Stir to combine, cover and cook 1 hour. Skim off excess fat.
5. To assemble the tacos: place about ¼ cup of pork on warmed tortilla. Top with cabbage and onions and serve. Refrigerate any leftover pork up to 3 days.

Nutrition Facts Per Serving

Calories 265 Total Carbs 14g Net Carbs 5g Protein 17g Fat 14g Sugar 3g Fiber 9g

Kielbasa & Lamb Cassoulet

Prep time: 1 hour, Cook time: 5 hours 30 minutes, Serves: 6

Ingredients:

12 oz. lamb stew meat, cut into 1-inch cubes
8 oz. kielbasa, cut into 1/4-inch slices
1 eggplant, peeled and chopped
1 green pepper, coarsely chopped
1 tbsp. fresh thyme

What you'll need from store cupboard:

2 cups low sodium beef broth
1 cup dried navy beans, rinsed well
6 oz. can tomato paste
3 cloves garlic, diced
fine
1 tbsp. olive oil
1 bay leaf
¼ tsp whole black peppercorn
Salt & pepper, to taste

Instructions:

1. Place beans in a large saucepan. Add enough water to cover by 2 inches. Bring to a boil; reduce heat. Simmer, uncovered, for 10 minutes. Remove from heat. Cover and let stand for 1 hour. Drain and rinse beans.
2. Heat oil in a large skillet over med-high heat. Add lamb and cook until brown on all sides. Drain off fat. Transfer to a crock pot.
3. Add beans, broth, kielbasa, thyme, garlic, peppercorns, and bay leaf. Cover and cook on high 4 to 5 hours.
4. Add the eggplant, pepper and tomato paste, stir well. Cook another 30 minutes until vegetables are tender. Discard bay leaf and serve.

Nutrition Facts Per Serving

Calories 391 Total Carbs 35g Net Carbs 22g Protein 32g Fat 14g Sugar 8g Fiber 13g

Beef & Broccoli Skillet

Prep time: 5 minutes, Cook time: 10 minutes, Serves: 4

Ingredients:

1 lb. lean ground beef

3 cups cauliflower rice, cooked

2 cups broccoli, chopped

4 green onions, sliced

What you'll need from store cupboard:

1 cup Teriyaki sauce (chapter 16)

Instructions:

1. Cook beef in a large skillet over med-high heat until brown. Add the broccoli and white parts of the onion, cook, stirring for 1 minute.
2. Add the cauliflower and sauce and continue cooking until heated through and broccoli is tender-crisp, about 3-5 minutes. Serve garnished with green parts of the onion.

Nutrition Facts Per Serving

Calories 255 total carbs 9g Net carbs 6g Protein 37g Fat 7g Sugar 3g Fiber 3g

Beef Picadillo

Prep time: 10 minutes, Cook time: 3-4 hour, Serves: 10

Ingredients:

1 ½ lbs. lean ground beef

1 onion, diced fine

1 red bell pepper,

diced

1 small tomato, diced

¼ cup cilantro, diced fine

What you'll need from store cupboard:

1 cup tomato sauce

3 cloves garlic, diced fine

¼ cup green olives, pitted

2 bay leaves

1 ½ tsp cumin

¼ tsp garlic powder

Salt & pepper, to taste

Instructions:

1. In a large skillet, over medium heat, brown ground beef. Season with salt and pepper. Drain fat. Add onion, bell pepper, and garlic and cook 3-4 minutes.
2. Transfer to crock pot and add remaining Ingredients. Cover and cook on high 3 hours.
3. Discard bay leaves. Taste and adjust seasonings as desired. Serve.

Nutrition Facts Per Serving

Calories 255 Total Carbs 6g Net Carbs 5g Protein 35g Fat 9g Sugar 3g Fiber 1g

Honey Bourbon Pork Chops

Prep time: 5 minutes, Cook time: 4 hours, Serves: 4

Ingredients:

4 pork chops, cut thick

What you'll need from store cupboard:

5 tbsp. honey

2 tbsp. lite soy sauce

2 tbsp. bourbon

2 cloves garlic, diced fine

Instructions:

1. In a small bowl, whisk together honey, soy sauce and bourbon. Stir in garlic.
2. Place pork chops in crock pot and top with sauce. Turn to make sure the pork chops are coated.
3. Cover and cook on low heat for 4 hours, or until the chops reach desired doneness. Serve.

Nutrition Facts Per Serving

Calories 231 Total Carbs 24g Protein 23g Fat 3g Sugar 20g Fiber 0g

Beef Goulash

Prep time: 15 minutes, Cook time: 1 hour, Serves: 6

Ingredients:

2 lb. chuck steak, trim fat and cut into bite-sized pieces

3 onions, quartered

1 green pepper,

chopped

1 red pepper, chopped

1 orange pepper, chopped

What you'll need from store cupboard:

3 cups water

1 can tomatoes, chopped

1 cup low sodium beef broth

3 cloves garlic, diced fine

2 tbsp. tomato paste

1 tbsp. olive oil

1 tbsp. paprika

2 tsp hot smoked paprika

2 bay leaves

Salt & pepper, to taste

Instructions:

1. Heat oil in a large soup pot over med-high. Add steak and cook until browned, stirring frequently. Add onions and cook 5 minutes, or until soft. Add garlic and cook another minute, stirring frequently.
2. Add remaining Ingredients. Stir well and bring to a boil. Reduce heat to med-low and simmer 45-50 minutes, stirring occasionally. Goulash is done when steak is tender. Stir well before serving.

Nutrition Facts Per Serving

Calories 413 Total Carbs 14g Protein 53g Fat 15g Sugar 8g Fiber 3g

Horseradish Meatloaf

Prep time: 15 minutes, cook time; 45 minutes, Serves: 8

Ingredients:

1 ½ lbs. lean ground beef
1 egg, beaten
½ cup celery, diced fine
¼ cup onion, diced fine
¼ cup skim milk

What you'll need from store cupboard:

4 slices whole wheat bread, crumbled
½ cup Sugar free ketchup, (chapter 16)
¼ cup horseradish
2 tbsp. Dijon mustard
2 tbsp. chili sauce
1 ½ tsp Worcestershire sauce
½ tsp salt
¼ tsp pepper
Nonstick cooking spray

Instructions:

1. Heat oven to 350 degrees. Spray an 11x7-inch baking dish with cooking spray.
2. In a large bowl, soak bread in milk for 5 minutes. Drain.
3. Stir in celery, onion, horseradish, mustard, chili sauce, Worcestershire, egg, salt, and pepper. Crumble beef over mixture and mix well.
4. Shape into loaf in the prepared baking dish. Spread ketchup over the top. Bake 45-50 minutes or a meat thermometer reaches 160 degrees. Let rest 10 minutes before slicing and serving.

Nutrition Facts Per Serving

Calories 213 Total Carbs 8g Net Carbs 7g Protein 29g Fat 7g Sugar 2g Fiber 1g

Beef Tenderloin with Roasted Vegetables

Prep time: 20 minutes, Cook time: 1 hour, Serves: 10

Ingredients:

3 lb. beef tenderloin halved
1 lb. Yukon gold potatoes, cut in 1-inch wedges
1 lb. Brussel sprouts,
1 lb. baby carrots
4 tsp fresh rosemary, diced

What you'll need from store cupboard:

¾ cup dry white wine
¾ cup low sodium soy sauce
3 cloves garlic, sliced
4 tsp Dijon mustard
1 ½ tsp ground mustard
Nonstick cooking spray

Instructions:

1. Place beef in a large Ziploc bag.
2. In a small bowl combine wine, soy sauce, rosemary, Dijon, ground mustard, and garlic. Pour half the mixture over the beef. Seal the bag and turn to coat. Refrigerate 4 ½ hours, turning occasionally. Cover and refrigerate remaining marinade.
3. Heat oven to 425 degrees. Spray a 9x13-inch baking dish with cooking spray.
4. Place the potatoes, Brussel sprouts and carrots in the prepared dish. Add reserved marinade and toss to coat. Cover and bake 30 minutes.
5. Remove tenderloin and discard marinade. Place over vegetables and bake 30-45 minutes or until meat reaches desired doneness.
6. Remove been and let stand 15 minutes. Check vegetables, if they are not tender bake another 10-15 minutes until done. Slice36 the beef and serve with vegetables.

Nutrition Facts Per Serving

Calories 356 Total Carbs 13g Net Carbs 10g Protein 43g Fat 13g Sugar 4g Fiber 3g

Mississippi Style Pot Roast

Prep time: 5 minutes, Cook time: 8 hours, Serves: 8

Ingredients:

3 lb. chuck roast

What you'll need from store cupboard:

6-8 pepperoncini
1 envelope au jus gravy mix
1 envelope ranch dressing mix

Instructions:

1. Place roast in crock pot. Sprinkle both envelopes of mixes over top. Place the peppers around the roast.
2. Cover and cook on low 8 hours, or high 4 hours.
3. Transfer roast to a large bowl and shred using 2 forks. Add it back to the crock pot and stir. Remove the pepperoncini, chop and stir back into the roast. Serve.

Nutrition Facts Per Serving

Calories 379 Total Carbs 3g Protein 56g Fat 14g Sugar 1g Fiber 0g

Beer Braised Brisket

Prep time: 10 minutes: Cook time: 8 hours, Serves: 10

Ingredients:

5 lb. beef brisket
1 bottle of lite beer
1 onion, sliced thin

What you'll need from store cupboard:

15 oz. can tomatoes, diced
3 cloves garlic, diced fine
1 tbsp. + 1 tsp oregano
1 tbsp. salt
1 tbsp. black pepper

Instructions:

1. Place the onion on the bottom of the crock pot. Add brisket, fat side up. Add the tomatoes, undrained and beer. Sprinkle the garlic and seasonings on the top.
2. Cover and cook on low heat 8 hours, or until beef is fork tender.

Nutrition Facts Per Serving

Calories 445 Total Carbs 4g Net Carbs 3g Protein 69g Fat 14g Sugar 2g Fiber 1g

Grilled Lamb & Apricot Kebabs

Prep time: 1 hour 10 minutes, Cook time: 15 minutes, Serves: 6

Ingredients:

2 ½ lbs. lamb stew meat
1 red onion, cut into
chunks
½ cup plain yogurt
Juice of 1 lemon

What you'll need from store cupboard:

2 cup dried apricots
1 ½ tsp smoked paprika
½ tsp oregano
Black pepper, to taste
Boiling water

Instructions:

1. In a large bowl, whisk together yogurt, lemon juice, smoked paprika, oregano and pepper. Add the lamb and toss until well coated. Cover and refrigerate for at least 1 hour.
2. Place the apricots in a medium bowl. Cover with boiling water and let sit for at least 30 minutes.
3. Heat grill to med-high heat. Thread 6 skewers with piece of lamb, then apricot, then onion. Repeat.
4. Grill 2-3 minutes per side, until lambs is nicely browned on the outside. Serve.

Nutrition Facts Per Serving

Calories 401 Total Carbs 10g Net Carbs 8g Protein 55g Fat 14g Sugar 7g Fiber 2g

Zucchini Lasagna

Prep time: 30 minutes, Cook time: 1 hour, Serves: 4

Ingredients:

1 lb. lean ground beef
2 medium zucchini, julienned
3 tomatoes, blanch in hot water, remove skins and dice
1 onion, diced
1 serrano chili, remove seeds and dice
1 cup mushrooms, remove stems and dice
½ cup low-fat mozzarella, grated

What you'll need from store cupboard:

2 cloves garlic, diced fine
½ cube chicken bouillon
1 tsp. paprika
1 tsp. dried thyme
1 tsp. dried basil
Salt and pepper
Nonstick cooking spray

Instructions:

1. Lay zucchini on paper towel lined cutting board and sprinkle lightly with salt. Let sit for 10 minutes.
2. Heat oven to broil. Blot zucchini with paper towels and place on baking sheet. Broil 3 minutes. Transfer to paper towels again to remove excess moisture.
3. Lightly coat a deep skillet with cooking spray and place over med-high heat. Add garlic, onion, and chili and cook 1 minute.
4. Add the tomatoes and mushrooms and cook, stirring frequently, about 4 minutes. Transfer vegetables to a bowl.
5. Add the beef to the skillet with the paprika and cook until no longer pink. Add the vegetables and bouillon to the beef along with remaining spices and let simmer over low heat 25 minutes.
6. Heat oven to 375 degrees. Line a small baking dish with parchment paper and place 1/3 of the zucchini in an even layer on the bottom. Top with 1/3 of the meat mixture. Repeat layers.
7. Sprinkle cheese over top and bake 35 minutes. Let rest 10 minutes before serving.

Nutrition Facts Per Serving

Calories 272 Total Carbs 11g Net Carbs 8g Protein 38g Fat 8g Sugar 6g Fiber 3g

Blue Cheese Crusted Beef Tenderloin

Prep time: 10 minutes, Cook time: 15 minutes, Serves: 4

Ingredients:

4 beef tenderloin steaks	4 ½ tsp fresh parsley, diced
2 tbsp. blue cheese, crumbled	4 ½ tsp chives, diced
	1 ½ tsp butter

What you'll need from store cupboard:

½ cup low sodium beef broth	1 tbsp. Madeira wine
4 ½ tsp bread crumbs	¼ tsp pepper
1 tbsp. flour	Nonstick cooking spray

Instructions:

1. Heat oven to 350 degrees. Spray a large baking sheet with cooking spray.
2. In a small bowl, combine blue cheese, bread crumbs, parsley, chives, and pepper. Press onto one side of the steaks.
3. Spray a large skillet with cooking spray and place over med-high heat.
4. Add steaks and sear 2 minutes per side. Transfer to prepared baking sheet and bake 6-8 minutes, or steaks reach desired doneness.
5. Melt butter in a small saucepan over medium heat. Whisk in flour until smooth. Slowly whisk in broth and wine. Bring to a boil, cook, stirring, 2 minutes or until thickened.
6. Plate the steaks and top with gravy. Serve.

Nutrition Facts Per Serving
Calories 263 Total Carbs 4g Protein 36g Fat 10g Sugar 0g Fiber 0g

French Onion Casserole

Prep time: 15 minutes, Cook time: 55 minutes, Serves: 8

Ingredients:

1 lb. lean ground beef	1 cup Swiss cheese, grated
6 eggs	½ cup onion, diced
2 cup skim milk	

What you'll need from store cupboard:

10 oz. can condensed French onion soup	1 tbsp. olive oil
6 oz. pkg. herb stuffing mix	1 tbsp. chili sauce
1 tbsp. Worcestershire sauce	2 tsp thyme
	Nonstick cooking spray

Instructions:

1. Heat oven to 350 degrees. Spray a 13x9-inch baking dish with cooking spray.
2. Heat oil in a large skillet over medium heat. Add beef and cook, breaking up with spatula, until no longer pink. Add onion, Worcestershire, and chili sauce, and cook 3-5 minutes, until onions are soft.
3. In a large bowl, beat eggs, soup, milk, ½ cup cheese, and 1 teaspoon thyme. Add the dry stuffing mix and beef. Stir well, making sure to coat the stuffing mixture.
4. Transfer to prepared baking dish. Sprinkle with remaining cheese and thyme and let rest 15 minutes.
5. Bake 45 minutes or until a knife inserted in center comes out clean. Serve.

Nutrition Facts Per Serving
Calories 327 Total Carbs 23g Net Carbs 22g Protein 30g Fat 12g Sugar 7g Fiber 1g

Creamy Braised Oxtails

Prep time: 10 minutes, Cook time: 4-6 hours, Serves: 6

Ingredients:

2 pounds oxtails	½ cup half-n-half
1 onion, diced	1 tsp margarine

What you'll need from store cupboard:

1 cup low sodium beef broth	2 tbsp. chili sauce
¼ cup sake	1 tsp Chinese five spice
4 cloves garlic, diced	Salt & pepper

Instructions:

1. Melt the margarine in a large skillet over med-high heat. Sprinkle oxtails with salt and pepper and cook until brown on all sides, about 3-4 minutes per side.
2. Add onion and garlic and cook another 3-5 minutes. Add the sake to deglaze the skillet and cook until liquid is reduced, 1-2 minutes.
3. Transfer mixture to the crock pot. Add the broth, chili sauce, and five spice, stir to combine. Cover and cook on low 6 hours, or high 4 hours, or until meat is tender.
4. Stir in the half-n-half and continue cooking another 30-60 minutes or sauce has thickened. Serve.

Nutrition Facts Per Serving
Calories 447 Total Carbs 4g Protein 48g Fat 24g Sugar 1g Fiber 0g

Cajun Beef & Rice Skillet

Prep time: 10 minutes, Cook time: 25 minutes, Serves: 4

Ingredients:

¾ lb. lean ground beef

2 cup cauliflower rice, cooked

1 red bell pepper, sliced thin

½ yellow onion, diced

1 stalk celery, sliced thin

1 jalapeño pepper, seeds removed and diced fine

¼ cup fresh parsley, diced

What you'll need from store cupboard:

½ cup low sodium beef broth

4 tsp Cajun seasoning

Instructions:

1. Place beef and 1 ½ teaspoons Cajun seasoning in a large skillet over med-high heat. Cook, breaking apart with wooden spoon, until no longer pink, about 10 minutes.

2. Add vegetables, except cauliflower, and remaining Cajun seasoning. Cook, stirring occasionally, 6-8 minutes, or until vegetables are tender.

3. Add broth and stir, scraping brown bits from the bottom of the pan. Cook 2-3 minutes until mixture has thickened. Stir in cauliflower and cook just until heated through. Remove from heat, stir in parsley and serve.

Nutrition Facts Per Serving

Calories 198 Total Carbs 8g Net Carbs 6g Protein 28g Fat 6g Sugar 4g Fiber 2g

Cajun Smothered Pork Chops

Prep time: 5 minutes, Cook time: 25 minutes, Serves: 4

Ingredients:

4 pork chops, thick-cut

1 small onion, diced fine

1 cup mushrooms,

sliced

1 cup fat free sour cream

2 tbsp. margarine

What you'll need from store cupboard:

1 cup low sodium chicken broth

3 cloves garlic, diced fine

1 tbsp. Cajun

seasoning

2 bay leaves

1 tsp smoked paprika

Salt & pepper to taste

Instructions:

1. Melt margarine in a large skillet over medium heat. Sprinkle chops with

salt and pepper and cook until nicely browned, about 5 minutes per side. Transfer to a plate.

2. Add onions and mushrooms and cook until soft, about 5 minutes. Add garlic and cook one minute more.

3. Add broth and stir to incorporate brown bits on bottom of the pan. Add a dash of salt and the bay leaves. Add pork chops back to sauce. Bring to a simmer, cover, and reduce heat. Cook 5-8 minutes, or until chops are cooked through.

4. Transfer chops to a plate and keep warm. Bring sauce to a boil and cook until it has reduced by half, stirring occasionally.

5. Reduce heat to low and whisk in sour cream, Cajun seasoning, and paprika. Cook, stirring frequently, 3 minutes. Add chops back to the sauce and heat through. Serve.

Nutrition Facts Per Serving

Calories 323 Total Carbs 13g Net Carbs 12g Protein 24g Fat 18g Sugar 5g Fiber 1g

Garlic Honey Pork Chops

Prep time: 5 minutes, Cook time: 10 minutes, Serves: 6

Ingredients:

6 boneless pork loin chops, trim excess fat

What you'll need from store cupboard:

¼ cup lemon juice

¼ cup honey

¼ cup low sodium soy sauce

¼ cup dry white wine

2 tbsp. garlic, diced fine

1 tbsp. vegetable oil

¼ tsp black pepper

Instructions:

1. Combine lemon juice, honey, soy sauce, wine, garlic, and pepper in a 9x13 baking dish. Mix well.

2. Add pork chops, turning to coat. Cover and refrigerate at least 4 hours, or overnight, turning chops occasionally.

3. Heat oil in a large skillet over med-high heat. Add chops and cook 2-3 minutes per side.

4. Pour marinade over chops and bring to a boil. Reduce heat to low and simmer 2-3 minutes, or chops are desired doneness. Serve topped with sauce.

Nutrition Facts Per Serving

Calories 436 Total Carbs 14g Protein 26g Fat 30g Sugar 12g Fiber 0g

Cheesesteak Stuffed Peppers

Prep time: 15 minutes, Cook time: 35 minutes, Serves: 4

Ingredients:

4 slices low-salt deli roast beef, cut into 1/2-inch strips	and blanch in boiling water 1 minute
4 slices mozzarella cheese, cut in half	1 ½ cup sliced mushrooms
2 large green bell peppers, slice in half, remove seeds,	1 cup thinly sliced onion
	1 tbsp. margarine

What you'll need from store cupboard:

1 tbsp. vegetable oil	¼ tsp salt
2 tsp garlic, diced fine	¼ tsp black pepper

Instructions:

1. Heat oven to 400 degrees. Place peppers, skin side down, in baking dish.
2. Heat oil and margarine in a large skillet over medium heat. Once hot, add onions, mushrooms, garlic, salt, and pepper, and cook, stirring occasionally, 10-12 minutes or mushrooms are tender.
3. Remove from heat and stir in roast beef.
4. Place a piece of cheese inside each pepper and fill with meat mixture. Cover with foil and bake 20 minutes.
5. Remove the foil and top each pepper with remaining cheese. Bake another 5 minutes, or until cheese is melted.

Nutrition Facts Per Serving

Calories 191 Total Carbs 10g Net Carbs 8g Protein 12g Fat 12g Sugar 5g Fiber 2g

Cheesy Beef & Noodles

Prep time: 10 minutes, Cook time: 15 minutes, Serves: 4

Ingredients:

1 lb. lean ground beef	grated
1 onion, diced	½ cup + 2 tbsp. fresh parsley diced
2 cup mozzarella,	

What you'll need from store cupboard:

Homemade Noodles, (chapter 15)	3 cloves garlic, diced fine
2 tbsp. tomato paste	1 tsp red pepper flakes
1 tbsp. extra-virgin olive oil	½ tsp pepper
1 tbsp. Worcestershire sauce	Salt, to taste

Instructions:

1. Heat oil in a large skillet over med-high heat. Add beef and cook, breaking up with a spatula, about 2 minutes.
2. Reduce heat to medium and season with salt and pepper. Stir in garlic, onion, pepper flakes, Worcestershire, tomato paste, ½ cup parsley, and ½ cup water. Bring to a simmer and cook, stirring occasionally, 8 minutes.
3. Stir in noodles and cook 2 minutes more. Stir in 1 cup of cheese, sprinkle the remaining cheese over the top and cover with lid, off the heat, until cheese melts. Serve garnished with remaining parsley.

Nutrition Facts Per Serving

Calories 372 Total Carbs 7g Net Carbs 6g Protein 44g Fat 18g Sugar 3g Fiber 1g

Deconstructed Philly Cheesesteaks

Prep time: 5 minutes, Cook time: 20 minutes, Serves: 4

Ingredients:

1 lb. lean ground beef	cheese
5-6 mushrooms, halved	3 green bell peppers, quartered
4 slices provolone	2 medium onions, quartered

What you'll need from store cupboard:

½ cup low sodium beef broth	1 tsp olive oil
1-2 tbsp. Worcestershire sauce	Salt & pepper, to taste

Instructions:

1. Heat oven to 400 degrees.
2. Place vegetables in a large bowl and add oil. Toss to coat. Dump out onto a large baking sheet and bake 10-15 minutes, or until tender-crisp.
3. Place beef in a large skillet and cook over med-high heat until no longer pink. Drain off fat.
4. Add broth and Worcestershire. Cook, stirring occasionally, until liquid is absorbed, about 5 minutes. Salt and pepper beef if desired. Top with sliced cheese, remove from heat and cover until cheese melts.
5. Divide vegetables evenly between 4 bowls. Top with beef and serve.

Nutrition Facts Per Serving

Calories 388 Total Carbs 15g Net Carbs 12g Protein 44g Fat 16g Sugar 9g Fiber 3g

Crock Pot Beef Roast with Gravy

Prep time: 15 minutes, Cook time: 5 ½ hours, Serves: 10

Ingredients:
3 lb. beef sirloin tip roast

What you'll need from store cupboard:

¼ cup lite soy sauce	pepper
¼ cup water	1 tbsp.
3 tbsp. balsamic	Worcestershire sauce
vinegar	2 tsp ground mustard
2 tbsp. cornstarch	1 ½ tsp garlic, diced
2 tbsp. coarse ground	fine

Instructions:
1. Rub roast with garlic and pepper. Cut in half and place in crock pot.
2. Combine soy sauce, vinegar, Worcestershire, and mustard, pour over roast.
3. Cover and cook on low heat 5 ½-6 hours or until beef is tender.
4. Remove roast and keep warm. Strain juices into a small sauce pan, skim off fat. Heat over medium heat.
5. Stir water and cornstarch together until smooth. Stir into beef juices. Bring to a boil, and cook, stirring, 2 minutes or until thickened. Serve with roast.

Nutrition Facts Per Serving
Calories 264 Total Carbs 3g Protein 37g Fat 12g Sugar 0g Fiber 0g

Crock Pot Carnitas

Prep time: 10 minutes, Cook time: 6 hours, Serves: 4

Ingredients:

4 lb. pork butt, boneless, trim the fat and cut into 2-inch cubes	Juice from 1 orange, reserve orange halves
1 onion, cut in half	2 tbsp. fresh lime juice

What you'll need from store cupboard:

2 cup water	1 tsp oregano
1 ½ tsp salt	2 bay leaves
1 tsp cumin	¾ tsp pepper

Instructions:
1. Place pork and orange halves in the crock pot. In a medium bowl, combine remaining Ingredients and stir to combine. Pour over pork.
2. Cover and cook on high 5 hours. Pork should be tender enough to shred with a fork. If not, cook another 60 minutes.
3. Transfer pork to a bowl. Pour the sauce into a large saucepan and discard the bay leaves and orange halves.
4. Bring to a boil and cook until it thickens and resembles a syrup.
5. Use two forks to shred the pork. Add pork to the sauce and stir to coat. Serve.

Nutrition Facts Per Serving
Calories 464 Total Carbs 3g Protein 35g Fat 35g Sugar 1g Fiber 0g

Italian Sausage & Zucchini Warm Salad

Prep time: 15 minutes, Cook time: 40 minutes, Serves: 6

Ingredients:
1 pkg. Italian sausage
3 small zucchinis, halved lengthwise

What you'll need from store cupboard:

12 oz. jar roasted red peppers, drain and cut into strips	grated ½ cup Italian Salad dressing (chapter 16)
6 oz. can black olives, drain	2 tbsp. olive oil, divided
1 cup reduced fat parmesan cheese,	Salt and pepper to taste

Instructions:
1. Heat 2 tsp. olive oil in a large non-stick frying pan. Add sausage and cook over medium-high heat until sausage is firm and well-browned on all sides. Transfer to cutting board and cut into ¾-inch slices.
2. Cut zucchini in ¾-inch slices.
3. Add another teaspoon of oil to the skillet, if needed, and cook sausage until browned on both sides. Transfer to a plate.
4. Add the remaining tablespoon of oil to the skillet along with the zucchini. Cook until it begins to soften, about 4-5 minutes. Remove from heat and cool slightly. Stir in Italian dressing and stir to coat the zucchini. Let marinate at least 5 minutes.
5. In a large bowl, combine sausage, olives, and peppers. Mix in the zucchini and dressing from the pan. Season with salt and pepper and fold in parmesan cheese. Serve immediately

Nutrition Facts Per Serving
Calories 399 Total Carbs 7g Net Carbs 5g Protein 19g Fat 32g Sugar 3g Fiber 2g

Crust Less Pizza

Prep time: 5 minutes, Cook time: 25 minutes, Serves: 4

Ingredients:

Pepperoni, ham, sausage, mushrooms, or toppings of your choice
8 oz. fat free cream

cheese, soft
1 ½ cup mozzarella cheese, grated
2 eggs

What you'll need from store cupboard:

½ cup lite pizza sauce
¼ cup reduced fat

parmesan cheese
1 tsp garlic powder
¼ tsp pepper

Instructions:

1. Heat oven to 350 degrees. Spray and 9x13-inch baking dish with cooking spray.
2. In a large bowl, beat cream cheese, eggs, pepper, garlic powder, and parmesan until combined. Spread in prepared dish and bake 12-15 minutes or until golden brown. Let cool 10 minutes.
3. Spread pizza sauce over crust. Top with cheese and your favorite pizza toppings. Sprinkle lightly with garlic powder. Bake 8-10 minutes or until cheese melts. Cool 5 minutes before serving.

Nutrition Facts Per Serving

Calories 164 Total Carbs 4g Net Carbs 3g Protein 12g Fat 11g Sugar 1g Fiber 1g

Easy Carbonara

Prep time: 5 minutes, Cook time: 10 minutes, Serves: 2

Ingredients:

1 slice bacon, thick cut
1 egg

½ tbsp. fresh parsley, diced

What you'll need from store cupboard:

Homemade Noodles, chapter 15
¼ cup reduced fat

parmesan cheese
Black pepper, to taste

Instructions:

1. Bring a large pot of salted water to a boil. Add the noodles and cook 1-2 minutes.
2. In a small bowl, beat the egg and parmesan cheese together.
3. Cook the bacon in a large pan until crispy. Remove the bacon (turn off the heat and leave the fat in the pan) and drain on a paper towel before cutting it into small pieces.
4. Once the noodles have boiled add them to the pan with the bacon fat. Pour the egg mixture over the hot pasta and toss together quickly (the heat from the pasta will cook the egg).
5. Add the chopped parsley, bacon and black pepper and continue tossing until combined. Serve.

Nutrition Facts Per Serving

Calories 237 Total Carbs 2g Protein 17g Fat 18g Sugar 0g Fiber 0g

Ham & Brie Turnovers

Prep time: 15 minutes, Cook time: 25 minutes, Serves: 8

Ingredients:

8 slices ham, diced
3 oz. brie cheese

1 egg

What you'll need from store cupboard:

2 9-inch pie crusts, unbaked
2 tbsp. sugar free fig preserves
2 tbsp. stone ground

mustard
1 tbsp. water
1/8 tsp salt
1/8 tsp pepper

Instructions:

1. Heat oven to 400 degrees. Line two cookie sheets with parchment paper.
2. On a lightly floured surface unroll one pie crust and cut 4 4-inch circles and place on prepared pan.
3. Gather up remaining dough, roll out and cut 4 more 4-inch circles and set aside
4. In a small bowl, combine fig preserves, mustard, salt, and pepper. Place a heaping teaspoon of fig mustard mixture in the center of dough on the pan and shape into a half dollar size
5. Use your hands to make a smaller circle of the brie and place on top of fig mixture. Place ham on top of the cheese, leaving ¼-inch edge.
6. In another small bowl, beat egg and water together. Brush around edge and top with 4-inch circle of dough. Repeat. Use a fork to seal the edges and cut a small X in the top. Brush with remaining egg wash.
7. Bake 25 minutes, or until golden brown. Remove from oven and cool on wire rack at least 5 minutes before serving. Repeat these steps with the second pie crust.

Nutrition Facts Per Serving

Calories 337 Total Carbs 25g Net Carbs 24g Protein 10g Fat 21g Sugar 2g Fiber 1g

Garlic Butter Steak

Prep time: 5 minutes, Cook time: 8 minutes, Serves: 4

Ingredients:

1 lb. skirt steak	diced, divided
1/4 cup fresh parsley,	5 tbsp. margarine

What you'll need from store cupboard:

6 tsp garlic, diced fine	Salt and pepper for taste
1 tbsp. olive oil	

Instructions:

1. Cut the steak into 4 pieces. Pat dry then season both sides with salt and pepper
2. Heat oil in a large, heavy skillet over med-high heat. Add steak and sear both sides, 2-3 minutes for medium rare, until it reaches desired doneness. Transfer to plate and cover with foil to keep warm.
3. Melt the margarine in a separate skillet over low heat. Add garlic and cook, stirring, until garlic is a light golden brown.
4. Pour the garlic mixture into a bowl and season with salt to taste. Slice the steak against the grain and place on plates. Sprinkle parsley over steak then drizzle with garlic mixture. Serve immediately.

Nutrition Facts Per Serving
Calories 365 Total Carbs 2g Protein 31g Fat 25g Sugar 0g Fiber 0g

Grilled Cajun Beef Tenderloin

Prep time: 10 minutes, Cook time: 1 hour, Serves: 12

Ingredients:

3 lb. beef tenderloin

What you'll need from store cupboard:

1 tbsp. paprika	½ tsp chili powder
4 tsp salt	1/8 tsp thyme
2 ¼ tsp onion powder	1/8 tsp ground
2 tsp cayenne pepper	mustard
1 ½ tsp garlic powder	Dash of cloves
1 ½ tsp white pepper	Nonstick cooking
1 ½ tsp black pepper	spray.
1 tsp basil	

Instructions:

1. Heat grill to medium heat. Spray rack with cooking spray.
2. In a small bowl combine spices.
3. Tie tenderloin with butcher string in 2-inch intervals. Rub outside of beef with spice mixture.
4. Place on the grill, cover and cook 50 minutes, or to desired doneness. Or roast in 425 degree oven 45-60 minutes.
5. Let rest 10 minutes before slicing and serving.

Nutrition Facts Per Serving
Calories 234 Total Carbs 2g Protein 33g Fat 10g Sugar 0g Fiber 0g

Grilled Pork Tenderloin Sandwiches

Prep time: 15 minutes, Cook time: 25 minutes, Serves: 6

Ingredients:

2 lb. pork tenderloin	cream
6 lettuce leaves	½ tsp fresh ginger,
¼ cup fat free sour	grated

What you'll need from store cupboard:

12 Flourless burger buns, (chapter 14)	brown sugar
2 cloves garlic, diced	1 ½ tsp lemon juice
¼ cup lite mayonnaise	1 tsp Splenda
2 tbsp. sunflower oil	1 tsp ground mustard, divided
2 tbsp. lite soy sauce	½ tsp Dijon mustard
2 tbsp. steak sauce	½ tsp horseradish
1 ½ tsp Splenda	Nonstick cooking spray

Instructions:

1. In a large Ziploc bag, combine oil, soy sauce, steak sauce, garlic, Splenda brown sugar, ½ tsp mustard, and ginger. Add pork and turn to coat. Refrigerate 8 hours or overnight.
2. Heat grill to med-high and spray grill rack with cooking spray. Place pork on the grill, cover, and cook 25-40 minutes, or meat thermometer reaches 160 degrees. Let rest 5 minutes before slicing.
3. In a small bowl, combine mayonnaise, sour cream, lemon juice, Splenda, remaining mustard, Dijon, and horseradish.
4. To serve, layer sliced pork on one bun, top with horseradish sauce, lettuce and another bun.

Nutrition Facts Per Serving
Calories 369 Total Carbs 7g Protein 44g Fat 16g Sugar 4g Fiber 0g

Herb Crusted Pork Tenderloin

Prep time: 5 minutes, Cook time: 4 hours, serves; 4

Ingredients:

1 lb. pork tenderloin	1 tsp thyme
What you'll need from store cupboard	½ tsp garlic, diced fine
2 tsp olive oil	Salt and pepper, to taste
1 tsp sage	

Instructions:

1. Stir the oil and seasonings together in a small bowl.
2. Place tenderloin in the crock pot and pour seasoning mix over the top. Cover and cook on high 3-4 hours, or until pork reaches desired doneness. Serve.

Nutrition Facts Per Serving

Calories 183 Total Carbs 0g Protein 30g Fat 6g Sugar 0g Fiber 0g

Lamb Ragu

Prep time: 15 minutes, Cook time: 8 hours, Serves: 8

Ingredients:

2 lbs. lamb stew meat	sliced thin
2 onions, diced	4 sprigs fresh rosemary
1 carrot, peeled and	3 tbsp. fresh sage

What you'll need from store cupboard:

28 oz. can whole plum tomatoes, peeled	8 cloves garlic, diced
	2 tbsp. olive oil
2 cups red wine	Salt & pepper, to taste

Instructions:

1. Sprinkle lamb with salt and pepper.
2. Heat oil in a large skillet over med-high heat. Add lamb and cook until brown on all sides.
3. Add onion, reduce heat, and cook 10 minutes, until onion is golden brown. Transfer mixture to a crock pot.
4. Crush the tomatoes with a fork and add to the crock pot with remaining Ingredients. Cover and cook on low 8 hours.
5. Use two forks to shred any chunks of lamb and stir well. Serve.

Nutrition Facts Per Serving

Calories 331 Total Carbs 11g Net Carbs 9g Protein 34g Fat 12g Sugar 6g Fiber 2g

Italian Pork Medallions

Prep time: 10 minutes, Cook time: 15 minutes, Serves: 2

Ingredients:

½ lb. pork tenderloin
¼ cup onion, diced

What you'll need from store cupboard:

1 clove garlic, diced	parmesan cheese
2 tbsp. Italian bread crumbs	2 tsp olive oil
	¼ tsp salt
1 tbsp. reduced fat	1/8 tsp pepper

Instructions:

1. Slice the tenderloin into 4 equal pieces. Flatten each piece to ¼-inch thick.
2. In a large Ziploc bag, combine bread crumbs, cheese, salt, and pepper.
3. Heat oil in a large skillet over medium heat. Add pork to the Ziploc bag, one piece at a time, and turn to coat.
4. Add the pork to the skillet and cook 2-3 minutes per side, or until no longer pink. Transfer to a plate and keep warm.
5. Add onion to the skillet and cook, stirring, until tender. Add garlic and cook 1 minute more. Serve pork topped with onions.

Nutrition Facts Per Serving

Calories 244 Total Carbs 7g Net Carbs 6g Protein 31g Fat 10g Sugar 1g Fiber 1g

Tangy Balsamic Beef

Prep time: 5 minutes, Cook time: 6 – 8 hours, Serves: 8

Ingredients:

3-4 lb. beef roast, boneless
½ onion, diced fine

What you'll need from store cupboard:

1 can low sodium beef broth	3 tbsp. honey
	1 tbsp. lite soy sauce
½ cup balsamic vinegar	1 tbsp. Worcestershire sauce
5 cloves garlic, diced fine	1 tsp red chili flakes

Instructions:

1. Place all Ingredients, except the roast, into the crock pot. Stir well. Add roast and turn to coat.
2. Cover and cook on low 6-8 hours. When the beef is done, remove to a plate and shred, using two forks. Add it back to the sauce and serve.

Nutrition Facts Per Serving

Calories 410 Total Carbs 9g Protein 45g Fat 20g Sugar 7g Fiber 0g

Maple Bourbon Glazed Ham

Prep time: 15 minutes, Cook time: 1 hour 30 minutes, Serves: 12
Ingredients:
10 lb. hickory smoked ham, butt portion
What you'll need from store cupboard:

1 ¼ cup Splenda	1 tsp maple extract
3 tbsp. bourbon	1 tsp dry mustard
1 tbsp. whole cloves	1 tsp white vinegar

Instructions:
1. Heat oven to 325 degrees.
2. Place ham face down in a shallow baking pan and cover loosely with aluminum foil. Place on lower rack of oven and bake for 1 hour.
3. In a small bowl, mix remaining Ingredients, except cloves, together.
4. After 1 hour of cooking, remove ham from oven, uncover and stand ham up on 1 side. With a sharp knife and in a "tic-tac-toe" fashion, score the fatty side of the ham, Insert single whole cloves in every corner of the squares created by the cuts.
5. Pour the glaze over the top and let drip down the ham. Place uncovered ham back in the oven and cook for another 30 minutes. Remove from oven and let stand 15 minutes before slicing.

Nutrition Facts Per Serving
Calories 417 Total Carbs 27g Net Carbs 25g Protein 31g Fat 16g Sugar 20gFiber 2g

Pasta Bolognese

Prep time: 10 minutes, Cook time: 2 hours, Serves: 8
Ingredients:

1 lb. lean ground beef	½ cup carrots, diced
4 oz. pancetta, chopped	½ cup half-n-half
	¼ cup fresh parsley, diced
1 small onion, diced	1 tbsp. margarine
½ cup celery, diced	

What you'll need from store cupboard:

2 28 oz. cans tomatoes, crushed	to taste
¼ cup white wine	Homemade pasta, cook and drain, (chapter 14)
1 bay leaf	
Salt & fresh pepper,	

Instructions:
1. Place a heavy, deep saucepan over med-high heat. Add pancetta and cook, stirring occasionally, until fat melts.
2. Add margarine, onions, celery and carrots, reduce heat to med-low and cook until soft, about 5 minutes.
3. Increase heat to med-high, add meat, season with salt and pepper and sauté until browned.
4. Add wine and cook until it reduces down, about 3-4 minutes.
5. Add tomatoes and bay leaf. Reduce heat to low, cover and simmer, at least 1-1/2 to 2 hours, stirring occasionally.
6. Stir in half & half and parsley, cook 2 minutes longer. Serve over pasta.

Nutrition Facts Per Serving
Calories 421 Total Carbs 23g Net Carbs 16g Protein 41g Fat 18g Sugar 13g Fiber 7g

Sirloin Strips & "Rice"

Prep time: 15 minutes, Cook time: 30 minutes, Serves: 6
Ingredients:
1 ½ lbs. top sirloin steak, cut in thin strips
3 cup Cauliflower Rice, cook, (chapter 14)
2 onions, slice thin
What you'll need from store cupboard:

14 ½ oz. tomatoes, diced, undrained	1 bay leaf
	2 tsp olive oil, divided
½ cup low sodium beef broth	1 tsp salt
	½ tsp basil
1/3 cup dry red wine	½ tsp thyme
1 clove garlic, diced	¼ tsp pepper

Instructions:
1. Sprinkle beef strips with salt and pepper.
2. Heat oil in a large skillet over medium heat. Add steak and cook, stirring frequently, just until browned. Transfer to a plate and keep warm.
3. Add remaining oil to the skillet along with the onion and cook until tender. Add the garlic and cook 1 minute more.
4. Stir in remaining Ingredients, except the cauliflower, and bring to a boil. Reduce heat and simmer 10 minutes.
5. Return the steak back to the skillet and cook 2-4 minutes until heated through and tender. Discard bay leaf and serve over cauliflower rice.

Nutrition Facts Per Serving
Calories 278 Total Carbs 9g Net Carbs 6g Protein 37g Fat 9g Sugar 5g Fiber 3g

Spicy BBQ Beef Brisket

Prep time: 10 minutes, Cook time: 5 hours, Serves: 14

Ingredients:

3 ½ lb. beef brisket	fine
½ cup onion, diced	1 tsp lemon juice

What you'll need from store cupboard:

2 cup BBQ sauce, (chapter 16)	Worcestershire sauce 1 tsp garlic, diced
1 pkt. Chili seasoning	fine
1 tbsp.	

Instructions:

1. Cut brisket in half and place in crock pot.
2. In a small bowl, combine remaining Ingredients, and pour over beef. Cover and cook on high heat 5-6 hours or until beef is fork tender.
3. Transfer brisket to a bowl. Use two forks and shred. Add the meat back to the crock pot and stir to heat through. Serve as is or on buns.

Nutrition Facts Per Serving

Calories 239 Total Carbs 7g Protein 34g Fat 7g Sugar 4g Fiber 0g

Pork Paprika

Prep time: 5 minutes, Cook time: 40 minutes, serves; 6

Ingredients:

1 lb. pork loin, trim fat and cut into 1-inch cubes	1 cup mushrooms, sliced thick 2/3 cup fat free sour cream
1 onion, diced fine	

What you'll need from store cupboard:

1 can petite tomatoes, diced	1 tbsp. garlic, diced fine
½ cup low sodium chicken broth	½ tsp thyme ½ tsp caraway seeds, ground
2 tbsp. olive oil	
2 tbsp. sweet paprika, divided	Salt & pepper to taste

Instructions:

1. Place pork in large bowl and sprinkle 1 tablespoon paprika, salt and pepper over meat, toss to coat.
2. Heat 1 tablespoon oil in a large, deep skillet over med-high heat. Add pork and cook, stirring frequently until brown on all sides, about 5-6 minutes. Transfer to a plate.
3. Add remaining tablespoon of oil to skillet and the mushrooms. Cook, stirring, till browned and no more liquid remains in the pan, about 5 minutes. Add the mushrooms to the pork.
4. Add more oil if needed and the onion. Cook about 3-5 minutes, or they just start to brown. Add garlic and spices and cook another 1-2 minutes. Add tomatoes with juice and broth, cook, stirring frequently, until mixture starts to thicken, about 5 minutes.
5. Stir the pork and mushrooms into the sauce. Reduce heat, cover, and simmer 15 minutes, or until pork is tender. Serve.

Nutrition Facts Per Serving

Calories 267 Total Carbs 8g Net Carbs 7g 23g Protein 15g Fat Sugar 3g Fiber 1g

One Pot Beef & Veggies

Prep time: 15 minutes, Cook time: 8 hours, Serves: 10

Ingredients:

3 lb. beef roast	1 green bell pepper, diced
1 lb. red potatoes, cubed	1 parsnip, diced
¼ lb. mushrooms	1 red onion, diced

What you'll need from store cupboard:

14 ½ oz. low sodium beef broth	¾ tsp salt ¾ tsp oregano
¼ cup water	¼ tsp pepper
3 tbsp. cornstarch	

Instructions:

1. Place the vegetables in a large crock pot. Cut roast in half and place on top of vegetables.
2. Combine broth, salt, oregano, and pepper, pour over meat.
3. Cover and cook on low heat 8 hours or until roast is tender.
4. Remove meat and vegetables to a serving platter, keep warm. Skim fat from cooking liquid and transfer to a small saucepan.
5. Place pan over medium heat and bring to a boil. Stir water and cornstarch together until smooth. Add to cooking liquid and stir 2 minutes until thickened. Serve with roast.

Nutrition Facts Per Serving

Calories 381 Total Carbs 28g Net Carbs 22g Protein 46g Fat 9g Sugar 12g Fiber 6g

Poblano & Cheese Burgers

Prep time: 5 minutes, Cook time: 15 minutes, Serves: 4

Ingredients:

1 lb. lean ground beef

4 slices Monterey jack cheese

2 poblano peppers, seeded and chopped

1 egg

2 tbsp. margarine

What you'll need from store cupboard

2 tbsp. dried minced onion

1 tbsp. liquid smoke

1 tbsp. Worcestershire sauce

Salt & pepper to taste

Instructions:

1. Heat up the grill.
2. In a large bowl, combine the beef, egg, onion, liquid smoke, Worcestershire, salt and pepper. Form into 6 patties and grill to desired doneness. Top with cheese.
3. Melt butter in a large skillet over med-high heat. Add pepper and cook until tender and it starts to char.
4. Place burgers on buns (chapter 14) top with peppers and your favorite burger toppings. Serve.

Nutrition Facts Per Serving

Calories 396 Total Carbs 4g Protein 43g Fat 22g Sugar 2g Fiber 0g

Shepherd's Pie

Prep time: 10 minutes, Cook time: 45 minutes, Serves: 8

Ingredients:

1 ½ lbs. ground lamb

3 carrots, grated

1 cauliflower, separated into small florets

1 red onion, diced

4 tbsp. margarine

2 tbsp. half-n-half

¼ cup low fat cheddar cheese, grated

What you'll need from store cupboard:

1 2/3 cups canned tomatoes, diced

4 tbsp. low sodium beef broth

2 cloves garlic, diced

fine

1 tbsp. olive oil

Salt & pepper, to taste

Instructions:

1. Heat oven to 350 degrees. Put a large saucepan of water on to boil.
2. Heat the oil in a large saucepan over med-high heat. Add onion and cook until soft. Add the lamb and cook, stirring occasionally, until brown on all sides.

3. Stir in the broth, tomatoes, and carrots. Reduce heat, and simmer 10 minutes, or until vegetables are tender and liquid evaporates.
4. Add the cauliflower to the boiling water and cook until soft, about 8-10 minutes. Drain well. Add the margarine, half-n-half, salt, and pepper and use an immersion blender to puree until smooth.
5. Pour the meat mixture into a large casserole dish. Top with cauliflower mash and sprinkle cheese over top. Bake 20 minutes, or until cheese is nicely browned. Serve.

Nutrition Facts Per Serving

Calories 262 Total Carbs 9g Net Carbs 6g Protein 27g Fat 13g Sugar 4g Fiber 3g

Southwest Braised Beef

Prep time: 20 minutes, Cook time: 2 hours 25 minutes, Serves: 6

Ingredients:

2 lb. eye of round beef roast, fat trimmed

What you'll need from store cupboard:

1 ¼ cup salsa

1 cup low sodium beef broth

¼ cup water

1 tbsp. vegetable oil

1 ½ tsp chili powder

1 tsp cumin

½ tsp garlic powder

½ tsp oregano

1 bay leaf

Instructions:

1. In a small bowl stir together the seasonings. Rub over the roast.
2. Heat oil in a large pot over med-high heat. Add roast and brown on all sides. Transfer to a plate.
3. Slowly pour broth into pot, stirring to scrape up brown bits off the bottom. Stir in salsa, water, and bay leaf. Return the roast to the pot.
4. Bring to a boil. Reduce heat, cover, and simmer 2 ¼-2 ½ hours or roast is tender.
5. Set meat aside and keep warm. Bring juices back to a boil. Cook 10-15 minutes or liquid is reduced to about 1 1/3 cups, skim fat off the top.
6. Discard bay leaf. Slice roast and serve topped with sauce.

Nutrition Facts Per Serving

Calories 297 Total Carbs 4g Net Carbs 3g Protein 46g Fat 10g Sugar 2g Fiber 1g

Moroccan Beef Skewers

Prep time: 15 minutes, Cook time: 10 minutes, Serves: 8

Ingredients:

2 lbs. top sirloin steak, cut in 1-inch pieces
1 cup fresh parsley, diced

1 cup cilantro, diced
¼ cup onion, grated
3 tbsp. fresh lemon juice
1 tsp ginger, grated

What you'll need from store cupboard:

2 cloves garlic, diced fine
2 tbsp. olive oil
1 tbsp. cumin
1 tbsp. coriander
1 tbsp. paprika
1 tbsp. cider vinegar
1 tbsp. sugar free

ketchup, (chapter 16)
1 tsp Thai red chili paste
Salt & pepper, to taste
Nonstick cooking spray

Instructions:

1. In a large Ziploc bag combine all Ingredients, except beef. Seal and shake to mix.
2. Add beef, seal and turn to coat. Refrigerate 8 hours or overnight.
3. Heat grill to med-high. Spray rack with cooking spray.
4. Place beef on 8 skewers and place on grill. Cover and cook 8-12 minutes, or beef reaches desired doneness. Serve.

Nutrition Facts Per Serving
Calories 251 Total Carbs 2g Protein 35g Fat 11g Sugar 1g Fiber 0g

Stuffed Flank Steak

Prep time: 20 minutes, Cook time: 30 minutes, Serves: 6

Ingredients:

1 ½ lb. flank steak
¼ cup fresh parsley, diced fine

¼ cup sun dried tomatoes

What you'll need from store cupboard:

½ cup boiling water
½ cup reduced fat parmesan cheese
1 tbsp. horseradish, drain

2 tsp vegetable oil
1 tsp coarse black pepper
Nonstick cooking spray

Instructions:

1. Heat oven to 400 degrees. Line a shallow roasting pan with foil and spray it with cooking spray.
2. Place tomatoes in a small bowl and pour boiling water over. Let stand 5 minutes.
3. Drain the tomatoes and add cheese,

parsley, horseradish, and pepper.

4. Cut steak down the middle, horizontally, to within 1/2-inch of opposite side. Open up to lay flat and flatten to ¼-inch thick.
5. Spread tomato mixture over steak leaving ½-inch edges. Roll up and tie with butcher string.
6. Place in prepared pan and cook 30-40 minutes, or until meat reaches desired doneness, 145 degrees on a meat thermometer is med-rare. Let rest 10-15 minutes then slice and serve.

Nutrition Facts Per Serving
Calories 267 Total Carbs 2g Protein 34g Fat 13g Sugar 0g Fiber 0g

Stuffed Grilled Pork Tenderloin

Prep time: 15 minutes, Cook time: 25 minutes, Serves: 6

Ingredients:

2 ¾ lb. pork tenderloins
½ tsp fresh ginger, grated

What you'll need from store cupboard:

"Cornbread" Stuffing, (chapter 15)
¾ cup dry red wine
1/3 cup Splenda brown sugar
¼ cup ketchup, (chapter 16)

2 tbsp. low sodium soy sauce
2 cloves garlic, diced
1 tsp curry powder
1/5 tsp pepper
Nonstick cooking spray

Instructions:

1. Slice the tenderloins down the center lengthwise to within ½-inch of the bottom.
2. In a large Ziploc bag, combine wine, sugar, ketchup, soy sauce, garlic, curry powder, ginger and pepper. Add the pork, seal and turn to coat. Refrigerate 2-3 hours.
3. Heat the grill to med-high. Spray the grill rack with cooking spray.
4. Remove the pork from the bag and discard marinade. Open the tenderloins to lie flat, spread stuffing down the center of each. Tie closed with butcher string in 1 ½-inch intervals.
5. Place tenderloins on the grill, cover and cook 25-40 minutes, or until a meat thermometer reaches 160 degrees. Let rest 5 minutes before slicing and serving.

Nutrition Facts Per Serving
Calories 452 Total Carbs 22g Net Carbs 19g Protein 36g Fat 18g Sugar 14g Fiber 3g

Sausage & Spinach Frittata

Prep time: 5 minutes, Cook time: 40 minutes, Serves: 6

Ingredients:

8 eggs, beaten	¾ cups baby spinach
1 1/3 cup sausage	¼ cup red onion, diced
1 ½ cup red bell pepper, diced	

What you'll need from store cupboard:

Salt and pepper, to taste
Nonstick cooking spray

Instructions:

1. Heat oven to 350 degrees. Spray a 9-inch pie pan with cooking spray.
2. Cook sausage in a medium skillet until no longer pink. Transfer to a large bowl with a slotted spoon.
3. Add remaining Ingredients and mix well. Pour into prepared pan and bake 30-35 minutes or until the center is completely set and top is starting to brown. Serve immediately.

Nutrition Facts Per Serving

Calories 156 Total Carbs 3g Net Carbs 2g Protein 12g Fat 10g Sugar 2g Fiber 1g

Tandoori Lamb

Prep time: 5 minutes, Cook time: 30 minutes, Serves: 6

Ingredients:

1 leg of lamb, butterflied
½ cup plain Greek yogurt

What you'll need from store cupboard:

1 tbsp. paprika	1 tsp garlic paste
1 tsp cumin	1 tsp ginger paste
1 tsp coriander	Salt & pepper, to taste
1 tsp onion powder	

Instructions:

1. In a large Ziploc bag, combine yogurt and spices. Zip closed and squish to mix Ingredients. Add the lamb and massage the marinade into the meat. Chill 1 hour or overnight.
2. Heat oven to 325 degrees. Transfer lamb to a baking sheet. Season with salt and pepper and roast 30 minutes, or until lamb is medium rare.
3. Remove from oven and let rest 5 minutes. Slice and serve.

Nutrition Facts Per Serving

Calories 448 Total Carbs 2g Protein 68g Fat 17g Sugar 1g Fiber 0g

Swedish Meatballs

Prep time: 10 minutes, Cook time: 20 minutes, Serves: 6

Ingredients:

1 lb. lean ground beef	5 tbsp. margarine
1 cup half-n-half	1 egg
¼ cup onion, diced fine	1 tbsp. fresh parsley, diced

What you'll need from store cupboard:

2 cup low sodium beef broth	1 tbsp. olive oil
¼ cup panko bread crumbs	1 tsp Dijon mustard
3 tbsp. flour	½ tsp garlic powder
1 tbsp. Worcestershire sauce	½ tsp salt
	¼ tsp allspice
	¼ tsp nutmeg
	1/8 tsp pepper

Instructions:

1. In a large bowl combine, beef, bread crumbs, egg and spices. Form into 12 large meatballs, or 20 small ones.
2. Heat oil and 1 tablespoon margarine in a large skillet. Add meatballs, in batches, and cook, stirring constantly, till browned and cooked through. Transfer to plate and cover.
3. Add remaining margarine and flour to skillet and stir constantly until it browns. Slowly stir in broth and half-n-half. Add Worcestershire and mustard and simmer till sauce starts to thicken. Salt and pepper to taste.
4. Add meatballs back to pan and cook another 1-2 minutes to heat through. Serve over noodles (chapter 14).

Nutrition Facts Per Serving

Calories 355 Total Carbs 9g Protein 28g Fat 22g Sugar 1g Fiber 0g

Spicy Grilled Flank Steak

Prep time: 15 minutes, Cook time: 15 minutes, Serves: 6

Ingredients:

1 ½ lb. flank steak

What you'll need from store cupboard:

3 tbsp. lite soy sauce
3 tbsp. sherry
3 tbsp. red wine vinegar
3 tbsp. Splenda brown sugar
1 tbsp. vegetable oil
1 ½ tsp paprika
1 ½ tsp red pepper flakes
1 ½ tsp chili powder
1 ½ tsp Worcestershire sauce
¾ tsp parsley flakes
¾ tsp garlic powder
¾ tsp salt
Nonstick cooking spray

Instructions:

1. In a small bowl, combine all Ingredients except steak. Pour 1/3 cup marinade into a large Ziploc bag and add steak. Seal and turn to coat. Refrigerate 1-3 hours. Save remaining marinade for basting.
2. Heat grill to medium heat. Spray rack with cooking spray.
3. Place steak on the grill and cook 6-8 minutes per side, basting every few minutes. Let rest 10 minutes, then slice against the grain and serve.

Nutrition Facts Per Serving

Calories 271 Total Carbs 7g Protein 35g Fat 9g Sugar 7g Fiber 0g

Pork Loin with Onion Beer Sauce

Prep time: 5 minutes, Cook time: 3 hours, Serves: 6

Ingredients:

1 ½ lb. pork loin
1 ½ cup dark beer
1 large onion, sliced

What you'll need from store cupboard:

2 cloves garlic, diced fine
3 tbsp. water
2 tbsp. cornstarch
1 tbsp. olive oil
1 tbsp. Dijon mustard
2 bay leaves

Instructions:

1. Heat oil in a large skillet over med-high heat. Add onions and cook until tender. Add the pork and brown on all sides. Transfer to the crock pot.
2. Add the beer, mustard, garlic, and bay leaves. Cover and cook on high 3 hours, or until pork is tender.
3. Transfer pork to a plate. Whisk together the corn starch and water and add to the

crock pot, stir well. Let cook until sauce thickens, about 30 minutes.
4. Slice the pork and serve topped with sauce.

Nutrition Facts Per Serving

Calories 342 Total Carbs 7g Protein 31g Fat 18g Sugar 1g Fiber 0g

Swedish Beef Noodles

Prep time: 10 minutes, Cook time: 20 minutes, Serves: 4

Ingredients:

1 lb. lean ground beef
8 oz. cremini mushrooms, sliced
1 cup onion, sliced thin
½ cup sour cream

What you'll need from store cupboard:

3 ½ cup low sodium beef broth
1 tsp garlic salt
1 tsp caraway seed
Homemade noodles, (chapter 14)
Nonstick cooking spray

Instructions:

1. Spray a large pot with cooking spray and heat over med-high heat. Add beef and cook, breaking up with spatula, 2 minutes. Add onions and mushrooms and cook until beef is browned and onions are soft.
2. Add the garlic salt, caraway seeds, and broth. Bring to a boil. Cover, reduce heat and simmer 10 minutes. Add noodles and cook another 3-5 minutes or noodles are done.
3. Stir in sour cream until blended and serve.

Nutrition Facts Per Serving

Calories 368 Total Carbs 12g Net Carbs 11g Protein 46g Fat 13g Sugar 5g Fiber 1g

Taco Casserole

Prep time: 5 minutes, Cook time: 40 minutes, Serves: 6

Ingredients:

1 lb. lean ground beef	½ cup cheddar cheese, grated
4 eggs	½ cup pepper jack cheese, grated
1 jalapeno, seeded and diced	¼ cup onion, diced
2 oz. low fat cream cheese	¼ cup half-n-half

What you'll need from store cupboard:

1 pkg. taco seasoning	1 tbsp. hot sauce
¼ cup water	Nonstick cooking spray
¼ cup salsa	

Instructions:

1. Heat oven to 350 degrees. Spray an 8x8-inch baking dish with cooking spray.
2. Place a large skillet over medium heat and cook beef until no longer pink
3. Add onion and jalapeno and cook until onion is translucent. Drain off fat.
4. Stir in taco seasoning and water and cook 5 minutes. Add the cream cheese and salsa and stir to combine.
5. In a medium bowl, whisk the eggs, hot sauce and half-n-half together.
6. Pour the meat mixture into prepared pan and top with egg mixture. Sprinkle with both cheeses and bake 30 minutes, or until eggs are set.
7. Let cool 5 minutes before slicing and serving.

Nutrition Facts Per Serving

Calories 307 Total Carbs 6g Net Carbs 5g Protein 34g Fat 15g Sugar 1g Fiber 1g

Chapter 14 - Meatless Main Dishes Recipe

Crispy Tofu with Chili Garlic Noodles

Prep time: 40 minutes, Cook time: 15 minutes, Serves: 8

Ingredients:

1 lb. extra firm tofu, cut in 1-inch slices & press 30 minutes	1 bell pepper, sliced thin
3 green onions, slice & separate white part from green	1 medium carrot, sliced thin
	4 tbsp. cilantro, diced

What you'll need from store cupboard:

1 recipe Homemade Pasta, cook & drain (chapter 15)	2 tbsp. cornstarch, plus more as needed
12 cloves garlic, diced fine	2 tbsp. sunflower oil
3 tbsp. lite soy sauce	1 tbsp. fish sauce
3 tbsp. oyster sauce	1 tsp Splenda
2 tbsp. red chili paste	Red chili flakes, to taste
	Sesame seeds, to top

Instructions:

1. In a small bowl, stir together soy sauce, oyster sauce, chili paste, fish sauce, and Splenda.
2. Crumble tofu into a medium bowl. Add cornstarch and toss to coat well.
3. Heat oil in a large skillet over med-high heat. Add tofu and cook until brown and crispy, break tofu up as it cooks. Transfer to a plate.
4. Add more oil, if needed, to the skillet and sauté carrot and bell pepper until they start to soften, about 3 minutes. Add to tofu.
5. Add the garlic and white parts of the onions and cook 30 seconds, stirring. Stir in sauce mixture and cook 2 minutes or until sauce coats the back of a spoon.
6. Add the pasta along with the tofu and vegetables. Stir to coat. Sprinkle with chili flakes. Serve garnished with green parts of onions, sesame seeds, and cilantro.

Nutrition Facts Per Serving

Calories 266 Total Carbs 26g Net Carbs 24g Protein 23g Fat 12g Sugar 12g Fiber 4g

Black Pepper & Garlic Tofu

Prep time: 25 minutes, Cook time: 40 minutes, Serves: 4

Ingredients:

14 oz. pkg. extra firm tofu	3 oz. Shiitake mushrooms, sliced
1 lb. asparagus, trim & cut in 1-inch pieces	1 onion, halved & slice in thin wedges
8 oz. kale, remove stems & slice leaves	1 green bell pepper, sliced

What you'll need from store cupboard:

½ cup low sodium vegetable broth	2 tsp cornstarch
8 cloves garlic, pressed, divided	2 tsp black pepper, freshly ground, divided
2 ½ tbsp. light soy sauce, divided	1 tsp rice vinegar
2 -4 tbsp. water	1 tsp sriracha

Instructions:

1. Heat oven to 400 degrees. Line a baking sheet with parchment paper.
2. Cut tofu in ½-inch slices and press between paper towels to remove excess moisture. Cut each slice into smaller rectangles.
3. In a Ziploc bag combine, 1 tablespoon soy sauce, water, 2 tablespoons garlic, rice vinegar, and 1 teaspoon pepper. Add tofu and turn to coat. Let marinate 15 minutes.
4. Place the tofu on the prepared pan and bake 15 minutes. Flip over and bake 15 minutes more. Remove from oven.
5. Place a large nonstick skillet over med-high heat. Add onion and cook until translucent, stirring frequently. Add bell pepper and cook 1 minute more.
6. Add garlic and mushrooms and cook 2 minutes, add a little water if the vegetables start to stick.
7. Stir in the kale and 2 tablespoons water and cover. Let cook 1 minutes, then stir and add more water if needed. Cover and cook another minute before adding asparagus and cook, stirring, until asparagus is tender crisp.
8. In a small bowl, stir together remaining soy sauce, broth, Sriracha, cornstarch, and pepper. Pour over vegetables and cook until heated through.
9. To serve plate the vegetables and place tofu on top.

Nutrition Facts Per Serving

Calories 176 Total Carbs 33g Net Carbs 27g Protein 16g Fat 4g Sugar 12g Fiber 6g

Tempeh Lettuce Wraps

Prep time: 5 minutes, Cook time: 5 minutes, Serves: 2

Ingredients:

1 pkg. tempeh, crumbled	½ red bell pepper, diced
1 head butter-leaf lettuce	½ onion, diced

What you'll need from store cupboard:

1 tbsp. garlic, diced fine	soy sauce
1 tbsp. olive oil	1 tsp ginger,
1 tbsp. low-sodium	1 tsp onion powder
	1 tsp garlic powder

Instructions:

1. Heat oil and garlic in a large skillet over medium heat.
2. Add onion, tempeh, and bell pepper and sauté for 3 minutes.
3. Add soy sauce and spices and cook for another 2 minutes.
4. Spoon mixture into lettuce leaves.

Nutrition Facts Per Serving

Calories 130 Total Carbs 14g Net Carbs 10g Protein 8g Fat 5g Sugar 2g Fiber 4g

Teriyaki Tofu Burger

Prep time: 15 minutes, Cook time: 15 minutes, Serves: 2

Ingredients:

2 3 oz. tofu portions, extra firm, pressed between paper towels 15 minutes	¼ red onion, sliced
	2 tbsp. carrot, grated
	1 tsp margarine
	Butter leaf lettuce

What you'll need from store cupboard:

2 100% whole wheat sandwich thins	marinade
	1 tbsp. Sriracha
1 tbsp. teriyaki	1 tsp red chili flakes

Instructions:

1. Heat grill, or charcoal, to a medium heat.
2. Marinate tofu in teriyaki marinade, red chili flakes and Sriracha.
3. Melt margarine in a small skillet over med-high heat. Add onions and cook until caramelized, about 5 minutes.
4. Grill tofu for 3-4 minutes per side.
5. To assemble, place tofu on bottom roll. Top with lettuce, carrot, and onion. Add top of the roll and serve.

Nutrition Facts Per Serving

Calories 178 Total Carbs 27g Net Carbs 20g Protein 12g Fat 5g Sugar 5g Fiber 7g

Crock Pot Stroganoff

Prep time: 10 minutes, Cook time: 2 hours, Serves: 2

Ingredients:

8 cups mushrooms, cut into quarters

1 onion, halved and sliced thin

4 tbsp. fresh parsley, chopped

1 ½ tbsp. low fat sour cream

What you'll need from store cupboard:

1 cup low sodium vegetable broth

3 cloves garlic, diced fine

2 tsp smoked paprika

Salt and pepper to taste

Instructions:

1. Add all Ingredients, except sour cream and parsley to crock pot.cover and cook on high 2 hours.
2. Stir in sour cream and serve garnished with parsley.

Nutrition Facts Per Serving

Calories 111 Total Carbs 18g Net Carbs 14g Protein 10g Fat 2g Sugar 8g Fiber 4g

Cauliflower "Mac" and Cheese

Prep time: 5 minutes, Cook time: 50 minutes, Serves: 6

Ingredients:

1 small head cauliflower, separated into small florets

1 ½ cup reduced-fat sharp cheddar cheese, grated

1 cup low-fat milk

1/2 cup chopped onion

2 tablespoons margarine, divided

What you'll need from store cupboard:

2 tbsp. whole wheat flour

2 tbsp. whole wheat bread crumbs

1 tsp olive oil

1 tsp yellow mustard

½ tsp garlic powder

¼ tsp salt

¼ tsp black pepper

Nonstick cooking spray

Instructions:

1. Heat oven to 400 degrees. Coat a baking sheet with cooking spray.
2. In a medium bowl, combine oil, salt, pepper, onion, and cauliflower. Toss until cauliflower is coated evenly. Spread on baking sheet and cook 25-30 minutes until lightly browned.
3. In a medium saucepan, over medium heat, melt 1 ½ tablespoons margarine. Whisk in flour until no lumps remain.

4. Add milk and continue whisking until sauce thicken. Stir in mustard, garlic powder, and cheese until melted and smooth. Add cauliflower and mix well.
5. Pour into a 1 ½-quart baking dish.
6. In a small glass bowl, melt remaining margarine in microwave. Stir in bread crumbs until moistened. Sprinkle evenly over cauliflower.
7. Bake 20 minutes until bubbling and golden brown on top.

Nutrition Facts Per Serving

Calories 154 Total Carbs 15g Net Carbs 12g Protein 8g Fat 8g Sugar 4g Fiber 3g

Mexican Scrambled Eggs & Greens

Prep time: 15 minutes, Cook time: 5 minutes, Serves: 4

Ingredients:

8 egg whites

4 egg yolks

3 tomatoes, cut in ½-inch pieces

1 jalapeno pepper, slice thin

½ avocado, cut in ½-inch pieces

½ red onion, diced fine

½ head Romaine lettuce, torn

½ cup cilantro, chopped

2 tbsp. fresh lime juice

What you'll need from store cupboard:

12 tortilla chips, (chapter 5), broken into small pieces

2 tbsp. water

1 tbsp. olive oil

¾ tsp pepper, divided

½ tsp salt, divided

Instructions:

1. In a medium bowl, combine tomatoes, avocado, onion, jalapeno, cilantro, lime juice, ¼ teaspoon salt, and ¼ teaspoon pepper.
2. In a large bowl, whisk egg whites, egg yolks, water, and remaining salt and pepper. Stir in tortilla chips.
3. Heat oil in a large skillet over medium heat. Add egg mixture and cook, stirring frequently, 3-5 minutes, or desired doneness.
4. To serve, divide lettuce leaves among 4 plates. Add scrambled egg mixture and top with salsa.

Nutrition Facts Per Serving

Calories 280 Total Carbs 10g Net Carbs 6g Protein 15g Fat 21g Sugar 4g Fiber 4g

Orange Tofu

Prep time: 15 minutes, Cook time: 2 hours, Serves: 4

Ingredients:

1 package extra firm tofu, pressed for at least 15 minutes, cut into cubes

2 cups broccoli florets, fresh

1 tbsp. margarine

What you'll need from store cupboard:

¼ cup orange juice

¼ cup reduced sodium soy sauce

¼ cup honey

2 cloves garlic, diced fine

Instructions:

1. Melt butter in a medium skillet, over medium high heat. Add tofu and garlic and cook, stirring occasionally until tofu starts to brown, about 5-10 minutes. Transfer to crock pot.
2. Whisk the wet Ingredients together in a small bowl. Pour over tofu and add the broccoli.
3. Cover and cook on high 90 minutes, or on low 2 hours.
4. Serve over cauliflower rice (chapter13).

Nutrition Facts Per Serving

Calories 137 Total Carbs 24g Net Carbs 22g Protein 4g Fat 4g Sugar 20g Fiber 2g

Grilled Tofu & Veggie Skewers

Prep time: 15 minutes, Cook time: 15 minutes, Serves: 6

Ingredients:

1 block tofu

2 small zucchinis, sliced

1 red bell pepper, cut into 1-inch cubes

1 yellow bell pepper,

cut into 1-inch cubes

1 red onion, cut into 1-inch cubes

2 cups cherry tomatoes

What you'll need from store cupboard:

2 tbsp. lite soy sauce

3 tsp BBQ sauce (chapter 16)

2 tsp sesame seeds

Salt & pepper, to taste

Nonstick cooking spray

Instructions:

1. Press tofu to extract liquid, for about half an hour. Then, cut tofu into cubes and marinate in soy sauce for at least 15 minutes.
2. Heat the grill to med-high heat. Spray the grill rack with cooking spray.
3. Assemble skewers with tofu alternating with vegetables.

4. Grill 2-3 minutes per side until vegetables start to soften, and tofu is golden brown. At the very end of cooking time, season with salt and pepper and brush with barbecue sauce. Serve garnished with sesame seeds.

Nutrition Facts Per Serving

Calories 64 Total Carbs 10g Net Carbs 7g Protein 5g Fat 2g Sugar 6g Fiber 3g

Tofu in Peanut Sauce

Prep time: 15 minutes, Cook time: 1 hour 25 minutes, serves; 4

Ingredients:

1 pkg. extra firm tofu, pressed 15 minutes and cut into cubes

1 pkg. fresh baby spinach

2 limes

1 tbsp. margarine

What you'll need from store cupboard:

½ cup raw peanut butter

2 tbsp. lite soy sauce

3 cloves garlic,

chopped fine

½ tsp ginger

¼ tsp red pepper flakes

Instructions:

1. Melt margarine in a large saucepan. Add tofu and garlic and cook, stirring occasionally, 5-10 minutes, or until tofu starts to brown.
2. Add remaining Ingredients, except spinach and bring to simmer. Reduce heat, cover and cook, stirring occasionally 30-35 minutes.
3. Stir in the spinach and cook 15 minutes more. Serve.

Nutrition Facts Per Serving

Calories 325 Total Carbs 15g Net Carbs 10g Protein 18g Fat 24g Sugar 5g Fiber 5g

Tofu Salad Sandwiches

Prep time: 15 minutes, total time 20 minutes, Serves: 4

Ingredients:

1 pkg. silken firm tofu, pressed

4 lettuce leaves

2 green onions, diced

¼ cup celery, diced

What you'll need from store cupboard:

8 slices bread, (chapter 14)

¼ cup lite mayonnaise

2 tbsp. sweet pickle relish

1 tbsp. Dijon mustard

¼ tsp turmeric

¼ tsp salt

1/8 tsp cayenne pepper

Instructions:

1. Press tofu between layers of paper towels for 15 minutes to remove excess moisture. Cut into small cubes.
2. In a medium bowl, stir together remaining Ingredients. Fold in tofu. Spread over 4 slices of bread. Top with a lettuce leaf and another slice of bread. Serve.

Nutrition Facts Per Serving

Calories 378 Total Carbs 15g Net Carbs 13g Protein 24g Fat 20g Sugar 2g Fiber 2g

Tofu Curry

Prep time: 10 minutes, Cook time: 2 hours, Serves: 4

Ingredients:

2 cup green bell pepper, diced
1 cup firm tofu, cut into cubes
1 onion, peeled and diced

What you'll need from store cupboard:

1 ½ cups canned coconut milk	2 tbsp. raw peanut butter
1 cup tomato paste	1 tbsp. garam masala
2 cloves garlic, diced fine	1 tbsp. curry powder
	1 ½ tsp salt

Instructions:

1. Add all Ingredients, except the tofu to a blender or food processor. Process until thoroughly combined.
2. Pour into a crock pot and add the tofu. Cover and cook on high 2 hours.
3. Stir well and serve over cauliflower rice.

Nutrition Facts Per Serving

Calories 389 Total Carbs 28g Net Carbs 20g Protein 13g Fat 28g Sugar 16g Fiber 8g

Pad Thai

Prep time: 15 minutes, Cook time: 30 minutes, Serves: 6

Ingredients:

12 oz. extra firm tofu organic, cut into 1-inch cubes	3 cups bean sprouts
	2 Green onions sliced
2 zucchini, shredded into long zoodles	1 cup red cabbage, shredded
1 carrot, grated	¼ cup cilantro, chopped

What you'll need from store cupboard:

¼ cup lime juice	2 tbsp. tamari
2 cloves garlic, diced fine	1 tbsp. sesame seeds
	½ tbsp. sesame oil
2 tbsp. reduced fat peanut butter	2 tsp red chili flakes

Instructions:

1. Heat half the oil in a saucepan over medium heat. Add tofu and cook until it starts to brown, about 5 minutes. Add garlic and stir until light brown.
2. Add zucchini, carrot, cabbage, lime juice, peanut butter, tamari, and chili flakes. Stir to combine all Ingredients. Cook, stirring frequently, until vegetables are tender, about 5 minutes. Add bean sprouts and remove from heat.
3. Serve topped with green onions, sesame seeds and cilantro.

Nutrition Facts Per Serving

Calories 134 Total Carbs 13g Net Carbs 11g Protein 12g Fat 6g Sugar 3g Fiber 2g

Tofu Bento

Prep time: 15 minutes, Cook time: 10 minutes, Serves: 4

Ingredients:

1 pkg. extra firm tofu	cooked
1 red bell pepper, sliced	2 cups broccoli, chopped
1 orange bell pepper, sliced	¼ cup green onion, sliced
2 cup cauliflower rice,	

What you'll need from store cupboard:

2 tbsp. low-sodium soy sauce	1 tsp garlic powder
	1 tsp onion powder
1 tbsp. olive oil	1 tsp chili paste
1 tsp ginger,	

Instructions:

1. Remove tofu from package and press with paper towels to absorb all excess moisture, let set for 15 minutes.
2. Chop tofu into cubes. Add tofu and seasonings to a large Ziploc bag and shake to coat.
3. Heat oil in a large skillet over medium heat. Add tofu and vegetables and cook, stirring frequently, 5-8 minutes, until tofu is browned on all sides and vegetables are tender.
4. To serve, place ½ cup cauliflower rice on 4 plates and top evenly with tofu mixture.

Nutrition Facts Per Serving

Calories 93 Total Carbs 12g Net Carbs 8g Protein 7g Fat 3g Sugar 5g Fiber 4g

Chapter 15 - Grains, Legumes & Pasta Recipe

"Flour" Tortillas

Prep time: 10 minutes, cook time 15 minutes, Serves: 4

Ingredients:

¾ cup egg whites

What you'll need from store cupboard:

1/3 cup water	½ tsp salt
¼ cup coconut flour	½ tsp cumin
1 tsp sunflower oil	½ tsp chili powder

Instructions:

1. Add all Ingredients, except oil, to a food processor and pulse until combined. Let rest 7-8 minutes.
2. Heat oil in a large skillet over med-low heat. Pour ¼ cup batter into center and tilt to spread to 7-8-inch circle.
3. When the top is no longer shiny, flip tortilla and cook another 1-2 minutes. Repeat with remaining batter.
4. Place each tortilla on parchment paper and slightly wipe off any access oil.

Nutrition Facts Per Serving

Calories 27 Total Carbs 1g Protein 5g Fat 0g Sugar 0g Fiber 0g

Fried Rice

Prep time: 5 minutes, Cook time: 15 minutes, Serves: 8

Ingredients:

2 cups sugar snap peas	2 egg whites
	1 egg

What you'll need from store cupboard:

1 cup instant brown rice, cooked according to	directions
	2 tbsp. lite soy sauce

Instructions:

1. Add the peas to the cooked rice and mix to combine.
2. In a small skillet, scramble the egg and egg whites. Add the rice and peas to the skillet and stir in soy sauce. Cook, stirring frequently, about 2-3 minutes, or until heated through. Serve.

Nutrition Facts Per Serving

Calories 107 Total Carbs 20g Net Carbs 19g Protein 4g Fat 1g Sugar 1g Fiber 1g

Flourless "Burger Buns"

Prep time: 10 minutes, Cook time: 35 minutes, Serves: 4

Ingredients:

4 egg yolks, room temp	temp
	¼ cup low fat ricotta
4 egg whites, room	cheese

What you'll need from store cupboard:

¼ cup reduced fat parmesan cheese

1/4 tsp cream of tartar

Instructions:

1. Heat oven to 300 degrees. Line a baking sheet with parchment paper.
2. In a large bowl, whisk egg yolks, ricotta and parmesan cheese until smooth.
3. In a separate bowl, beat egg whites until foamy, then add in cream of tartar and beat until stiff peaks form.
4. Add some beaten egg white to the egg yolk mixture and mix lightly. Slowly and lightly fold in the remaining egg white to the egg yolk mixture until just blended.
5. Spoon the batter onto prepared pan to make 8 buns. Bake 35 minutes. Use as bread for sandwiches or eat on its own.

Nutrition Facts Per Serving

Calories 50 Total Carbs 1g Protein 4g Fat 3g Sugar 1g Fiber 0g

Cheesy Cauliflower Puree

Prep time: 5 minutes, Cook time: 15 minutes, Serves: 6

Ingredients:

2 ½ lbs. cauliflower florets, steamed	cheese, grated
	2 tbsp. half-n-half
4 oz. reduced fat sharp cheddar	1 tbsp. butter

What you'll need from store cupboard:

½ tsp salt	½ tsp pepper

Instructions:

1. Steam the cauliflower until it is fork tender, drain.
2. Add the cauliflower and remaining Ingredients to a food processor. Pulse until almost smooth. Serve warm.
3. You can make it ahead of time and just reheat it as needed also.

Nutrition Facts Per Serving

Calories 145 Total Carbs 10g Net Carbs 5g Protein 9g Fat 9g Sugar 5g Fiber 5g

Cauliflower Puree

Prep time: 10 minutes, Cook time: 15 minutes, Serves: 6

Ingredients:

2 ½ lbs. cauliflower florets, halved
½ leek, white and pale green part, 4 tbsp. butter
2 tsp fresh parsley, diced

What you'll need from store cupboard:

2 tbsp. low sodium chicken broth
2 tsp extra virgin olive oil
4 cloves garlic, diced fine
¼ tsp salt
¼ tsp pepper

Instructions:

1. Place the cauliflower in a steamer basket over boiling water. Cover and steam 10-15 minutes or until fork tender.
2. Rinse the leek under water and pat dry. Chop into thin slices.
3. Heat oil in a large skillet over med-low heat. Add the leek and cook 2-3 minutes, or until soft. Add the garlic and cook 1 minute more.
4. Add all Ingredients to a food processor and pulse until almost smooth. Serve warm, or refrigerate for a later use.

Nutrition Facts Per Serving

Calories 146 Total Carbs 14g Net Carbs 8g Protein 5g Fat 9g Sugar 6g Fiber 6g

Mexican "Rice"

Prep time: 5 minutes, Cook time: 10 minutes, Serves: 6

Ingredients:

2 cups cauliflower rice, cooked
1 small jalapeño, seeded and diced fine
½ white onion, diced

What you'll need from store cupboard:

½ cup water
½ cup tomato paste
3 cloves garlic, diced
fine
2 tsp salt
2 tsp olive oil

Instructions:

1. Heat oil in skillet over medium heat. Add onion, garlic, jalapeno, and salt and cook 3-4 min, stirring frequently.
2. In a small bowl, whisk water and tomato paste together. Add to skillet. Cook, stirring frequently, 3-5 minutes.
3. Stir in cauliflower, and cook just until heated through and most of the liquid is absorbed. Serve.

Nutrition Facts Per Serving

Calories 46 Total Carbs 7g Net Carbs 5g Protein 2g Fat 2g Sugar 4g Fiber 2g

Cauliflower "Rice"

Prep time: 5 minutes, Cook time: 10 minutes, Serves: 4

Ingredients:

1 small head cauliflower, separated into small florets

What you'll need from store cupboard:

1 tablespoon olive oil
1 clove of garlic, diced fine
½ tsp salt

Instructions:

1. Use a cheese grater to rice the cauliflower, using the big holes. Or, use a food processor and short pulses until it resembles rice.
2. In a nonstick skillet, over med-high heat, heat oil until hot. Add garlic and cook 1 minutes, stirring frequently. Add cauliflower and cook, stirring, 7-9 minutes, or until it is tender and starts to brown.
3. Serve as is or use in your favorite recipes.

Nutrition Facts Per Serving

Calories 48, Total Carbs 4g Net Carbs 2g Protein 1g Fat 4g Sugar 2g Fiber 2g

No Corn "Cornbread"

Prep time: 10 minutes, Cook time: 25 minutes, Serves: 16

Ingredients:

4 eggs, room temperature
1/3 cup butter, melted

What you'll need from store cupboard:

1 ½ cup almond flour, sifted
1/3 cup Splenda
1 tsp baking powder

Instructions:

1. Heat oven to 350 degrees. Line an 8-inch baking dish with parchment paper.
2. In a large bowl, whisk together eggs, butter, and Splenda. Stir in the flour and baking powder until no lumps remain.
3. Pour batter into prepared dish and smooth the top. Bake 25-30 minutes or until edges are golden brown and it passes the toothpick test.
4. Let cool 5 minutes before slicing and serving.

Nutrition Facts Per Serving

Calories 121 Total Carbs 6g Net Carbs 5g Protein 3g Fat 9g Sugar 4g Fiber 1g

Chickpea Tortillas

Prep time: 5 minutes, Cook time: 10 minutes, Serves: 4
Ingredients:
1 cup chickpea flour   Nonstick cooking
1 cup water   spray
¼ tsp salt
Instructions:
1. In a large bowl, whisk all Ingredients together until no lumps remain.
2. Spray a skillet with cooking spray and place over med-high heat.
3. Pour batter in, ¼ cup at a time, and tilt pan to spread thinly.
4. Cook until golden brown on each side, about 2 minutes per side.
5. Use for taco shells, enchiladas, quesadillas or whatever you desire.

Nutrition Facts Per Serving
Calories 89 Total Carbs 13g Net Carbs 10g Protein 5g Fat 2g Sugar 3g Fiber 3g

Cheese Biscuits

Prep time: 20 minutes, Cook time: 20 minutes, Serves: 16
Ingredients:
8 oz. low fat cream   4 eggs
cheese   2 tbsp. margarine,
3 cup mozzarella   melted
cheese, grated
What you'll need from store cupboard:
1-1/3 cup almond   powder
flour   Nonstick cooking
4 tbsp. baking   spray
Instructions:
1. Heat oven to 400⁰ degrees. Spray a 12-inch cast iron skillet with cooking spray
2. In a saucepan over low heat, melt the cream cheese and mozzarella together. Stir until smooth. Remove from heat.
3. In a large bowl, combine the melted cheese, eggs, baking powder, and flour. Mix until smooth. Let rest for 10 to 20 minutes.
4. Use a large cookie scoop, to scoop dough and place in prepared skillet. Refrigerate 10 minutes.
5. Bake for 20 to 25 minutes, until golden brown. Brush biscuits with melted margarine.

Nutrition Facts Per Serving
Calories 106 Total Carbs 5g Net Carbs 4g Protein 7g Fat 8g Sugar 0g Fiber 1g

Light Beer Bread

Prep time: 5 minutes, Cook time: 55 minutes, Serves: 14
Ingredients:
¼ cup butter, soft
What you'll need from store cupboard:
12 oz. light beer   mix
3 cup low carb baking   1/3 cup Splenda
Instructions:
1. Heat oven to 375 degrees. Use 1 tablespoon butter to grease the bottom of a 9x5-inch loaf pan.
2. In a large bowl, whisk together beer, baking mix, and Splenda. Pour into prepared pan.
3. Bake 45-55 minutes or until golden brown. Cool in pan 10 minutes, remove from pan and cool on wire rack.
4. In a small glass bowl, melt remaining butter in a microwave and brush over warm loaf. Cool 15 minutes before slicing.

Nutrition Facts Per Serving
Calories 162 Total Carbs 16g Net Carbs 12g Protein 9g Fat 5g Sugar 5g Fiber 4g

Quick Coconut Flour Buns

Prep time: 5 minutes, Cook time: 20 minutes, Serves: 4
Ingredients:
3 eggs, room temperature
2 tbsp. coconut milk, room temperature
What you'll need from store cupboard:
¼ cup coconut flour   1 tbsp. honey
2 tablespoons   ½ tsp baking powder
coconut oil, soft   ½ tsp salt
Instructions:
1. Heat oven to 375 degrees. Line a cookie sheet with parchment paper.
2. In a small bowl, sift together flour, baking powder and salt.
3. In a medium bowl, combine eggs, coconut oil, milk, and honey, mix well. Slowly add dry Ingredients to the egg mixture. Batter will be thick but make sure there is no lumps.
4. Form into 4 balls and place on prepared pan. Press down into rounds ½-inch thick. Bake 15-20 minutes or until buns pass the toothpick test.

Nutrition Facts Per Serving
Calories 143 Total Carbs 6g Protein 4g Fat 12g Sugar 5g Fiber 0g

Cauliflower Pizza Crust

Prep time: 15 minutes, Cook time: 30 minutes, Serves: 8
Ingredients:
1 ½ lb. cauliflower, separated in florets
1 egg
What you'll need from store cupboard:
1 ½ cup reduced fat parmesan cheese
½ tbsp. Italian seasoning
½ tsp garlic powder
Instructions:
1. Heat oven to 400 degrees. Line a pizza pan, or stone, with parchment paper.
2. Place the cauliflower in a food processor and pulse until it resembles rice.
3. Cook the cauliflower in a skillet over medium heat, stirring frequently, until soft, about 10 minutes.
4. In a large bowl, whisk the egg, cheese and seasonings.
5. Place the cauliflower in a clean kitchen towel and squeeze out any excess moisture. Stir into cheese mixture to form a soft dough, press with a spatula if needed.
6. Spread the dough on the prepared pan about ¼-inch thick. Bake 20 minutes, or until top is dry and firm and edges are golden brown.
7. Let cool 5-10 minutes, the crust will firm up as it cools. Add desired toppings and bake 5-10 minutes more. Slice and serve.

Nutrition Facts Per Serving
Calories 158 Total Carbs 10g net Carbs 6g
Protein 12g Fat 9g Sugar 4g Fiber 4g

"Cornbread" Stuffing

Prep time: 15 minutes, Cook time: 40 minutes, Serves: 6
Ingredients:
1 strip bacon, diced
1 egg
1 cup onion, diced
1 cup celery, diced
2 tbsp. margarine, divided
What you'll need from store cupboard:
1 cup almond flour
¼ cup low sodium chicken broth
3 cloves garlic, diced fine
2 tbsp. stone-ground
cornmeal
1 tsp thyme
1 tsp sage
¾ tsp salt
Fresh ground black pepper, to taste
Instructions:
1. Heat the oven to 375 degrees.

2. Melt 1 tablespoon margarine in a skillet over low heat. Add onions and celery and cook, stirring, until soft, about 10 minutes. Add garlic and seasonings and cook 1-2 minutes more. Remove from heat and let cool.
3. Place the almond flour, cornmeal and bacon in a food processor and pulse until combined. Add the broth and egg and pulse just to combine. Add the onion mixture and pulse just until mixed.
4. Place remaining tablespoon of margarine in a cast iron skillet, or baking dish, and melt in the oven until hot. Swirl the pan to coat with melted margarine.
5. Spread the dressing in the pan and bake 30 minutes or until top is nicely browned and center is cooked through. Serve.

Nutrition Facts Per Serving
Calories 177 Total Carbs 9g Net Carbs 6g
Protein 6g Fat 14g Sugar 2g Fiber 3g

Garlic Basil Breadsticks

Prep time: 10 minutes, Cook time: 10 minutes, Serves: 4
Ingredients:
2 eggs, beaten
2 cup mozzarella cheese, grated
2 tbsp. cream cheese
2 tbsp. fresh basil, diced
What you'll need from store cupboard:
4 tbsp. coconut flour
4 cloves garlic, crushed
Nonstick cooking spray
Instructions:
1. Heat oven to 400 degrees. Spray a baking sheet with cooking spray.
2. Add mozzarella, cream cheese, crushed garlic and basil to a microwaveable bowl. Mix and then cook for 1 minute. Stir well to make sure the cheeses are melted and then add in the flour and egg.
3. Mix well, use your hands if needed to form into a dough.
4. Break off pieces of the dough and roll into a long finger shapes. Place on prepared pan.
5. Bake 8-10 minutes or until the dough begins to brown. Remove from heat and let cool slightly before serving.

Nutrition Facts Per Serving
Calories 153 Total Carbs 10g Net Carbs 5g
Protein 9g Fat 8g Sugar 1g Fiber 5g

Healthy Loaf of Bread

Prep time: 10 minutes, Cook time: 30 minutes, Serves: 20

Ingredients:

6 eggs, separated   4 tbsp. butter, melted

What you'll need from store cupboard:

1 ½ cup almond flour, sifted   1/8 tsp salt

3 tsp baking powder   Butter flavored cooking spray

¼ tsp cream of tartar

Instructions:

1. Heat oven to 375 degrees. Spray an 8-inch loaf pan with cooking spray.
2. In a large bowl, beat egg whites and cream of tartar until soft peaks form
3. Add the yolks, 1/3 of egg whites, butter, flour, baking powder, and salt to a food processor and pulse until combined.
4. Add remaining egg whites and pulse until thoroughly combined, being careful not to over mix the dough.
5. Pour into prepared pan and bake 30 minutes, or until bread passes the toothpick test. Cool 10 minutes in the pan then invert and cool completely before slicing.

Nutrition Facts Per Serving

Calories 81 Total Carbs 2g Net Carbs 1g Protein 3g Fat 7g Sugar 0g Fiber 1g

Homemade Pasta

Prep time: 20 minutes, Cook time: 5 minutes, Serves: 8

Ingredients:

1 egg + 2 egg yolks

What you'll need from store cupboard:

1 ¾ cup soy flour   3-4 tbsp. cold water

¼ cup ground wheat germ   1 tsp light olive oil

        ½ tsp salt

Instructions:

1. In a large bowl, whisk egg, egg yolks, oil and 3 tablespoons water until smooth.
2. In a separate bowl, combine flour, wheat germ, and salt. Stir into egg mixture until smooth. Use the last tablespoon of water if needed to make a smooth dough.
3. Turn out onto a lightly floured surface and knead 5-8 minutes or until smooth. Cover and let rest 10 minutes.
4. Divide dough into 4 equal pieces and roll out, one at a time, as thin as possible,

or run it through a pasta machine until it reaches the thinnest setting.

5. Let dough dry out for 30 minutes. Cut into desired size with pasta machine or pizza cutter. It not using right away, let it dry overnight on a pasta or cooling rack. Fresh pasta should be used within 3 days.
6. It will store in the freezer, after drying for just an hour, in an airtight bag, 6-8 months. Pasta dried overnight can be stored in an airtight container for up to 1 week.
7. To cook it when fresh, add to a pot of boiling water for 4-5 minutes or until tender. Dried pasta will take a couple minutes longer.

Nutrition Facts Per Serving

Calories 152 Total Carbs 12g Net Carbs 9g Protein 16g Fat 5g Sugar 6g Fiber 3g

Homemade Noodles

Prep time: 5 minutes, chill time; 4 hours, Serves: 2

Ingredients:

1 cup mozzarella cheese, grated

1 egg yolk

Instructions:

1. Add the mozzarella to a bowl and microwave for 1-2 minutes, until melted. Let cool for 30 seconds.
2. With a rubber spatula, gently fold the egg yolk into the cheese.
3. Turn the mixture out onto a parchment paper-lined baking sheet. Place another piece of parchment paper on top of the dough and press down with your hand until thin.
4. Remove the top piece of parchment and cut the dough into thin strips. Place the "pasta" on a rack and refrigerate for four hours or overnight.
5. To cook, place in boiling water for 1 minute. Drain and run cool water over to prevent sticking. Serve with your favorite sauce.

Nutrition Facts Per Serving

Calories 67 Total Carbs 1g Protein 5g Fat 5g Sugar 0g Fiber 0g

Pizza Crust

Prep time: 20 minutes, Cook time: 40 minutes, Serves: 4

Ingredients:

1 ½ cup mozzarella cheese, grated   2 oz. cream cheese
1 egg, beaten

What you'll need from store cupboard:

¾ cup almond flour   ½ tsp salt
½ tsp Italian seasoning   ½ tsp garlic powder
                                              ½ tsp onion powder

Instructions:

1. Heat oven to 400 degrees. Line a large baking sheet with parchment paper.
2. In large bowl, microwave cream cheese and mozzarella for 60 seconds. Remove from microwave and stir. Return to microwave and cook another 30 seconds. Stir until well combined.
3. Add flour, salt, onion powder, garlic powder, and egg. Stir until almond flour is well incorporated into cheese. If mixture becomes too sticky, microwave another 10-15 seconds to warm up.
4. Place dough on parchment paper and roll out thin. Poke holes in crust with fork. Bake 10 minutes.
5. Remove from oven and turn over. Bake another 10 minutes.
6. Remove from oven and top with desired pizza toppings.
7. Return to oven and bake another 10 minutes, until toppings are hot and cheese is melted.

Nutrition Facts Per Serving

Calories 198 Total Carbs 5g Net Carbs 3g Protein 9g Fat 17g Sugar 1g Fiber 2g

Chapter 16 - Sauces, Dips & Dressings Recipe

Alfredo Sauce

Prep time: 5 minutes, Cook time: 10 minutes, Serves: 6

Ingredients:

1 ½ cup heavy cream
1 tbsp. margarine

What you'll need from store cupboard:

½ cup reduced fat parmesan cheese   Black pepper
4 cloves garlic, diced fine   Salt
                                              Nutmeg

Instructions:

1. Melt butter in a medium saucepan over medium heat. Add garlic and sauté for about 30 seconds, until fragrant.
2. Add the heavy cream. Bring to a gentle simmer, then continue to simmer for about 5 minutes, until it begins to thicken and sauce is reduced by about 1/3.
3. Reduce heat to low. Gradually whisk in the Parmesan cheese. Keep whisking over low heat, until smooth. Add salt, pepper, and nutmeg to taste. (If sauce is thicker than you like, thin it out with more cream.)

Nutrition Facts Per Serving

Calories 147 Total Carbs 2g Protein 2g Fat 14g Sugar 0g Fiber 0g

Creamy Poppy Seed Dressing

Total time: 5 minutes, Serves: 6

Ingredients:

⅓ cup light mayonnaise
¼ cup skim milk

What you'll need from store cupboard:

3 tbsp. Splenda   2 tsp poppy seeds
4 tsp cider vinegar

Instructions:

1. In a small bowl, whisk all Ingredients together until thoroughly combined. Store in an airtight jar in the refrigerator.

Nutrition Facts Per Serving

Calories 90 Total Carbs 10g Protein 1g Fat 5g Sugar 7g Fiber 0g

Almond Vanilla Fruit Dip

Prep time: 5 minutes, Total time: 10 minutes, Serves: 10

Ingredients:

2 ½ cup fat free half-n-half

What you'll need from store cupboard:

4-serving size fat-free sugar-free vanilla instant pudding mix	1 tbsp. Splenda
	1 tsp vanilla
	1 tsp almond extract

Instructions:

1. Place all Ingredients in a medium bowl, and beat on medium speed 2 minutes. Cover and chill until ready to serve. Serve with fruit for dipping. Serving size is ¼ cup.

Nutrition Facts Per Serving

Calories 87 Total Carbs 4g Protein 2g Fat 7g Sugar 1g Fiber 0g

Garlic Dipping Sauce

Prep time: 5 minutes, Total time: 5 minutes, Serves: 4

Instructions:

1 cup Greek yogurt

1 tbsp. fresh dill, diced fine

What you'll need from store cupboard:

2 cloves garlic, diced fine

Instructions:

1. In a small bowl, whisk all Ingredients together.
2. Serve warm or cover and chill until ready to use.

Nutrition Facts Per Serving

Calories 40 Total Carbs 2g Protein 5g Fat 1g Sugar 2g Fiber 0g

Orange Marmalade

Prep time: 30 minutes, Cook time: 30 minutes, Serves: 48

Ingredients:

4 navel oranges	1 lemon

What you'll need from store cupboard:

2 ½ cup water	4 tbsp. Splenda
¼ cup warm water	1 oz. gelatin

Instructions:

1. Quarter the oranges and remove all the pulp. Scrap the white part off the rind and cut it into thin 2-inch strips. Remove as much of the membrane between orange segments as you can and place

the seeds in a small piece of cheesecloth, pull up the sides to make a "bag" and tie closed.

2. Repeat with the lemon but discard the seeds. Cut the lemon rind into smaller strips than the orange rind.
3. Chop the orange and lemon pulp and add it to a medium saucepan along with 2 ½ cups water. Bring to a rapid boil over med-high heat.
4. Reduce heat to med-low and add the bag of seeds. Boil gently for 30 minutes, or until the citrus fruit is soft. Remove and discard the seed bag.
5. Dissolve the gelatin in the warm water. Add it to the orange mixture with ½ the Splenda. Being careful not to burn yourself, taste the marmalade and adjust sweetener as desired.
6. Spoon the marmalade into 3 ½-pint jars with air-tight lids. Seal and chill.

Nutrition Facts Per Serving

Calories 15 Total Carbs 3g Protein 1g Fat 0g Sugar 3g Fiber 0g

Basic Salsa

Prep time: 15 minutes, chill time: 1 hour: Serves: 8

Ingredients:

8 tomatoes	spicy you like it
2-3 jalapeno peppers, depending on how	2 limes, juiced

What you'll need from store cupboard:

4 cloves garlic	Nonstick cooking spray
1 tbsp. salt	

Instructions:

1. Heat oven to broil. Spray a baking sheet with cooking spray.
2. Place tomatoes, peppers, and garlic on prepared pan and broil 8-10 minutes, turning occasionally, until skin on the vegetables begins to char and peel way.
3. Let cool. Remove skins.
4. Place vegetables in a food processor and pulse. Add salt and lime juise and pulse until salsa reaches desired consistency.
5. Store in a jar with an airtight lid in the refrigerator up to 7 days. Serving size is ¼ cup.

Nutrition Facts Per Serving

Calories 31 Total Carbs 7g Net Carbs 5g Protein 1g Fat 0g Sugar 4g Fiber 2g

Herb Vinaigrette

Prep time: 5 minutes, mix time: 5 minutes, Serves: 12

Ingredients:

2 tbsp. shallot, diced fine	1 tbsp. fresh oregano, diced
1 tbsp. fresh basil, diced	1 tbsp. fresh tarragon, diced

What you'll need from store cupboard:

¼ cup extra virgin olive oil	vinegar
¼ cup low sodium chicken broth	¼ teaspoon salt
¼ cup red-wine	¼ teaspoon freshly ground pepper

Instructions:

1. Place all Ingredients in a jar with an air tight lid. Secure lid and shake vigorously to combine.
2. Refrigerate until ready to use. Will keep up to 2 days. Serving size is 1 tablespoon.

Nutrition Facts Per Serving

Calories 39 Total Carbs 0 Protein 0g Fat 4g Sugar 0g Fiber 0g

Blueberry Orange Dessert Sauce

Prep time: 5 minutes, Cook time: 10 minutes, Serves: 16

Ingredients:

1 ½ cup orange segments	1 cup blueberries
	¼ cup orange juice

What you'll need from store cupboard:

¼ cup water	3 tbsp. Splenda
1/3 cup almonds, sliced	1 tbsp. cornstarch
	1/8 tsp salt

Instructions:

1. In a small saucepan, combine Splenda, cornstarch, and salt. Whisk in orange juice and water until smooth.
2. Bring to a boil over med-high heat, cook, stirring frequently, 1-2 minutes or until thickened.
3. Reduce heat and stir in fruit. Cook 5 minutes. Remove from heat and let cool completely.
4. Store in an airtight jar in the refrigerator until ready to use. Serving size is 1 tablespoon.

Nutrition Facts Per Serving

Calories 46 Total Carbs 8g Protein 1g Fat 1g Sugar 6g Fiber 0g

Spaghetti Sauce

Prep time: 20 minutes, Cook time: 30 minutes, Serves: 6

Ingredients:

1 onion, diced	1 stalk celery, diced
1 carrot, grated	1 zucchini, grated

What you'll need from store cupboard:

1 (28 oz.) Italian-style tomatoes, in puree	½ tbsp. oregano
	1 tsp olive oil
1 (14 ½ oz.) diced tomatoes, with juice	1 tsp basil
	1 tsp thyme
½ cup water	1 tsp salt
2 cloves garlic, diced fine	¼ tsp red pepper flakes

Instructions:

1. Heat oil in a large saucepan over medium heat. Add vegetables and garlic. Cook, stirring frequently, until vegetables get soft, about 5 minutes.
2. Add remaining Ingredients, use the back of a spoon to break up tomatoes. Bring to a simmer and cook, partially covered, over med-low heat 30 minutes, stirring frequently.
3. Store sauce in an air-tight container in the refrigerator up to 3 days, or in the freezer up to 3 months.

Nutrition Facts Per Serving

Calories 47 Total Carbs 8g Net Carbs 6g Protein 2g Fat 1g Sugar 3g Fiber 2g

All Purpose Beef Marinade

Prep time: 10 minutes, Total time: 10 minutes, Serves: 8

Ingredients:

6 limes zested
1 bunch cilantro, diced

What you'll need from store cupboard:

¼ c olive oil
6 cloves garlic, diced fine

Instructions:

1. Mix all Ingredients in an airtight container.
2. Keep refrigerated for up to 3 months or frozen up to 6 months. Serving size is 1 tablespoon.

Nutrition Facts Per Serving

Calories 78 Total Carbs 1g Protein 0g Fat 8g Sugar 0g Fiber 0g

All Purpose Chicken Marinade

Prep time: 5 minutes, total time, 5 minutes, Serves: 24

Ingredients:

1 onion, quartered
½ lemon, with skin
½ orange, with skin
3 tbsp. rosemary, diced
2 tbsp. thyme, diced

What you'll need from store cupboard
½ cup olive oil
6 cloves garlic, diced fine

Instructions:

1. Place all Ingredients in a food processor and pulse until combined.
2. Store in an air tight container in the refrigerator up to 3 months. Serving size is 1 tablespoon.

Nutrition Facts Per Serving
Calories 41 Total Carbs 1g Protein 0g Fat 4g Sugar 1g Fiber 0g

Apple Cider Vinaigrette

Total time: 5 minutes, Serves: 8

What you'll need from store cupboard:

½ cup sunflower oil
¼ cup apple cider vinegar
¼ cup apple juice, unsweetened
2 tbsp. honey
1 tbsp. lemon juice
½ tsp salt
Freshly ground black pepper, to taste

Instructions:

1. Place all Ingredients in a mason jar. Screw on lid and shake until everything is thoroughly combined. Store in refrigerator until ready to use. Shake well before using.

Nutrition Facts Per Serving
Calories 138 Total Carbs 4g Protein 0g Fat 13g Sugar 4g Fiber 0g

BBQ Sauce

Prep time: 5 minutes, minutes, Serves: 20 Cook time: 20

What you'll need from store cupboard:

2 1/2 6 oz. cans tomato paste
1 ½ cup water
½ cup apple cider vinegar
1/3 cup swerve confectioners
2 tbsp. Worcestershire sauce
1 tbsp. liquid hickory smoke
2 tsp smoked paprika
1 tsp garlic powder
½ tsp onion powder
½ tsp salt
¼ tsp chili powder
¼ tsp cayenne pepper

Instructions:

1. Whisk all Ingredients, but water, together in a saucepan. Add water, starting with 1 cup, whisking it in, until mixture resembles a thin barbecue sauce.
2. Bring to a low boil over med-high heat. Reduce heat to med-low and simmer, stirring frequently, 20 minutes, or sauce has thickened slightly.
3. Taste and adjust seasoning until you like it. Cool completely. Store in a jar with an airtight lid in the refrigerator. Serving size is 2 tablespoons of sauce.

Nutrition Facts Per Serving
Calories 24 Total Carbs 9g Net Carbs 8g Protein 1g Fat 0g Sugar 7g Fiber 1g

Pear & Poppy Jam

Prep time: 2 hours, Cook time: 30 minutes, Serves: 32

Ingredients:

3 pears, peeled, seeded and chopped
½ lemon

What you'll need from store cupboard:

¾ cup Splenda   1 tbsp. poppy seeds

Instructions:

1. Place pears in a large bowl. Sprinkle with Splenda and toss to coat. Squeeze the lemon over the pears and toss again. Let sit for 2 hours so the fruit will release its juice.
2. Place poppy seeds in a medium saucepan over medium heat. Cook, stirring, 1-2 minutes to lightly toast the. Transfer them to a bowl.
3. Add the pears, with the juice, to the saucepan and bring to a boil, stirring frequently. Reduce the heat and let boil 10 minutes or until thickened.
4. Spoon ½ the pears into a blender and process until smooth. Add the puree back to the saucepan along with the poppy seeds. Continue cooking 5-10 minutes or the jam is thick.
5. Spoon into 2 pint sized jars with air tight lids. Let cool completely, screw on the lids and store in the refrigerator. Serving size is 1 tablespoon.

Nutrition Facts Per Serving
Calories 36 Total Carbs 8g Net Carbs 7g Protein 0g Fat 0g Sugar 6g Fiber 1g

Bacon Cheeseburger Dip

Prep time: 5 minutes, Cook time: 30 minutes, Serves: 8

Ingredients:

1 lb. lean ground beef	grated
1 pkg. cream cheese, soft	1 cup fat free sour cream
2 cups low fat cheddar cheese,	2/3 cup bacon, cooked crisp and crumbled

What you'll need from store cupboard:
10 oz. can tomatoes with green chilies

Instructions:
1. Heat oven to 350 degrees.
2. Place a large skillet over med-high heat and cook beef, breaking it up with a wooden spoon, until no longer pink. Drain off the fat.
3. In a large bowl, combine remaining Ingredients until mixed well. Stir in beef.
4. Pour into a small baking dish. Bake 20-25 minutes or until mixture is hot and bubbly. Serve warm.

Nutrition Facts Per Serving
Calories 268 Total Carbs 9g Protein 33g Fat 10g Sugar 2g Fiber 0g

Caramel Sauce

Prep time: 5 minutes, Cook time: 10 minutes, Serves: 12

Ingredients:

2/3 cup heavy cream	1/3 cup margarine

What you'll need from store cupboard:

3 tbsp. Splenda	1 tsp vanilla

Instructions:
1. Add the margarine and Splenda to a medium saucepan and place over low heat. Once the margarine melts, cook 3-4 minutes, stirring occasionally, until golden brown.
2. Stir in the cream and bring to a low boil. Reduce heat and simmer 7-10 minutes, stirring occasionally, until mixture is a caramel color and coats the back of a spoon.
3. Remove from heat and whisk in the vanilla. Cool completely and pour into a jar with an air tight lid. Store in the refrigerator. Serving size is 1 tablespoon.

Nutrition Facts Per Serving
Calories 84 Total Carbs 3g Protein 0g Fat 7g Sugar 3g Fiber 0g

Berry Dessert Sauce

Prep time: 5 minutes, Cook time: 3 hours, Serves: 12

Ingredients:

8 oz. strawberries, hulled and halved	6 oz. blackberries
	4 oz. blueberries

What you'll need from store cupboard:
¼ cup Splenda

Instructions:
1. Add the berries and Splenda to the crock pot. Stir to mix.
2. Cover and cook for 3 hours on a low heat.
3. Ladle the sauce into a jar with an air tight lid, and let cool completely before screwing on the lid and storing in the refrigerator. Serving size is 1 tablespoon.

Nutrition Facts Per Serving
Calories 48 Total Carbs 10g Net Carbs 8g Protein 1g Fat 0g Sugar 8g Fiber 2g

Blackberry Spread

Prep time: 5 minutes, Cook time: 30 minutes, Serves: 16

Ingredients:
1 lb. blackberries
1 lemon, juiced

What you'll need from store cupboard:
¼ cup Splenda

Instructions:
1. Place blackberries, Splenda and lemon juice in a medium sauce pan over med-high heat. Cook berries down, stirring occasionally, about 30 minutes, or mixture resembles a thick syrup.
2. Scoop 1/2 cup of the mixture out and place it in a bowl.
3. Place a fine mesh sieve over the bowl and strain the rest of the mixture through, pressing and scraping to get as much of the moisture out that you can.
4. Discard solids. Stir jam in bowl and place in a jar with an air-tight lid.

Nutrition Facts Per Serving
Calories 28 Total Carbs 6g Net Carbs 4g Protein 0g Fat 0g Sugar 4g Fiber 2g

Cheesy Jalapeno Dip

Prep time: 5 minutes, cook time; 3 hours, Serves: 10

Ingredients:

4 pkgs. cream cheese, soft
1 ½ cups low fat cheddar cheese, grated
1 cup bacon, cooked and crumbled
1 cup fat free sour cream

1 fresh jalapeño, sliced
What you'll need from store cupboard
2 cans jalapenos, diced
1 packet ranch dressing mix

Instructions:

1. In a large bowl, mix cream cheese, 2/3 cup bacon, diced jalapenos, 1 cup cheddar cheese, sour cream and dressing.
2. Spread in crock pot. Top with remaining bacon and cheese. Arrange sliced jalapeno across the top.
3. Cover and cook on low 3 hours. Serve warm.

Nutrition Facts Per Serving

Calories 233 Total Carbs 12g Protein 24g Fat 9g Sugar 2g Fiber 0g

Chinese Hot Mustard

Prep time: 15 mins, Total time: 15 minutes, Serves: 4

What you'll need from store cupboard:

1 tbsp. mustard powder
1½ tsp hot water
½ tsp vegetable oil

½ tsp rice vinegar
⅛ tsp salt
⅛ tsp white pepper

Instructions:

1. In a small bowl, mix together the dry Ingredients. Add water and stir until mixture resembles liquid paste and dry Ingredients are absorbed.
2. Stir in oil and vinegar until thoroughly combined. Cover and let rest 10 minutes.
3. Stir again. Taste and adjust any seasonings if desired. Cover and refrigerate until ready to use.

Nutrition Facts Per Serving

Calories 19 Total Carbs 1g Protein 1g Fat 1g Sugar 0g Fiber 0g

Cinnamon Blueberry Sauce

Prep time: 5 minutes, Cook time: 10 minutes, Serves: 16

Ingredients:

2 cup blueberries
2 tbsp. fresh lemon juice

What you'll need from store cupboard:

¼ cup Splenda
¼ cup water

2 tsp corn starch
½ tsp cinnamon

Instructions:

1. In a small saucepan, over medium heat, Splenda and cornstarch. Stir in remaining Ingredients and bring to a boil, stirring frequently.
2. Reduce heat and simmer 5 minutes, until thickened. Let cool completely.
3. Pour into a jar with an airtight lid and refrigerate until ready to use. Serving size is 1 tablespoon.

Nutrition Facts Per Serving

Calories 27 Total Carbs 6g Protein 0g Fat 0g Sugar 5g Fiber 0g

Citrus Vinaigrette

Prep time: 5 minutes, Total time: 10 minutes, Serves: 6

Ingredients:

1 orange, zested and juiced
1 lemon, zested and juiced

What you'll need from store cupboard:

¼ cup extra virgin olive oil
1 tsp Dijon mustard
1 tsp honey

1 clove garlic, crushed
Salt & pepper, to taste

Instructions:

1. Place the zest and juices, mustard, honey, garlic, salt and pepper in a food processor. Pulse to combine.
2. With the machine running, slowly pour in the olive oil and process until combined.
3. Use right away, or store in a jar with an airtight lid in the refrigerator.

Nutrition Facts Per Serving

Calories 94 Total Carbs 6g Net Carbs 5g Protein 0g Fat 8g Sugar 4g Fiber 1g

Cranberry Orange Compote

Prep time: 5 minutes, Cook time: 10 minutes, Serves: 8
Ingredients:
1 lb. fresh cranberries, rinsed and drained
1 large orange, halved
What you'll need from store cupboard:
1 tsp vanilla   1 tsp cinnamon
Instructions:
1. Add cranberries to a medium saucepan and place over medium heat. Squeeze both halves of the orange, with pulp, into the berries. Stir in vanilla and cinnamon.
2. Cook, stirring frequently, until berries start to open. Reduce heat and continue cooking for 10 minutes, or until mixture starts to thicken.
3. Let cool 15 minutes, then spoon into a jar with an airtight lid. Refrigerate until ready to use.

Nutrition Facts Per Serving
Calories 43 Total Carbs 8g Net Carbs 5g Protein 0g Fat 0g Sugar 4g Fiber 3g

Marinara Sauce

Prep time: 10 minutes, Cook time: 30 minutes, Serves: 6
What you'll need from store cupboard:
28 oz. can diced tomatoes, undrained   olive oil
4–6 cloves garlic, diced fine   2 tbsp. tomato paste
4 tbsp. extra virgin   1 tbsp. basil,
1 tsp Splenda
1 tsp salt
Instructions:
1. Heat oil in saucepan over medium heat. Add the garlic and cook 1 minute.
2. Stir in the tomato paste and cook 1 minute more. Add the tomatoes and basil and simmer 10-15 minutes, breaking up the tomatoes as they cook.
3. Stir in Splenda and salt. Use an immersion blender and process to desired consistency.
4. Let cool and store in a jar with an airtight lid in the refrigerator up to 7 days. Or use right away.

Nutrition Facts Per Serving
Calories 179 Total Carbs 13g Net Carbs 10g Protein 2g Fat 14g Sugar 8g Fiber 3g

Dry Rub for Pork

Prep time: 5 minutes, Total time: 5 minutes, Serves: 16
What you'll need from store cupboard:
2 tbsp. ground coffee, extra fine ground   1 tbsp. Splenda brown sugar
2 tbsp. chipotle powder   1 tbsp. salt
1 tbsp. smoked paprika   1 tsp ginger
1 tsp mustard powder
1 tsp coriander
Instructions:
1. Mix all Ingredients together.
2. Store in airtight container in cool, dry place for up to 1 month.

Nutrition Facts Per Serving
Calories 5 Total Carbs 1g Protein 0g Fat 0g Sugar 1g Fiber 0g

Easy Cheesy Dipping Sauce

Prep time: 2 minutes, Cook time: 5 minutes, Serves: 2
Ingredients:
¾ cup skim milk   cheddar cheese
¾ cup reduced-fat   1 tbsp. margarine
What you'll need from store cupboard:
1 tbsp. flour   Salt and pepper
Pinch of cayenne
Instructions:
1. Melt margarine in a small saucepan over medium heat. Whisk in flour and cook, whisking constantly, until golden brown, about 1 minutes.
2. Slowly add milk and continue whisking until no lumps remain. Cook, whisking constantly, until mixture thickens and starts to bubble, 3-4 minutes.
3. Stir in cheese until smooth. Season with cayenne, salt and pepper to taste.

Nutrition Facts Per Serving
Calories 219 Total Carbs 8g Protein 16g Fat 15g Sugar 5g Fiber 0g

Horseradish Mustard Sauce

Prep time: 5 minutes, Total time: 5 minutes, Serves: 8

Ingredients:

¼ cup fat free sour cream

What you'll need from store cupboard:

¼ cup lite mayonnaise	½ tsp ground mustard
1 ½ tsp lemon juice	½ tsp Dijon mustard
1 tsp Splenda	½ tsp horseradish

Instructions:

1. In a small bowl, combine all Ingredients until thoroughly combined.
2. Store in an air tight jar in the refrigerator until ready to use. Serving size is 1 tablespoon.

Nutrition Facts Per Serving

Calories 36 Total Carbs 2g Protein 0g Fat 2g Sugar 1g Fiber 0g

Italian Salad Dressing

Prep time: 5 minutes, Total time: 5 minutes, Serves: 8

Ingredients:

2 tbsp. lemon juice

What you'll need from store cupboard:

¾ cup olive oil	1 tsp oregano
¼ cup red wine vinegar	½ tsp honey
2 cloves of garlic, diced	½ tsp salt
2 tsp Italian seasoning	¼ tsp black pepper
	¼ tsp red pepper flakes

Instructions:

1. Combine all Ingredients in a measuring cup or jar. Whisk well.
2. Store in jar or bottle with an air tight lid for up to 1 week. Serving size is 1 tablespoon.

Nutrition Facts Per Serving

Calories 167 Total Carbs 1g Protein 0g Fat 18g Sugar 0g Fiber 0g

Italian Salsa

Prep time: 10 minutes, chill time: 1 hour, Serves: 16

Ingredients:

4 plum tomatoes, diced	fine
½ red onion, diced	2 tbsp. fresh parsley, diced

What you'll need from store cupboard:

12 Kalamata olives, pitted and chopped	vinegar
2 cloves garlic, diced fine	1 tbsp. olive oil
	2 tsp capers, drained
1 tbsp. balsamic	¼ tsp salt
	¼ tsp pepper

Instructions:

1. In a medium bowl, combine all Ingredients and stir to mix. Cover and chill 1 hour before using.
2. Store in a jar with an airtight lid in the refrigerator up to 7 days. Stir before using.

Nutrition Facts Per Serving

Calories 21 Total Carbs 2g Protein 0g Fat 1g Sugar 1g Fiber 0g

Maple Mustard Salad Dressing

Total time: 5 minutes, Serves: 6

What you'll need from store cupboard:

2 tbsp. balsamic vinegar	maple syrup
2 tbsp. olive oil	1 tsp Dijon mustard
1 tbsp. sugar free	1/8 tsp sea salt

Instructions:

1. Place all the Ingredients in a jar with a tight fitting lid. Screw on lid and shake to combine. Store in refrigerator until ready to use.

Nutrition Facts Per Serving

Calories 48 Total Carbs 2g Protein 0g Fat 5g Sugar 0g Fiber 0g

Walnut Vinaigrette

Total time: 5 minutes, Serves: 4

What you'll need from store cupboard:

½ cup water	¼ cup raisins
¼ cup balsamic vinegar	1 clove garlic
	1 tsp Dijon mustard
¼ cup walnuts	¼ tsp thyme

Instructions:

1. Place all Ingredients in a blender or food processor and pulse until smooth. Store in a jar with an air tight lid in the refrigerator.

Nutrition Facts Per Serving

Calories 53 Total Carbs 2g Net Carbs 1g Protein 2g Fat 5g Sugar 0g Fiber 1g

Maple Shallot Vinaigrette

Prep time: 3 minutes, Total time: 5 minutes, Serves: 4

Ingredients:

1 tbsp. shallot, diced fine

What you'll need from store cupboard:

2 tbsp. apple cider vinegar

1 tbsp. spicy brown mustard

1 tbsp. olive oil

2 tsp sugar free maple syrup

Instructions:

1. Place all Ingredients in a small jar with an airtight lid. Shake well to mix. Refrigerate until ready to use. Serving size is 1 tablespoon.

Nutrition Facts Per Serving

Calories 45 Total Carbs 5g Protein 0g Fat 2g Sugar 0g Fiber 0g

Pizza Sauce

Prep time: 5 minutes, Cook time: 5 minutes, Serves: 8

Ingredients:

½ cup yellow onion, diced

What you'll need from store cupboard:

15 oz. tomatoes, crushed, no sugar added

1/3 cup + 1 tbsp. olive oil

3 cloves garlic, diced

2 tsp parsley

1 tsp rosemary

1 tsp thyme

1 tsp smoked paprika

Salt, to taste

Instructions:

1. Heat 1 tablespoon oil in a small skillet over medium heat. Add onion and garlic and cook until onions are translucent.
2. In a medium saucepan, over medium heat, stir all Ingredients together, along with onions. Bring to a simmer and cook 2-3 minutes, stirring constantly.
3. Remove from heat and let cool completely. Store in a jar with an air tight lid in the refrigerator up to 2 weeks. Or in the freezer up to 6 months.

Nutrition Facts Per Serving

Calories 179 Total Carbs 8g Net carbs 6g Protein 2g Fat 17g Sugar 5g Fiber 2g

Pineapple Mango Hot Sauce

Prep time: 10 minutes, Cook time: 20 minutes, Serves: 16

Ingredients:

2 cherry peppers, diced

1 ghost pepper, diced

1 cup pineapple,

diced

½ cup mango, diced

2 tbsp. cilantro, diced

What you'll need from store cupboard:

1 cup water

½ cup vinegar

1 tsp olive oil

1 tsp Splenda

1 tsp paprika

Salt, to taste

Instructions:

1. Heat oil in a large saucepan over medium heat. Add peppers and fruit and cook 8 minutes to soften.
2. Add remaining Ingredients and bring to a boil. Reduce heat and simmer 20 minutes. Remove from heat and let cool.
3. Add mixture to a food processor and pulse until smooth. Pour into sterilized bottles, secure lids and refrigerate until ready to use.

Nutrition Facts Per Serving

Calories 16 Total Carbs 3g Protein 0g Fat 0g Sugar 2g Fiber 0g

Peach Pepper Relish

Prep time: 10 minutes, chill time: 2 hours, Serves: 16

Ingredients:

2 peaches, peeled and diced

1 green onion, diced fine

1/3 cup bell pepper,

diced

1/3 cup red pepper, diced

2 tbsp. fresh mint, diced

What you'll need from store cupboard:

1 tbsp. lemon juice

1 tbsp. sugar free peach preserves

Instructions:

1. In a medium bowl, stir together peaches, onion, peppers, and mint.
2. In a small bowl, combine lemon juice and preserves. Pour over peach mixture and toss to coat.
3. Place in an airtight container and refrigerate up to 2 hours or overnight. Serving size is 2 tablespoons.

Nutrition Facts Per Serving

Calories 10 Total Carbs 3g Protein 0g Fat 0g Sugar 2g Fiber 0g

Queso Verde

Prep time: 10 minutes, Cook time: 30 minutes, Serves: 10

Ingredients:

½ package cream cheese, soft

½ cup white American cheese, cubed

½ cup white cheddar cheese, cubed

½ cup pepper Jack cheese, cubed

¼ cup skim milk

What you'll need from store cupboard:

½ cup salsa verde

½ cup green chilies, diced

Nonstick cooking spray

Instructions:

1. Heat oven to 325. Spray a small baking dish with cooking spray.
2. In a medium mixing bowl, combine all Ingredients. Add to prepared baking dish.
3. Bake 30 minutes, stirring every 8-10 minutes, until cheese is melted and dip is hot and bubbly. Serve warm.

Nutrition Facts Per Serving

Calories 105 Total Carbs 3g Net Carbs 2g Protein 7g Fat 7g Sugar 1g Fiber 1g

Raspberry & Basil Jam

Prep time: 5 minutes, Cook time: 20 minutes, Serves: 24

Ingredients:

2 lbs. fresh raspberries

1/3 cup fresh basil, diced fine

2 tbsp. lemon juice

What you'll need from store cupboard

½ cup Splenda

Instructions:

1. Add berries and lemon juice to a large saucepan and place over medium heat. Use a wooden spoon to break up the berries. Bring to a low boil and simmer 5-6 minutes, or until mixture starts to bubble.
2. Stir in Splenda and cook, stirring frequently, until Splenda is dissolved and mixture resembles syrup, about 15 minutes.
3. Remove from heat and stir in the basil. Spoon into glass jars with air tight lids. Let cool completely then add lids and refrigerate. Serving size is 1 tablespoon.

Nutrition Facts Per Serving

Calories 40 Total Carbs 8g Net Carbs 6g Protein 0g Fat 0g Sugar 6g Fiber 2g

Roasted Tomato Salsa

Prep time: 10 minutes, Cook time: 30 minutes, Serves: 8

Ingredients:

6 plum tomatoes

1 ¼ cup cilantro

What you'll need from store cupboard:

2 tsp olive oil

1 tsp adobo sauce

½ tsp salt, divided

Nonstick cooking spray

Instructions:

1. Heat oven to 425 degrees. Spray a broiler pan with cooking spray.
2. Cut tomatoes in half and remove seeds. Place, cut side up, on broiler pan. Brush with oil and sprinkle with ¼ teaspoon salt. Turn tomatoes cut side down and bake 30-40 minutes or until edges are browned.
3. Place cilantro in food processor and pulse until coarsely chopped. Add tomatoes, adobo, and remaining salt. Process until chunky. Store in jar with air tight lid and refrigerate until ready to use. Serving size is 2 tablespoons.

Nutrition Facts Per Serving

Calories 33 Total Carbs 5g Net Carbs 4g Protein 1g Fat 1g Sugar 4g Fiber 1g

Spicy Asian Vinaigrette

Prep time: 5 minutes, Total time: 10 minutes, Serves: 4

Ingredients:

1-inch piece fresh ginger, peel & quarter

1 tbsp. fresh lemon juice

What you'll need from store cupboard:

¼ cup sesame oil

2 cloves garlic, peeled

2 tbsp. rice vinegar

1 tbsp. hot Chinese

hot mustard, (chapter 16)

1 tsp light soy sauce

1/8 tsp red pepper flakes

Instructions:

1. Place all Ingredients in a food processor or blender and process until smooth.
2. Store in a jar with an airtight lid. Serving size is 2 tablespoons

Nutrition Facts Per Serving

Calories 172 Total Carbs 7g Protein 2g Fat 17g Sugar 2g Fiber 0g

Spicy Peanut Sauce

Prep time: 5 minutes, Cook time: 5 minutes, Serves: 20

Ingredients:
¼ cup fresh lime juice
2 tbsp. fresh ginger, peeled and grated

What you'll need from store cupboard:

1 ½ cups reduced-sodium, low-fat chicken broth	brown sugar
	2 tbsp. low-sodium soy sauce
1 cup reduced-fat peanut butter	½ tsp crushed red pepper flakes
3 tbsp. Splenda	

Instructions:
1. In a small saucepan, over medium heat, heat peanut butter until melted. Add broth and stir until combined.
2. Add remaining Ingredients, and cook over med-low heat 5 minutes, stirring frequently, until thickened.
3. Use over shrimp, scallops, chicken, turkey or beef. Serving size is 2 tablespoons.
4. Store in air-tight container in the refrigerator up to 3 days.

Nutrition Facts Per Serving
Calories 90 Total Carbs 9g Net Carbs 8g Protein 3g Fat 5g Sugar 4g Fiber 1g

Spicy Sweet Dipping Sauce

Prep time: 5 minutes, total time 5 minutes, Serves: 16

Ingredients:
¼ tsp habanero pepper, diced fine
1 tbsp. lime juice

What you'll need from store cupboard:

1 cup sugar free orange marmalade	flakes
	¼ tsp sesame oil
1 tbsp. fish sauce	Pinch of salt
½ tsp red pepper	

Instructions:
1. Mix all Ingredients together in a small bowl. Spoon into a jar with an air tight lid and store in the refrigerator.
2. Serving size is 1 tablespoon. Will last up to one week in the refrigerator.

Nutrition Facts Per Serving
Calories 12 Total Carbs 5g Protein 0g Fat 0g Sugar 0g Fiber 0g

Sriracha Dipping Sauce

Prep time: 1 minute, Total time: 2 minutes, Serves: 6

Ingredients:
2 tsp fresh lime juice

What you'll need from store cupboard:

½ cup lite mayonnaise	1 tbsp. Splenda
2 tbsp. Sriracha sauce	1 tsp Worcestershire sauce

Instructions:
1. In a small bowl, stir all the Ingredients together until smooth.
2. Use right away, or cover and refrigerate until ready to use. Serving size is 1 ½ tablespoons.

Nutrition Facts Per Serving
Calories 83 Total Carbs 5g Protein 0g Fat 7g Sugar 2g Fiber 0g

Strawberry Rhubarb Jelly

Prep time: 15 minutes, Cook time: 15 minutes, serves; 64

Ingredients:
5 cups rhubarb, cut in ½-inch slices
2 cups strawberries, hulled and halved
1 tbsp. fresh lemon juice

What you'll need from store cupboard:
2 ¼ cup Splenda

Instructions:
1. Add all Ingredients to a large sauce pan and place over medium heat. Bring to a boil, stirring frequently.
2. Reduce heat, cover, and simmer 15-20 minutes, until rhubarb is soft and mixture has thickened, stirring occasionally.
3. Spoon into 2 pint sized jars and let cool completely. Add the lids and store in refrigerator. Serving size is 1 tablespoon.

Nutrition Facts Per Serving
Calories 37 Total Carbs 7g Protein 0g Fat 0g Sugar 7g Fiber 0g

Sugar Free Ketchup

Prep time: 5 minutes, Total time: 5 minutes, Serves: 28

What you'll need from store cupboard:

12 oz. tomato paste   1 tbsp. salt
1 ½ cup water   3 tsp Splenda
1/3 cup white vinegar   1 tsp onion powder

Instructions:

1. In a large bowl, combine water, vinegar, Splenda, onion powder, and salt. Whisk in tomato paste until smooth.
2. Pour into a glass jar with an air tight lid and store in refrigerator until ready to use. Serving size is 2 tablespoons.

Nutrition Facts Per Serving

Calories 15 Total Carbs 3g Protein 0g Fat 0g Sugar 2g Fiber 0g

Teriyaki Sauce

Prep time: 5 minutes, Cook time: 10 minutes, Serves: 16

What you'll need from store cupboard:

1 ¼ cup water, divided   stevia
¼ cup lite soy sauce   1 ½ tbsp. corn starch
2 tbsp. + ½ tsp liquid   ½ tsp ginger
   ¼ tsp garlic powder

Instructions:

1. Combine soy sauce, 1 cup water, ginger, garlic powder, and stevia in a small saucepan. Place over med-low heat and bring to a simmer.
2. Whisk the corn starch with the ¼ cup water until smooth. Add it to the sauce in the pan and mix thoroughly. Let sauce simmer until it starts to thicken, about 1 minute.
3. Remove from heat and cool completely. Sauce will continue to thicken as it cools. Use as a marinade or dipping sauce. Serving size is 1 tablespoon.

Nutrition Facts Per Serving

Calories 5 Total Carbs 1g Protein 0g Fat 0g Sugar 0g Fiber 0g

Tangy Mexican salad dressing

Total time: 5 minutes, Serves: 8

Ingredients:

½ cup cilantro, diced fine
3 tbsp. fresh lime juice

What you'll need from store cupboard:

½ cup sunflower oil   1 tsp garlic salt
2 tbsp. water   ½ teaspoon Mexican
1 tbsp. apple cider   oregano
vinegar   Freshly ground black
2 tsp honey   pepper, to taste

Instructions:

1. Add all Ingredients to a food processor or blender. Pulse until well blended and emulsified. Taste and adjust seasonings as desired.
2. Store in an air-tight container in the refrigerator. To serve, bring to room temperature and shake well.

Nutrition Facts Per Serving

Calories 127 Total Carbs 2g Protein 0 Fat 14g Sugar 2g Fiber 0g

Warm Bacon Vinaigrette Dressing

Prep time: 5 minutes, Cook time: 10 minutes, Serves: 4

Ingredients:

6 pieces thick sliced   and crumbled
bacon, cooked crisp   1 shallot, diced fine

What you'll need from store cupboard:

½ cup red wine   brown sugar
vinegar   ¾ tsp Dijon mustard
2 cloves garlic, diced   Salt
fine   Fresh ground black
1 ½ tsp Splenda   pepper

Instructions:

1. After cooking the bacon, pour out all but 3 tablespoons grease into a jar, save for later.
2. Add the garlic and shallot to remaining hot grease and cook 2-3 minutes, or until soft.
3. Add Splenda and stir until it dissolves. Whisk in remaining Ingredients and season with salt and pepper to taste. Use immediately with your favorite salad.

Nutrition Facts Per Serving

Calories 115 Total Carbs 2g Protein 7g Fat 8g Sugar 1g Fiber 0g

Appendix 1 Measurement Conversion Chart

VOLUME EQUIVALENTS(DRY)

US STANDARD	METRIC (APPROXIMATE)
1/8 teaspoon	0.5 mL
1/4 teaspoon	1 mL
1/2 teaspoon	2 mL
3/4 teaspoon	4 mL
1 teaspoon	5 mL
1 tablespoon	15 mL
1/4 cup	59 mL
1/2 cup	118 mL
3/4 cup	177 mL
1 cup	235 mL
2 cups	475 mL
3 cups	700 mL
4 cups	1 L

VOLUME EQUIVALENTS(LIQUID)

US STANDARD	US STANDARD (OUNCES)	METRIC (APPROXIMATE)
2 tablespoons	1 fl.oz.	30 mL
1/4 cup	2 fl.oz.	60 mL
1/2 cup	4 fl.oz.	120 mL
1 cup	8 fl.oz.	240 mL
1 1/2 cup	12 fl.oz.	355 mL
2 cups or 1 pint	16 fl.oz.	475 mL
4 cups or 1 quart	32 fl.oz.	1 L
1 gallon	128 fl.oz.	4 L

TEMPERATURES EQUIVALENTS

FAHRENHEIT(F)	CELSIUS(C) (APPROXIMATE)
225 °F	107 °C
250 °F	120 °C
275 °F	135 °C
300 °F	150 °C
325 °F	160 °C
350 °F	180 °C
375 °F	190 °C
400 °F	205 °C
425 °F	220 °C
450 °F	235 °C
475 °F	245 °C
500 °F	260 °C

WEIGHT EQUIVALENTS

US STANDARD	METRIC (APPROXIMATE)
1 ounce	28 g
2 ounces	57 g
5 ounces	142 g
10 ounces	284 g
15 ounces	425 g
16 ounces (1 pound)	455 g
1.5 pounds	680 g
2 pounds	907 g

Appendix 2 Recipe Index

A

African Christmas Stew 73
Alfredo Sauce 162
Alfredo Sausage & Vegetables 134
All Purpose Beef Marinade 164
All Purpose Chicken Marinade 165
Almond Cheesecake Bites 30
Almond Coconut Biscotti 39
Almond Flour Crackers 30
Almond Vanilla Fruit Dip 163
Apple Cheddar Muffins 15
Apple Cider Vinaigrette 165
Apple Cinnamon Muffins 15
Apple Cinnamon Scones 16
Apple Crisp 63
Apple Filled Swedish Pancake 16
Apple Pear & Pecan Dessert Squares 55
Apple Topped French Toast 17
Apple Walnut Pancakes 17
Apricot Soufflé 57
Arroz Con Pollo 91
Asian Beef Bowls 135
Asian Chicken Wings 30
Asian Fried Eggplant 127
Asian Meatball Soup 73
Asian Noodle Salad 53
Asian Roasted Duck Legs 92
Asian Style Slaw 46
Asparagus & Bacon Salad 46
Autumn Skillet Cake 57
Autumn Slaw 46
Avocado & Citrus Shrimp Salad 47

B

Bacon & Cabbage Soup 73
Bacon & Cauliflower Casserole 134
Bacon Cheeseburger Dip 166
"Bacon" & Egg Muffins 26
Baked "Potato" Salad 47
Baked Maple Custard 59
Baked Salmon with Garlic Parmesan Topping 113
Baked Seafood Casserole 114
Balsamic Chicken & Vegetable Skillet 91
Banana Nut Cookies 30
Basic Salsa 163
BBQ Chicken & Noodles 92
BBQ Oysters with Bacon 116
BBQ Pork Tacos 135

BBQ Sauce 165
Beef & Broccoli Skillet 136
Beef & Lentil Soup 74
Beef & Sweet Potato Stew 79
Beef & Veggie Quesadillas 134
Beef Burgundy & Mushroom Stew 74
Beef Goulash 136
Beef Picadillo 136
Beef Tenderloin Steaks with Brandied Mushrooms 132
Beef Tenderloin with Roasted Vegetables 137
Beef Vegetable Soup 75
Beef Zoodle Stew 75
Beer Braised Brisket 138
Beer Cheese & Chicken Soup 76
Berry Breakfast Bark 16
Berry Dessert Sauce 166
Black Pepper & Garlic Tofu 153
Blackberry Crostata 60
Blackberry Soufflés 61
Blackberry Spread 166
Blackened Shrimp 117
BLT Stuffed Cucumbers 31
Blue Cheese Crusted Beef Tenderloin 139
Blueberry Cinnamon Muffins 15
Blueberry English Muffin Loaf 18
Blueberry Lemon "Cup" Cakes 56
Blueberry No Bake Cheesecake 57
Blueberry Orange Dessert Sauce 164
Blueberry Stuffed French Toast 18
Breakfast Pizza 19
Broccoli & Bacon Salad 48
Broccoli & Mushroom Salad 48
Broiled Stone Fruit 56
Buffalo Bites 31
Butternut Fritters 128

C-D

Cafe Mocha Smoothies 15
Café Mocha Torte 70
Cajun Beef & Rice Skillet 140
Cajun Catfish 112
Cajun Chicken & Pasta 90
Cajun Flounder & Tomatoes 112
Cajun Seafood Stew 77
Cajun Shrimp & Roasted Vegetables 116
Cajun Smothered Pork Chops 140
Candied Pecans 31
Cantaloupe & Prosciutto Salad 46

Cappuccino Mousse 55
Caprese Salad 49
Caramel Pecan Pie 61
Caramel Sauce 166
Carrot Cupcakes 70
Cauliflower "Mac" and Cheese 154
Cauliflower "Rice" 158
Cauliflower Breakfast Hash 18
Cauliflower Hummus 34
Cauliflower Mushroom Risotto 126
Cauliflower Pizza Crust 160
Cauliflower Puree 158
Celery Apple Salad 49
Cheese Biscuits 159
Cheese Crisp Crackers 31
Cheese Spinach Waffles 19
Cheesecake 59
Cheesesteak Stuffed Peppers 141
Cheesy Beef & Noodles 141
Cheesy Cauliflower Puree 157
Cheesy Chicken & "Potato" Casserole 93
Cheesy Chicken & Spinach 92
Cheesy Ham & Broccoli Soup 79
Cheesy Jalapeno Dip 167
Cheesy Onion Dip 40
Cheesy Pita Crisps 32
Cheesy Stuffed Chicken 93
Cheesy Taco Chips 32
Chestnut Stuffed Pork Roast 132
Chewy Granola Bars 33
Chicken & Pepper Stew 78
Chicken & Shrimp Satay 95
Chicken & Spinach Pasta Skillet 98
Chicken Cordon Bleu 101
Chicken Guacamole Salad 49
Chicken Marsala 96
Chicken Pappardelle 72
Chicken Stuffed with Mushrooms 94
Chicken Tuscany 96
Chicken Zucchini Patties with Salsa 97
Chickpea Tortillas 159
Chili Lime Tortilla Chips 33
Chili Relleno Casserole 129
Chinese Hot Mustard 167
Chipotle Bacon & Chicken Chowder 77
Chipotle Chicken & Corn Soup 75
Chocolate Cherry Cake Roll 58
Chocolate Chip Blondies 34
Chocolate Orange Bread Pudding 62
Chocolate Torte 62
Chopped Veggie Salad 47
Chorizo & Corn Chowder 78
Chunky Chicken Noodle Soup 80
Chutney Turkey Burgers 98
Cilantro Lime Grilled Shrimp 117

Cinnamon Apple Chips 34
Cinnamon Apple Granola 20
Cinnamon Apple Popcorn 35
Cinnamon Blueberry Sauce 167
Cinnamon Bread Pudding 63
Cinnamon Rolls 21
Cioppino 74
Citrus Vinaigrette 167
Clam & Bacon Soup 76
Coconut Breakfast Porridge 17
Coconut Cream Pie 64
Coconut Milk Shakes 61
Coconut Shrimp 117
Coconutty Pudding Clouds 64
"Cornbread" Stuffing 160
Cottage Cheese Pancakes 20
Crab & Cauliflower Bisque 76
Crab & Spinach Dip 35
Crab & Spinach Frittata 21
Crab Cakes 118
Crab Frittata 118
Cranberry & Almond Granola Bars 36
Cranberry Coffeecake 19
Cranberry Orange Compote 168
Cream Cheese Pound Cake 55
Creamy Braised Oxtails 139
Creamy Chicken & Cauliflower Rice Soup 80
Creamy Chicken Tenders 99
Creamy Crab Slaw 48
Creamy Italian Chicken & Pasta 89
Creamy Pasta with Peas 129
Creamy Poppy Seed Dressing 162
Creamy Sweet Potato & Cauliflower Bisque 78
Creamy Turkey & Peas with Noodles 99
Creole Chicken 102
Crispy Baked Cheese Puffs 35
Crispy Baked Flounder with Green Beans 121
Crispy Italian Chicken with Zucchini 103
Crispy Tofu with Chili Garlic Noodles 152
Crock Pot Beef Roast with Gravy 142
Crock Pot Carnitas 142
Crock Pot Fish & Tomatoes 119
Crock Pot Stroganoff 154
Crunchy Apple Fries 36
Crunchy Grilled Chicken 100
Crunchy Lemon Shrimp 119
Crust Less Broccoli Quiche 128
Crust Less Pizza 143
Curried Chicken & Apples 100
Curried Chicken Soup 81
Dark Chocolate Coffee Cupcakes 60
Deconstructed Philly Cheesesteaks 141
Dill Smoked Salmon over Noodles 119
Double Chocolate Biscotti 41
Dry Rub for Pork 168

E-F

Easy Carbonara 143
Easy Cheesy Dipping Sauce 168
Easy Seafood Chowder 81
Eggnog Breakfast Pudding 22
Eggplant-Zucchini Parmesan 129
Faux Chow Mein 130
Festive Holiday Salad 48
Fiesta Casserole 131
Fig Cookie Bars 37
Fisherman's Pie 116
Florentine Pizza 130
"Flour" Tortillas 157
Flourless "Burger Buns" 157
Fluffy Lemon Bars 37
Freezer Fudge 39
French Onion Casserole 139
French Onion Chicken & Vegetables 103
French Onion Soup 82
Fried Rice 157
Fried Zucchini 40

G

Garden Vegetable Pasta 127
Garlic Basil Breadsticks 160
Garlic Butter Steak 144
Garlic Dipping Sauce 163
Garlic Honey Pork Chops 140
Garlic Shrimp with Sun Dried Tomatoes 121
German Chocolate Cake Bars 60
Gingerbread Cookies 38
Gingerbread Soufflés 65
Grilled Cajun Beef Tenderloin 144
Grilled Lamb & Apricot Kebabs 138
Grilled Pork Tenderloin Sandwiches 144
Grilled Portobello & Zucchini Burger 129
Grilled Tofu & Veggie Skewers 155
Grilled Tuna Steaks 117
Grilled Vegetable & Noodle Salad 50
Guinness Beef Stew with Cauliflower Mash 72

H-I

Ham & Brie Turnovers 143
Ham & Broccoli Breakfast Bake 23
Ham & Cheese Breakfast Biscuits 17
Ham & Jicama Hash 23
Harvest Salad 52
Harvest Vegetable Soup 84
Hawaiian Breakfast Bake 23
Hawaiian Chicken 96
Healthy Loaf of Bread 161
Healthy Taco Salad 50
Healthy Turkey Chili 103
Hearty Beef Chili 133
Hearty Bell Pepper Stew 82

Herb Crusted Baked Ham 133
Herb Crusted Pork Tenderloin 145
Herb Vinaigrette 164
Holiday Apple & Cranberry Salad 54
Holiday Strata 20
Homemade Cheetos 42
Homemade Noodles 161
Homemade Pasta 161
Honey & Cinnamon Shortbread 43
Honey Bourbon Pork Chops 136
Honey Garlic Chicken 90
Honey Roasted Pumpkin Seeds 43
Honeydew & Ginger Smoothies 32
Horseradish Meatloaf 137
Horseradish Mustard Sauce 169
Hot & Spicy Mixed Nuts 36
Hot Chicken Salad Casserole 90
Hot Maple Porridge 24
Irish Stew 82
Italian Breakfast Bake 22
Italian Eggplant Rollups 33
Italian Pork Medallions 145
Italian Salad Dressing 169
Italian Salsa 169
Italian Sausage & Zucchini Warm Salad 142
Italian Sausage Soup 83
Italian Steamed Mussels 125
Italian Veggie Soup 83

J-K

Jalapeno Turkey Burgers 93
Jambalaya 113
Jicama Hash Browns 27
Kielbasa & Lamb Cassoulet 135
Korean Beef Soup 84
Korean Chicken 101

L

Lamb Ragu 145
Layered Salad 50
Lemon Chicken 102
Lemon Glazed Blueberry Bread 29
Lemon Meringue Ice Cream 63
Light Beer Bread 159
Lobster Chowder 123
Lobster Roll Salad with Bacon Vinaigrette 51

M-N

Mango Strawberry Smoothies 24
Maple Bourbon Glazed Ham 146
Maple Glazed Salmon 122
Maple Mustard Salad Dressing 169
Maple Orange Salmon 123
Maple Shallot Vinaigrette 170
Margarita Chicken Dip 44
Margarita Grilled Salmon 125

Marinara Sauce 168
Mediterranean Grilled Chicken 102
Mediterranean Shrimp Pasta 124
Mediterranean Stuffed Chicken 104
Mexican "Rice" 158
Mexican Beef Stew 81
Mexican Scrambled Eggs & Greens 154
Middle East Chicken Skewers 91
Mini Bread Puddings 69
Mini Eggplant Pizzas 43
Mini Key Lime Tarts 65
Mini Mushroom Egg Stacks 25
Mississippi Style Pot Roast 137
Mocha Java Smoothies 18
Moist Butter Cake 66
Monterey Crab Quiche 114
Moroccan Beef Skewers 149
Mozzarella Sticks 32
Mustard "Potato" Salad 51
No Bake Lemon Tart 64
No Corn "Cornbread" 158
No-Bake Chocolate Swirl 64

O

Oatmeal Peanut Butter Bars 40
Olive & Mushroom Frittata 25
One Pot Beef & Veggies 147
Onion Rings 44
Orange Chicken 100
Orange Marmalade 163
Orange Oatmeal Cookies 39
Orange Tofu 155

P-Q

Pad Thai 156
Paella 120
Pan Seared Trout & Salsa 113
Parmesan Truffle Chips 44
Pasta Bolognese 146
Peach Custard Tart 56
Peach Ice Cream 66
Peach Pepper Relish 170
Peanut Butter Oatmeal Cookies 42
Peanut Butter Pie 58
Peanut Butter Waffles 23
Pear & Poppy Jam 165
Pecan Chicken Enchiladas 104
Pecan Pear Salad 52
Peppered Duck Breasts with Grilled Plums109
Pesto Stuffed Mushrooms 38
Pickled Cucumber & Onion Salad 52
Pickled Cucumbers 40
Pineapple Frozen Yogurt 67
Pineapple Mango Hot Sauce 170
Pistachio Cookies 45
Pizza Crust 162

Pizza Sauce 170
Pizza Stuffed Portobello's 130
Poached Eggs & Grits 26
Poblano & Cheese Burgers 148
Pomegranate & Brussels Sprouts Salad 50
Pomegranate Panna Cotta 68
Popcorn Style Cauliflower 34
Pork Chops with Creamy Marsala Sauce 133
Pork Loin with Onion Beer Sauce 151
Pork Paprika 147
Pork Posole 84
Pumpkin Ice Cream with Candied Pecans 67
Pumpkin Muffins 21
Pumpkin Pancakes 26
Pumpkin Pie Smoothie 28
Pumpkin Spice French Toast 27
Queso Verde 171
Quick Coconut Flour Buns 159

R

Ranch Chicken Casserole 97
Raspberry & Basil Jam 171
Raspberry & Dark Chocolate Mini Soufflés 67
Raspberry Almond Clafoutis 69
Raspberry Lemon Cheesecake Squares 68
Raspberry Peach Cobbler 69
Raspberry Walnut Parfaits 35
Red Clam Sauce & Pasta 124
Roast Turkey & Rosemary Gravy 98
Roasted Cauliflower with Tomatoes 128
Roasted Duck Legs with Balsamic Mushrooms 94
Roasted Mushroom & Cauliflower Soup 83
Roasted Tomato Salsa 171
Rosemary Potato Chips 45
Rum Spiced Nuts 41

S

Salmon Dill Soup 77
Salmon Milano 125
Sangria Jello Cups 65
Sausage & Pepper Soup 85
Sausage & Spinach Frittata 150
Seafood & Broccoli Pasta 124
Seafood Enchiladas 115
Seafood Gumbo 120
Seafood Medley over Pasta 122
Seared Duck Breast with Red Wine & Figs 106
Shepherd's Pie 148
Shrimp & Artichoke Skillet 119
Shrimp & Avocado Salad 49
Shrimp in Coconut Curry 118
Shrimp Pasta in Red Pepper Sauce 122
Shrimp with Pumpkin Risotto 123
Sirloin Strips & "Rice" 146
Slow Cooker Lemon Chicken with Gravy 105

Slow Cooker Poblano Soup 89
Smoky Lentil & Leek Soup 86
Smoky Pumpkin Soup 88
Soft Pretzel Bites 42
South American Fish Stew 88
South of the Border Chicken Casserole 106
Southwest Braised Beef 148
Southwest Chicken Salad 47
Southwest Chicken Soup 80
Southwest Turkey Lasagna 107
Spaghetti Sauce 164
Spanish Halibut 115
Spiced Chicken Breasts with Peach Pepper Relish 105
Spicy Asian Vinaigrette 171
Spicy BBQ Beef Brisket 147
Spicy Grilled Flank Steak 151
Spicy Grilled Turkey Breast 109
Spicy Lettuce Wraps 99
Spicy Peanut Sauce 172
Spicy Shrimp Soup 85
Spicy Sweet Dipping Sauce 172
Spicy Tomato Chicken Soup 88
Spinach & Tomato Egg Muffins 25
Spinach Cheddar Squares 24
Sriracha Dipping Sauce 172
Steak & Broccoli Soup 86
Sticky Ginger Cake 62
Strawberry & Avocado Salad 51
Strawberry & Ricotta Crepes 24
Strawberry Cheesecake 54
Strawberry Coconut Scones 22
Strawberry Kiwi Smoothies 28
Strawberry Rhubarb Jelly 172
Strawberry Sorbet 58
Stuffed Flank Steak 149
Stuffed Grilled Pork Tenderloin 149
Sugar Free Ketchup 173
Summer Breakfast Parfait 26
Summer Corn Salad 54
Sunrise Smoothies 27
Swedish Beef Noodles 151
Swedish Meatballs 150
Sweet & Sour Chicken 105
Sweet & Spicy Seafood Pasta 121
Sweet Potato Crème Brule 71

T

Taco Casserole 152
Tandoori Lamb 150
Tangy Almond Shortbread Cookies 45
Tangy Asparagus Bisque 86

Tangy Balsamic Beef 145
Tangy Mexican salad dressing 173
Tangy Orange Roughy 123
Tempeh Lettuce Wraps 153
Teriyaki Sauce 173
Teriyaki Tofu Burger 153
Teriyaki Turkey Bowls 108
Tex Mex Breakfast Bake 29
Tex Mex Popcorn 36
Tex Mex Veggie Bake 127
Thai Turkey Stir Fry 108
Tiramisu 59
Toffee Apple Mini Pies 68
Tofu Bento 156
Tofu Curry 156
Tofu in Peanut Sauce 155
Tofu Salad Sandwiches 155
Tomato Soup with Seafood 85
Tortilla Chips 38
Tropical Fruit Tart 71
Tuna Carbonara 126
Turkey & Bacon Chowder 86
Turkey & Mushroom Casserole 101
Turkey & Pepper Skillet 110
Turkey Enchiladas 112
Turkey Meatballs with Spaghetti Squash 97
Turkey Noodle Casserole 110
Turkey Roulade 111
Turkey Sloppy Joes 105
Turkey Stuffed Peppers 107
Turkey Stuffed Poblano Peppers 95
Tuscan Sausage Soup 79

V-W

Vanilla Mango Smoothies 28
Vegetable Noodle Soup 87
Waffle or Pancake Mix 27
Walnut Vinaigrette 169
Warm Bacon Vinaigrette Dressing 173
Warm Portobello Salad 53
Watermelon & Arugula Salad 52
Watermelon & Shrimp Ceviche 37
Watermelon Ice 66
White Bean & Chicken Soup 87

Y--Z

Yogurt & Granola Breakfast Popsicles 28
Zesty Chicken & Asparagus Pasta 111
Zucchini "Pasta" Salad 53
Zucchini Chips 41
Zucchini Fritters 131
Zucchini Lasagna 138

Lightning Source UK Ltd.
Milton Keynes UK
UKHW050652130421
381910UK00002B/71